Frank Nitti

The True Story of Chicago's Notorious "Enforcer"

RONALD D. HUMBLE

BARRICADE
BOOKS

FORT LEE, NEW JERSEY

Published by Barricade Books Inc.
185 Bridge Plaza North
Suite 308-A
Fort Lee, NJ 07024

www.barricadebooks.com

LIBRARY OF CONGRESS CATALOGING-IN-PUBLICATION DATA

Humble, Ronald.
  Frank Nitti / Ronald D. Humble.
    p. cm.
  Includes bibliographical references and index.
  ISBN 978-1-56980-342-4 (hardcover)
   1. Nitti, Frank, d. 1943. 2. Criminals—Illinois—Chicago—Biography.
3. Organized crime—Illinois—Chicago—History. I. Title.

HV6248.N625H86 2007
364.1092—dc22
[B]

                                        2007049104

ISBN 13: 978-1-56980-342-4
ISBN 1-56980-342-0

10 9 8 7 6 5 4 3 2 1

Manufactured in the United States of America

To Max Allan Collins,
who has helped keep Nitti alive.

CONTENTS

INTRODUCTION

THIS IS ONE of the first books written on Frank "the Enforcer" Nitti. While I was initially researching this project, it was my intention to restrict my focus on the actual, historical Frank Nitti, and this remains an important objective of this biography. There are many documented historical bits and pieces of Nitti's career (although close examination reveals that many of these are apparently derived from a few common sources), but until now, these have not been pulled together and analyzed in a major serious work such as a biography specifically dedicated to Nitti's life and criminal career.

However, in the course of my research, it became obvious that the popularized Frank Nitti of television series and movie fame was a fixation of many people, and furthermore, these dramatic interpretations have steadily become merged with the life of the real man. While this has resulted in much inaccurate and confused "knowledge" concerning Frank Nitti, there is also a growing body of purely fictionalized spin-offs of the Nitti legend that are in many cases quite fantastic. At the same time, there are apparently obscure aspects of the real Nitti's career that are fantastic enough in themselves to intrigue the most dedicated Kennedy assassination-conspiracy theorist.

Instead of just rejecting this historically inaccurate media and fictional material as something that could only contaminate my database of biographical knowledge, I decided that something important enough had happened here to warrant further analysis. Also, I decided it was important that the apparent schisms between his actual and fictional lives be addressed in detail and somehow reconciled. Hence, this book has embraced Hollywood's and other fictionalized accounts of Frank Nitti in dedicated chapters as a framework for understanding why his character, out of so many Prohibition-era gangsters, seems so popular to this day. This seems only fitting because the real Frank Nitti was obsessed with Hollywood and the entertainment industry as an innovative avenue for criminal enterprise, and he had an important influence on the motion-picture industry's development.

Frank Nitti is arguably the most media-glamorized gangster in history, and his character remains very popular with the general public. The evidence speaks for itself: Nitti's character has appeared in more television series episodes and motion pictures than any other modern gangster in history, even Al "Scarface" Capone himself. At one time, Nitti was universally portrayed as a vicious gunman and tough guy, while today some Mafia historian revisionists claim he was little more than a harmless frontman with an eye for accounting records. Where lies the truth?

Strangely, very few books have dealt specifically with his actual life. Many of the elements of his life have been there for almost any competent researcher and writer to produce a satisfactory accounting. It soon dawned on me that the Frank Nitti persona is popular in the same sense as a familiar cartoon character or a Japanese computer-generated *idoru* celebrity that everyone assumes is a real person: the big, tough guy in shades of gray-and-black pinstriped suits who Eliot Ness managed to defeat every week within sixty minutes; the mean guy in an all-white suit who Ness threw from the roof of a building because he had killed his best pal "Malone"; or the wise guy who was Al Capone's right-hand man and best gunman but didn't seem to have much of a personal life.

Nitti's story is profoundly American in nature and context—immigrants struggling for success beyond the confines of the law in the dog-eat-dog social melting pots of Chicago and New York; the liberal use of intimidation and violence as the ultimate solution to almost any problem; politicians, police, and government officials of all stripes; plus the glitter and luxury of Hollywood and Miami. But it should also be made clear at the onset that this is not intended to be a cliché-ridden history of stereotypical "godfathers" and punch-drunk gunsels in loud pinstriped suits wearing white spats over their shoes and carrying violin cases—there is enough of this type of material around for those who are interested. It should also be noted that this work does not attempt to recount the countless gangland internecine feuds that took place during the Roaring Twenties and Dirty Thirties, only those considerable number that Frank Nitti had a direct involvement or influence with in a major way.

However, the related myth of Eliot Ness as somehow being Frank Nitti's archenemy is tackled and, perhaps, debunked for the final time. This is a study of ruthless and highly intelligent men whose lives were predicated upon constant danger to themselves and others, but who often had the outward appearance of successful businessmen, which in a sense they were except that their business was crime. Such men—and self-educated Nitti was their archetype—dealt with the interrelated commodities of crime of any type: terror, revenge, extortion, hostile business and union takeovers, torture, murder and assassinations, secret societies, and interlocking conspiracies at many levels of apparent reality.

In addition to Nitti's life, it was felt important to include vignettes concerning some of the more interesting characters he was closely involved with over the course of his criminal career. The final book has ultimately resulted in an analysis not only of Frank Nitti's life and career, but also of the many consequences and repercussions of his life and actions, some of which continue to this day.

This work represents my first analysis of American crime lords, my past work having focused on international security and intelligence issues including some aspects of the Asian organized-crime associations known as triads. However, during the course of my research, I soon discovered that Asian and American crime organizations share much in common including arcane customs and traditions specific to each group, violent enforcement methods combined with astute business practices, and factional politics in which subgroups within each organization constantly jockey for power. This last point is particularly pertinent to Nitti's leadership term over Chicago's most important organized-crime syndicate (commonly known as the Outfit) because it has been claimed, I believe erroneously, by some that Nitti was just a figurehead leader.

In regard to reference and data sources, the references used in this book are derived from official government sources, newspaper sources, previous studies, and mob-derived anecdotal sources, with a preference for primary sources wherever possible. Thousands of pages of digital and hard-copy references were researched over the course of three years. Some of the most interesting sources are passed-down oral histories, as well as Web sites that can only be described as *de-facto* mob official histories that offer a wealth of material.

The creative approach taken was to synthesize as much of this data as possible and apply analytical techniques commonly used for national-security and intelligence issues using open-source data from past studies; databases; the Internet; police, government, and newspaper files, and combining all this to produce an intelligence estimate of a most plausible causation and course of events, specifically related to the life and times of Frank Nitti and his legacy.

While quantitative facts were desired and much more official information is available today on global organized crime compared with what was available even a decade or so ago, much of the secret inner workings and history of the various factions of the Outfit, the Mafia, and la Cosa Nostra still remain shrouded in mystery. Even official information when passed on to the public is suspected of containing some intended disinformation and when it in turn is passed on by others, further misinformation. However, rejecting anecdotal evidence, rumors, and hearsay would in the case of this subject matter be a waste of rich source material. Whenever possible, multiple sources have been used to verify major claims.

The problem in the study of organized crime is compounded by the difficulty in obtaining direct experience with or even access to the subject matter (i.e. underworld mobsters), particularly when the subject has been dead for more than six decades. This often results in a focus on the historical record of highly visible events and material made available by law-enforcement agencies such as transcripts of wiretapped conversations between organized criminals.

Government evidence is subject to wide interpretations, while media accounts are often suspect because journalists tend to oversimplify some more mundane issues while emphasizing sensational events. Government reports, court files, and data collected by regulatory bodies are difficult to access and are also often biased because they only reflect official positions. Such agencies are often uncooperative with researchers who they perceive as a distraction from their primary mission of enforcing the law. Often media reports are summaries of official police reports, and when errors have been made in reporting, retractions, if any, are usually obscure.

It is not unusual for criminal autobiographies to include contradictions, self-glorifications, and attempts at vindications of their actions. Similarly, the unofficial accounts of law-enforcement officials may be biased toward self-glorification, as well as the dehumanization and exaggerated demonization of their criminal opponents. Nevertheless, the information used herein is of a diverse enough nature to provide a high level of confidence that the more important details of Frank Nitti's life have been captured accurately.

A lot of people and organizations helped out with this challenging project. The U.S. Federal Bureau of Investigation's

online "Electronic Reading Room" library of famous criminals
proved very useful and after an analysis of some six thousand
pages of its documents, provided many new insights and facts
on Frank Nitti, his times, and key associates. Janis Wiggins
and Tim Rives of the National Archives and Records Administration provided invaluable assistance in obtaining elusive
files, as did David M. Hardy of the FBI's Records Management Division for providing a good portion of the bureau's
files on Nitti, and Martin Lesley and Bryan McDaniel of
the Chicago Historical Society and Museum. Jim Hornstra
of NewsBank, Inc. did a great favor and opened a floodgate
of new material when he provided me open access to the
online *Chicago Tribune* Historical Archive...many thanks.
Photographic contributions and related design assistance were
provided by Silvana Gallardo and Billy Drago, Leonard Hill
of Leonard Hill Films, Tiffany Humble, Ron Frick, Scott
Deitche, Kimberly Murray@Corbis, Liz Latrobe, Allan
Eaglesham, James Richards, Troy Taylor, Tom Hunt, Walter
E. Janzen of Janzen Photography, and Daniel Brandt of Public
Information Research; Web-site design (see my Web site at
underworldicons.com) and original artwork by Boyd Speer at
BoydSpeer.com; and computer troubleshooting by Dan Lu. Gus
Russo provided some useful professional writing pointers, as
did Mark Winegardner and Allen (W. A.) Harbinson. Various
members of the University of Chicago staff were very helpful.
The services of *amazon.com* and *alibris.com* were invaluable in
researching and obtaining rare and out-of-print books. Special
thanks to Dr. Walter Willborn for his copyediting and editorial
assistance, and thanks to all other friends and family members
who provided timely assistance and helpful encouragement for
what, at times, appeared to be an all-but-impossible task, and
to any others who have inadvertently been left out.

Previous studies contained very useful information on Frank
Nitti and related issues, in particular the works of Herbert

Aller, Laurence Bergreen, John J. Binder, Ovid Demaris, Jim Doherty, Andy Edmonds, Marc Eliot, Claudia Furiati, Sam and Chuck Giancana, Robert J. Groden and Harrison Edward Livingstone, the Illinois Association for Criminal Justice, Elmer L. Irey and William J. Slocum, Estes Kefauver, John Kobler, Allan May, Hank Messick, Dan E. Moldea, Clark R. Mollenhoff, John Morgan, George Murray, Ed Reid, Ed Robertson, William F. Roemer Jr., Gus Russo, David E. Scheim, Robert J. Schoenberg, John William Tuohy, and Lee David Zlotoff. Thanks goes out to all those who made personal anecdotes and other special information available. Any inaccuracies, misinterpretations, or omissions are entirely my own responsibility.

My sincere gratitude is offered to publisher Carole Stuart for turning my dream into reality, and for the editorial assistance of Ivy McFadden and Sandra Stuart, who made it even more real.

And finally, a very special word of thanks and appreciation for Max Allan Collins, whose assistance and advice greatly facilitated the publication of this book, and whose own work has continued to cultivate the historical legacy of Frank Nitti over the years in new and innovative ways. Perhaps more than anyone else, Max has done the most work to keep this historical figure remembered in a manner true to the real man.

TODAY'S CHICAGO POLICE Department officially had surprisingly little to say to me concerning Frank Nitti when access was requested to their archives. Perhaps they'd just as soon forget he had ever existed? The FBI, the U.S. Department of Treasury, and the U.S. Secret Service all apparently still retain some files on Frank Nitti that rate a restricted-access-only classification for reasons that will soon become apparent to the reader.

—*Ronald D. Humble, 2008*

Frank Nitti: "The Enforcer"

No better friend. No worse enemy.
—Sulla the Dictator, Rome 80 B.C.

Origins

Frank "the Enforcer" Nitti was an infamous real-life Chicago gangster from the 1920s to the early 1940s, as well as being perhaps the most fictionalized American underworld character in history. He eventually rose to command Chicago's premier underworld organization, "the Outfit." A feared gangster, the sobriquet the Enforcer stuck throughout and, as we shall see, well after his criminal career and life. His criminal projects included the assassination of a Chicago mayor standing next to the president-elect of the United States, the faked kidnapping of an international con artist who was the brother of cosmetic-industry tycoon Max Factor, and the grand extortion of Hollywood that included brushes with such luminaries as Walt Disney and Bing Crosby. Nitti's actions touched on the lives of several future U.S. presidents. He died under very unusual and mysterious circumstances.

The life of Nitti was the portrait of a man of seemingly enormous contradictions, simultaneously warm and loving with his friends and family, but ruthless and cruel with his numerous enemies. An Italian immigrant who began his career as a barber, he became an enormously powerful man in organized crime. While it is true that Nitti's profession was one of violence and murder, for the most part, such acts were directed against fellow members of the underworld rather than innocent civilians. Nitti has been portrayed in Hollywood and in fiction as a tough "made man" and gangland killer—in truth, he was to various degrees all of these things, plus much more. However, the main difference was that, unlike most of his fictionalized versions, the actual Nitti wasn't always just an aggressive gangster. He was a complex human being, subject to changes in mood, temperament, humor, illness, and with varied personal interests and a private family life just like most people.

WHO WAS FRANK Nitti the real person? Born in Italy as Francesco Raffaele Nitto on January 27, 1886, his family came from a small town called Angori, near Salerno, Sicily. Frank's parents were Rose and Luigi (Louis) Nitto. He immigrated with his mother to the United States through the port of New York at age five on July 1, 1891, onboard the steamship *Guerra*. His family first settled at Harrison, New Jersey, and then moved on to Brooklyn, New York. Young Nitti made his declaration of intention for U.S. naturalization on March 9, 1921, request number 129102, and was naturalized as an American citizen on February 25, 1925, naturalization certificate number 191944, through the naturalization office in Chicago's federal building.[1]

Frank Nitti's prison records indicated that he only received a seventh-grade education from the Number 14 School at the corner of Navy and Concord streets, although he is believed by some to have had a full formal education in advanced chemistry.[2] Nevertheless, in later life, he projected an image of being well educated, intelligent, and quite urbane. At an early age, Nitti chose to reject science or any other legitimate profession as a career and became increasingly involved with criminal pursuits. During this process, he gained plenty of street smarts, initially through associations with street gangs.[3] Somewhere along the line of his criminal career, perhaps early on as a jewelry fence, he also reportedly became a talented watchmaker, likely the sign of a keen, analytical intellect.

Nitti's intelligence and capacity for learning begs the question of why he became a criminal in the first place. Poverty would be an easy answer, but there does not appear to be a ready sociological solution that would truly satisfy a criminologist. Nitti became a self-educated man, a dilettante of sorts, surrounded by colleagues who were in most cases his exact opposite. It is possible that he was an individual with a genetic or social predisposition for criminal activities, but it was also likely he was in it simply for the money, which after he entered organized crime's upper echelons, he was certainly never in short supply until his death.

His organized-crime career debuted when he was a part-time barber and jewelry fence in the large New York Italian community, but his keen business and accounting acumen soon helped him rise through the syndicate ranks. He learned the barbering trade before and after school. After leaving school, he claimed to have worked for eleven years at various jobs that included positions at the Brooklyn Palmers Cooperage Factory, Arbuckle Cooperage Factory, a shoe factory at Forty-eighth Street and Third Avenue, and other locations, giving his earnings to his mother and family.

His prison record indicates that he never had any military service. Nitti possibly worked as a barber and fence in John "Jake the Barber" Factor's barbershop, and he would maintain their relationship decades later when Factor had become a famous international con artist. In his prison records, Nitti claims that from 1919 to 1925, he worked for an R. Russo and then Giuseppi "Diamond Joe" Esposito, nominally as a barber for only $40 to $42 per week, although by the end of this period, he was in actuality fully operational within the Outfit. Once Prohibition began, he also established his own illegal alcohol-distillery operations.[4]

Nitti's crime roots were with street gangs. In Brooklyn, during a period around 1907, Nitti headed the Navy Street Boys juvenile gang, for which the eight-year-old Al Capone became the gang's mascot.[5] During the pre-Great War period, Nitti also was a youthful member of the infamous New York Five Points Gang, described as a "school for gangsterism," again along with the young Al Capone; there they forged a lasting friendship and partnership.[6] Louis Campagna, Frankie Yale, and John Torrio also had their gangster roots with this gang, which had been established by Irish thug Paul Kelly near the turn of the century with a strength of some fifteen hundred teenaged members.[7] The young Nitti might have been a member of the Forty Thieves Juniors youth wing of the Five Points Gang.

Besides Nitti and Capone, other future Mafia bosses such as Charles "Lucky" Luciano and Meyer Lansky had their roots with the Five Point Gang, which had a territory that included the east side of Manhattan and an area bounded by the Bowery and Broadway, Fourteenth Street and City Hall Park. Nitti's association with the Five Points Gang proves quite clearly that he became a member of the Mafia at an early age, as this gang was a training ground for its future made men. The FBI specifies that the Black Hand gangs and the Five Points Gang in New York City during the first decades of the twentieth century were at the roots of the growth of the American Mafia and Italian organized crime.[8]

At some point, Nitti joined the infamous Combination Network gang established by Luciano and Lansky in New York, which was closely associated with the Murder Inc. mercenary group of contract killers.[9] Nitti began fencing hot jewelry via lifelong friend and associate Alex Louis Greenberg, who he may have met through John Factor.[10] Records are lacking on his specific criminal activities during the formative years prior to the mid-1920s, but these likely included the traditional organized-crime areas of gambling, vice, extortion, loansharking, and robbery. He became a firearms and weapons expert. Nitti didn't relocate to Chicago until 1919, but he was soon favored in this city by its new underworld boss and personal friend, Al Capone, and rapidly became his second-in-command.

Frank Nitti's original surname was believed to have been misspelled by the press from Nitto to Nitti, likely a typesetting error in the *Chicago Tribune*. Nitti was also the surname of a well-known Italian politician of the era, Francesco Saverio Nitti, who had become prime minister of Italy in June 1919, which may have also contributed to Nitti's use of this alias. Throughout his career, he was commonly known by this surname, which he supposedly preferred because it "sounded more American," in addition to the nickname embellishment, the Enforcer, possibly relating to his keenness for correctly implementing orders entrusted to him by Capone, plus an aptitude for organizing violent and lethal activities. Specific activities of a Chicago Outfit enforcer would include maintaining internal discipline and supervising intimidation and violence, including murdering underworld rivals and outsiders as necessary.[11] Such underworld nicknames are often coined by rival mobsters, frustrated detectives, or creative news reporters, and rarely, if ever, by the individual criminal himself. Nitti also used the aliases "Frank Raddo" and "Frank Novelli," among others. Nicknames given him by fellow mobsters are said to have included "Screwy" and "Chi-chi."[12]

Looks and Attitude

A short, slight man—"diminutive" by some descriptions—he was by different accounts just five feet four and three-quarters inches to five feet six inches tall and weighed only about 145 pounds. Frank Nitti may have had a nervous twitch and has been described by some, perhaps unfairly, as looking like a nervous bank teller rather than a Chicago gangster.[13] He was introspective and often had a worried look to his appearance. He was considered by some to be handsome in a dark, rugged sort of way and has been compared in appearance to period movie-star bad-guy George Raft.[14] His face had some slight scarring, particularly under the lower lip, and an old nose injury.

His prison record indicated that he was in excellent health, but with a three-inch appendectomy scar. Nitti was always carefully groomed with meticulously styled black hair and had dark, large, liquid eyes.[15] He never wore prescription eyeglasses throughout his life. While he usually did not appear or act particularly tough, he, perhaps, provided an even more unsettling appearance because of his compact stature and cunning nature and was feared by many of his contemporaries.

Nitti was known as a high-strung stickler for details and for forcefully expressing his opinions to Capone and other senior gangsters. He could become quite abusive to subordinates who did not carefully follow his precise orders. The adjectives "smart," "cunning," "arrogant," and "obnoxious" have all been used to describe Nitti, although some of his closer associates such as John Roselli also described him as "one fabulous guy."[16] Nitti was certainly more intelligent than anyone else in the organized-crime community of the era with the possible exception of Meyer Lansky.

Nitti's photos showed him to be exceedingly well dressed and meticulous in his personal appearance and with either a pensive or slightly bemused expression on his face. The police called him "a classy little fellow."[17] Nitti usually wore his hair slicked straight back and parted to one side in the style of the period (usually to the right), but in an effort to change his appearance, he was known to use disguises that incorporated changes in hair styles and growing or shaving off mustaches.

This latter habit was unique among modern underworld leaders (although during the late stages of his life, Sam Giancana wore a full beard), because mustaches were associated with the "moustache Pete" image of Sicilian Mafiosos and the Camorra from the Old World and were usually a social no-no for progressive American gangsters. The custom of not wearing mustaches was likely started by Lucky Luciano in 1931 when he eliminated the Mafia old-guard leaders. A government agent once claimed that Nitti's mustache made him look like Adolf Hitler while others thought it increased his "rabbity" appearance.[18]

Frank Nitti completely trusted few people.[19] In fact, Nitti had relatively few friends among his gangster colleagues and often preferred the company of professional, educated people who were not directly involved with crime. Many other gangsters thought of him as being "snotty."[20] He was usually a quiet, thoughtful man "not much given to talking" who did not easily share his emotions with others, although later in life, he was likely torn by personal and emotional conflicts.[21] Nitti was known to speak in a somewhat condescendingly precise diction to his subordinates in the Outfit, who found him to be cold, humorless, and colorless and simply not as much fun when compared to Big Al. In fact, he often gave the distinct impression that he despised other criminals. He is remembered as even talking to Al Capone on occasion in a quite abrupt manner, once when discussing a problem and telling Capone, "I'll handle it, you just keep out of it," to the amazement of the other gangsters present.[22] However, Nitti's personal relationship with Capone, until Capone was sent to prison for the final time, was almost that of a brother.

NITTI OFTEN MADE efforts at projecting the image of a Mafia wise guy through his speech and mannerisms, which were sometimes gruff and menacing in tone.[23] He was widely known as an articulate and forceful speaker who would use phrases such as "We've got the world by the tail with a downhill start," and "The goose is in the oven waiting to be cooked."[24] If Nitti did have an accent, it would have been a Brooklyn accent rather than Italian. His handwriting was almost elegant.

Frank Nitti apparently did not have the type of personal vices that many other gangster leaders such as Al Capone often fell victim to: casually frequenting prostitutes, gambling, heavy drinking, or using drugs of any type. He simply loathed other members of the Outfit who drank heavily and made fools of themselves in public, would not tolerate them and often encouraged them to get on the wagon or face potentially fatal consequences.[25] He did chain-smoke cigarettes and was a moderate drinker, enjoying the occasional glass of wine.[26]

However, Nitti routinely made decisions that would increase and expand the business activities of the Outfit in precisely these vices in which he did not personally partake, and he made victims of many innocent, and some not-so-innocent, people. He also routinely ordered the intimidation, beating, maiming, and murder of his enemies and may have had a direct hand in some of these violent activities. Some of Nitti's subordinates were exceedingly brutal, and he felt no hesitation in using them when he deemed it necessary.

Professional Expertise

Frank Nitti was likely the best strategist ever produced by organized crime, and he was one of the few underworld leaders of the period with an expert knowledge of business and accounting.[27] The press described him as being "crafty, artful, subtle and ruthless, Nitti is a man made to order for stratagems and spoils."[28] He soon became known as the "so-called financial genius of the Capone liquor and vice syndicate."[29] Nitti was unique in his ability to develop alternative innovative solutions for problems, and he had an extensive knowledge of firearms.[30] Some knowledge of the sciences is apparent in the manner in which he developed his modus operandi and his common use of "lateral thinking." Nitti did not like to make mistakes in his projects and was as adept as any police detective at seeking important clues and background evidence. He carefully researched his criminal business activities and was an avid reader of daily financial newspapers and other business publications. For example, prior to his large Hollywood shakedown operation, Nitti learned from his research that the motion-picture industry was ripe for extortion and for entertainment-union wage-increase shakedowns, and he used this hard data to target specific companies and industry leaders. When undertaking union takeovers, he would study union constitutions and bylaws.[31]

For many years, Nitti served as Al Capone's enforcer, business manager, and second-in-command. Not only did he avoid being prosecuted by U.S. Treasury Agent Eliot Ness's the Untouchables as has often been portrayed on film, but he likely planned the Saint Valentine's Day Massacre for Capone, took command of the Outfit in Chicago when Capone went to prison, and steered organized crime into new and innovative territories, such as rackets involving unionized labor and Hollywood's motion-picture industry.

Once he was the boss of the Outfit, it is likely that Nitti thought of himself as a corporate CEO rather than a criminal leader because he brought a businesslike style of leadership to Chicago organized crime that has not been duplicated to this day. Nitti was the level-headed businessman that the glamor-seeking Capone never could be, and he regularly worked in his relatively spartan office from early in the morning until late at night, although it was apparent he enjoyed business lunches at expensive restaurants, some of which he owned. He also liked to frequent nightclubs such as Chicago's Arigan Ballroom, which offered entertainment by musicians such as Wayne King, and with wife Anna, Nitti often enjoyed a night dancing and dining at "the better class hotels." Nitti is known to have played golf with Al Capone and Jack McGurn and attended the Strand movie theater in Lansing, Michigan, with his FBI records also indicating an affiliation with the Illinois Golf Association, Miami.[32]

Arrest Record

Frank Nitti was never quite a stranger to the law and the police, but neither was he what could be termed a jailbird. Up until at least 1930 and his prosecution for income-tax evasion, he did not have a widely known police or FBI criminal record and did not yet qualify for Chicago's "who's who" list of criminals and public enemies.[33] To the chagrin of J. Edgar Hoover, information on Nitti was also not to be found in the extensive records of the National Division of Identification and Information. Initially, the police took an interest in him because of his well-known association with Al Capone, but later his photograph was often splashed in the newspapers, and he soon became infamous. After he was imprisoned for income-tax evasion, the Board of Parole took the unusual step—without apparent success—of making inquiries to various state identification bureaus and police forces in states and cities where Nitti had spent time to learn something more on his criminal past.

Strangely, Nitti never was included on the Chicago Crime Commission's "Public Enemies List" when even relative nonentities within the Outfit were often featured prominently.[34] Nitti's Chicago Police Department criminal identification number in 1936 was C-25924 and group number 2219, while his official FBI fingerprint classification was 31/28 MM/01 14/.[35] While in a Chicago court appearance on September 26, 1933, Nitti answered questions in a clear, low voice and claimed that he was a restaurateur, owning Chicago restaurants at 901 South Halsted Street (Naples Restaurant) and 5829 Madison Street.[36] Usually to arrest an Outfit leader such as Nitti for even a short time, the authorities had to resort to the degrading charge of vagrancy, which provided a legal loophole to arrest someone who found it difficult to prove that he had an honest occupation.[37] Nitti was arrested on a vagrancy charge following the Saint Valentine's Day Massacre in 1929 and was released on a $10,000 bond. He was again arrested for vagrancy after he was released during his income-tax trial on November 7, 1930, on a $50,000 bond. The new charge forced him to put up an additional $10,000. John H. Lyle was the presiding judge in both of these instances, and he took credit for developing the vagrancy charge as a method of quickly removing criminals from the streets of Chicago.[38] Once Nitti became the head of the Chicago syndicate, he was placed under almost constant police surveillance and harassment.[39]

FRANK NITTI'S MAJOR incarceration resulted from his March 1930 indictment by a federal district court on charges of income-tax evasion for the years 1925 to 1927, for which he was sentenced to eighteen months at the United States Penitentiary Leavenworth, Kansas. After receiving several months off for good behavior, he was released March 24, 1932. Frank Nitti also spent short times in jail for lesser offenses. However, Nitti's 1930 FBI file noted that "this Subject has been arrested by the local police on numerous occasions but has always managed to secure his release and a court order destroying his photograph and fingerprint records." He briefly went to jail in 1925 along with the mob's youthful politician Johnny Patton.[40] The Cook County, Chicago Illinois Division prison opened in 1929 as the first building of a new 1,160-prisoner complex that had as prisoners such senior Outfit leaders as Al Capone, Frank Nitti, and Tony Accardo.[41]

NITTI WAS ARRESTED in 1940 as a result of a federal gambling investigation and subpoenaed to appear before a federal grand jury, and he was also indicted for violations of the U.S. Radio Communications Act for operating a racing-wire service, but was soon free, and the charges had no apparent effect on his operations.[42]

Frank Nitti was never convicted or tried for murder, but was linked to numerous such cases. While FBI and associated local police files do not reveal any specific murder or physical assault charges ever having been laid against Nitti, he was certainly suspected of being the brains behind various such lethal acts. In 1933, Nitti was arrested for questioning concerning the murders of North Side gangster Teddy Newberry and Chicago Mayor Anton Cermak, events that we shall see he was, in fact, closely linked to behind the scenes.[43]

Nitti certainly had a reputation for being tough.[44] An FBI source indicates that Nitti had, indeed, personally killed, but was not one of the top Outfit men with confirmed kills.[45] He was said to be handy with a straight razor resulting from his short career as a barber. Nitti may not have been the greatest American gunman since Wyatt Earp, but neither was he just the mob accountant or frontman as some current crime writers and historical apologists have painted him. Nitti certainly ordered many murders of fellow criminals, and his was likely the Machiavellian mind that planned complex, major Outfit hits such as the Hymie Weiss murder, the Saint Valentine's Day Massacre, and the assassination of Chicago Mayor Anton Cermak.

Family Life

By all accounts, Frank Nitti was a loving husband and doting father, a skillful businessman, as well as being a ruthless killer. His father died in Italy when Frank was just eighteen months old, and his mother brought him to the United States when he was five. He once claimed in court that he had worked at various jobs just to support his mother and the rest of the Nitti clan in Brooklyn. His mother remarried, and he could not get along with his stepfather, which was a major reason for his leaving home as a young man.

Nitti stated in his prison records that "I was raised in a good Christian home and taught to be a Catholic." A November 1933 newspaper article claimed that Frank Nitti was Al Capone's cousin, but this appears unlikely (the Fischetti brothers were Al's cousins).[46] He reported to the FBI in 1930 that he had a sister named Mrs. Anna Vollaro who lived in Brooklyn, while his sister, Marie (likely a half-sister), was the wife of fellow Outfit member Anthony "Tough Tony" Capezio, a suspect in the Saint Valentine's Day Massacre.[47]

In his prison record, Nitti indicated that he partially supported sister Anna "owing to her large family." It is also likely that Frank Nitti had at least one half-brother from his mother's second marriage and, through this half-brother, other nephews and nieces. He had other cousins, but it is unlikely Capone was one of these. Frank Nitti undoubtedly has descendants today in the United States including those through his adopted son and his grandchildren. Romeo Jack Nitti, a small-time associate of the Outfit, was believed to be a relative of Frank Nitti's, possibly a nephew, and was sent to Dallas with Paul Roland Jones to work with Outfit associate Jack Ruby prior to the President John F. Kennedy assassination.[48] Frank Dolendi was a Nitti nephew.

Frank Nitti's first wife, Anna Theresa Ronga, has been characterized as an innocent and loyal spouse. Federal agent Elmer L. Irey described the first Mrs. Nitti as a "very pretty woman."[49] Nitti met her by the mid-1920s, and they were married on February 16, 1929 in St. Louis, just two days after the Saint Valentine's Day Massacre. She came from a very good family and was the daughter of a medical doctor. Because she was a divorcee, she could not marry in a Roman Catholic Church.

She remained loyal to her husband throughout his criminal career, including his stretch in prison, until her untimely death. His marriage to her was a logical connection given Nitti's thinly veiled aspirations to be considered part of decent society. In fact, his father-in-law, Dr. Gaetano Ronga, operated on Frank Nitti and saved his life after Chicago police officers under the personal orders of Mayor Anton Cermak attempted to murder him in 1932. Dr. Ronga was a "prominent civic leader" in Chicago. [50] However, Dr. Ronga also was a known mob physician and in addition to providing medical services to Nitti, did so for other known gangsters such as Samuel Samuzzo "Samoots" Amatuna, "one of the most treacherous and cold-blooded killers in gangland," in November 1925 at Chicago's Jefferson Park Hospital. Amatuna had been shot and later died.[51]

In 1934, Frank and Anna are believed to have adopted a son from a young unwed mother because Anna could not conceive, which supposedly was the reason she had been divorced from her previous husband.[52] The boy was named Joseph, and while Nitti was tough with other gangsters, he went to great lengths to spoil his son, who reportedly became a successful legitimate businessman as an adult. Such adoptions in Italian organized-crime families are considered commonplace, and Anna and Frank proved to be wonderful parents. Unfortunately, Anna died in Chicago on November 19, 1940, at thirty-eight from an internal ailment, likely colitis, which was often fatal during this era.[53] Frank Nitti may have become seriously depressed over his wife's death, and he often wore black until his own death several years later.

Nitti's second wife was Antoinette (Toni) M. Caravetta, the former secretary and fiancée of gambler and horse- and dog-track owner Edward "Fast Eddie" O'Hare.[54] Fast Eddie, a former attorney, was an Al Capone business-ventures adviser who passed on information to the Internal Revenue Service that helped sentence and convict Capone to prison for income-tax evasion. In return, O'Hare likely escaped an income-tax conviction himself. His rise within the Outfit really began after Capone was imprisoned and Nitti took control.

O'Hare was president of the Sportsman's Park Race Track and Hawthorne Kennel Club dog-racing facilities, which he operated for Frank Nitti along with Johnny Patton, the "boy mayor" of Burnham, Illinois.[55] However, on November 8, 1939, O'Hare was reportedly executed by the Outfit for crossing Nitti on a business transaction and possibly as overdue payback for informing on Capone. Big Al was enraged upon hearing while in prison of O'Hare's treason and had sworn to have him killed. The pragmatic Nitti recognized that O'Hare was an important "money getter" and allowed him to operate as long as possible, but likely ordered his execution to coincide with Capone's release from prison.[56] Nitti married Eddie's former fiancée in July 1942. Chicago's O'Hare International Airport was named after Edward O'Hare's son from an earlier marriage, Butch, a World War II naval aviation hero.[57]

Antoinette, an attractive woman with auburn hair, was thirty-seven when they married and some two decades Nitti's junior. It is possible that earlier she had been Nitti's mistress; she had corresponded with him while he was in prison in 1931. By a few accounts, the marriage was unhappy, and Nitti had entered into it for little more than the convenience of providing a caring mother for young Joseph. On the other hand, there are also many indications that theirs was a close and sincere relationship and that she truly loved him.[58] In any case, Nitti died nine months after they were married, although she continued to raise Joseph and apparently remained Mrs. Nitti for the rest of her life.[59] She also continued to be involved with Chicago and Florida racetrack activities until at least the 1950s and was subpoenaed to appear as a witness before federal grand juries investigating organized crime, as well as numerous investigations into the tax situation of her late husband's estate.[60]

Mistresses?

It has been rumored that Frank Nitti was involved with other women as perhaps mistresses or girlfriends, but there is very little detail on such relationships and how these might have affected his apparently rock-solid first marriage and his short second one. Certainly, even when single, Nitti never had Al Capone's boisterous reputation of partying with large numbers of young women of dubious backgrounds. Anna is said to have claimed that she and Nitti were inseparable during the first three years of their marriage before he went to prison in January 1931. As related, it is possible that Nitti's second wife, Antoinette, had been his mistress at some point, because they had known each other since at least the early 1930s.

Nitti's flames are said to have included Virginia Hill, a thrice-divorced aspiring actress who came to Chicago from Alabama to be a burlesque dancer for the 1933-34 Chicago World's Fair (an event with which Nitti became quite involved) and who was also a girlfriend of an array of other hoods including Frank Costello, Charlie Fischetti, Anthony Accardo, Carlos Marcello, and Joey Adonis, as well as being Bugsy Siegel's infamous paramour.[61] Not surprisingly, the footloose Hill was known to many as "the Queen of the Mob." She owned two hundred pairs of shoes and was devoted to high fashion and expensive jewelry.[62] There is a popular story that at an executive session of a Senate investigating committee on organized crime, Hill was asked why so many men gave her so much money and expensive gifts, to which she replied, "Senator, I'm the best goddamned cocksucker in the world."[63]

Hill was also known to be a money runner for the Chicago mob and to have a penchant for blackmailing Hollywood stars. It seems difficult to believe that the elitist Nitti could have been seriously attracted to such a "vulgar and obscene" opportunistic harlot. The FBI records on Hill do not indicate that Nitti was one of her numerous lovers, but do hint that she was both a narcotics user (she liked smoking opium in Chinatown dens) and trafficker, as well as being linked to a prostitution ring.[64] She also liked spending large sums of money on parties, clothes, jewelry, and accessories, frequently moved between luxury accommodations, and sometimes changed her hair color on a daily basis. For petty expenses, she kept $100 bills in hatboxes.[65]

Following Siegel's unsolved murder at her Beverly Hills home in 1947, she attempted suicide several times with drug overdoses, but not surprisingly survived each attempt. Then fearing for her life because of money she allegedly stole from the New York mob that commanded the feared Murder Inc. hit squad, Hill slipped away into obscurity to Mexico. Notorious Chicago Outfit killers David Yaras, Leonard Patrick, and William Block have been linked to the Siegel hit because of the modus operandi used in the shooting. Hill may have been skimming money from the Las Vegas casino operations with Siegel, which led to his death, and saving it in a Swiss bank account.[66] However, Hill did not even bother to attend Siegel's funeral.[67] She later reportedly became a "Mrs. Hans Hauser," a skiing instructor living in Spokane, Washington, and the mother of a child.[68] Another report has it that Hill fatally poisoned herself on March 24, 1966, in Kopple, Austria, where she was living on a Mafia widow's "pension." Others agree that her suicide attempts were ultimately successful.[69] Beautiful women and gangland leaders have an almost natural attraction—Chicago boss Sam Giancana's girlfriends included movie actress Marilyn Monroe and singing star Phyllis McGuire of the McGuire Sisters.

Hangouts

Frank Nitti when single may have occupied an apartment at Gladys and Lotus avenues in Chicago and liked to take infrequent winter holidays in Florida.[70] In Miami, Nitti would sometimes stay at Charlie Fischetti's showcase home on Biscayne Bay.[71] Later, Nitti, like Capone, would own a Miami family home he used for winter vacations with his wife and son.[72] Nitti eventually sold his Florida house for $45,000 to Max Caldwell, head of the Chicago retail clerks' union, who was in cahoots with Outfit labor-racketeering schemes.[73] Nitti also had a summer home at Benton Harbor at Lake Michigan. However, in general, Nitti was a compulsive worker who put in long hours on an almost daily basis and expected the same behavior from his top men.[74]

Nitti's prison records and other sources indicate the following as some places of personal residence or nominal business:

- Harrison, New Jersey (1891-1893, residence)
- 148 Navy Street, Brooklyn, New York (1907-1911, residence)
- 104 Garfield Place, Brooklyn (1911-1919, residence and later residence of sister Anna Vollaro)
- 2653 North Halsted Street, Chicago, Illinois (1919-1923, residence)
- 852 South Halsted Street, Chicago (1919-1923, employed as barber by R. Russo)
- 3167 Clybourne Avenue, Chicago (1923-1924, employed as barber by G. Esposito)
- 2425 North Cicero Avenue, Cicero, Illinois (1924-1925, employed as barber by G. Esposito)
- 800 South Oakley Boulevard, Chicago (1924-1930 period, business)
- 1127 South Troop Street, Chicago (1924-1925, residence)

- 833 South Marshfield Avenue, Chicago (1925-1927, residence)
- 1801 Fiftieth Avenue, Cicero (1927-1928, residence)
- 3201 South Clinton Street, Berwyn, Illinois (fall of 1930, residence)
- 1200/1208 McAlister Place, Chicago (1929-1942, residence)
- 712 Selbourne Road, Chicago (1942-1943, residence)

Nitti bought his second wife a lavish gift of a twenty-room Chicago mansion that was much more extravagant than the modest residence Al Capone had maintained in Chicago, although Capone also owned a very upscale estate in Miami. This, Nitti's final home, was located in Chicago's posh west Riverside district at 712 Selbourne Road and is apparently still occupied in pristine condition today. Nitti personally supervised the design and remodeling of this home.[75] The respectable, quiet, and tree-shaded neighborhood of Riverside was also the home of other gangsters including John "Screwy" Moore (a.k.a. Claude Maddox), owner of the Paddock Lounge; Francis Maritote; Joey Glimco; Louis Campagna; and Nitti's bent politician pal, Harry Hochstein.[76]

Nitti's home and all visitors were under constant police and FBI surveillance. His neighbors said the Nittis were a quiet family who kept to themselves, but Frank Nitti often took long walks about his neighborhood and exchanged pleasant greetings with them.[77] In 1940, Nitti had lived with his first wife at 1208 McAlister Place next to his in-laws.[78]

Much of the Outfit's activities under Nitti took place in the downtown Chicago business district commonly called the Loop. The name Loop is said to have originated from the route of a cable-car line that encircled Chicago's central business district in 1882 prior to the construction of the Loop elevated railroad tracks of the Chicago Transit Authority in

1897. The Loop has since become a term for the city's historic downtown, an area roughly bounded by the Chicago River on the north and west, Grant Park on the east, and Congress Parkway to the south. Chicago's First Ward has always been a strategic district for organized crime, containing the Loop, the Near West Side, and the Near South Side, and has been the site of businesses as diverse as brothels, gambling houses, fine department stores, restaurants, skyscrapers, five-star hotels, and major banks.

One of Nitti's Chicago headquarters was located in the Loop's massive La Salle-Wacker Building at 221 North La Salle Street in a cramped three-room office suite, number 554. The La Salle-Wacker Building is an art-deco skyscraper that today is used as a multitenant commercial office building and is one of Chicago's most high-tech wired structures for Internet, multimedia, and telecommunications applications. Nitti's cramped space became the location of music radio station WAAF during the 1950s.

This office complex in Nitti's era was the location of a legitimate and somewhat innocuous enterprise that he called the Quality Flour Company, but was also used as a front by the Outfit for nonbaking activities such as a gambling-wire service. Its location in the heart of downtown Chicago's central business district in a commercial office high-rise was a far cry from Capone's luxurious headquarters in the Four Deuces bordello at 2222 South Wabash (disguised as a used-furniture store), Cicero's Anton Hotel at 4835 West Twenty-second Street, the Hawthorne Hotel (Inn) at 4823 Twenty-second Street in Cicero during 1924 to 1926 (complete with bulletproof metal window shutters and nicknamed "the Castle"), the Metropole Hotel (owned by the Capone family) located at 2300 South Michigan Avenue from 1926 to 1928, and finally the Lexington Hotel on 2135 South Michigan Boulevard. Outfit headquarters and operations were sometimes fronted by an antique dealer or a doctor's office, and Nitti used several places for gambling headquarters, such as the Ace News Service located over a furniture store at 6233 Cottage Grove Avenue. Another Nitti apartment headquarters was at 33 West Kinzie Street in a "striking, 100-year-old brick building" that is now the home of Harry Caray's restaurant in the Make Carrosse office building. It is likely that Capone maintained others.[79]

Often known as the Fort, the Lexington Hotel headquarters was abandoned by Nitti shortly after Capone was sentenced to imprisonment in 1931, but it is possible that a lower-key Outfit presence was subsequently reestablished. It was built as one of Chicago's first high-rise luxury hotels to house dignitaries during the World's Columbian Exposition in 1893. Through the decades, it decayed until it turned into a flophouse and was demolished in the late 1980s. Nitti was known to keep suites at such hotels as the Carleon at 2138 South Wabash Avenue, Antonette (Cicero), Auditorium, Seneca, La Salle, Congress, Sherman, and the Bismarck (often the location of Outfit board of directors' meetings). The third floor of the Capri Restaurant at 123 North Clark Street, which was owned by Nitti and was across the street from the Chicago City Hall and County Building and known to some as "little city hall," was also a favorite secret meeting place and mob hangout because it had a private elevator entrance that could be used to control access to its large dining room.[80]

Some of Nitti's most important meetings were held at his home or the homes of close associates such as his neighbor, Harry Hochstein. Having different meeting places meant Nitti could not be easily found by underworld enemies or law-enforcement officials. Hotels also provided a neutral ground for Nitti's frequent meetings with politicians, union leaders, and other gangsters. Capone once threw Nitti a birthday party at the New Florence Restaurant where champagne, spiced steak, and an impressive cake were served.[81]

Heritage

Frank Nitti remained proud of his ethnic heritage throughout his life, but usually referred to himself as being Italian-American rather than Sicilian. There are stories that he endured beatings by Irish-American policemen rather than deny he was of Italian origin. Yet Nitti's story is a profoundly American one, just as the Mafia has become an inarguable part of American society. He was a rare thinking-man's gangster with a philosophical bent.

Throughout Nitti's long criminal career as he rose first as Al Capone's lead enforcer and adviser and then himself became the leader of perhaps the greatest organized-crime syndicate the world has ever known—the Chicago Outfit—a series of events conspired to raise him to an increasingly legendary status. Following his death, this process continued through the entertainment industry's use of his character that played upon the legends—which were based on some facts—and resulted in new myths to the point where today it is increasingly difficult to separate fact from fiction.

APPENDIX A PROVIDES a complete chronology of the life and times of Frank Nitti.

2

The Outfit

...the Mafia is powerful, so powerful that entire police forces or even a mayor's office can be under Mafia control. That's why Hoover was afraid to let us tackle it. He was afraid that we'd show up poorly. Why take the risk, he reasoned, until we were forced to by public exposure of our shortcomings?
—William C. Sullivan, *The Bureau: My Thirty Years in Hoover's FBI*

Corporation is good for business.
—Johnny Torrio

Organized Crime

The Mafia, the mob, the underworld, la Cosa Nostra, and the Outfit are some of the terms associated with organized crime in the United States, and to most people, usually mean the same thing. But what exactly are these organizations and others like them, who participates in them, and in what activities? Frank Nitti led the largest underworld organization in Chicago and one of the most powerful Mafia groups in America, the Outfit. However, when people talk about organized crime, it sometimes has different meanings:

The term "organized crime" can be used in two very different senses. It can simply mean systematic and illegal activity for power or profit. Today, however, the term is usually used in a second sense, and has become virtually synonymous with gangsters in general or the "Mafia" or mafia-type organizations in particular.

It is usually implied or stated by those using the term in this latter sense that gangster organizations have gained an unacceptable level of power through violence and the ability to corrupt weak, greedy and therefore passive public officials; organized crime in this sense is a threat to rather than part of the rest of society.[1]

THE FEDERAL BUREAU of Investigation today defines organized crime as any group having some manner of a formalized structure and whose primary objective is to obtain money through illegal activities.[2] Such groups maintain their position through the use of actual or threatened violence, corrupt public officials, graft, or extortion, and generally have a significant impact on the people in their locales, region, or the nation as a whole. The FBI defines a "criminal enterprise" as a group of individuals with an identified hierarchy, or comparable structure, engaged in significant criminal activity. These organizations often engage in multiple criminal activities and have extensive supporting networks. The FBI believes the terms "organized crime" and "criminal enterprise" to be similar, and they are often used synonymously.

These definitions are just as applicable to Frank Nitti's era as they are today and include the criminal activities of murder, extortion, drug trafficking, corruption of public officials, gambling, infiltration of legitimate businesses (e.g. vending machines, unions, securities, waterfront activities, bars and clubs, garment industry, food produce, garbage disposal, restaurants, and real estate), labor racketeering, "vigorish" high-interest loansharking, prostitution, pornography, tax fraud schemes, and most notably today, stock-manipulation schemes. As we shall see, following the repeal of Prohibition, Frank Nitti emphasized gambling, union racketeering, vice, loansharking, and extortion operations.[3]

Racketeering refers to an illegal business or fraudulent scheme such as those dealing in stolen property, insurance frauds, fraudulent bankruptcies, securities frauds, credit frauds, forgery, counterfeiting, illegal gambling, trafficking in drugs or liquor, or various forms of extortion.[4] Major rackets today include the global trafficking of arms of all types and of migrant people who are seeking a new homeland or who are tricked or pressured to become indentured laborers or prostitutes in new lands—in essence, wageless slaves.

Organized crime's illegal profits are in turn laundered in a range of legitimate enterprises such as real estate, construction ventures, restaurants, fuel-oil companies, meat-packing/distribution companies, concrete plants, trucking companies, garbage/carting companies, the telephone calling-card industry, and Wall Street. Key activities of organized crime are summarized in Table 2.1. Today, the Racketeer Influenced and Corrupt Organizations Act (RICO) of the United States Code defines a criminal enterprise as "any individual, partnership, corporation, association, or other legal entity, and any union or group of individuals associated in fact although not a legal entity," active in organized crime. The Continuing Criminal Enterprise statute further defines a criminal enterprise as any group of six or more people where one of the six occupies a position of organizer, a supervisory position, or any other position of management with respect to the other five and which generates substantial income or resources and is engaged in a continuing series of criminal violations of the United States Code. The FBI defines significant racketeering activities as those undertaking criminal acts that are chargeable under the RICO act. While RICO and related legislation came into effect considerably after Frank Nitti's reign, it provides a useful framework for understanding past and current organized-crime activities.

Table 2.1 Activities of Organized Crime	
FEDERAL CRIMES	STATE CRIMES
• Bribery • Sports bribery • Counterfeiting • Embezzlement of union funds • Mail fraud • Wire fraud • Money laundering • Obstruction of justice • Murder for hire • Drug trafficking • Prostitution and other areas of sexual exploitation • Alien smuggling • Trafficking in counterfeit goods • Weapons trafficking • Theft from interstate shipment • Interstate transportation of stolen property	• Murder • Kidnapping • Gambling • Arson • Robbery • Bribery • Extortion • Drugs

The Mafia

The Mafia is a secret criminal organization that historically has had significant economic and political power both in criminal and legitimate enterprises first in its native Sicilian society and then in America following the paths of immigration to the United States in the nineteenth and twentieth centuries.

It likely originated in Palermo and western Sicily during the late Middle Ages as a mercenary band of strong-arm enforcers hired by gentry landowners and as a local reaction against long periods of foreign misrule.[5]

These secret societies of "Men of Honor" (*Uomo d' Onore*) eventually evolved into a domestic networked organization of near-autonomous rural groups that lorded over peasants who had little or no allegiance to their often foreign legitimate rulers. It became a widespread and powerful enshrined secret society of bandits who fought against foreign oppressors and much later in its history, developed its organized-crime characteristics as we know these today.

Similar secret Italian societies include the Camorra or Neapolitan Mafia, 'Ndrangheta or Calabrian Mafia, and the Sacra Corona Unita or United Sacred Crown, which are all categorized by the FBI as "Italian Organized Crime."[6] Some claim that by 1900, the Mafia in Sicily controlled virtually the entire western third of the island, taking control of all local governments, factories, and landed estates.[7] The Camorra and other Italian societies have now for all intents and purposes been absorbed by the mainstream Mafia.[8]

The American Mafia is believed to have been established by Don Vito Cascio Ferro, who fled to New York City in 1893 following the murder of banker Emanuele Notarbartolo in Sicily. It was subsequently greatly strengthened when large numbers of its members fled to the United States during the 1920s to escape oppression by the Fascist dictator, Benito Mussolini.[9] In addition to New York, New Orleans was a cradle for the Mafia, which soon spread to all major cities in America and Canada. The term Mafia is often used loosely to refer to all American organized-crime groups, but in fact, the actual Sicilian family-based Mafia is only one element within a much broader stream of related Italian organized-crime groups that includes such organizations as Chicago's Outfit, which historically has not been family based. In general, the Mafia is a fraternal organization divided into many different gangs or mobs, rings, syndicates, or conspiracies. Members can belong to one or more such groups simultaneously, and the organization may be permanent or temporary.[10]

The rise of the modern American Mafia has often been traced to Charles "Lucky" Luciano who in 1935 became considered by many as the "boss of bosses," the number one in command of a national syndicate, often termed la Cosa Nostra. Luciano chaired a so-called Mafia Commission of organized-crime leaders from across the nation and enforced his leadership through Murder Inc., a group of professional contract killers who worked nationally. Luciano founded Murder Inc. with Ben Siegel, Louis Buchalter, and Meyer Lansky. Under the Mafia Commission's guidelines for the use of Murder Inc., organized crime across America had the right to contract one of its hit men to liquidate any problem individuals, although there were restrictions on killing innocent civilians (i.e. those not directly involved with organized crime), corrupt politicians, police officers, reporters, and others whose elimination would generate too much publicity and interfere with business operations. Frank Nitti was a customer of such services provided by Bugsy Siegel and Meyer Lansky.[11] The organization supposedly went into decline when Abe "Kid Twist" Reles, a top lieutenant in Murder Inc., was charged with murder by police in 1940 and proceeded to rat on his fellow hit men with details of more than two hundred Mafia-sanctioned murders. Reles was subsequently murdered in Coney Island under mysterious circumstances.[12] Currently, there exists a revisionist school of thought that believes "that there was no such thing as Murder Inc. with hired killers sitting around waiting for killing assignments."[13]

Through its history, leading American Mafia families continued to monopolize illegal activities related to alcohol, vice, gambling, and vigorish loansharking, with competing families establishing mutually recognized and agreed upon territories either by negotiation or if all else failed, violent intimidation. Loansharking was practiced by Italian and Jewish mob members, with sometimes tens of millions of dollars on the street being run by a single syndicate. Yet, the very existence of the American Mafia continued to be ignored or denied in the first half of the twentieth century. For example, during court questioning in 1947, Jake "Greasy Thumb" Guzik, a high-level member of the Outfit for decades, was asked if a Chicago organized-crime syndicate existed. He replied, "Not that I know of. I never heard of it…I take that back, I read about it, but I don't believe it. I don't know of any. There might be a few people friendly to each other, but that is all."[14]

During the peak of Frank Nitti's leadership in the 1930s, the Mafia formed the institutionalized structure that is now the pattern for American organized crime, but it continued operations in relative obscurity from the general public for decades. In 1957, the New York State Police uncovered and disrupted a meeting of sixty-four high-ranking members of the Mafia Commission at Joseph Barbara's sprawling estate near the small upstate New York town of Apalachin, proving its existence definitively. Joseph Barbara was the millionaire president of the Canada Dry Bottling Company of Endicott, New York.

This Mafia Commission meeting had representatives of Mafia groups from New York, Buffalo, Chicago, Detroit, and Philadelphia. New Orleans had traditionally been considered more independent in most areas. Chicago's Outfit dominated smaller Midwestern groups from Kansas City, St. Louis, Milwaukee, Rockford, and Detroit, while Cleveland was under the Genovese family from New York City.

The Apalachin revelation forced FBI Director J. Edgar Hoover to finally admit the existence of organized crime in America, and he then formed the Top Hoodlum Program to counter it in the public eye. The specific FBI effort against the Outfit had been termed the "Reactivation of the Capone Gang" project. Its name illustrated the FBI's lack of knowledge concerning the Outfit, which had been quietly maintained and expanded by Nitti and others after Al Capone's imprisonment and was certainly never required to be reactivated in any manner.[15]

During the early 1960s, Attorney General Robert Kennedy, against father Joe Kennedy's advice, began an obsessive campaign against the American underworld that may have contributed to the deaths of his brother, President John F. Kennedy, and himself. The 1963 testimonies of Mafia informant Joseph Valachi, a soldier in the Genovese family who was one of the first to break the code of *omerta* in a major way, turned further detailed evidence on the secret workings of the underworld that included names of members, structures, power bases, codes, swearing-in ceremonies, and other guarded secrets.

In the late 1980s, the Mafia Commission's power was supposedly weakened from a series of federal racketeering charges under the RICO statutes resulting in the various city syndicates taking on more independent operations. However, the Mafia Commission apparently still exists and is today largely centered around the East Coast region of the United States and Canada. The commission reportedly reconvened in 2001 to formulate policy and agree on areas of cooperation.[16]

The FBI under J. Edgar Hoover did not admit the existence of the Mafia and organized crime in general until late in his career although the agency's files are replete with case histories and studies of such organizations dating back to the 1920s. The FBI had even undertaken a major study on the topic called the "Mafia Monograph" in 1958, which Hoover rescinded and called "baloney."[17] The "Mafia Monograph" was written by crime experts contracted by the FBI as a study of the origin, nature, and activities of the Mafia in its native Sicily and how it was transplanted to the United States and further developed.[18] It is notable that the first American government agency to credit the existence of an organized criminal underworld was the U.S. Secret Service, which is tasked with the security of the president and other key executive leaders, as well as with maintaining the sanctity of U.S. currency.

In 1950-1951, a U.S. Senate committee, led by Estes Kefauver, a Democratic senator from Tennessee, demonstrated beyond a reasonable doubt that such a "sinister criminal organization" operated throughout the nation.[19] However, this series of hearings across America perhaps produced a somewhat naive and contrived set of conclusions as its final product:

> We can lick organized crime. We can correct the evils plaguing our country if the good citizens will open their eyes to our danger. We can lick it if we recognize the alliance of criminals and their "respectable" front men for what they are—hoodlums and despoilers rather than glamorous figures or heroes—and go after them with the same determination and ruthlessness that they employ in milking and perverting our society for their own gains.... There is nothing that the American people cannot overcome if they know the facts.[20]

THIS HIGH-SOUNDING RHETORIC did not stop the Kefauver Senate Crime Investigation Committee (Kefauver Committee) from milking the maximum media sensationalism from the testimony of key witnesses such as Virginia Hill, characterizing her as a hysterical "fading underworld queen" and a "ravaged looking woman with a mottled complexion and loose flesh that is beginning to wrinkle around the neck."[21] Under the committee's relentless questioning, New York Mafia boss Frank Costello's spirit supposedly broke, and he took on the appearance of "an old, beaten man" whose "grammar failed him" and who "garbled his words" in a parody of gangster-speak, according to Kefauver.[22]

Nitti was referred to as a "stalwart" lieutenant of Al Capone who "succeeded him as leader of the mob...but in 1943...was found dead under circumstances that indicated he had committed suicide."[23] The committee was very interested in the leadership and organizational structure of the Outfit, an area that had been virtually ignored by the FBI under J. Edgar Hoover for decades.[24]

Nevertheless, Mafia boss Meyer Lansky lived at liberty until his death in 1983 and was never convicted of even an income-tax evasion, let alone his involvement with Murder Inc. The most common explanation for this strange state of affairs was claims that the mob (possibly Meyer Lansky, Frank Costello, Carlos Marcello, or gay mob lawyer Roy Cohn) had some incriminating material such as photographs of J. Edgar Hoover likely related to his now widely known homosexual and cross-dressing transvestite tendencies. There is today simply too much documented circumstantial evidence and eyewitness testimony in support of such claims for the theory to be ignored.

Hoover and his assistant director and longtime companion, Clyde Tolson, used the nicknames "Speed" and "Junior" between themselves, went to Miami together for vacations (traveling everywhere in each other's company), spent weekends together at home in Washington, D.C., never married, dressed alike, had very personal photographs of each other, and were at the end of their lives buried side by side. On New Year's Eve 1936, after dinner at the New York Stork Club attended by Hoover, Tolson, Walter Winchell, and others, Hoover was seen holding hands with Tolson. The two were also seen by numerous witnesses holding hands at racetracks. Outfit West Coast operative Johnny Roselli spoke specifically of an occasion in the late 1920s when Hoover was arrested on charges of homosexuality in New Orleans. As will be detailed in Chapter Six, Roselli was one of Nitti's most important subordinates. However, rampant public gossip concerning this arrest was suppressed by Hoover, and if

FBI subordinates even suggested in private that Hoover and Tolson were homosexual, Hoover would demand a retraction.

The photo(s) in question involved Hoover in drag and/or having sex with Clyde Tolson and other males. These photos may also have been in the possession of the OSS and its offspring, the CIA. Meyer Lansky was believed to have had close wartime ties with the OSS.

Hoover and Tolson may have been participants in at least two orgies at the Plaza Hotel that were also attended by Roy Cohn and Lewis S. Rosensteil, the Schenley liquor mogul and benefactor of Brandeis University who had ties to Frank Costello and Meyer Lansky. Rosensteil's fourth wife, Susan, has supported such claims as a witness.[25]

Strangely, some academics still refute the existence of the Mafia as a cohesive international crime syndicate.[26] In fact, the contemporary Mafia may in part be an artificial organization that has taken on the form as others have seen it over a period of decades. As we shall see in the specific development of the Nitti legend, it is not beyond the realm of possibility that fictional literature and Hollywood portrayals of Mafia and other organized-crime stereotypes have reinforced actual specific patterns of behavior and customs in what otherwise might have remained much less refined and loosely knit family-based criminal groupings. The FBI today defines la Cosa Nostra, which in English simply means "this thing of ours," as a "nationwide alliance of criminals, linked through both familial and conspiratorial ties that is dedicated to pursuing crime and protecting its members" consisting of "different 'families' or groups that are generally arranged geographically and engaged in significant and organized racketeering activity."[27] Chicago's Outfit is perhaps the model for organized-crime syndicates that go above and beyond traditional Mafia families. Chicago, the New York metropolitan area, Philadelphia, New England, and Detroit are all major centers of American Mafia crime groups. However, to get a grass-roots feel for what the Mafia or la Cosa Nostra really means to those directly involved with it, an excerpt from an FBI wiretapped egomaniacal monologue by the former New York Gambino crime family boss, "Dapper Don" John Gotti, to some of his subordinates is instructive for its emotional intensity and group solidarity:

> I'm not in the mood for the toys, or games, or kidding…I'm not in the mood for clans. I'm not in the mood for gangs. I'm not in the mood for none of that stuff there. This is gonna be a Cosa Nostra 'til I die. Be it an hour from now, or be it tonight, or a hundred years from now when I'm in jail. It's gonna be a Cosa Nostra.[28]

THE MAFIA IS still a loosely networked alliance of family-based groups bound by kinship ties, implicit codes such as that of *omerta* (i.e. absolute silence to all outsiders about anything concerning criminal activities, the provision of disinformation to authorities, and the strict maintenance of social codes such as the prohibition of a made man having an affair with another made man's girlfriend or wife), and complete submission to its hierarchical family-based authority structure upon the pain of an individual member's death that has a near-religious significance and is considered to have precedence even over personal family and national loyalties. Other Mafia virtues are humility, providing reciprocal aid to all other Mafia members in any and all cases, absolute obedience to all Mafia leaders, considering an offense to one member an offense to all and requiring revenge at all costs, never seeking government justice assistance under any circumstances, and never revealing the names of members or any other secrets.

There are other perhaps less apparent characteristics of a good Mafioso: politeness; a reserved nature; discipline; living a relatively modest lifestyle regardless of his actual worth; being pious; and being a faithful, kind, and loving father and husband. Other similar values are: be loyal to members of the organization; don't interfere with each other's interests, and don't be an informer; be a man of honor, and always do right; respect womanhood and your elders; do not rock the boat; be rational; be a member of the team; do not engage in battle if you can't win; be a stand-up guy; keep your eyes and ears open and your mouth shut; don't sell out; have class; be independent; and know your way around the world.[29] One made man does not harm another except on express orders of his boss. Frank Nitti would have scored high on these virtues and characteristics as perceived by his criminal brotherhood.

THE MAFIA'S OVERALL framework of organization is predicated upon having a substantial membership that works toward subverting the government and the order of law through bribery and corruption, and toward dominating areas of organized crime such as gambling, narcotics, prostitution, racketeering, loansharking, the infiltration of legitimate businesses, etc. The life span of the Mafia is indefinite, although some partnerships may be temporary, and the areas of criminal activity became habitual and a primary source income for its members. The top leadership of the Mafia deals primarily in crimes of conspiracy and is isolated from actual operations by a buffer of two or more levels of underlings including a trusted aide such as an underboss. Another trusted aide is the "money mover" who is used to handle illicit funds, hiding their true sources, and investing through commercial connections in legitimate areas such as real estate, stocks and bonds, and other types of business. Sometimes the mob does not choose well for this money-mover task. Virginia Hill, Ben Siegel's paramour, was trusted as a cash courier until it was discovered she was skimming millions of dollars intended for Las Vegas casino and hotel developments.[30] The bulk of all profits clandestinely go to bosses.

A MAFIA BOSS is also known as a "don," a term of respect. The top-level leadership avoids involvement in actual crimes and limits social contacts and obvious links to criminal activities. Bosses must be protected at all costs. Deference is given to position, authority, and seniority (e.g. tone of voice used, opening doors, offering seats, and other obvious displays of respect). Bosses must grant permission for all illicit activities undertaken by his Mafia group based upon family criteria and the avoidance of activities that would cause an obvious public outcry.

Maintaining a public-relations front of propriety and respectability at all times is a priority. "Sit downs" are meetings held within a Mafia organization or with another family or associates usually at lower levels of authority. Infrequent meetings between bosses are held, and their decision on any matter is final.

Discipline is kept within the group and is total, ranging from warnings and sanctions to murder. Violence and murder may be committed upon any individual within the organization who becomes an informer and any outsider who threatens the security of the organization. Such murders often involve not just killing a victim, but his or her total disappearance, preferably with no trace of violence and no publicity. The victim simply becomes a missing person. The Mafia does not recognize geographical, government, and political boundaries that could restrict its activities and partnerships with other similar groups.[31] A Mafia boss has strict control over his family's territory that cannot be lightly interfered with by another family, whether his organization is large or small or has a seat on the Mafia Commission.

While the Mafia family is sacrosanct, it is expected that a made man would kill his actual son or brother if he was an informant or some other detriment to the group. During the arcane initiation ceremony for a new member becoming a made man, the trigger finger of the initiate is cut, and the blood oath is administered in Italian: *Io voglio entrare in questa organizzazione per proteggere la mia famiglia e per proteggere I miei amici.* ("I want to enter into this organization to protect my family and to protect all my friends.")[32]

The Chicago Outfit has never stood much on secret initiations and other traditional Mafia ceremonies, perhaps because of its more cosmopolitan nature.[33] In Capone and Nitti's era, the Outfit's made-man ceremony was even simpler and more to the point: "So I 'make' you. You are now one of us. If you fuck up, we take it out on…your sponsor."[34]

OTHER QUAINT MAFIA customs include the "kiss of death," which is exchanged between the executioner and victim—it is preferable that the latter is lured into a benign state for his remaining hours of life—as well as slashing off a murdered man's genitals and leaving them in his mouth as a show of contempt. Ritualized greetings are also commonly used between made men. Perhaps the only comparable (and equally contradictory in practice) codes of conduct that come to mind are in the militaristic Japanese cult of bushido developed by the samurai-warrior elite, which not coincidentally are maintained today by the Japanese yakuza organized-crime syndicates and the arcane, mystic organization and practices of the Chinese triads. One becomes a Mafia member through family sponsorships, and Mafia fraternal ties are strengthened through intermarriages among different Mafia families.[35] Strangely and somewhat contradictorily, Mafia members and police officers share a bond because they each live by strict paramilitary codes of conduct, duty, and loyalty, that while diametrically opposed to each other, set them apart from average "civilians" and often result in a grudging, respectful admiration of each other.[36]

TO BE A full member of the Mafia, it is still likely necessary to be of at least partial Sicilian or Italian ethnic origin. This appears to be based on the theory that desirable organized-crime characteristics (from the Mafia's perspective) can be conveyed genetically, an ancient code known as *Sangre Nostru* (Our Blood).[37] Some claim that the Mafia's operational field organization is based largely on the structure of the ancient Roman legion.[38] Indeed, with its family structure of boss (don), underboss (second-in-command), *consiglieri* (chief adviser), capos (captains) commanding capo *regimes* (captain's teams or crews), and *soldati* (soldiers) at the bottom of the made-man pecking order, the Mafia is run along paramilitary lines as an army of captains and soldiers, which is also a reason why police forces find it so intimidating.[39] Mafia groups are also thought to be organized into units of ten men (sometimes called "crews" in modern parlance) that are commanded by a group chief, or capo *decina*, who in turn is commanded by an area chief.[40] Membership in this paramilitary organization is formally granted through a social initiation and associated rites that result in a chosen member becoming a made man, an honorific generally restricted to ethnic Italians.

IN GENERAL, THE Mafia's most violent activities are restricted to members of competing criminal organizations, although the social fallout from its illegal rackets affects all levels of modern society. The organization employs secret rules, elaborate systems of prearranged codes and communications systems that are difficult to infiltrate, and trusted friends and relatives who are only used as couriers to avoid electronic surveillance. To influence politicians, the Mafia uses direct funding contributions and fundraising schemes. In addition, efforts are made to help friends and relatives achieve positions at all levels of elected government, courts, and appointed bureaucracies to have influence over the executive and judiciary decision-making process.

The Mafia has a superb internal intelligence-gathering system, and undertakes covert special operations such as assassinations, kidnappings, propaganda, media influencing and personal defamation, bribery, faked illnesses, intimidation, torture, etc.[41]

The fix is at the heart of every organized-crime racket, which consists of some means of controlling key politicians, senior police officials, and business and union executives through physical intimidation, murder, sexual blackmail, bribes, high-interest loans, etc., and is the domain of the specialist "corruptor."[42] However, despite its reputation for strong-arm tactics, people are rarely forced to enter into such illegal Mafia-related activities against their will and initially are more often willing victims.[43] A new organized-crime specialty is "cybercrime" such as lucrative and sophisticated "denial of service" attacks against business computer systems around the world as a form of extortion, the electronic laundering of illegal gains, as well as electronic counterfeiting and fraud systems and on-line gambling schemes.

Efforts over the decades by Italian and American authorities to eradicate the Mafia, despite some temporary successes, have generally met with failure. In the U.S. and Sicily, it continues as a virtual state within a state. There is also a current effort to recruit new American Mafia members directly from Sicily because they are believed to be more trustworthy in an Old World sense and less likely to cooperate with authorities when under the pressure of interrogation.[44] The American Mafia within the United States and Canada is for all intents and purposes fully integrated and ignores the border separating the two nations.[45] For example, Montreal is believed to fall under the jurisdiction of New York families and Toronto under Buffalo. Today there are some ten major Italian-American Mafia families.

The FBI currently estimates that Italian organized-crime groups have approximately 25,000 members and 250,000 affiliate members worldwide, with more than 3,000 members and affiliates in the United States. Other estimates place the number of American Mafia members as high as 14,600 full members and 63,100 associate members during the mid-1980s.[46] Another recent estimate has the number of American Mafia members at some 1,700 in twenty-four major and minor families falling under the authority of the national Mafia Commission, but this figure might be unduly conservative.[47] Italian organized crime is also present in South America, Australia, and parts of Europe besides Italy.

Of course, it should be emphasized that not all immigrant Italians, or even Italian criminals, are linked to the Mafia, and in the traditional fraternal society sense, not all members of the Mafia are necessarily criminals. This mob stereotype has often been incorrectly applied to Jews, Irish, and other immigrant groups within America. Virtually all nationalities participate in organized crime—senior Outfit frontman Murray "the Camel" Humphreys, for example, was a Welshman.

Today, well-established international organized-crime organizations must also include the Russian *mafiya*, Chinese triad gangs, Japanese yakuza, Vietnamese street gangs, Indochinese "Golden Triangle" narco-mercenary armies, Colombian drug cartels, and other South American and Asian narco-terrorist groups. Many of these groups cooperate with each other and the traditional Mafia. However, traditional American organized-crime syndicates, now into their fourth and fifth generations, remain the preeminent underworld powerhouse, and it is very difficult to judge their full impact and influence today because they have been so successful in laundering illegal revenues into totally legitimate enterprises. A September 1994 conference for high-level American law-enforcement and intelligence-community personnel in Washington, titled Global Organized Crime: The New Empire of Evil, concluded:

> The dimensions of global organized crime present
> a greater international security challenge than any-
> thing Western democracies had to cope with during

the cold war. Worldwide alliances are being forged in every criminal field from money laundering and currency counterfeiting to trafficking in drugs and nuclear materials. Global organized crime is the world's fastest growing business, with profits estimated at $1 trillion.[48]

ALL THESE TRANSNATIONAL organized-crime gangs have been very quick to capitalize on the widespread and unprecedented series of global political, economic, social, and technological changes during the last several decades. However, drug trafficking and money laundering are still the crimes of choice, with other important activity areas being illegal gambling, sports bribery and fixing, political corruption, extortion, kidnapping, fraud, counterfeiting, infiltration of legitimate businesses, murders, bombings, and weapons trafficking.

The FBI estimates that global organized crime has annual profits close to $1 trillion with perhaps a tenth of this attributed to Italian organized crime.[49] Without a doubt, the American Mafia controls very sinister criminal activities that prey upon some of the weakest elements of society. However, one can question whether such disreputable activities would disappear without the Mafia, perhaps resulting in even greater social harm without the element of regulation and control provided by organized crime. As we shall see, Frank Nitti had a greater influence on the development of the modern patterns of organized crime than any other underworld leader of his era.

The Outfit's Origins and Development

The Outfit is Chicago's premier organized-crime organization, and while not traditionally based upon Mafia family groupings per se, it is organized along the same lines and with the same customs as the Mafia. The origins of the Outfit begin in about 1915 under Giacomo "Big Jim" Colosimo in Chicago's First Ward district. The name Outfit actually became widely used in the early 1950s, replacing or supplementing other terms such as the syndicate, the Capone mob, Chicago criminal syndicate, and the Capone syndicate because it "had a nice ring to it."[50] However, the term was used as early as the 1930s during Frank Nitti's term of power, and it is possible that it originated with Nitti himself. It is the Chicago Mafia's own term to describe their organization.[51] Many within the syndicate, including Nitti, also simply termed their organization "the boys."

Colosimo, a so-called "white slaver," influenced local politicians and police through bribes, organized city workers, and established lucrative bordellos in red-light districts. White slavery as defined under the Mann Act has racial connotations, but specifically refers to the practice of trading and selling women as prostitutes across state lines, hence making it a federal crime.[52] Some of Colosimo's classier brothels were French Emma's, the Casino, Utopia, Sappho, and Everleigh Club.[53]

Colosimo's relative, Johnny Torrio, had organized-crime experience from New York City, which he applied to Colosimo's operations in Chicago. Colosimo was liquidated in 1920, possibly by Al Capone on Torrio's orders, because he was uninterested in taking advantage of the new illegal alcoholic-beverage opportunities presented by Prohibition. Al Capone, who had served under Joe Masseria and Frankie Yale (Uale) in New York, became Torrio's underboss. Capone bought out and inherited the Outfit in 1925 when Torrio took early retirement after nearly being murdered by the O'Banion-Moran-Weiss North Side syndicate, at the time the Outfit's major opposition.

Under Capone, the Outfit was extremely aggressive in its expansion activities and emphasized sheer violence as a means toward these ends, while at the same time, Capone liked to bask in media publicity. Capone heightened the rivalries between opposing gangs, systematically eliminating all competition through hitting their top leadership, until the conflict with the rival group under George "Bugs" Moran erupted into a full-scale gang war. This war to a large extent culminated in the famous Saint Valentine's Day Massacre of 1929, after which Moran left town for good. With the defeat of the Aiello gang by 1930-1931, most of Chicago's underworld came under the control of the Outfit. The Irish North Side Gang in its various manifestations proved to be the Outfit's major persistent opponent under the successive reigns of Dion O'Banion, George Moran, Teddy Newberry, and Roger Touhy.

By 1936, the FBI identified the following organized-crime power structure in Chicago:

- The Outfit (Capone Gang) (South Side)
- Saltis Gang (Southwest Side)
- O'Donnell Gang (West Side)
- Moran Gang (North Side)
- Ghetto Gang (West Side)
- Vinci Gang (South Side)
- Valley Gang (West Side)
- Ragen Colts Gang (Southwest Side)
- Red Bolton Gang (West Side)
- Circus Gang (a.k.a. Circus Café Gang) (Northwest Side)
- Northwest Side Gang[54]

THE OUTFIT QUICKLY expanded into Chicago's suburbs using terror, as in Forest View (which subsequently became known as "Caponeville"), as well as bribing public officials and the police in Cicero. The success of mob boss Johnny Torrio, and his successors Al Capone and Frank Nitti, in taking over town government in the Chicago suburb of Cicero provided Chicago-area organized crime a defining characteristic: "a weedlike resilience based on its ability to take over entire governmental offices" that exists to this very day. Cicero continues to provide the Outfit a dependable base of operations and sanctuary during bad times.[55]

Cicero was completely in the Outfit's pocket. It was used as a gangster sanctuary and a center for alcohol distribution and vice, and the local government and police force were all under Capone's control. Because of a public outcry over Cicero's immoral nature, the forces of law and order decided to study this situation scientifically using some of the best academic minds available. The resulting Illinois Crime Survey was a 1929 attempt at providing "a detailed history of organized crime over a period of twenty-five years in the city of Chicago and surrounding communities" and at formulating specific recommendations in reaction to the growing lawlessness in the region that was unprecedented in America at that time. It is a 1,108-page pedantic report with numerous detailed statistical tables, graphs, maps, and examples and case studies related to organized and individual crime and related law-enforcement efforts in Chicago.[56] It classified the Outfit as a "medieval feudal system" governed by warlords with small armies of mercenaries.[57]

Money was and still is what the Outfit is all about. An April 1925 police raid on an Outfit headquarters provided evidence that it was receiving millions of dollars annually from illegal alcohol, gambling, and prostitution, and that Frank Nitti was one of the main beneficiaries of these profits.[58] In 1931, Chicago labor and other racketeering was worth $200 million per year, or more than a half-billion dollars in constant dollars, according to the Chicago Crime Commission. The Employers' Association of Chicago listed ninety-one different types of such related rackets.[59]

However, in practice, it was difficult to pinpoint the exact yearly revenues of the Outfit, although various attempts have been made, with another estimate being $100 million from

1925 to 1930. When Al Capone was indicted in 1931, the federal government claimed that the Outfit had total receipts of $200 million over ten years.[60] Yet another estimate by the Cook County State's Attorney Office was $105 million for 1927 alone.[61] One claim is that Capone grossed $60 million from bootlegging in 1927, but there is no way to verify the veracity of all such estimates. However, the high figures were quite possible as the Outfit was reportedly dealing with some four million gallons of illegal alcohol per year for Illinois, Iowa, Minnesota, and South Dakota during Prohibition. In October 1939, Al Capone claimed to an FBI agent interviewing him prior to his release from Alcatraz that he had personally made profits of $10 million from alcohol sales during Prohibition, but it is likely he was mentally unstable at that point, and his claims must be taken with a grain of salt, although some, indeed, believe Capone was making as much as approximately $1 million per day at the height of his power during Prohibition.[62]

Whatever the exact amount of money earned by the Outfit, profits were obviously huge. For example, it cost $3 to produce a barrel of beer that was sold to a speakeasy for $55 or directly used in an Outfit club at many times this profit. The Outfit had an average of ten breweries in operation at all times during Prohibition, each churning out about one hundred barrels of beer per day, so daily gross receipts were at least $55,000. Standardized brewing equipment purchased at the same manufacturer was used by all Outfit breweries: 15,000-gallon steel-vat plant units, motors, compression tanks, and racking machines. Equipment seized by government raids would often be repurchased by Outfit agents at U.S. Marshals' auctions.[63] Bootlegging was the major activity in Cook County during Prohibition with "pinchbacks," not quite a half-pint of booze, being sold for 75 cents each, with "the second swallow from the bottle untying your shoes." The Outfit also controlled as many as twelve hundred speakeasies in the greater Chicago region.[64]

During Nitti's term as boss, Prohibition was repealed, and overall profit margins became resultantly tighter. Consequently, a greater effort had to be made to expand other existing profit centers, such as gambling and labor rackets, and to find new activity areas and markets. Gambling remained a major profit center. Outfit ledger sheets from 1941, which were probably prepared by mob accountant Fred Evans, indicate that Cook County gambling was bringing in almost $4 million in gross income per year, of which more than $2.6 million were profits divided among senior members. The major beneficiaries were Nitti, Jake Guzik, Murray Humphreys, and Edward Vogel.[65]

So where did all the Prohibition profits go? Outfit leaders such as Nitti lived comfortable personal lives, but not excessively so because this was against their code. Neither were the assets passed to their families apparently all that great. In later years, Al Capone's widow and son could barely get by with their Miami restaurant, and Al's old Palm Island estate had to be sold by Mae Capone. The government did not recover much of these vast sums, just the amounts they could pin on personal income-tax evasions by leaders such as Nitti and Capone. It is likely that much of the vast profits had been reinvested for the syndicate by financial wizard Jake "Greasy Thumb" Guzik into legitimate businesses with this investment pattern being maintained to this day.[66]

Guzik grew up around the Chicago brothel district of Twenty-second Street and Wabash Avenue and had little formal schooling.[67] Businesses through which he laundered illegal profits included those related to the legitimate food and beverage sector such as hotels, bakeries, restaurants, nightclubs, towel and apron services, cleaning services, dry cleaning and laundry, ice, soft drinks, mixers, lunch foods, cheese, pasta, and flour.[68] The reinvestment process undertaken by Guzik must also have been carefully managed by Nitti because it began during his long term as boss.

The Outfit's operations were, and are, predicated upon the establishment of numerous political-patronage connections between its various rackets and government and judiciary organizations at the national (Congress), state (Illinois State Legislature at Springfield, state courts), and local levels (Chicago City Council, ward committeemen, suburban town councils, police officials, municipal courts), as well as political-party representatives at all levels and from all political stripes. In 1931, the Chicago Civic Safety Committee claimed that there were six thousand city, state, and federal officials in the Outfit's pay, as were 80 percent of Chicago's magistrates and judges.[69]

Chicago's local politicians, perhaps best exemplified by Mayor William Hale "Big Bill" Thompson, were for the most part firmly in the pocket of the Outfit during Capone and Nitti's reigns—his successor, Anton Cermak, wasn't, but as we shall see, he didn't last very long. Following Cermak's death, Nitti preferred to keep relationships with politicians active, but low key and out of the public's eye.[70]

The political and business influence wielded by the Outfit during Nitti's leadership term was enormous in Illinois. Frank Nitti and Louis Campagna were said to have exerted enough pressure in the Illinois State Legislature to prevent the passage of state law-enforcement wiretapping bills during the 1930s and early 1940s.[71] Nitti was once described not as simply the boss of a criminal syndicate, but as the "chief of the crime-labor-politics alliance."[72] The Kefauver Committee during the early 1950s was amazed at the level of political corruption in Chicago: "Everywhere we went [across America] the committee found a certain amount of political immorality, but in Chicago the rawness of this sort of thing was particularly shocking."[73]

William Hale Thompson (1868-1944) was one of Chicago's most interesting, colorful, and eccentric mayors. He was a political showman who brought excitement and theatrics to the mayor's office. He once announced that he was quitting politics to lead an expedition to the South Seas to find tree-climbing fish. "I have strong reason to believe that there are fish that come out of the water, can live on land, will jump three feet to catch a grasshopper, and will actually climb trees." But he soon returned to Chicago politics.

A vocal supporter of the women's suffrage movement, he frequently changed his position on issues to suit the times. Prohibition was one of these issues, and he ran for office in 1927 on a platform of reopening closed speakeasies and won by a landslide. During his terms of office, the Chicago police were ineffective in combating organized crime, and bribery and corruption were rampant. The U.S. Department of Justice was believed to have kept files on Thompson, wiretapping and bugging his hotel suites. He died a millionaire, nevertheless.

By 1932 when Capone was finally incarcerated, the Outfit's leadership mantle next fell on Frank "the Enforcer" Nitti, who held the position until his death in 1943. Like Capone, Nitti maintained close relations with politicians, particularly the First Ward Democratic organization; he often liked to hang around Michael "Hinky Dink" Kenna's cigar store and meet with other underworld characters.[74]

Strangely, many law-enforcement agencies, most notably the FBI, seemed to have seriously believed that the Outfit had somehow disintegrated after Capone was incarcerated, and they did not begin serious wide-scale investigations into it again until the 1950s and 1960s. In fact, Nitti was followed briefly by Paul "the Waiter" Ricca and then Tony "Big Tuna" Accardo, both former Nitti associates.[75] Accardo began his climb in the underworld as a loyal and trusted gunman guarding the Lexington Hotel (often in the lobby with a machine gun in his lap) and as a specially selected personal bodyguard for Al Capone under the direction of Frank Nitti. Accardo then became a capo under Nitti and subsequently an underboss for Paul Ricca.[76]

In 1956, Sam "Momo" Giancana took control with Accardo still providing advice behind the scenes as a senior *consigliere*. Sam Battaglia, "Milwaukee Phil" Alderisio, and Jackie Cerone all had short terms at the helm. Joey Aiuppa was boss from 1971 to 1986. During Frank Nitti's era, the thick-witted Aiuppa controlled the mob's operations in Cicero and the western suburbs of Chicago. He began his career guarding the lobby of the infamous Hawthorne Hotel in Cicero, his submachine gun also often prominently displayed. In the early 1970s, Aiuppa had, in fact, bought the old Hawthorne Hotel, and it was renamed the Towne Hotel, and with its adjoining Turf Lounge that at one time was owned by Frank Nitti and managed by Alex Louis Greenberg, became a major hangout for the upper echelons of the Outfit. Such acts of sentimentality and respect for their history are not uncommon among the leadership of the Outfit. Some say that after the execution of the retired but still flamboyant Sam Giancana in 1975 at his Oak Park home, Tony Accardo resumed full leadership behind the scenes. Accardo had a reputation for violence. In 1978, while Accardo was on vacation in California, his River Forest home was burglarized. Within a month, the five suspected burglars were found slain gangland-style.[77]

By this time, the Outfit's key interests were in the Teamsters' Union, union pension funds, and Las Vegas gambling. Scandals with Frank Sinatra, Jimmy Hoffa, Marilyn Monroe, and other celebrities had come and gone, as had all-but-forgotten possible links with Cuban exiles and the assassination of President John F. Kennedy. Joe Ferriola was briefly boss until 1989, when he died at age sixty-one from a heart attack. Most of the remaining old-timers faded away toward the end of the 1980s. Accardo was still active during this period, but because of age and ill health, he began to lose influence. He died in 1992 from congestive heart failure, acute respiratory failure, pneumonia, and chronic obstructive pulmonary disease without ever serving prison time or having an attempt made on his life despite a long list of charges against him that included murder, kidnapping, extortion, tax fraud, union racketeering, and gambling. Accardo was never even convicted of a felony, and he boasted that he had never spent a night in jail. Although never imprisoned, Accardo was constantly under the scrutiny of the law; he had been cited for contempt at the 1950s Kefauver Committee hearings and had taken the Fifth Amendment 172 times before the McClellan Committee, more properly known as the Select Senate Committee on Improper Activities in the Labor or Management Field, which conducted investigations of labor union racketeering from 1957 to 1960. A major tax conviction against Accardo was overturned in 1960, and he is believed to have remained a major force behind the Outfit until his death. With Accardo dead, the last direct link between Nitti and the Outfit had also died.[78]

At a term of twelve years (including 1929-1930, when Al Capone was imprisoned for the first time) suddenly cut short, Nitti had the longest leadership office term except for Joey Aiuppa's fifteen years. However, Accardo was active behind the scenes for longer than anybody as a "chairman emeritus," while Aiuppa was not known for his brilliance and could very well have been a figurehead boss.

It was during Nitti's term as boss that the Outfit's most far-reaching and incredible activities and criminal accomplishments took place, but these were for the most part lost with Nitti in his grave. None of the men who followed Nitti, as colorful as they may have been, will ever likely be the repeated subjects of movies, television series, novels, and more, six decades following their deaths, with the possible exception of Sam Giancana. However, it is important to note that essentially the same organization that Capone and Nitti led decades ago has never gone away and has had a continuous history for almost a century. The Outfit's bosses are summarized in Table 2.2. As usual, the Chicago police and the current administration of the Chicago Crime Commission still seem to be unsure who exactly is the real boss of the Outfit at any given time.

Table 2.2 The Outfit's Bosses 1910-1997, and Their Length of Term in Office

1910 "Big Jim" Colosimo (1910-1920) (ten years)

1920 Johnny Torrio (1920-1925) (five years)

1925 "Scarface" Al Capone (1925-1931) (six years)

1932 Frank "the Enforcer" Nitti (1929-1930 and 1932-1943) (twelve years)

1943 Paul "the Waiter" Ricca (1943 to 1950) (seven years)

1950 Tony "Big Tuna" Accardo (1950 to 1957) (seven years)

1957 Sam "Momo" Giancana (1957 to 1966) (nine years)

1966 Sam "Teets" Battaglia (1966) (about one year)

1966 John "Jackie" Cerone (1966 to 1969) (three years or less)

1969 Felix "Milwaukee Phil" Alderisio (1969 to 1971) (two years)

1971 Joseph "Joey the Doves" Aiuppa (1971 to 1986) (fifteen years)

1986 Joseph Ferriola (1986 to 1989) (three years)

1989 Sam Carlisi (1989 to 1993) (six years)

Current The current leadership structure is uncertain.

References: Anon., (*http://www.suntimes.com/special_sections/crime/cst-nws-mobtop18r.html*); Russo, Gus, *The Outfit: The Role of Chicago's Underworld in the Shaping of Modern America.* (New York: Bloomsbury, 2001), p. 475; and others.

Nitti's Outfit

During Nitti's reign, the Outfit was an "equal opportunity employer" based upon what you could do, not who or what you were, and was multiethnically integrated and included Italians from various regions, Irish, and Jews, plus some Asians, blacks, and others, many in positions of considerable power.[79] For example, Ken Eto, an Asian-American, was in charge of the Outfit's *bolita* gambling (a type of Cuban numbers lottery) for many years until he was suspected of turning informant for the FBI and attempts were made on his life.[80] The Outfit under Capone and Nitti pioneered the inclusion of non-Italians such as Jake Guzik, Gus Alex, and Murray Humphreys in positions of extreme power. However, the core of the senior leadership, including all the bosses such as Capone, Nitti, and their successors, were Italian and made men within the Mafia.

Arguably, the multiethnic character of the Outfit peaked under the leadership of Capone and Nitti and then reverted to a more traditional Italian organized-crime character. In the old Sicilian Mafia, it was necessary to be from Sicily to be made, but modern Italian crime organizations have considerably broadened this geographical eligibility criterion to include all of Italy. There were members of the Outfit who simply would reserve judgment on an order from a boss who was non-Italian and not a made man. Members such as "Machine Gun" Jack McGurn (a.k.a. Vincenzo De Mora, Jack Demore, Vincent Gebardi) with non-Italian sounding names were actually Italians who had changed their names.

While multiethnic in character, the core of the Outfit remained Italian and linked to the Italian-American population in Chicago. The *Unione Siciliano*, later known as the Italian-American National Union, was an ethnic Italian fraternal society closely linked to the Mafia and the Outfit and was a prime recruiting ground for new organized-crime members.

Frank Nitti was the *Unione*'s president from 1930 to 1937 following the death of its former leader, Joe Aiello, an Outfit rival, and had previously been considered Capone's chief link with the *Unione* and the Mafia.[81] This position clearly demonstrated Nitti's status within the Sicilian Mafia hierarchy, a prestige that Al Capone did not himself enjoy.

Following Nitti's term, his associate, Philip "Dandy Phil" D'Andrea, was president of this organization from 1937 to 1939.[82] D'Andrea, Al Capone's former bodyguard, also gained control of the Chicago Italian language newspaper, *L'Italia*. When the paper's previous owner brought a lawsuit against D'Andrea, this individual was mysteriously assassinated before the case was settled.[83] D'Andrea became infamous when he carried a concealed handgun into Al Capone's final court hearing, packing a loaded semiautomatic .45-caliber pistol in a shoulder holster. Untouchable agent Paul Robsky was the one who made the discovery. Unlike in the 1987 movie version of *The Untouchables* where Frank Nitti wore the weapon to court (the real Nitti was serving a prison sentence during Capone's trial), in reality, D'Andrea did not shoot anybody and was not pushed from the roof of the courthouse by Eliot Ness.[84] Furthermore, D'Andrea may actually have had a legal argument for being permitted to carry the gun because he was also a duly appointed deputy sheriff and had a permit to carry the weapon. Nevertheless, he was arrested and held without bail before being sent to a six-month Leavenworth prison term for contempt of court.[85]

At the 1950 Kefauver Committee hearings when asked if he knew of the Mafia, D'Andrea stated he had only "heard of it as a child," and when further queried if it was ever discussed by Italian-American families: "Oh, God, no. No, sir! It's not discussed out of the home."[86] Nitti and D'Andreas' Sicilian background and role with the *Unione Siciliano* were sure indicators that they were full-fledged members of the Mafia, although some have questioned whether Capone and Nitti were traditional Mafia members.[87]

In 1930, Al Capone had established the Outfit's board of directors with Frank Nitti as its chief executive officer in his absence and in charge of operations, and Jake Guzik in charge of administration.[88] Other important board and senior management members under Nitti included Charlie Fischetti (nightclubs and gambling casinos); Murray Humphreys ("legitimate rackets" such as labor unions, cleaning plants, laundries); Joe Fusco (legal liquor distribution); Jake Guzik (with an additional responsibility for overseeing racehorse betting); Eddie Vogel (coin-operated machines such as slot machines, cigarette machines, jukeboxes, and vending machines); and Hymie Levine (race wire).

This organization's structure was dynamic. For a complete summary of the leading figures in the Outfit during Nitti's term as boss, see Appendix B, p. 317. It would become significantly more streamlined after Capone went to prison the final time and following Nitti's purges during 1936-1937. Some individuals in minor positions in 1931 would rise to senior positions during the next twelve years, while others died of natural and unnatural causes. Some such as Al's brother, Ralph "Bottles" Capone (described as "sloppy, greedy, and dumb" and who had been in charge of soft drinks and tavern supplies), were sidelined by Nitti and slipped into obscurity.

Those on the board met often, sometimes on a daily basis, usually putting in twelve-hour working days, and had to dress and act the corporate-executive role. Nitti believed in having frequent presentations made to the board by specialists within the Outfit who were in charge of new projects. Most of the top-management echelon were entrepreneurs with other business interests such as clubs, hotels, and restaurants in addition to Outfit projects. The mass of low-level members were paid on a salary basis.[89] Families were deliberately isolated from illegal activities. Womanizing was frowned upon, particularly during working hours. Alcoholism and drug abuse were forbidden both from an ethical point of view and to prevent intoxicated members from revealing Outfit secrets.[90]

Nitti greatly streamlined the bloated Capone organization he inherited, which had numbered some one thousand members. However, by the mid-1930s, the Outfit under Nitti could still muster five hundred to six hundred gunmen within a week's notice. Membership in the Outfit was then comparable to being part of an elite military unit, and this was expected to be reflected in a member's attitude, capabilities, and appearance. Al Capone had instituted a militarylike fitness regimen for all members of the Outfit including the provision of gyms at headquarters locations for regular workouts and secret gun ranges for target practice.[91] In addition, Outfit gunmen were expected to dress the part—stylish business suits with clean shirts and ties, polished shoes, and preferably pearl-gray hats with black hatbands. As one federal agent from the era commented, "Capone hoods were not only gaudy, they were neat to the point of being sartorial fops."[92] Coincidentally, like the military, the Outfit at this time was seen by many down-and-out young men as a means of bettering themselves, at least in the eyes of their peers.

The Outfit had an intelligence system of paid informants that federal officials such as George E. Q. Johnson deemed to be "remarkable." It seemed as if the Outfit had placed "spies everywhere."[93]

The Outfit also maintained representatives in Miami, Havana (before the communist takeover), Los Angeles, Dallas, and Las Vegas after the gambling casinos were established. In regard to their payroll system, it had a corporate-style general bankroll, as well as individual bankrolls for its top members. Nitti required that Outfit executives hand in receipts to claim personal expenses and encouraged expense accounts be used for legitimate purposes by senior members. There was even a mob accounting system with income referred to as "ins" and expenses as "kick outs," and the monthly payment of the net profits divided among the top Outfit members as the "divvy."[94] However, Nitti was far from being a bureaucrat and throughout his life, left no incriminating trails of memos, compromising photographs, or damning tape-recorded conversations.

Operationally, the Outfit was a conglomerate of enterprises and activities. The majority of the Outfit's other ranks were people used for operations activities such as gunsels, bootleggers, bodyguards, spies, wiretappers, collectors, and watchmen. Everybody from newspaper boys to policemen formed an Outfit spy network. In addition to the personnel outlined, the Outfit employed legal advisers, police and politicians on the take, prostitutes, panders and pimps, dancers, singers, entertainment managers, "watchers" (lookouts), bouncers, croupiers, waiters, chefs, chauffeurs, and others. Specialist positions included enforcers to ensure internal and external mob rule, informants who warned about criminal investigations and impending police raids, and corrupters to provide payoffs and help secure immunity for the organization and its members.[95] It should be noted that in the underworld, the position of chauffeur is an important job, and many of the leading Outfit bosses began their climb to the top by chauffeuring their superiors.

There were many personality types in the Outfit, varying from certified psychopaths to men who would be considered outstanding and an asset in many professional fields. One Outfit character outstanding in his own way was the stalwart Frankie "Slippery" Rio, whose main attribute was loyalty. Frankie Rio has been characterized as a classic "torpedo," "a brain-dead thug" who was simply loyal and willing to put his life on the line for Capone while acting as one of his key henchmen. He was a natural killer, but lacked the imagination and strategic planning skills that Frank Nitti excelled at during his career. Rio was Al Capone's most important bodyguard and was almost constantly at his side.[96] Rio once saved Capone's life by pulling him to the ground and shielding him with his own body when North Side Gang enemy machine-gunners led by the soon-to-be-dead Hymie Weiss poured more than one thousand rounds into the Hawthorne Hotel on September 20, 1926.[97] Rio once faked a falling-out with Capone, going so far as slapping him. The charade successfully exposed the anti-Capone plot of John Scalise, Albert Anselmi, and Joseph Guinta, all later tortured and bludgeoned to death by Capone at the instigation of Frank Nitti.[98]

On May 17, 1929, Al Capone and Frankie Rio made a Philadelphia stopover on their way home from a national Mafia Commission conference in Atlantic City. They were arrested leaving a theater for carrying concealed deadly weapons. Sentenced for terms of one year each, they were released after nine months on March 17, 1930, for good behavior.[99] Rio is believed to have voluntarily accompanied Capone to prison because at this time Capone was seeking a refuge from the uproar that the Saint Valentine's Day Massacre had caused in Chicago.[100] On another occasion several years later, Rio attempted to barter the release of Capone from prison so his boss could solve the kidnapped Lindbergh baby case.[101] Rio was also an expert in sales promotions and helping to solve grievances among the ethnic street gangs, and he also took over Nitti's old job as enforcer when Capone went to prison for the final time.[102] At one point, Capone might have considered Rio as his successor, but "loyal soul" that he was, he just didn't have what it took to be the boss, so Capone picked Nitti instead.[103] Frankie Rio died of a heart attack in 1935 at age forty, one of the rare underworld leaders of the period who died of natural causes.[104]

Other Outfit men such as Lawrence "Dago" Mangano were typical of the gunmen working for Nitti. Mangano was listed

by the Chicago Crime Commission as a "public enemy" as early
as 1923 and eventually rose to be "Public Enemy Number Four"
and was arrested more than two hundred times. Still, he didn't
seem to have spent any time in prison for activities that included
pandering, vice, larceny, and gambling. Mangano grew up in
Chicago's notorious Patch district along with mob colleagues
Jack McGurn, Frankie Pope, Albert Anselmi, and Giuseppi
"Diamond Joe" Esposito, among others. During Capone's war
with the Aiello brothers, Mangano and fellow Outfit gunman
Phil D'Andrea warned Dominic Aiello to leave town and shot
up his bakery. Mangano, Ralph Capone, and Charles Fischetti
later controlled beer distribution for the syndicate.

Mangano and James Aducci were primary suspects in the
prominent 1931 torch murder of aging pimp "Mike de Pike"
Heitler, who had become a problem for the Outfit, and with
help from Tony Accardo and Frankie Rio, in the liquidation
of West Side vice-monger Jack Zuta. In the case of the Heitler
murder, Mike de Pike had prepared a letter as an instrument of
vengeance in the event of his death. In it, he named a number
of key Outfit men, Frank Nitti being one of them, as being
linked to his own, Zuta's, and *Chicago Tribune* reporter Alfred
"Jake" Lingle's murders.[105] In 1944, Mangano was finally killed
in a hail of bullets in Chicago, likely over a disagreement with
Tony Accardo concerning the leadership of the Outfit, at that
time in disarray after most of its top leadership structure was
either in prison or dead. Another favorite gunman used by
Nitti was Sam Giancana, who eventual rose to become the
Outfit's boss himself.[106]

Between 1919 and 1963, 976 gangland-style murders were
committed in Chicago, but only two were cleared by the arrest
and conviction of the killers. In many cases, these murders were
committed by professional killers from other organized-crime
centers.[107] During one four-year period in Prohibition, 215 murders were committed in Chicago.[108] One must assume this lack

of murder convictions is a result of the code of *omerta* and the swift underworld punishment inflicted upon any informers, giving police few facts with which to work.[109] Most victims of gang violence in Chicago were of Italian descent by far.[110]

Criminal Legacy

The Outfit may have been down for some periods of its history, but never completely out of the picture. Supposedly, the young members of the Outfit now don't know much Italian and talk and dress like any other businessmen, but still crave the big money as in Nitti's day. Many descendants of Nitti and other underworld leaders are now part of the mainstream "upperworld" and likely have nothing to do with the syndicate because their fathers simply did not want their children to be involved with crime.[111]

Currently, the Outfit is still running rackets and scams and is still in cahoots with local politicians. The FBI's Chicago office ranks the Outfit's "big three"' profit centers as the traditional rackets of a "street tax" on gambling, "juice loans" (i.e. loans where the mob squeezes the debtor until no more "juice" remains), and narcotics, as well as legitimate enterprises used to launder the proceeds of illegal activities.

The Outfit's so-called street tax (dating from the late 1920s) is extorted from illegal gambling and vice operators, more often than not under an explicit threat of violence. Juice loans have annual interest rates (or vigorish) ranging from 120 percent to 520 percent that are payable weekly and are, in effect, a form of extortion. Other rackets include skimming profits from legal casinos.[112] The police simply do not have a handle on many Outfit activities, as much today as in the past.

The Outfit is much smaller than in Nitti's day with perhaps a tenth of its former strength, about fifty made mobsters by the last FBI count, and the group, perhaps, does not have Nitti's far-reaching aspirations. It is now a much more insular organization, apparently not even having much to do with the East Coast-dominated Mafia Commission. The Outfit's outposts in Miami, Hollywood, and Las Vegas are now believed by some to be under the control of local mobs in those cities.[113] However, some estimates of the Outfit's current strength are much higher.[114]

When recently questioned by the press whether a culture of corruption existed in Cicero, a U.S. Attorney replied, "There does seem to be a persistent problem." By some accounts, modern Chicago still remains a "mob oasis," complete with "crooked cops and shady business dealings" with the same Chicago Crime Commission as from Nitti's day investigating the same illegal activities.[115] Today, the federal government heads an Organized Crime Strike Force that could easily be something Eliot Ness might have thought up more than seventy years ago.[116]

The FBI has found out the hard way that even if key underworld figures are removed, the depth and financial strength of these syndicates more often than not allows them to continue on for all practical purposes untouched. While its apparent top leadership is now facing criminal prosecution and sentencing, there are rumors that the Outfit may soon be thinking big once again and is reportedly forging new alliances with other ethnic organized-crime syndicates, including the Russian *mafiya* and Chinese triad gangs.

Frank Nitti's legacy lives on.

3

Capone's Enforcer

Frank Nitti: Hey, Al, how come you get to keep most of the money?
Al Capone: Because I'm the boss.
Frank Nitti: How come you're the boss?
Al Capone: Because I have most of the money.
—Anonymous Internet joke

Plug 'em. That's what I would do.
—Paul Regina as Frank Nitti
in *The Untouchables* (1993)

Prohibition

Frank Nitti became a prominent gangster during a great historical social maelstrom that encompassed the aftermath of the Great War with both rampant economic growth and the advent of the criminalization of alcoholic beverages in America, followed by the misery of the Great Depression. The federal government's Volstead Act of October 28, 1919, and the 1920 Prohibition Eighteenth Amendment to the Constitution outlawed alcoholic beverages and were closely related to women's suffrage and temperance-religious social movements such as the Women's Christian Temperance Union and the Anti-Saloon League. Major cities—Chicago, New York, and

Detroit—were seen by these reformers as bastions of sin and temptation where vice went hand in hand with alcohol consumption, which also was perceived as a major cause of crime, social violence, poverty, and low-economic productivity. Labor unions were opposed to these temperance measures because of the thousands of distillers, brewers, waiters, and bartenders who were suddenly unemployed.

Specifically, the Eighteenth Amendment outlawed the manufacture, sale, and transportation of alcohol. The Volstead Act, introduced by U.S. Congressman Andrew Volstead, defined an alcoholic beverage as anything with more than 5 percent of alcohol and also made the very consumption of alcohol illegal. However, there were many means of bypassing these new laws. For example, those who required alcohol for "medical reasons" were allowed to purchase a rationed supply.[1] Legal alcohol was also readily available in America for export trade, medicinal purposes, and as a by-product of such consumer products as hair tonic, cosmetics, and perfume. Government "permits for withdrawal" were needed to purchase legal alcohol stocks. Bribing officials was one way of obtaining them. Another popular method was simply hijacking the right railway boxcar.[2]

On October 24, 1929, Wall Street collapsed, and an industrial paralysis spread across the United States, the richest nation in the world, until by 1933, twenty million Americans were facing starvation.[3] By 1931, the nation was experiencing its most severe economic devastation in history resulting in suffering and misery for wide segments of the population. Stock-market losses in October 1929 alone amounted to $16 billion, and in the same year, more than half of all Americans were living below a minimum subsistence level. During the same year, the gross national product fell 8.5 percent, and more than 20 percent of the U.S. population would become unemployed over the next several years.

This crisis was not natural, not caused by disaster, war, flood, or famine, but was an artificially created economic state. There was no immediate relief from government for the aggrieved populace until President Franklin D. Roosevelt's "New Deal" of economic reform and recovery in 1933, just in the nick of time for the battered working class and not coincidentally when Prohibition was also repealed on March 15, 1933. This was the environment of social and economic repression in which born-opportunistic entrepreneurs such as Frank Nitti and Al Capone seized the moment.

A combination of economic depression, a lack of social safeguards, Prohibition's Eighteenth Amendment and the Volstead Act, and rampant police corruption acted to spawn a new breed of violent and highly organized criminals. During these times of pinstriped suits and Tommy guns, these criminals included not only Al Capone and Frank Nitti, but many others such as the infamous Ma Barker, Alvin "Creepy" Karpis, Bonnie and Clyde, George "Machine Gun" Kelly, Giuseppe "Joe the Boss" Masseria, Charles "Lucky" Luciano, Benjamin "Bugsy" Siegel, Meyer Lansky, and John Dillinger. Such criminals, with colorful popular images that included Thompson submachine guns carried in violin cases and gaudy suits, along with media-conscious law-enforcement officers, most prominent among them Eliot Ness and his Untouchables, brought interest to the otherwise often depressing headline news of the times. Beyond the newspaper stories and popularized household words, bloody urban warfare in Chicago and New York by organized-crime factions resulted in increasingly structured and powerful gangs.

However, the major change occurring as a result Prohibition was the organization of crime on a national or even international scale, mostly dominated by mob figures of Italian ethnicity, but also involving people of all ethnic backgrounds. Organized crime resulted primarily from the complicated logistical demands of illegally importing (from Canada or Europe) liquor and setting up distribution networks and consumer outlets such as speakeasies. The most successful crime organizations were dominated by men of recent immigrant backgrounds such as Italians, Jews, and Irish because their cultures, unlike those of staid Anglo-Saxon heritage, reinforced the idea of eluding and defying government and police authority as a positive and desirable characteristic. Far from being isolated socially, many of these gangsters became folk heroes and often associated with the famous and wealthy. The ultimate results of the social-engineering experiment of Prohibition was that crime rates skyrocketed, organized crime was strengthened, corruption flourished at all official levels, and large numbers of ordinary people were arrested, while it failed to achieve any of its original objectives and was finally repealed in defeat. As soon as legitimate bars were closed, they were simply replaced by undercover speakeasies. Some make the same comparison with today's war on drugs.

While it became illegal for American companies to sell, buy, distribute, or manufacture alcoholic beverages, Prohibition did not curb the public's appetite for the product. As dictated by basic economic principles of supply and demand, a supplier comes into being for any product that has a great enough demand. International suppliers from Canada and Europe, who were breaking no law in their countries, as well as illegal domestic suppliers, began production to meet this U.S. demand. At first, illicit alcohol enterprises were inefficient small-time operators, but in time, these were replaced by well-managed ethnic minority (mostly Italian and Jewish) syndicates in major American cities. Ethnic ties made such organizations very difficult for police organizations to penetrate, as well as fostering increasingly complex and formalized organizational networks that eventually formed the organizations of the Mafia and its branches such as the Outfit.

Liquor profits allowed these organizations to expand into every major American city and to eventually horizontally and vertically integrate their means of production and distribution. The new flexible transportation system created by the innovations of automobiles, trucks, and aircraft were also crucial for the development of these underworld networks and regional crime centers. Automobiles, unlike public forms of transportation, provided criminals a unique blend of independent mobility, anonymity, speed, and specialized applications such as armored and glass plating. As with today's U.S. border, American security could not possibly cope with the thousands of miles of U.S. territory adjacent to Canada, Mexico, and Cuba from which a steady supply of alcohol was produced for the American market. Legal industrial alcohol was another source of product, although wood-based alcohol often proved fatal to those drinking it. Because of the organizational and financial strength they gained during Prohibition, organized-crime organizations were able to carry on in new rackets once alcohol was legalized.

However, many people other than overt immigrant gangsters made their fortunes during Prohibition, among them the respectable father of a future president of the United States, one Joseph P. Kennedy. Well educated (a Harvard man), well heeled, and accepted as part of high society, Kennedy's involvement with illegal booze began in 1924 when he first entered the bootlegging business likely because it presented an almost-sure method to increase his existing fortune. Joe Kennedy, a banker and investor, already knew the business through his father, P. J. Kennedy, who had owned saloons and liquor dealerships in Massachusetts. Joe, too, benefited from the many judiciary and legal contacts from his mother's side of the family who were also involved in the liquor trade. He adapted this knowledge to converting existing legal saloons and liquor distributorships to illegal speakeasies and international-smuggling operations similar to those used today to distribute cocaine and heroin from South America and Asia.

Kennedy funneled his existing wealth into liquor-smuggling operations from Canada and Europe, and his initial partner was Frank Costello, the New York wise guy who would someday rise to Mafia boss status. The Costello-Kennedy partnership would eventually sour, and Costello and other underworld leaders were persecuted by Joe Kennedy's sons, John and Robert, when they rose to political preeminence and whose assassinations have been linked by many conspiracy theorists to their father's failed mob connections. Add to that the related issue of President John F. Kennedy's failure to adequately protect organized-crime investments in Cuba. However, the major Nitti-Kennedy connection would arise when the Outfit helped finance Joe Kennedy's big investments in Hollywood, which helped gain a foothold for their Hollywood extortion scam discussed in Chapter Six.[4]

Chicago Beginnings

At the beginning of Prohibition in Chicago, there existed thousands of members of the local Italian community who were making alcohol mostly in home stills. Bootlegging was an easy source of money for these people and soon led to conflict between organized-crime gangs that each sought to control a segment of the Chicago market. In addition to serving its own large regional market, Chicago became the entrepot for much of the American Midwestern market. These opportunities, however, soon led to strife and violence between underworld factions, often drawn along Italian- and Irish-ethnic lines. For example, when Antonio D'Andrea, a pillar of Chicago's Italian community, but closely tied to organized crime and in competition with Irish gangs, announced his candidacy as a nonpartisan alderman for Chicago's Nineteenth Ward, on February 11, 1921, a powerful bomb exploded at his political rally at approximately 9:30 p.m. "just after a speech by prominent civic leader Dr. Gaetano Ronga." (Ronga would be the future father-in-law of Frank Nitti and was a pallbearer at D'Andrea's funeral.)[5] Illegal liquor was a natural tie-in with vice, gambling, extortion, and organized-crime activities.

In 1922, Al Capone began working for Chicago boss Johnny Torrio as a bodyguard and bouncer. Capone was originally from Brooklyn, New York. Torrio was the successor to Big Jim Colosimo, who had been liquidated in 1920. Torrio sold a franchise to Capone in 1923–1924 for operations in the Chicago industrial suburb of Cicero, and when Torrio left for Italy in 1925, Capone bought the remainder of his business interests. At this time, the Outfit only controlled bootlegging in Chicago's South Side, a chain of brothels in a crescent of west and southwest suburbs, plus dozens of gambling dens. North Side bootlegging was in the hands of Irish gangsters Dion O'Banion and George "Bugs" Moran, while North Side operations were controlled by the six Sicilian Genna brothers.

Frank Nitti and Al Capone had known each other since their youth in Brooklyn when Capone was a member of Nitti's Navy Street Boys teenage gang. Al Capone's brothers, Vincenzo, Ralph, and Frank, were also full members of this gang.[6] There is some evidence that Nitti and Capone together made their way from New York and sought their fortune in Chicago by 1919 in an area of the South Side known as Little Hell.[7] It is likely that in the early 1920s, Nitti made the transition from fencing stolen goods and small-time bootlegging to organized crime and joined the Outfit under Johnny Torrio.[8]

In the early 1920s, Nitti was also associated with Chicago gang leader Giuseppi "Diamond Joe" Esposito, who sponsored many other important future members of the Outfit. Nitti's prison records indicate that he was nominally employed by

Esposito as a barber from 1923 to 1925. Esposito remained close friends with Nitti. The two often vacationed at Esposito's palatial summer home at Bass Lake, Indiana, and Esposito let Nitti and his wife stay in his mansion, "Bella Napoli." Nitti became a gunman and enforcer along with William "Klondike" O'Donnell, William "Three Fingers Jack" White, "Machine Gun" Jack McGurn, and Charles Fischetti.[9] By 1923-1924, Nitti had joined Capone and Johnny Torrio in the takeover of the Chicago suburb of Cicero.[10]

Frank Nitti was Al Capone's bodyguard from 1924 to 1926, supposedly at a salary of some $7,800 per year (while Capone may have been clearing upward of $33,000 a week), and his success at this task led to successive quick promotions with increasingly greater responsibilities and financial incentives that included a cut of overall profits. Some believe that Nitti became an emotional substitute for Capone's brother, Frank, following his death at the hands of the Chicago police in 1923. In 1926, Nitti and Jack McGurn were the only trusted bodyguards allowed to accompany Capone to his Michigan retreat at Round Lake near Lansing. Nitti packed a .45-caliber semiautomatic pistol as a personal weapon.[11]

Nitti must have had income from other sources because when he was sentenced to a prison term in 1930 for income-tax evasion, his estimated income for the years 1925 to 1927 was well over $200,000 per year. To place these amounts of money in the context of the salaries of the day, a Chicago police inspector during Prohibition had a yearly salary of about $3,000, which was considered to be a very high-paying job; a federal agent had an annual salary of $1,800 to $2,400 per year; and a new automobile could be purchased for around $500.

Nitti soon became an expert at smuggling Canadian whiskey into distribution points throughout Chicago and had a proven network of underworld customers to whom he could market the illegal booze. This organizational and logistical ability helped earn his rapid promotion to the top echelon of the Outfit, and following a few years that saw a rapid rise from chief enforcer and *consigliere* to underboss of the Outfit, for all intents and purposes, he ran the syndicate for Capone.[12] Nitti soon emerged as Capone's top gang-war officer and tactician.[13] Some early reports also claimed Nitti was the Outfit's treasurer, but it is now widely believed that Jake Guzik and others were the dedicated financial experts in charge of this area, although Nitti certainly had a keen knowledge and a hands-on involvement with financial matters and acted as Capone's business manager.[14]

Between 1925 and 1929, at least four major attempts were made on Al Capone's life. Frank Nitti was in charge of Capone's security, and none of these attempts were successful. (At one point, the North Side Gang had pumped more than one thousand rounds into Capone's headquarters at the Hawthorne Hotel, but he emerged unscathed.) In 1925, Capone's top associates included Frank Nitti, Jake "Greasy Thumb" Guzik, Louis "Little New York" Campagna, the Fischetti brothers, and the leader of his execution squad, Fred "the Brain" Goetz. The political and police protection and intergang cooperation system that Torrio had built broke down under the antagonistic leadership of Capone, and a fierce series of "beer wars" erupted. However, by the end of the 1920s, Capone and the Outfit were the undisputed major force behind organized crime in Chicago.[15]

The FBI classified Capone's official occupation as being a "professional gambler."[16] While Capone was not particularly intelligent, he made a point of surrounding himself with men who were, such as Frank Nitti, Jake Guzik, and Murray Humphreys. Nitti was described as Capone's treasurer, second vice president, and general adviser by a February 1936 issue of the *Chicago Sunday Tribune* that provided a special exposé of the Outfit's organization (in fact, by that time Nitti had long since been the Outfit's boss). He was also described as being "well informed, presentable and handled much money."[17] As *consigliere*, he was Capone's right-hand man and trusted adviser, a position that could not easily be obtained.

Adviser and Underboss

Frank Nitti first became Capone's *consigliere* and then his underboss or second-in-command by 1930-1931.[18] During the 1920s, Nitti was in charge of directing much of Capone's liquor and vice enterprises. These were not only in Chicago, for the Outfit and East Coast mobs had operations in other cities (particularly Miami, which had a strong Outfit presence during the Capone and Nitti eras) with drug-smuggling-and-processing operations for marijuana, cocaine, and heroin, prostitutes, underground porn shops, and adult massage parlors. Gambling operations established and controlled by Nitti were found in Cicero, the Loop, and other greater Chicago locations. Under the leadership of Nitti, the Outfit would take a more corporate approach to the vertical and horizontal integration of such rackets from top to bottom and expanding operations on a large-scale national basis.

Some historians have portrayed Frank Nitti as standing in the shadow of Al Capone, of Nitti only being Capone's student. This is completely false. Frank Nitti had a completely different personality than that of Al Capone and a completely different business-management style, but he could stand alone as a very competent leader. Nitti was self-educated with a methodical, analytical business mind, while Capone dropped out of school during the sixth grade, but had street smarts and was a natural leader and organizer of such rackets as distilleries, breweries, nightclubs, brothels, speakeasies, bookie joints, gambling houses, racetracks, and more. Capone felt he was providing the people a social service that they demanded—wine, women, and song—while Nitti always considered the Outfit's many illegal activities as simply another business. Capone was a big and burly brawler (called "the Big Fellow" by many). While Nitti was physically unprepossessing, he projected an intimidating presence through his personality.

Capone preferred the quick fix to problems, usually by the use of violence, while Nitti, although certainly capable of decisive violent action when required, preferred long-term solutions through bribes and strategic alliances, combined with just the right amount of physical intimidation – the so-called low-profile "iron fist in the velvet glove" approach. Capone never quite understood that the general public would only tolerate violence to a certain point, but Nitti fully grasped this principle of restraint.

Capone's clothing style tended toward outrageous publicity-gathering outfits such as banana-yellow suits and shocking-pink silk shoes, and sporting personal accessories such as a 11-½ carat diamond pinkie ring. Nitti avoided such ostentatious "pimp gear" in favor of immaculately tailored, conservative, dark three-piece business suits. Capone actively sought attention and adoration from the general public (whom he wished would view him in the same light as a movie star), the press, and even the police, while Nitti shunned such flamboyant displays as a prudent standard practice.

According to various sources, Capone liked to keep court in the manner of a medieval king inside his extravagant suites on the third, fourth, and fifth floors of the Lexington Hotel from 1928 until he was imprisoned (fifty-four rooms in all; Treasury Agent Elmer L. Irey claimed that the Outfit occupied the sixth, seventh, and eighth floors, so perhaps at some point, they had moved between floors).[19] Whatever the exact arrangements were in "the Lex," there was always a massive presence of Capone's assistants, gunmen, women, and other hangers-on of his entourage. When the Outfit was put on a high-security alert, it would establish a four-block cordoned "no go zone" surrounding its headquarters that it would not even allow police officers or federal agents to cross.[20]

While Nitti had an office in the Lexington and was a familiar presence when he worked for Capone, he preferred the use of functional front companies often located in office buildings or anonymous hotel suites; and eventually he moved the Outfit's headquarters out of the Lex when he became boss. The Chicago Police Department wasted no time in raiding the Fort following Capone's final prison conviction in 1931, but found these headquarters totally deserted with no records or other evidence remaining. In 1986, a nationally broadcasted television special, "The Mystery of Al Capone's Vault," was hosted by Geraldo Rivera to examine a long-locked vault that supposedly belonged to Capone in the Lexington. Not surprisingly, nothing was discovered in the vault after it was dramatically cracked. Rivera also fired a submachine gun into the walls of a second-floor gymnasium where Capone's bodyguards used to work out. They were also unable to find any of the rumored hidden tunnels or staircases some said Capone and his men used to escape detection by police and rival bootleggers.[21]

Capone's Palm Island estate in Miami had a bathroom washbowl with solid gold legs.[22] Capone also traveled in style in a seven-ton custom-made armored Cadillac limousine that had cost him $20,000 in 1928 (complete with a machine-gunner's station, steel-plated gas tank, bulletproof glass, police siren, and secret gun locker) amid much fanfare and an entourage that often included eighteen bodyguards and a bevy of beautiful women. Nitti's residences were also impressive, but never ostentatiously so. When Nitti traveled, it was usually in secret, and the police and press had much difficulty keeping track of even his approximate whereabouts.

Capone thought of himself as a modern Robin Hood stealing from the rich to give to the poor and did things like opening soup kitchens during the Depression to feed Chicago's poor and unemployed by providing three free meals per day. (The "soups" were also used to conveniently launder criminal proceeds by making their cash flow appear as charitable donations; Nitti also used them to launder the take from the Hollywood extortion scam.)[23] Even though Capone was a murderer, pimp, extortionist, and bootlegger, he was, indeed, beloved by a general public who cheered him at public events, while the same public had little if any feeling for Nitti at the time and would only respect him out of fear when he became boss. Capone was outgoing, emotional, and warm in his own way. Nitti was always the outwardly cold and clinical professional.

Under Capone, the Outfit's activities focused on the popular ones of booze, prostitution, and gambling. Capone, who wanted so much to legitimize himself and be accepted as a contributing member of the community, was enraged, humiliated, and thoroughly insulted when he was branded Public Enemy Number One in Chicago. Nitti was never a declared public enemy and always thought of himself as a businessman running a business for profit, who moved the organization on to new criminal frontiers such as labor rackets on a big scale, as well as narcotics, which Capone opposed. Capone sought to be constantly in the limelight, in the company of movie stars, important businessmen, and major political figures, while Nitti preferred to quietly use and extort such people. Capone was a notorious womanizer who was infected with an advanced form of syphilis. Nitti's prison records indicated that he had tested negative for syphilis and gonorrhea. Nitti shunned publicity and was easily irritated by newspaper articles that even mentioned his name. Unlike Capone, Nitti, a very private man who did not easily share his personal emotions, would never have desired the continuing media coverage that would be his six decades after his death.

Enforcement

There is no specific legal evidence or criminal convictions that prove Frank Nitti actually killed anyone himself as so often has been portrayed by Hollywood, but it is still likely that he did so, particularly during the early part of his organized-crime career. He was familiar with weapons and certainly ordered many hits to be undertaken by his soldiers, and he played key roles in various important jobs. While some modern authors have claimed Nitti was a career "front office strategist" who sent others to do the dirty work, others have termed him a "crack triggerman," and the police characterized him as a "murder agent."[24] Top federal agent Elmer L. Irey wrote in his memoirs that Nitti's nickname "the Enforcer" was completely accurate for his role of enforcing discipline within the Outfit, that Nitti was Capone's right-hand man and second-in-command, and that he "had what it takes" to provide the "quick, cruel discipline Al needed to keep the faithful and the competitor dormant."[25] Irey further related that "Capone doesn't kill any more. He brings in thugs to do it for him. Frank Nitti, 'The Enforcer,' handles the arrangements and if the thugs fail 'The Enforcer' has them knocked off."[26]

An Outfit member talked about Nitti and his operations under Capone:

> Everything is business-like. Take The Enforcer, he keeps everybody in line for Al. Somebody gets out of line, Al tells The Enforcer, the next thing you know a couple of guys get off a train from Detroit or New York or St. Louis, and The Enforcer tells them who has to go. The guys do the job and go home. The price is $2,500 a job. . . . When the guys from out of town louse up a job and only "hurt" somebody, The Enforcer don't fool around none.

He has one of his own guys get the two guys who
blew the job. That's why very few fellows get hurt
around here. They get kilt. [sic][27]

ALTHOUGH SHORT, NITTI was capable of intimidation. On one
occasion during a disagreement, he backed his rotund and
boozy union frontman, George Browne, into a hotel washroom and almost pushed him out of an upper-story window.[28]
Nitti's lack of physical stature would not have been much of
a handicap in his role as an enforcer as he was precisely the
type of small tough man that had formed the ranks of the
deadly ancient Roman legions. In fact, many successful Sicilian mobsters were even shorter than Nitti. Nitti was thought
to have had "the Look," also called the "evil eye," which is
difficult to describe, but you know what it is when you have
it, and it alone is said to stop men dead in their tracks. This
claim is supported by some of the existing photographs of
Nitti where he exhibits an intense, penetrating, and often
indirect gaze.

As will be related in detail, the legal convictions that stuck
to Nitti were related to monetary crimes such as income-tax
evasion and extortion, although violence was implicit in each
of these cases. However, as in the case of Capone, the lack of
murder charges and convictions was likely due to the organized-crime community's traditional policy of not cooperating with authorities and of prosecuting internally. Some have
directly concluded that Nitti "had killed so many to maintain
Al Capone's power."[29]

Nitti also had an important role in the Outfit's takeover
of Chicago bartender, factory worker, truck driver, construction, and service-industry unions by organizing intimidation
and violence to frighten union members, infiltrating existing
unions, and organizing new unions where none existed.[30] An
attorney, A. C. Lewis, had this to say about Nitti:

He was high in the councils of the Capone gang and was generally reputed to be the person who carried out the executions decreed by the gang and became known as Nitti the Enforcer. In the course of time Al Capone was sent to prison on an income tax charge. His gang was so well established that it continued to function, and continued to take on new activities. It became known as the Syndicate and the aforesaid Frank Nitti became the titular head thereof.[31]

IN ALL, THE evidence indicates that Frank Nitti deserved the sobriquet the Enforcer. Nitti's most prominent trademarks for covert "wet work" operations were precise detailed planning that left nothing to chance, multiple shooters using interlocking fields of fire against their target, and sometimes the use of a patsy as a fall guy for a highly visible assassination. Wet work is commonly used to describe the violent clandestine operations employed by modern government intelligence and criminal organizations, including assassination, murder, kidnapping, torture, and other forms of violent tactics. Nitti may have also planned and possibly participated in high-end robberies as late as 1939.[32]

Some of the murders and assassinations that Nitti was probably involved with to some degree were those of Louis Alterie; George Barker; John M. Bolton; Estelle Carey; Anton Cermak; Mike de Pike Heitler; Jacob Kaufman; Alfred "Jake" Lingle; Tommy Maloy; Jack McGurn; Teddy Newberry; Edward O'Hare; Albert J. Prignano; James A. Ragen, Sr.; Saint Valentine's Day Massacre victims—Frank Gusenberg, Peter Gusenberg, Adam Heyer, Albert Kachellek (a.k.a. James Clarke), John May, Albert Weinshank, and Dr. Reinhardt Schwimmer; John Scalise, Albert Anselmi, and Joseph Guinta; Hymie Weiss and Patrick Murray; Gus Winkler; and Jack Zuta.

The major weapons of the internecine gang wars of the period were the ice pick, which could be used to conceal the cause of death by sticking it in the ear of the victim to scramble the brains and make the resulting death, with its small puncture wound, appear as a cerebral hemorrhage; knives for slitting throats and for torture; strangulation by hand, piano wire, or rope (e.g. the "Italian rope trick" where an unsuspecting victim was lured into a room to be grabbed and strangled by two men, one on each end of the rope); often fatal beatings by fist, blackjack, pipe, or baseball bat; axes for dismembering victims' bodies; and guns of all types (e.g. semiautomatic handguns and sawed-off shotguns).[33]

By the summer of 1927, small explosive bombs known as "pineapples" were widespread organized-crime weapons in Chicago and became the preferred weapon for intimidation and extortion. In the 1928 Cook County primary campaign, such bombs were used as a political weapon to intimidate voters and candidates. Bombing victims included a U.S. senator and a circuit court judge.[34] However, for the most part, these bombing campaigns resulted in no casualties; the majority of the victims of the internecine Chicago gang wars were mostly restricted to mobsters and mob-related individuals rather than innocent civilians, plus the odd policeman. (Nitti was never responsible for the bombing death of a little girl, as has been depicted by Hollywood, or the deliberate murder of any civilians.) Furthermore, these killings were largely restricted to specific rough areas of Chicago.[35] At one point between 1931 and 1933, the Outfit under Nitti was losing one soldier per day as a direct result of conflicts with rival gangs, most notably the North Side Gang.[36]

By the mid-1920s, the .45-caliber M1928 Thompson submachine gun had become the weapon of choice for the many drive-by shootings that were first perfected during the Capone-Nitti era. Thompsons and shotguns were used in many mob hits that followed the same pattern: The victim's car would be tailed by another car, and when the victim stopped, at a red light for example, the other car would pull up alongside it and blast away at the victim through his side window and windshield. The Thompson was also ideal for street fighting and could use an eighteen-, twenty-, and thirty-round box magazine or the fifty- and one-hundred-round drum magazines beloved by gangsters, but often troublesome in actual service. The original Tommy gun owed much of its fame to Hollywood, as well as to the real mob, but had a complex blow-back mechanism and required expert maintenance because of its precision-craftsmanship design. It was designed by U.S. Army Gen. John Thompson to meet the requirements of trench warfare during World War I and became widely adopted by the American military, where undoubtedly much of the related expertise of organized crime was originally sourced. Alex Korecek, an arms dealer, was identified as a major supplier of submachine guns to the Outfit while Peter von Frantzius was another.[37]

When Capone took command of the Outfit, violent crime increased significantly in Chicago, as did related political corruption with the election of William "Big Bill" Thompson as the city's mayor. The election of Thompson allowed Capone to increase the pace of his operations by buying businesses that could be used as fronts for numerous illegal activities. This almost immediately increased tension between the Outfit and rival gangs, most notably Dion O'Banion's and George "Bugs" Moran's North Side Gang. On November 3, 1924, Frank Nitti was a triggerman during the meeting at the Ship gambling den in Cicero. The session led to the November 10 murder of Dion O'Banion at his flower shop on North State Street.[38] Relations with the Genna brothers' gang were also strained at this point.

Frank Nitti is believed to have been the key player in the planning and execution of the 1926 Hymie Weiss hit, an effort by Capone to eliminate one of his most important gangster opponents who was allied with Bugs Moran's North Side Gang and who had made attempts on Capone's and Torrio's lives.[39] This operation was planned by Nitti along military lines and established his credentials as a wet-work master. Frankie Rio, Tony "Mops" Volpe, and Louis Barko were thought to be key members on this assassination team, and the size of this overall team was possibly larger than has often been estimated.

The Weiss assassination was a masterpiece of complex planning, coordination, and execution. Nitti had Weiss under constant surveillance deep in his own North Side territory for weeks to understand his movements and location patterns at all given times. Weiss lacked an effective personal security system. Outfit operatives tracked Weiss everywhere he went. Weiss was attacked at exactly the right place at the right time. The front and back of the location were covered by spotters and gunmen. Perhaps more than one dozen men were involved in the operation at any given time. It is reasonable to believe that the men on the team were the Outfit's best and could have included Frankie Rio, John Scalise, Albert Anselmi, Jack McGurn, Francis Maritote, Tony Volpe, Louis Campagna, Sam Hunt, and Phil D'Andrea. Nitti himself may have been at the scene as a gunman.

At the time of the assassination, the careful planning and precise practice paid off, and everything came together.[40] The operation included the innovative use of interlocking fields of fire against the target and even the possible use of additional out-of-town gunmen to compartmentalize operations. Up to three separate gunmen teams are believed to have attacked Weiss and his party. On October 11, 1926, Earl "Hymie" Weiss and Patrick Murray were killed and three others wounded on North State Street by some fifty rounds from submachine gun, shotgun, and high-powered rifle fire by six or more shooters from the second story of 740 North State Street across from

Dion O'Banion's old flower shop, which was still being used by Weiss as a headquarters.[41] Subsequently, Nitti directed other offensive actions against the North Side Gang.

Frankie Yale was the target of the next assassination Nitti probably had a major role in planning. Yale had been an old Capone ally, but fell into disfavor. In early 1928, Al Capone and his family had taken an extended vacation at their new Palm Island estate leaving Nitti in charge in Chicago.[42] On the night of the Frankie Yale hit, July 1, 1928, it is believed that a long-distance phone call was placed to Frank Nitti's headquarters at the Metropole Hotel from the Brooklyn home of Louis Campagna's mother, who happened to live near the Yale residence. Campagna happened to be Nitti's bodyguard.[43] Yale was killed as he was driving down Forty-fourth Street in Brooklyn. His car was forced to pull over by another car from which a hail of bullets riddled Yale and his car in the standard fashion. Some of the weapons and spent shell casings recovered at the scene were traced to a Chicago arms dealer. Campagna was a prime suspect in this hit in which a Thompson submachine gun was used for the first time in New York.[44]

"Lefty Louie" Campagna (also known as "Little New York"), who remained loyal to Nitti until his boss's death, had a violent criminal record stemming back to a December 20, 1917, bank robbery of $100,000, and over the decades he was a prime suspect for a long string of murders. Like Frankie Rio, Campagna was typical of many Outfit men in that he was reputed to be both a vicious professional torpedo and a loving family man. In 1928, Campagna pulled a gun on the chief of the Chicago police force while his men surrounded police headquarters in an attempt to capture and liquidate the imprisoned Joseph Aiello. Campagna and his men were never charged for this fantastic feat of arms, but Chicago newspaper headlines screamed the next day: "Gunmen Defy Police: Invade Law's Stronghold."[45]

While sometimes portrayed by Hollywood as just being Nitti's gunsel flunky, Campagna actually became a senior member of the Outfit and was quite often involved in its key decision-making process.[46] He was always greatly feared in underworld circles, and just the threatening mention of his name was "known to turn rough customers into slobbering yesmen."[47] Along with Frankie Rio, he was visually the original stereotype for every Hollywood hit man named "Lefty," "Mugsy," and "Rocky." Campagna had been a Five Points gang member in New York along with Nitti and Capone and likely came to Chicago with them. At some point between 1924 and 1926, he became Capone's bodyguard and personal hit man, and carried on in this capacity for Nitti after Capone was imprisoned.[48] He survived Nitti and remained active with illegal Chicago gambling establishments such as the A&R Lounge and the Austin Club after serving prison time related to Nitti's failed Hollywood extortion racket.[49] A nature lover, Campagna owned farms and was an enthusiastic gardener and fisherman.

The next infamous hit would firmly establish Nitti as a master of the art although it is likely he was assisted by Jack McGurn in planning the operation. Such assistance was probably ordered by Capone against Nitti's advice, a humiliation that McGurn surely paid for with his life once Nitti became boss. The Saint Valentine's Day Massacre took place on February 14, 1929, and remains one of the most remembered and violent organized-crime multiple murders in history. It was intended to eliminate Capone's major enemies at one stroke and decapitate the North Side Gang's leadership. According to mobsters Johnny Roselli and Sam Giancana, it was Nitti who planned the fine details of this successful, but exceedingly brutal, hit that was to take place at a garage used by George Moran's North Side Gang at 2122 North Clark Street.

The operation was marked by the innovative use of two of the hit men arriving dressed in Chicago police uniforms and the others in civilian clothes, but with detective's badges. Moran's men had been carefully observed by the Outfit for weeks prior to the hit to establish their patterns of behavior, and it was discovered that the garage where the murders eventually took place was a hub for North Side Gang alcohol-distribution activities. Outfit lookouts infiltrated and surrounded the garage. More than 150 rounds from two shotguns and two Thompson submachine guns were methodically pumped into the seven hapless victims, who were literally torn apart. However, the main objective of the hit, Bugs Moran, had luckily missed the event.[50]

There has been much speculation on the identities of the gunmen including theories that some were gunsels hired from Detroit, possibly from the infamous Purple Gang, or the Karpis-Barker gang, or some local men such as Murray Humphreys, Jack McGurn, Claude Maddox, John Scalice, and Albert Anselmi. Alvin Karpis, notorious bank robber and kidnapper, confessed to federal officials after he was taken into custody in May 1936 that Louis Campagna had offered him a job in 1933 for strong-arm work for the Outfit at a salary of $250 a week, but he had refused the offer. Other sources indicate that Karpis had, in fact, worked for Frank Nitti as a labor goon during 1931 and 1932, had seen Nitti during the same period at the boss's Benton Harbor summer home on Lake Michigan, and discussed Mayor Anton Cermak's recent attempt on Nitti's life. Karpis may have participated in earlier operations for the Outfit.[51]

The Purple Gang was a loosely organized confederation of Detroit mobsters who undertook nationwide criminal activities that included bootlegging from Canada in partnership with the Outfit, kidnapping, and labor racketeering. The Purple Gang self-destructed by the time of World War II, but a number of former members continued as national and even international underworld figures, with some being indicted and convicted as recently as 1996. One of its members, Nathan Rabin, was even employed by Japanese intelligence services during World War II in Shanghai as a professional hit man, extortionist, and blackmailer.[52] Other gangs continued to use the name Purple Gang, but the original gang had an all-Jewish membership.[53]

Chicago's Circus Café Gang, whose members were affiliated with the Outfit, were also suspects in the Saint Valentine's Day Massacre.[54] The use of such outside help is a likely indicator of Nitti's key role in the planning of the attack as McGurn would have been more inclined to use Outfit members and do the job himself.

The official Chicago police record of the event noted:

> ...seven Moran gangsters who were lined up facing a brick wall and mowed down with machine guns and shotguns in a garage at 2122 N. Clark Street at 10:40 A.M., 2/14/29. When the killers left two of them had their hands in the air and the other two followed pointing the machine guns at their backs. They all got into an auto disguised as a police squad car and escaped.[55]

SIX OF THE seven killed were Moran gang members. The seventh, Dr. Schwimmer, was quite possibly innocent. He was an optometrist and "a crony and admirer of Moran" who ended up with too much of a visceral thrill that day.[56] Unfortunately for Capone, the main target of the hit, George Moran, was not at the garage when the massacre took place. Moran was lucky that morning because he was running late, and the hit men had mistaken his brother-in-law and co-leader, Albert Weinshank, for him. When Moran arrived at the garage, he probably thought it was being raided by the police. So he ducked into a coffee shop across the street to lay low. A German shepherd chained in the garage (Moran's mascot) was left unharmed although some Hollywood portrayals have incorrectly had it shot, too. The gunshots plus the dog's howling alerted nearby people that something was amiss. The only man alive when the authorities arrived was Frank Gusenberg, but he had twenty bullets in his body and died shortly after.[57]

The FBI reported that Nitti was in charge of operations when Capone went to Miami in February 1929 before the Saint Valentine's hit went down. Nitti was briefly seized by the police at this time on a vagrancy charge, but released on a $10,000 bond (the normal bond of the time was $300). On February 16, 1929, two days after the murders, he married Anna, his first wife, in St. Louis.[58] At this time, the Chicago Police Department's chief of detectives was reportedly on the Outfit's payroll for $5,000 per week and kept Capone informed on Moran's whereabouts. The Outfit's relationship with the Chicago police was always very close and cordial under Capone and Nitti. In 1930, for example, a confidential police memo calling for the arrest of forty-one Outfit members was in Capone's possession, apparently for his approval and editing, prior to the actual arrests being made.[59] The implication was that the Outfit had strategically placed operatives within the police department who were leaking sensitive information as part of a syndicate intelligence system.

Two of the Capone gunmen used for the Saint Valentine's hit, John Scalice and Albert Anselmi, along with another confederate, Joseph Guinta, were subsequently liquidated by Capone for disloyalty upon Nitti's specific recommendation to use an Outfit top-leadership banquet as the venue for this deed.[60] It is believed by some that this multiple execution was performed personally by Capone, who used a baseball bat to smash their skulls at the mob banquet on May 7, 1929, at the Hawthorne Inn, although there is some debate as to the exact location. The victims were then repeatedly shot at close range for good measure, possibly by Nitti and Frankie Rio. Other sources indicate that the execution was done at The Plantation Club, "a roadhouse and casino that dripped Old South magnolia charm near Hammond, Indiana, just over the line from Burnham."[61] Federal agent Elmer L. Irey placed the location at the New Florence Restaurant across the street from Capone's Lexington Hotel headquarters.[62]

Some believe that the executions were performed by Tony "Big Tuna" Accardo, himself a future boss, who was then rewarded with a rare mob honor, a second nickname—"Joe Batters"—by Al Capone in the presence of Nitti and other top Outfit men.[63] Scalise and Anselmi are believed to have been the innovative hit men who were first to coat their bullets with garlic for a poisonous effect and the first to use the "handshake shot" murder technique such as was used on Dion O'Banion.

Nitti's career soared following the massacre. The killings Nitti would organize in the future when he was boss would generally be much more subtle than those he orchestrated for Capone, but just as deadly and setting the stage for modern covert-intelligence operations. One man besides Nitti is believed to have benefited from the massacre: Peter von Frantzius, a Diversey Parkway arms merchant who is thought to have supplied the submachine guns and other weapons used for the Saint Valentine's killings, as well as Alfred "Jake" Lingle's and other murders.[64]

On the other hand, Capone's fortunes generally declined thereafter. It was in May 1929 that Capone and Frankie Rio were arrested in Philadelphia on a concealed weapons charge. While Capone served his sentence, Frank Nitti took charge of the Outfit from the headquarters at the Lexington Hotel. Some suggest that Capone and Rio deliberately got themselves arrested so the public heat stemming from the Saint Valentine's Day Massacre could cool down, possibly at the request of the national Mafia Commission. The commission's head, Charles Luciano, is believed to have unsuccessfully cautioned

Capone to stall giving in to any such a demand and to leave the conference.[65]

During Capone's absence, Nitti was in charge of the Outfit's internal discipline and decided who would be hit and bombed, and whose booze trucks would be hijacked, with the major targets being the remnants of the Aiello-Moran gang.[66] Nitti visited Capone in prison on a regular basis, and they used the warden's office for private conferences.[67] At this time, Nitti sponsored the career of Paul "the Waiter" Ricca, who someday would supersede him as boss.[68] Ricca's rise with Nitti's support came as a surprise for some other senior members of the Outfit because Ricca was then virtually an unknown.[69]

Officially, the Saint Valentine's Day Massacre and its equally bloody aftermath remains unsolved, but it did turn some public opinion against Capone and focused increased law-enforcement efforts against him.[70] There are Chicago residents today who claim that the site of the massacre is haunted.[71]

Stint in Prison

U.S. District Attorney George E. Q. Johnson considered Frank Nitti as one of Chicago's top echelon organized-crime figures, "an important gangster." Johnson was the driving force behind Nitti and Capone's prison sentences resulting from convictions for tax avoidance. In the landmark 1927 Sullivan ruling, the U.S. Supreme Court had decided that all illegal profits derived from criminal activities were taxable and could be used by the federal government to charge organized-crime figures with income-tax evasion. As early as 1928, Johnny Torrio had warned the Outfit's top leadership to be careful with their income-tax returns. At this point, senior organized-crime figures never filed income-tax returns, legally owned nothing in their own names, never made declarations of personal assets or income, and undertook all their business through frontmen to retain this income anonymity. Besides Nitti and Al Capone, others who would go to prison after being prosecuted for income-tax avoidance included Terry Druggan, Frank Lake, Murray Humphreys, Jake Guzik (long-time bookkeeper, business manager, organizer, go-between, fixer, schemer, and chief statistician for the Outfit), and Al's brother, Ralph "Bottles" Capone.[72] Investigators supposedly traced some $370 million of turnover between the business activities of Nitti, Guzik, and Ralph Capone.[73]

Nitti certainly had to pay his prison dues during his rise to leadership in the Outfit, his imprisonment resulting from the federal efforts to destroy the Capone mob. Nitti may have taken temporary refuge in Italy during 1930 on a fake passport to avoid arrest, but was charged by federal agents upon his return to the U.S. Nitti had reportedly told Al Capone, "I'll scram. I'll go back to the old country. That'll take the heat off the mob, and I'll get a little fun out of my dough."[74]

Following charges of income-tax avoidance, Nitti went into hiding in a series of locations including Miami, various Outfit brothels such as the Carleon Hotel in Chicago and the Roamer Inn, and a hideout in Berwyn County, west of Cicero, using an alias in the company of Anna before he was apprehended by a task force of two FBI agents, an Internal Revenue Bureau agent, and fifteen to twenty Chicago policemen. Elements of the U.S. Secret Service in Chicago may also have been involved in Nitti's national manhunt. Approximately 150,000 wanted posters with Nitti's photograph and details of a $1,000 reward offered by the Citizens' Committee for the Prevention and Punishment of Crime of the Chicago Association of Commerce for information leading to his capture were distributed nationally in post offices, police stations, and other public facilities, with 10,000 distributed in Chicago alone. The reward for Nitti was offered in the belief that he was connected to the murders of *Chicago Tribune* reporter Alfred "Jake" Lingle and North Side Gang leader Jack Zuta, although charges were never brought to bear. Nitti's FBI file indicates that his investigation was to a large extent personally orchestrated by Director Hoover, who feared that a key witness was under a death threat by the Outfit. H. H. Clegg, the FBI special agent in charge for Chicago at the time, coordinated matters from that end. FBI manpower shortage—and a consequent lack of agents available for the case—was a major issue and a constant source of friction with George E. Q. Johnson.

Berwyn was a Chicago suburban area where many Outfit types made their family homes and in return kept the community clean from their criminal enterprises. Federal agent Elmer Irey recounted that Frank Nitti was apprehended in Berwyn after an agent spotted Mrs. Frank Nitti, "a very pretty woman," driving a car going shopping and to a beauty parlor. Nitti's wife apparently took actions to avoid being tailed, but was still followed by federal agents to apartment 3-D at 3201 South Clinton Street, South Berwyn. The G-men staked out the apartment from an adjacent church belfry and learned that Mrs. Nitti was using the cover name of "Belmont."

Early in the morning of October 31, 1930, Frank Nitti was taken into custody in the "richly furnished apartment" after the arresting officer inquired at the entrance "Which Belmont?" Nitti gave this curt answer: "The well-known Belmont, you son of a bitch. Come on in." Some reports indicate that he was in bed. Nitti surrendered without any trouble. Presumably his wife remained free, although she also may have been arrested and then released.

It should be noted that the FBI was involved because Nitti crossed state lines when he holed up at the Roamer Inn. The inn, which included an Outfit bordello called the Japanese Garden and offered prostitutes, gambling, drugs, and alcohol to its clientele, was located just outside Michigan City, Indiana, forty miles from the Illinois border.[75]

Nitti himself was soon free on $50,000 bail, rearrested on a vagrancy charge, and then released once again.[76]

Treasury Department agent Frank J. Wilson compiled an income-tax avoidance case against Nitti based upon coded records seized from Outfit distilleries, gambling casinos, speakeasies, and brothels over a decade.[77] Nels Tessem, a high-powered U.S. Internal Revenue Service agent who had helped imprison Ralph Capone and Jake Guzik for income-tax evasion through wiretapping and other investigative methods, has been given credit, in part, for Nitti's conviction. Pat Roche, chief investigator for the U.S. Attorney's office in Chicago, headed the police investigation. It is also possible that informers within the Outfit contributed to Nitti's case, as well as those of Jake Guzik, Ralph Capone, and ultimately Al Capone, with the heavily censored official FBI and prison records of the case indicating that one key individual, "a man of very poor character," was involved.[78]

A specific example used in the federal case built against Nitti was a check for $1,000 from the take of Cicero gambling operations that Nitti endorsed. It was deposited in the Pinkert Bank and used to buy cashier's checks for a fictional "J.C. Dunbar." These checks were later deposited in the Schiff Trust and Savings Bank in Cicero. The bank managers had entered into an agreement with Nitti to clear checks and deliver cash without showing Nitti's name on any bank records.[79] Between March 14 and March 22, 1930, a federal grand jury in Chicago had formally charged the fugitive Nitti on five counts of tax evasion on income derived from unexplained sources in indictment Number 21246 *United States v. Frank R. Nitto*, with bail set at $50,000.[80] The specifics of this case were that Nitti had a spending pattern, and hence personal income, totaling $743,000 for the years 1925, 1926, and 1927, without filing and paying income tax on this income.[81] This was a very large income for the time, and today would be equivalent to many millions of dollars of purchasing power. For this gross income, Nitti had failed to pay an estimated $159,000 in income tax due to Uncle Sam.[82] The ultimate source of this money, whether legal or illegal, was irrelevant to the case brought against Nitti, who simply claimed that he hadn't filed and paid taxes because the earlier income-tax laws were unclear.[83]

Congressman Joseph "Hinky Dink" Parrillo was Al Capone's personal representative in Washington, and being a lawyer by trade, he was soon approached to fix Frank Nitti's rap.[84] However, the popular mood on the Hill at the time was to clean organized crime from the streets of America in general and Chicago in particular, and Hinky Dink's bribes went nowhere before Nitti's final sentencing.

The social background to Nitti's conviction was that Chicago's traditional oligarchic upper classes, outraged by the ongoing cycle of criminal violence, simply wished that the likes of Nitti and Capone would disappear from *their* fine city, and a charge of income-tax evasion, to be used again successfully against Capone, was as good a means as any. The rising fortunes of such gangsters were also perceived as a future economic threat to upper-classes' entrenched legitimate business operations. Irony was added to hypocrisy because many members of this social elite, including judges and government attorneys, were some of the best customers of the Outfit's numerous speakeasies and other services during Prohibition. Almost without exception, the men leading the attack on the Outfit, such as U.S. Attorney George E. Q. Johnson, were staunch Anglo-Saxons while their opponents were portrayed as dark, Latin foreigners. The so-called "Secret Six" establishment businessmen who founded the Chicago Crime Commission to directly tackle the Outfit beyond the boundaries of normal law enforcement is another prime example of this period's ethnic stratification.

Following his arrest, Nitti pleaded guilty as a result of an attempted plea-bargaining ploy for a lighter sentence. "Nitti hadn't even argued the point, but quietly pleaded guilty and happily took a year and a half."[85] Dispirited, he is said to have simply wanted to "get it over with."[86] In his prison records, Nitti admitted his conundrum to parole officials when asked why he had not paid any income tax whatsoever:

> There were times there I would have been more than glad to have paid. It was so complicated, I didn't understand it myself. I consulted several attorneys there and some advised me one way and some advised me another way. There was one time there I wanted to try to make a whole settlement, but just couldn't do it. If I would go in, if I wanted to make a settlement, I didn't know where to get all that money from. After it was all over, I held the bag, that is the way the story turned out.

NITTI'S TEAM OF high-priced lawyers, led by attorney Benjamin P. Epstein, tried to keep their client out of jail by saying he would pay all taxes owed plus double that amount to cover penalties and interest. For most people, such an offer would have been accepted. But Nitti was not "most people." He was an enemy of the state and what was considered decent society. His federal indictment was so generic that he was required to do time regardless of whether the mechanism itself was a miscarriage of justice. Some effort was made at deporting him due to an apparent lack of naturalization records, but nothing came of this. A major trial case was made of the uncertainty of whether Nitti's offense was a misdemeanor or a felony.

On December 20, 1930, he was sentenced to eighteen months at Leavenworth prison plus the maximum $10,000 fine. This fine was not paid until November 1931 although Nitti was willing to pay it immediately upon conviction. He also claimed that there was an agreement with District Attorney Johnson that was never honored whereby he would receive favorable recommendation for parole after serving one year and a day upon payment of the fine.

Arriving in January 11, 1931, Nitti served most of his stretch as prisoner Frank Nitto, register number 38021-L, with several months (108 days) off for good behavior. Nitti's prison file indicates that loyal wife Anna spearheaded a largely unsuccessful drive for his early release and pleaded to the authorities that Frank would from now on follow only the "straight and narrow path" and "she would accompany him West where they would reside, thereby removing him from his former associates and environment." She wrote to parole board officials in November 1931 when she paid her husband's $10,000 fine:

> My husband notwithstanding all that might be said against him, acted in good faith with the government and in the future, I know he will conduct himself as we promised the district attorney, as all good citizens should conduct themselves. I am ready to stand by him in helping him in his future conduct...I am sure that my husband in view of all that has happened in Chicago and in his case, has learned his lesson, and I am only standing by him because I know that I shall have no occasion to feel ashamed of anything that he will do in the future.

NITTI HAD MADE an agreement with the authorities that he was "not to return to Chicago, and that he would leave his gang connections and lead a useful, upright life."

> All I want to try to do if I get a chance, I want to start all over again. This has been enough for

me....I don't want to go back to Chicago because there is nothing there for me. It would be very embarrassing on my part and also my wife. I want to start over again and keep away from past associates and go straight.

JOHNSON, IREY, AND Wilson remained closely involved with Nitti's case after his senior status with the Outfit was finally determined by federal authorities, and they offered Mrs. Nitti an outward display of sympathy, but did little to help parole Nitti. He was eligible for parole on July 10, 1931. This was refused first on July 3, 1931, and again on November 30, 1931. While in prison, Nitti worked at soft jobs such as driving a car for the superintendent of the prison farm and working around his house in such capacities as laundryman, one of the best prisoner's jobs available because it involved regular outings to the outside world and other perks, and he was dressed mostly in civilian clothes. In his confidential work report, Nitti was rated as an excellent worker with a "trustworthy," "friendly," "pleasant," "energetic," and "faithful" character, almost the ideal prisoner. He also worked in the hospital kitchen and was appointed a prison trusty of the outer east gate. According to his parole officer, he had a "perfect conduct record" during his entire confinement, and the prison psychiatrist gave him similar stellar grades.

On several occasions, a "William Nitto," probably an Outfit colleague masquerading as a brother, paid him visits, which would have been how Nitti maintained close communications with the syndicate. (Another man claiming to be a "Tony Nitto" of Chicago was denied a visit.) Wife Anna Nitti, father-in-law Dr. Gaetano Ronga, his attorney Benjamin P. Epstein, Johnny Patton, and Edward O'Hare were other visitors. Sister Anna Vollaro corresponded with him on a regular basis, as did "brother" William. He also received letters from and corresponded with

Antoinette M. Caravetta, who would become his second wife. Guests other than family members had to be approved by the warden. Nitti was released on March 24, 1932.[87]

Nitti's supposed discomfort at being confined even in relatively plush prison conditions would much later fuel the rumors that he committed suicide rather than face jail time again. A seemingly strange condition of Nitti's parole was that he pursue a business career running Forest Dairy commercial dairy farm in Kansas City, Missouri, as a "Route Foreman and Solicitor" at a wage of $150 per month. This was perhaps not as outlandish as it may first seem because other senior Outfit members like Paul Ricca and Louis Campagna owned large working farms, possibly as money-laundering fronts. The Outfit at the time did own Chicago's Meadowmoor Dairies at 1334 South Peoria.

Al Capone had reportedly promoted the passage of an ordinance through the Chicago City Council that Grade A milk could not be sold as fresh more than seventy-two hours after it left the cow. A resulting law stipulated that the expiration date by which milk was to be sold must be clearly stamped on the milk container where the consumer could read and understand it, as is now many decades later a common practice internationally.[88]

However, Frank Nitti was not an agriculturalist by nature and was soon in thick again with the Outfit, heading straight back to Chicago and taking the leadership chair from Al Capone, who was himself soon off to serve a long stretch in prison for income-tax avoidance.[89] It should be noted that Nitti's tenure with the Outfit was solid enough at this point that he had no difficulty in resuming his position of authority within the organization after he had served his prison sentence. There was some press speculation shortly after his return to Chicago that Murray Humphreys was leading an armed revolt against Nitti's assumption of control, but this never materialized.

Following his income-tax conviction, Nitti made a point of carefully completing his income-tax returns and showing legitimate annual sources of income that included coin-operated vending machines, dog racetracks, and company stocks.[90] However, in 1935, well after he had become the Outfit's boss, Nitti was again the subject of a little-known federal income-tax civil action resulting from claiming $59,500 under "miscellaneous receipts," which were, in fact, related to gambling and slot-machine incomes, but he was not successfully prosecuted.[91] Nitti paid income tax on "honest" annual incomes of $87,079 for 1935, $82,756 for 1936, $103,469 for 1937, $107,112 for 1938, $63,674 for 1939, and $39,903 for 1940. In fact, his actual annual income was many times these amounts from various under-the-table sources. There was no tax complaint against Nitti at the time of his death in 1943, but by 1945, a lien related to the Hollywood extortion case was put on the estate he left his wife and son, and related IRS investigations continued for many years.[92]

Move to Power

Frank Nitti found when he was released from prison that the official heat on him had not entirely dissipated. Earlier in 1930, an official Chicago Police Department listing of thirty-one gangsters targeted for prosecution had been found by police officials and Internal Revenue and FBI agents at the Carleon Hotel at 2138 South Wabash Avenue, a known Outfit hangout and brothel in Cicero. The agents went there searching for Nitti when he was on the run prior to his income-tax prosecution. This secret police document had likely been obtained through bribery or a spy in the detective bureau, and an edited list omitting key Outfit members had been substituted. The resulting public uproar had the effect of encouraging a continued investigation of Nitti and his senior associates. The Outfit

members omitted from the list were Louis Campagna, Claude
Maddox, Ted Newberry, Tony Accardo, Sam Hunt, Marty
Guilfoyle, Murray Humphreys, and Anthony Capezio. Nitti
had never been on the list.[93]

On October 25, 1931, Al Capone was convicted of evading
$215,000 in income tax and was sentenced to eleven years in
prison. He successfully delayed serving his prison sentence
until Nitti had finished his and could take control of the
Outfit. Capone hoped that he would be released early from
prison. Once out, he would reclaim his position as boss. This
futile hope demonstrated his continued faith in the loyalty of
Nitti, whom he personally anointed as the heir to the throne.
While Hollywood has made the frequent error of having Nitti
present during Capone's trial and its aftermath, Nitti was still
in prison. In fact, the FBI believed that Capone feigned an
illness to delay serving his sentence until Nitti's release.

Controversy continued to dog the flamboyant Scarface
even in prison. During 1933, while Capone was in the U.S.
penitentiary at Atlanta, Georgia, it was charged that he ran
a narcotics-smuggling operation by knocking a tennis ball
beyond the prison wall while playing on the prison tennis
courts and having a substitute ball returned that had illegal
drugs hidden inside. Other prisoners supposedly tried to extort
large sums of money from him.

Subsequently, he was jailed at the new Alcatraz Island
Prison, off San Francisco, where he was almost murdered
during a prison riot. His outside communications privileges
were severely limited in Alcatraz.[94] FBI records clearly indicate
that Frank Nitti made a specific effort not to associate himself
with Capone during or after his trial, and while other well-
known gangsters such as Frankie Rio, Murray Humphreys,
Jake Guzik, and Louis Campagna visited Capone in jail,
Nitti did not during Capone's second prison sentence. Capone
made an initial effort at continuing to direct the Outfit from

behind bars, but this was soon ended by the increased security surrounding him, as well as Nitti's concerted efforts to fully assume direct command.

There has been a longstanding rumor that Frank Nitti somehow orchestrated Al Capone's final conviction on income-tax evasion so he could supplant Capone as the Outfit's boss. Part of this lore is that Nitti handed over to authorities the accounting ledgers used against Capone, and in return, the federal government allowed Nitti to consolidate his leadership of the Outfit without interference. Nitti and Louis Campagna may, indeed, have stopped an effort to fix Capone's trial. There was a general feeling in the Outfit's leadership that Capone was becoming a severe liability because of his continuing outlandish and highly visible behavior, as well as his steadily deteriorating mental condition.[95]

Nitti was closely linked to Edward "Fast Eddie" O'Hare, who did provide information used by federal authorities to convict Capone. O'Hare was later liquidated, probably on Nitti's order, when Capone was finally released from prison. This speculative theory has been popularized first by the 1975 movie *Capone* starring Sylvester Stallone as Frank Nitti and again in the 1993-1994 television series of *The Untouchables* starring Paul Regina as Nitti. It has also been explored in fictional literature, such as Max Allan Collins's *The Million-Dollar Wound* (1986).[96]

While there is no definitive evidence to support this theory, it was very apparent that once Capone was behind bars for the long stretch, Nitti did little, perhaps nothing, to help him shorten his prison sentence or conceivably regain control of operations upon his release in 1939. As it turned out, Capone was released early because he was suffering from a degenerative medical condition caused by an advanced case of syphilis (*general paresis*). The condition made his return to power impractical, if not impossible. In addition, Nitti apparently had little, if anything, to do with Capone following his release.

In 1934, Al Capone's brother, Ralph Capone, had made some tentative efforts to assume control over the Outfit, but nothing came of these weak attempts, and he was soon sidelined by Nitti. In 1939, Gus Winkler's wife is believed to have informed the FBI that Frank Nitti had said "to leave well enough alone... it was better for everyone if Capone stayed in jail." By the time Capone was set free, his mental state had deteriorated to the point that information he provided the FBI concerning current leadership and activities of the Outfit was largely discounted by J. Edgar Hoover.[97]

Capone's illness prevented any realistic possibility of his challenging Nitti in an attempt to regain power. Capone did not receive the Outfit's traditional "coming out" party for members just released from prison, symbolic of his now-reduced status. After he was released, Al Capone, according to brother Ralph, spent his final years "reading newspapers" and "walking the grounds to get some sunshine" at his Florida estate with his long-suffering and loyal wife Mae.

Al Capone's final imprisonment led to a widespread and naive expectation by Chicago's general public that the Outfit and organized crime in general was at last somehow finished in their city. This perception was also apparently shared by some law-enforcement and federal officials who should have known better. By early 1932, Frank "the Enforcer" Nitti was the Outfit's new leader, and the syndicate was very much alive.

4

Chicago Boss

Al Capone: Some reporter come up to me the other day
and say, "So Eliot Ness finally got you."
You know what he's talking about?
Frank Nitti: Never heard of him.
　　　　　—Lee David Zlotoff, *Nitti:*
　　　　　The Story of Frank Nitto, "The
　　　　　Enforcer": A Movie for Television

You heard Ness is in town, Nitti said.
Fuck Ness, Accardo said, and there were nods
and grunts of agreement, all around.
　　　　　—Max Allan Collins, *Road to Purgatory*

In Command

Any hope that organized crime had left Chicago with the imprisoned Al Capone was just wishful thinking. Correspondence of November 30, 1936, to FBI Director J. Edgar Hoover stated that the Outfit was "bigger, (and) more powerful than at any time in its history" and "is ruled with an iron hand by Frank Nitti."[1]

It was a challenging time for Nitti to assume command as illegal Prohibition revenues were drying up. The Outfit was largely overstaffed, often with nonessential personnel, and continued to command the attention of government and law-enforcement authorities. The infiltration of labor unions had become a major organized-crime activity, but the syndicate also controlled a large part of gambling, breweries, alcohol retailing, and narcotics, and many dyeing, cleaning, linen, and laundry businesses in Chicago. Outfit headquarters were now at the Sherman Hotel, the Congress Hotel, and in the 33 West Kinzie Street office building. Under Nitti, the Outfit was downsized, with many of Capone's numerous cronies and hangers-on removed, and an emphasis was placed on having a competent core group with hired help being brought on as required.

Nitti de-emphasized the dramatic drive-by shootings that thrilled Capone in favor of more sophisticated and less obtrusive methods. An interesting "personal and confidential" memorandum of December 6, 1939, from FBI Special Agent in Charge for Chicago W. S. Devereaux to J. Edgar Hoover, succinctly summarized the state of affairs of the Outfit at the time of Al Capone's release from prison.

> [censored] believes that FRANK NITTI alias FRANKIE THE ENFORCER is well set in Cleveland, Florida, and other sections of the country as a result of so-called legitimate businesses and also as a result of his interest in various labor unions, etc. NITTI, JACK GUZIK, LITTLE NEW YORK CAMPAGNA, as well as other so-called "big-wigs" of the syndicate organization, are now pretty well settled with the strong arm type of employee or "muscle man". In other words, most of the syndicate's desires have been in recent years and are at the present time carried out as a result of threats to do physical harm by the administration of beatings to those who will not comply with their wishes. After AL CAPONE went to jail it appears that there was a wholesale

elimination of the employee who resorted to the use of the gun or knife ... [censored] also stated that the general rumor has it that CAPONE will have to be content with whatever monies or power that are thrown to him merely out of goodness of heart on the part of NITTI and other top men of the syndicate ... RALPH CAPONE is, of course, nowhere near as active as AL CAPONE was during his heyday, nor does he wield the power and authority that NITTI and other members of the organization presently wield. ... It might here be stated [censored] opinion of NITTI is to the effect that NITTI at one time was of the killer type but after AL CAPONE was sent up by the government he was more or less converted to the muscle type of practice and now is well satisfied with this procedure and sees the dangers of wholesale killings. [censored] believes that NITTI will resist any effort on the part of AL CAPONE to come back into a position of authority with the syndicate.[2]

HOWEVER, TO THIS day there is a widespread public belief that has been propagated by Hollywood that once federal agent Eliot Ness had vanquished Capone, he either continued to battle Frank Nitti in Chicago or soon after, personally killed him. This belief could not be further from the truth.

Eliot Ness

Decades after Nitti's death, key Outfit member Johnny Roselli asked Los Angeles mobster Jimmy "the Weasel" Fratianno a rhetorical question on the role of Eliot Ness versus Frank Nitti in the original television series of *The Untouchables*. "...what did he ever have to do with Frank Nitti?"³ The general consensus is that they did not have very much to do with each other. Famous criminologist Saul Alinsky, who knew Nitti personally and had worked for him as a university graduate student, also debunked Hollywood's version of Ness quite bluntly. "Forget all that Eliot Ness shit… The only real opposition to the mob came from other gangsters, like Bugs Moran or Roger Touhy. The federal government could try to nail 'em on an occasional income-tax rap, but inside Chicago they couldn't touch their power."⁴

TWO TELEVISION SERIES and a major motion-picture version of *The Untouchables* have long portrayed Federal Prohibition Agent Eliot Ness and Frank "the Enforcer" Nitti as deadly enemies at a very personal level. Ness's small team of agents were dubbed "Untouchables" by Chicago newspapers because they were supposedly incorruptible and above taking a bribe (and has nothing to do with the Hindu caste system that classifies its lowest members as "untouchables").

The general consensus of organized-crime historians is also that Nitti and Ness had very little to do with one another, and an independent FBI source confirms that Nitti and Ness likely did not even directly meet each other.⁵ Ness was successful with some telephone wiretaps into the Outfit, but these were mostly aimed at Ralph Capone rather than Nitti, who tended to be paranoid about such things and always took careful countermeasures. Ness's major triumph was in 1931 when he anonymously contacted Capone on the telephone and had him watch a parade of confiscated beer trucks parade past the Lexington Hotel. About the worst act the Outfit ever actually committed against Ness was one night stealing the front wheels from his car.⁶

By the height of Nitti's reign during the mid-1930s, G-man Ness had left Chicago for good and was working in Cleveland with the Cleveland Safety Council. He had become mostly concerned with the rates of venereal-disease infections among

U.S. military servicemen who had sexual relations with prostitutes and with enforcing the White Slave Traffic Act rather then trying to close down the Outfit. Ness did not work directly for the FBI, but during his relatively brief stint as a federal Prohibition agent, he indirectly reported to J. Edgar Hoover's agency. Ness was employed as a Prohibition agent, Internal Revenue Service, from August 26, 1926, to June 5, 1929, when he was transferred to the Bureau of Prohibition, Department of Justice, where he worked from July 1, 1930, to August 10, 1933, as a senior Prohibition investigator. The detailed FBI records on Eliot Ness give no hint that he ever spoke or met with Frank Nitti, let alone laid hands on him as has been portrayed in television series and motion pictures.[7]

There were three original books written about Eliot Ness and his Untouchables that were used as a basis for all subsequent fictionalized treatments in books, television, and movies. Frank Nitti is only mentioned four times in passing in Eliot Ness's original book co-written with professional writer Oscar Fraley: Once Nitti is referred to as the head of Capone's "Department of Justice" when he supposedly called a meeting in 1929 with the top brass of the Outfit on how best to deal with Ness; when Nitti and the explosives expert James "Bomber" Belcastro were having an intimidating conversation with a Ness informant over a drink "on how to 'take care' of people"; when Nitti watched the famous parade of confiscated beer trucks with Capone, Frankie Rio, and others from the Lexington Hotel; and in reference to Nitti's eighteen-month prison sentence for income-tax evasion that Ness had no role in by all accounts.[8] Nitti is also incorrectly referred to as Al Capone's cousin in a newspaper quote from the *Boston Traveler*. There are no indications in this account that Ness had any actual personal interactions with Frank Nitti during his term as the leader of the Untouchables.

Some of Ness's accounts of scrapes with low-level underworld characters seem to lack a convincing sense of danger and unintentionally provide comic relief. Ness did provide interesting observations at the field level, such as referring to Outfit gunsels as "pearl gray hats" because of their common choice of headgear. However, it is difficult to comprehend how the type of small-scale actions described in his book could have had any major impact on the Outfit during Prohibition other than to fuel the government's propaganda effort.

Rather than being the man who directly put Capone in prison, the actions of Ness and his Untouchables could be more accurately described as pinpricks against the fringes of the Outfit's empire. Some claim that in reality, the syndicate provided Ness with the addresses of minor warehouses to raid, along with the names of some expendable minor hoods to arrest, so that more important operations could continue without interference while Ness obtained the media coverage he apparently keenly desired.[9]

The second book was written by Fraley after Ness died and concerns Ness's work in Cleveland from 1935 to 1941 based upon his personal records. In Cleveland, Ness's team of elite cops was dubbed "the Unknowns" and included a woman named Virginia Allen, "a tall stately blonde who was well known in Cleveland society circles."[10] This book makes no mention of Frank Nitti although this time span was his peak period as boss of the Outfit.

The final book in the trilogy was written by Fraley and one of Ness's Untouchables, Paul Robsky, and is concerned with Robsky's duties in Chicago and New Orleans from 1929 to 1932. He makes references to Nitti when discussing the organizational structure of the Outfit and some very interesting observations on the Mayor Anton Cermak assassination.[11] Robsky's book is the most engaging and frankly honest of the three. He freely admitted that he both enjoyed drinking liquor during Prohibition and frequenting women of questionable reputation.

However, there are some hints that Frank Nitti may have indirectly interacted with Eliot Ness and his agents at some

level more than is generally documented before Ness was sent
to Cleveland. Ness was present at the 1933 trial related to the
attempted murder of Nitti by Chicago police detectives under
the order of Mayor Anton Cermak, and contemporary newspaper coverage shows Ness questioning everyone involved.
In the aftermath of the shooting, which Ness investigated,
it would be unthinkable that the surviving victim wouldn't
be questioned. Hence, it is unlikely that Nitti and Ness had
absolutely nothing to do with each other.

This author heard a radio interview with one of the last surviving members of the Untouchables, probably Paul Robsky,
who recounted a story in which he was dining with a friend in
a fine Chicago restaurant when Frank Nitti and his entourage
entered the establishment and were seated at a reserved table.
Nitti's men cased the room and immediately recognized the
federal agent. The resulting tension could have been cut with a
knife. The Untouchable feared for his life when Nitti sent one of
his men over to request that he come to Nitti's table. However,
Nitti told the Untouchable he knew who he was, he thought
he was a good man, and that if he ever really wanted to make
some serious money, he should come work for the Outfit. This
was no small offer at a time when the FBI Special Agent in
Charge of Chicago Melvin H. Purvis, famous for being part of
the ambush that laid low John Dillinger, was making less than
$500 per month. The Untouchable thanked Nitti for his offer,
returned to his table, and everything went back to normal.

Many elements of the popular Eliot Ness myth concern
the accomplishments of other federal and police officials that
have been synthesized by Hollywood. U.S. District Attorney
George E. Q. Johnson had a lot more to do with putting away
Capone than Ness, and Johnson worked closely with Chicago's
established ruling class to fight the Outfit. Other federal officials instrumental in putting Capone behind bars were IRS
agents Frank J. Wilson and Elmer L. Irey. Irey had been a

male stenographer and postal inspector who rose to head the U.S. Internal Revenue Service Intelligence Unit by 1937. He served as chief coordinator of all Treasury Department law-enforcement agencies, including the Secret Service, Customs Service, Foreign Funds Control, and Narcotics, Alcohol Tax and Intelligence, and was found to be an honest and generally likable man even by some of his organized-crime opponents.[12] Frank Wilson eventually became head of the U.S. Secret Service's atomic-research security organization.[13]

Honest Chicago cops of the era who fought hard against organized crime included Capt. John Stege, in charge of the West Side police division, and Lt. Bill Drury, a highly deco-rated and controversial detective whose unorthodox methods of leaking mob secrets to the Chicago and Miami newspapers cost him his life. By 1952, he was an equally controversial newspaper reporter and was shot-gunned to death. Another tough police detective was Lt. Theodore F. Tierney whom Frank Nitti nicknamed "Little Seizer" because he took delight in beating up hoods twice his own size with his bare fists in front of their friends.[14]

The Chicago Crime Commission was a nonprofit organiza-tion established by upper-class businessmen members of the Chicago Association of Commerce to fight organized crime. The commission was also known as the Citizens' Committee for the Prevention and Punishment of Crime or simply the Secret Six because its lawyer and businessman members refused to reveal their identities to the public although its founder was even then known to be Col. Robert Isham Randolph.[15] Other members are now known to have included Julius Rosenwald, the head of Sears; Samuel Insull, an oil-and-gas magnate; Frank F. Loesch; Edward E. Gore; and George A. Paddock. This organization touted laudable values such as public decency and an abhorrence of urban violence, but was also essentially a reaction by vested big-business interests to the increased clout organized crime gave to unionized labor and the business threat represented by Prohibition alcohol profits once these were reinvested into legitimate enterprises.

One of the commission's main covert actions was hiring Alexander G. Jamie, the future brother-in-law of Eliot Ness, to conduct a series of sting operations that it financed and that were coordinated with Eliot Ness's raids and arrests, and which received extensive media coverage.

The commission also gave $75,000 to federal treasury agent Irey to help penetrate the Outfit.[16] A primary economic objective of all this was to clean up Chicago's distinct image as a "gangster town" in time for the 1933 Chicago World's Fair.[17] In any event, the Outfit's activities continued almost without pause when Capone went to prison for the final time and following the repeal of Prohibition.

Eliot Ness has been consistently portrayed in film and television as a moralistic supercop in counterpoint to a personally violent, often crude Nitti. Many accounts of the real Ness indicate that he was an alcoholic with a string of broken marriages. Ness was not a married man with a family during his Chicago operations against Capone as has been so often portrayed (he lived with his parents), whereas Frank Nitti, usually pictured by Hollywood as a free-living bachelor residing in hotel rooms, was a family man with a very nice home. Rather than moving on to the stunning police career many have assumed, Ness's law-enforcement career, by all accounts, declined and fizzled after his Capone-stalking days. A major problem for Ness was that he was so keen on personal publicity from the media that mobsters often referred to him as "Eliot Press."[18]

FBI Director J. Edgar Hoover is thought to have detested the headline-grabbing Ness because he preferred to be the focus of positive media attention himself, and Hoover had much to do with Ness's reassignment during the Second World War to the position of head of the Federal Social Protection Agency, which had the mandate of suppressing prostitution near U. S. military bases in an effort to keep sexually transmitted diseases from decimating the country's armed forces. After Prohibition was repealed, Ness had been reassigned to the federal Alcohol Tax Unit and essentially became a "revenuer" enforcing tax laws in the "Moonshine Mountains" against the impoverished hill folk of Ohio, Kentucky, and Tennessee. He resigned this position to become Cleveland's Public Safety Director in December 1935 where in addition to tackling the venereal-disease epidemic among American servicemen, he went after corruption and inefficiency in the police department, gambling and extortion rings, violent youth gangs, fire protection and traffic safety, and other law-enforcement reforms.[19] His career was marred by incidents that included drunken driving and leaving the scene of an accident in which he hit a pedestrian with his car.

A close perusal of the FBI's historical files on Ness soon reveals the true tedious and bureaucratic nature of his day-to-day career and lack of any actual frequent interaction with major underworld figures such as Nitti. The record of Capone's income-tax evasion trial that sent him to prison for the final time makes little mention of Ness and his Untouchables. Far from being hailed a hero following Capone's incarceration, Ness was required to take a comprehensive exam to qualify for continued service with the federal government. Ness died in obscurity and near poverty on May 16, 1957, from a heart attack following a long history of bouts of depression, obesity, alcoholism, disillusionment, and being deeply in debt following a number of failed business ventures. Unfortunately for Ness, he also died before his initial book and the subsequent television series caught the public's imagination.

Author Max Allan Collins believes that Ness "was a flawed man but probably as close to a real-life Dick Tracy or Sherlock Holmes as this country ever had; the tough thing about researching him is that there has been so much negative post-*Untouchables* TV show revisionist history—much coming from jealous fellow law-enforcement officers or mob guys wanting to play him down—that it's hard to know the truth.... Ness stayed very active against the Outfit right up until the end of Prohibition. Also, the notion that he was a press hound in Chicago, announcing raids to the media, does not appear to be true."[20]

Liquor Activities

In 1934, the Outfit began moving part of its assets such as nightclubs and taverns from Cicero County to Berwyn County following the end of Prohibition and the need to diversify revenue-generating activities.[21] It was felt that to continue being a force in the alcohol industry, it would be essential to control unions related to hotels, saloons, and cabarets and others representing waiters, waitresses, cooks, bakers, and nightclub performers and musicians.[22] The Outfit also made a concerted effort to remain in the consumer alcohol business through the ownership of legitimate production facilities managed by frontmen with relatively clean records who would have no difficulties in obtaining the required government licenses and permits; maintaining unlicensed breweries; competing unfairly by not paying alcohol taxes; forcing retailers to purchase their product using strong-arm methods; and attempting the takeover of alcoholic-beverage brands from legitimate breweries and distillers.[23]

Of course, syndicate clubs and bars would use Outfit brands as much as possible while attempting to meet consumer demand in a much more competitive environment. The Outfit's draft-beer brands were Manhattan and Great Lakes, bottled beer Badger and Cream Top, and its hard liquor and wines Gold Seal Liquors, Fort Dearborn Products, and the Capitol Wine and Liquor Company.[24] Some of these products were quite competitive based on their quality alone. Frank Nitti once testified that the Outfit hoped to see the day when "We would make a profit on every olive in every martini served in America."[25]

In 1919, Johnny Torrio bought the Malt-Maid Brewery in Chicago, which occupied almost an entire city block at 3901 South Emerald Street. The name was changed to the Manhattan Brewing Company when Alex Louis Greenberg, a close friend of Capone and Nitti, was hired as resident manager. Greenberg was a once-penniless refugee from Czarist Russia who became a reputed financial wizard and longtime adviser to the Outfit.[26] Greenberg also owned Chicago's Seneca Hotel and was associated with gangster Charles "Cherry Nose" Gioe who was liquidated in 1954. In 1955, Greenberg himself was the victim of an Outfit hit.[27]

Greenberg became the legal owner of the brewery in 1933, and the brewery was subsequently renamed the Canadian Ace Brewing Company and was headquartered at 3954 South Union. Frank Nitti is believed to have owned a significant share of this brewery and its outgrowth, the Atlas Brewing Company.[28] However, competition from national beer giants such as Anheuser-Busch, Schlitz, Pabst, and Miller and the major brand-name hard-liquor distillers, and a corresponding shift in consumer taste preferences, doomed Chicago's domestic breweries by the 1970s despite the best efforts of the Outfit to maintain a market niche. For example, Canadian Ace, which had turned to the low-end beer market, folded in 1968.[29]

Even after the repeal of Prohibition, an illegal alcohol market of sorts still existed and provided revenue for the Outfit for many years to come. In one 1942 case, a mysterious "Manhattan Company" with offices and large warehouses had been established in Miami and was the subject of an FBI investigation. Beer trucks were observed leaving a warehouse at night accompanied by black limousines, reportedly with guards who were armed with submachine guns. It was discovered that the Manhattan Company was an Outfit front with Frank Nitti its president and Charlie Fischetti its secretary. Investigations revealed that trainloads of beer were being shipped in from mob breweries in Chicago to Miami, where famous beer labels were applied to the cheap generic product and sold in Florida hotel bars at premium prices. The principals were served subpoenas and ordered to appear before a federal court with the company's books, but the night before the scheduled court appearance, the Manhattan Company was gutted by fire, and all its records were destroyed. Other incriminating evidence in warehouses had also conveniently vanished. A smiling Nitti reportedly said "he felt badly about the loss of the books."[30]

Diversification

Under Nitti, the Outfit further diversified its activities in such areas as gambling, unionized labor, vice, and loansharking following the decrease in alcohol-related business. Narcotics smuggling, processing, and distribution was another activity area that was quietly maintained. While not the violent breed of gangster Al Capone epitomized, Frank Nitti did not shun extreme violence when he thought it was necessary. A December 17, 1932, quote from the *Chicago Daily News* could not have been further from the truth: "Murray 'The Camel' Humphreys and Frank 'The Enforcer' Nitti are ready to surrender. They have had enough of the blood-letting. 'Too many of our friends are being killed.'"[31]

After recovery from an assassination attempt in late 1932, Nitti conducted a seventy-five-day bombing campaign that began on February 1, 1933, to immediately reassert his underworld authority. Some forty Outfit pineapple bombs were exploded in the offices and warehouses of small businessmen who were tardy with their protection money.[32] These small bombs were not particularly powerful or destructive, but were effective warnings of worse things to come. They were likely planted under the direction of James Belcastro, the syndicate explosives expert. The Outfit also wanted to secure its sources of business tribute in preparation for the lucrative Century of Progress 1933-1934 Chicago World's Fair, including the marketing and distribution of its now-legal alcohol products.

Besides alcohol, the Outfit cornered food, nonalcoholic beverages, transportation services, parking, hat and coat checking, washroom supplies, and many other products and service contracts used by the World's Fair, as well as control of the related labor unions. The fair's San Carlo Italian Village, a collection of upscale Italian eateries, was a mob meeting place of sorts. When adult visitors tired of the fair, there were Outfit all-night bars, nightclubs, burlesque shows, massage parlors, and gambling casinos waiting. The Outfit during this period largely pioneered the concept of adult, nontherapeutic massage parlors as fronts for prostitution.[33] It also owned blatant bordellos such as the Four Deuces and gambling and vice dens such as the Ship, the Stockade, and the Hawthorne Smoke Shop.[34] In a very real sense, it was the Outfit that built and successfully ran this world's fair.

In 1933, syndicate leaders from across America, including Meyer Lansky from New York and Jack Dragna from Los Angeles, came to meet Frank Nitti in Miami and pay homage to him for his actions against Chicago's Mayor Anton Cermak and for his lead role in coordinating the lucrative Chicago World's Fair operations.[35] Some believe it was at this point that Nitti had securely cemented his position as boss of the Outfit and proceeded to move the organization into areas that Capone had for the most part avoided, such as narcotics.[36] It was not a coincidence that Nitti's assumption of firm command should have almost exactly coincided with the repeal of Prohibition—new conditions required new and innovative thinking.

As outlined in the Kefauver Committee hearings on organized crime two decades later, it was agreed at this Miami meeting that national action should be taken to control the U.S. legal liquor trade through investments; market syndicate brands of beer and liquor through the control of bartender and restaurant unions and employer associations; expand bookmaking operations and control race-wire news services and scratch sheets; invest in the legitimate food and beverage industry, hotels, restaurants, cocktail lounges, saloons, and retail liquor stores; and seek to influence and control unions in the entertainment field, such as those for musicians, nightclubs, and theaters. The Mafia leaders present at this meeting agreed not to compete against one another and to cooperate in ventures when feasible. Nitti's national conference, in fact, duplicated the function of the Mafia Commission that had recently been established by Charles Luciano in New York and likely began or aggravated a longstanding rivalry and enmity between the two bosses.

Nitti also met with the Outfit's board of directors during the fall of 1933 on the third floor of the Capri Restaurant at 123 North Clark Street, across the street from Chicago City Hall and County Building, again to discuss strategies for new opportunities.[37] The important decision to prioritize the takeover of entertainment and service industry unions in Chicago, Los Angeles, and other major cities was made at this meeting attended by key participants Paul Ricca, Charlie Fischetti, Louis Campagna, and Murray Humphreys. Communications with Al Capone in prison had by this time become increasingly less frequent, his varied efforts for an early parole were unsuccessful, and his last semblance of command steadily faded away in parallel with the incurable disease affecting his mind.

Gambling

By 1937, Frank Nitti and his associates directly controlled the lucrative Chicago and Cook County gambling operations, but also had implemented a steady plan to expand these operations into new and improved areas in the post-Prohibition environment.[38] As early as 1931, Nitti, along with Al and Ralph Capone and Jake Guzik, was the owner of a Cicero gambling combine that profited $30,000 per month.[39] Part of Nitti's duties as boss was the oversight of all gambling operations and skimming off his significant share of the profits.[40] Jake Guzik later became Nitti's gambling underboss, responsible for granting permission for new operators to open banking casinos on a percentage commission and providing protection services.[41] Gambling became the major single source of illegal income for the Outfit and all American organized crime during Nitti's term as boss.[42] Outfit bookmaking joints were set up in a territory from the Wisconsin state line on the north, to Kankakee in the south, and from Lake Michigan to past Aurora in the west.

Most of the Chicago action took place in the Loop under the management of senior Nitti associate Lawrence Mangano, with the political protection of local politicians that supposedly included Mayor Edward J. Kelly; Patrick A. Nash, chairman of the Cook County Democratic Central Committee; James Aducci, Republican member of the Illinois House of Representatives; Alderman William V. Pacelli; and state Senator Daniel A. Serritella. Aducci was a full member of the Outfit and had been arrested eighteen times between 1920 and 1934.[43]

Under Nitti, the Outfit was permitted by the Kelly political machine to operate gambling houses and bordellos in Chicago and Cook County in return for strong-arming the voting pattern of ethnic-Italian wards and precincts.[44] In addition to their control of many aspects of local Chicago government and politics, a significant Outfit presence was felt at the state capital of Springfield. Under Nitti's leadership, Jake Guzik masterminded the syndicate's major investment into gambling and various legitimate or quasi-legitimate activities of the vast amounts of capital the Outfit accumulated during Prohibition.[45]

The Outfit had gambling action in casinos and nightclubs (dice, roulette, handbooks, bingo, and slots), horse-race betting, as well as betting on baseball, football, basketball, and other sports. These gambling activities were often the focus of intense, and sometimes murderous, rivalries between the Outfit and other organized-crime syndicates. Personnel involved with gambling rackets included "ropers" who solicited or directed patronage to a gambling club; "friskers" who examined patrons at the club's entrance for hidden weapons; "stickmen" who drew in dice with a curved stick; "bankers" who took in and paid out money; and "shills" who played with the house's money, but appeared to be patrons in order to keep the game going and increase the odds in favor of the house.[46] By the early 1950s, gambling under the control of organized crime was a $25-billion annual racket in the U.S.[47]

Another area of gambling that Nitti made major inroads on was the "numbers policy racket," a lottery-type game favored by the poor African-American community of the time and played in large volumes by ordinary people who were thus permitted a very small chance of making, for example, $1,000 from a $2 bet.[48] Edward P. Jones was the acknowledged African-American policy boss on Chicago's South Side.[49] By 1943, it was a $3-million-per-year racket in Chicago.[50] Nitti's successors, in particular Sam Giancana, further increased activities in this market segment, and it became largely dominated by the Outfit.[51]

Frank Nitti was not always successful in his efforts to expand gambling operations outside of Chicago. During the mid-1930s, at Galveston, Texas, he attempted to muscle in on illicit gambling-house operations, but supposedly "barely made it out of town, and back to Chicago, after messing with the local Galveston power brokers."[52] However, by the late 1940s, the Outfit, using Nitti's former messenger boy, Jack Ruby, and others, had cemented a hold on rackets in Dallas.

Chicago's first gambling casino was Indiana Harbor's famous Big House, which operated from 1929 to 1950 at 3326 Michigan Avenue. Historian Archibald McKinlay called the Big House "…Chicagoland's casino of casinos, thanks to the early backing of Frank Nitti."[53] The Big House was one of the Midwest's most lavish gambling emporiums, providing free taxi service to and from Chicago's South Side and amenities such as oriental rugs on the second floor and costly mahogany roulette and dice tables. It was also one of the Outfit's key national race-wire nerve centers for bookie establishments across the nation. Employing 125 personnel, it had fifteen branch handbooks (bookie joints), with six in Hammond, two in Whiting, and seven in East Chicago. Virgil Peterson, a head of the Chicago Crime Commission, reported to the Kefauver Committee in 1950 that the Big House had a gross annual profit of approximately $9 million.

The Big House was succeeded by others such as the 825 Club (or the South Shore Smoker) at 825 West Chicago Avenue. Other plush gambling resorts controlled by Nitti were the Colony Club, Club Alabam on Rush Street, the Esquire roadhouse on Waukegan Road near Winnetka Road, and the Rock Garden Club in Cicero. Approximately nine hundred illegal gambling establishments were to be found in the greater Chicago region by 1941 with the most profitable headed by the Outfit and producing millions of dollars in annual revenues. Gambling-house keepers were usually fined a mere $5 or $10 when arrested, which represented a minimal deterrent for the ongoing operation of such lucrative establishments.[54]

At one point, Nitti was the owner of Chicago's Sportsman's Park Race Track and likely had other interests in horse and dog tracks in Chicago and Miami.[55] Nominal ownership of the track was through the Chicago Business Men's Racing Association.

The Outfit under Nitti also demanded a 25-percent interest in every handbook operation in Chicago.[56] This policy eventually resulted in the syndicate's effective control of the major handbook operations in the city, allegedly with the cooperation of police officials and the local telephone company. Six syndicate nerve centers served some 350 handbook joints with information services. The absorption of handbooks by the Outfit was usually accomplished through intimidation and simply announcing "we're in" and "everything will be taken care of" for a 50-percent split plus a fixed amount of money off the top for "the fix," which could be increased if the bookie did not fully cooperate from the beginning. A refusal was met with a cutoff of wire-service information, an increase in police harassment, and finally, physical beatings and possible death. As part of the syndicate fix, the bookie would be warned of infrequent police arrests and provided with immediate legal and bondsman services in court.

The syndicate would provide its handbooks nerve-center data, clerical staff and telephone operators, and all required equipment and services including switchboards, unauthorized telephone installation and repair, chalk, matches, pencils, charts, scratch sheets, and refreshments. Elaborate measures were taken to spread the risk of large bets among different bookies and to network information, including miles of unauthorized direct telephone wires between different centers to maintain communications security. Bets were accepted in many cigar and grocery stores and by bellboys. Mob slot machines and restaurants were installed in handbook locations.[57] Racetrack news-service entrepreneur James A. Ragen Sr. claimed to police that the Outfit was intending to gain control of every handbook operation in the United States during the 1940s through the control of crucial racing-information services.[58]

Nitti's term in office saw the creation of a gambling- and racing-information wire-distribution service (i.e. horse-racing results and tip sheets with scratches, selections, and estimated-odds data) called the Trans-American Publishing and News Service, Inc., under Gus Greenbaum and Moses Annenberg (father of future media tycoon, Walter Annenberg).[59] This wire service, also known as the Transamerican News Service and Publishing Company, eventually superseded or supplemented competing services—the Daily Racing Form, Continental Press Service, Nationwide News Service, and others—by the early 1940s.[60] Race wires were of particular importance to bookmakers to speed the results of horse races across the nation. Al Capone with his gambling boss, Jimmy Mondi, first started to muscle in on gambling-wire services that Mont Tennes established after World War I as the General News Bureau. Tennes eventually quit the rackets, and Annenberg soon picked up the majority of its operations.[61] Frank Nitti had started a "Blue Scratch Sheet" with Annenberg prior to Trans-American.[62] Another earlier Outfit racing-wire news service was Chicago's R&H Publishing Company.

This early form of the information highway provided a virtual monopoly on the transmission of gambling news and related bookmaking operations throughout the U.S., Canada, Mexico, and Cuba, and had major offices in Chicago, Los Angeles, New York, Las Vegas, Reno, Salt Lake City, and other big cities. Trans-American received support from other organized-crime leaders such as Benjamin "Bugsy" Siegel, Meyer Lansky, and Mickey Cohen. The wire service was very effective. In 1942, when California had fears that it might soon be attacked by the Japanese, a vital telegraph service providing communications for the U.S. Fourth Army was knocked out by an aircraft crash for three hours while the gambling wire service was restored within fifteen minutes.[63]

Annenberg, a Hearst newspaper chain and racing-form publisher, had been affiliated with senior Mafia leaders Meyer Lansky, Charles Luciano, and others since the early 1920s, although he made great efforts to distance himself from the more violent aspects of this relationship. He did, however, employ mob goons and bribes against his business competitors. Annenberg may have been present at a May 1929 meeting of the Mafia Commission at Atlantic City to promote his idea of a gambling wire service, but he supposedly rebuffed early partnership offers from the Outfit. Annenberg was assisted in establishing these services in Chicago by the infamous *Chicago Tribune* crime reporter Alfred "Jake" Lingle, who was murdered on June 9, 1930, under mysterious circumstances.[64] Minor hood Leo Brothers was convicted of the Lingle murder, but it is widely believed that Lingle, who was closely connected to the Outfit, was eliminated because he double-crossed Al Capone on a dog-track development deal and may have actually been hit by Ted Newberry and other Outfit men.[65]

However, Annenberg himself faced a June 1939 indictment and sentencing by a federal jury for more than $5.5 million in avoided income taxes, interest, and penalties, plus three years in prison.[66] Much deadly infighting had developed among wire-service partners. By 1934, Nitti had decided that the Outfit should enter bookmaking (which provided round-the-clock gambling revenue as opposed to gambling clubs, which were mostly active at night) in a big way to make up for much of the profits lost with the repeal of Prohibition. This decision put him at odds with Annenberg.

Jake Guzik, Murray Humphreys, and Tony Accardo had unsuccessfully tried to persuade James A. Ragen Sr., an Annenberg business associate in a competitive race-wire service, Nationwide News Service and Continental Press Service, to partner with the Outfit. Ragen had fruitlessly sought protection from the FBI and prepared affidavits that named Frank Nitti and others involved in a supposed plot to murder Annenberg.[67] Nitti had reportedly told Ragen, "The syndicate is trailing Annenberg…If you come along with us, we will kill Annenberg in twenty-four hours."[68] By 1936, Annenberg is believed to have reached an agreement with the Outfit in which he paid $1 million a year for protection and freedom to pursue his own business interests.[69] Additional deals had been made with the Outfit. On January 2, 1935, following Frank Nitti's death threats against him, Annenberg, through his associate Ragen, had couriered $100,000 in $100 bills to Frank Nitti for "services rendered" in helping "convince" a minority shareholder in Nationwide News Service to see things his way.[70] However, the implication was that this, too, was protection money.

Trans-American really began to pick up pace in 1946, several years after Nitti's death, under Murray Humphreys, Jake Guzik, and Tony Accardo, and nominally run by Ralph O'Hara, once an Outfit-installed head of the movie-operators' union.[71] James A. Ragen Sr. was probably liquidated by the Outfit because he opposed working with their senior man in Los Angeles at that time, Jack Dragna, following a chain of events initiated by Nitti years earlier. Ragen was the operator of the Continental Press Service, another sports-wire service engaged in the dissemination of racing information to handbooks, and he supposedly had refused to surrender the control of this business through a 40-percent cut to Chicago organized-crime figures.[72]

Chicago Police Department records indicate that on June 24, 1946, James Ragen was shot in his car by unknown persons in a moving truck (that was later abandoned and found to be heavily armored and able to withstand the returned shots from Ragen's bodyguards in another car) at the corner of Pershing Road and

State Street in Chicago. This followed an earlier assassination attempt on April 29, 1946, during a high-speed car chase. Later, while in hospital seriously wounded after the second attack, but recovering and under heavy guard, Ragen was poisoned by large amounts of mercury placed in his hospital food and drink, and he soon died. There is also a possibility that Ragen was eliminated as part of an effort to secure the release from prison of Paul Ricca, Louis Campagna, Phil D'Andrea, and the others convicted in 1943 in the Hollywood extortion case that had been organized by Frank Nitti.[73]

On March 8, 1947, Outfit operatives David Yaras, Leonard Patrick, and William Block were indicted on charges of murdering Ragen on the basis of three African-American witnesses to the shooting.[74] Initially, one of these witnesses had reported Block as the man who had fired shots, Yaras as kneeling with another weapon, and Patrick as the driver of the truck. However, on April 3, 1947, the indictment against Yaras, Patrick, and Block was quashed by Chief Justice Harold G. Ward in criminal court after one of the three murder witnesses was slain and the other two witnesses quickly recanted.

The case was also tainted by allegations of related improprieties by Chicago police officers. Guzik, Accardo, and Humphreys were directly linked to orchestrating Ragen's murder, but never charged.[75] As we shall see in the next chapter, David Yaras, while not a personality familiar to most, is a recurring figure linked to important Outfit assassination conspiracies with unusual methodologies over a three-decade period starting with the "madman" Giuseppe Zangara's assassination of Chicago Mayor Anton Cermak in 1933 and ending with President John F. Kennedy's assassination in 1963 by another supposed leftist "lone nut," Lee Harvey Oswald.

Key Nitti associate on the West Coast, John Roselli, once testified that the wire service, gambling handbook, slot machines, and other Outfit gambling rackets depended on political corruption to successfully operate.[76] Police efforts to close such gambling activities were futile or merely symbolic. The closure of the Big House in 1950 apparently "did not seriously harm the timely communication of racing results to Hammond, East Chicago or Whiting because the wire service continued from a hideout in Cedar Lake."[77] Eventually, the gambling wire services were legislated out of existence by the Wire Act of 1960 and to a large extent supplanted by Las Vegas casinos well after Nitti's era. Trans-American itself ended on June 13, 1947, although on February, 28, 1951, the Kefauver Committee announced that James Ragen's Continental Press Service was now controlled by the Outfit. Such wire services were completely disbanded during the 1950s when improved mass-communications technologies made the odds and racetrack winners instantly known across the country.[78]

Nitti controlled all his gambling rackets with an iron fist. At one point, Paul Battaglia of the Battaglia brothers gang had made a bad habit of robbing Outfit gambling houses. His brother, Frank Battaglia, was best known for shooting a pregnant woman during an attempted robbery. Nitti was considerably less tolerant of such matters compared to Al Capone, and on August 27, 1938, assigned some of his men to kidnap Paul Battaglia, who was then shot twice in the head and tossed into a back alley from a speeding car.[79]

In 1941, much of Nitti's involvement with Chicago gambling operations was revealed by police investigations that indicated he and his senior partners, Jake Guzik, Murray Humphreys, and Edward Vogel, were each making $139,000 in profits per month through handbooks, lavish gambling resorts, and other games-of-chance operations. However, the evidence was insufficient to convict Nitti.[80]

By the 1940s, coin-operated vending machines of various types were an important and steady source of quasi-legitimate Outfit revenue. These slot-machines (or one-armed bandits), cigarette machines, jukeboxes, and food-and-beverage vending machines were installed in hundreds of taverns, golf clubs, dance halls, and other public entertainment locations. The venues only received 40 percent of the profits from the syndicate, which retained the other 60 percent. According to his tax records, Nitti personally took in thousands of dollars annually from the vending-machine operation, making it, company stock, and dog-track racing his primary legal sources of income.

Nitti claimed to have sold his slot-machine operations to Edward Vogel in 1939.[81] The early war years of 1939-1942 by some accounts brought particularly hard times for Outfit gambling activities, particularly handbooks and wire services. Police raids on Outfit gambling establishments supposedly became more serious by 1941 with a stated objective of choking off this lucrative source of syndicate income.[82] However, syndicate financial records from 1941 indicated that over a one-month period alone, the Outfit made $323,000 in gross profits from slot machines, gambling houses, punchboard lotteries, etc., just in Cook County. More than $26,000 a month was paid at this time in police graft for noninterference with such gambling operations.[83] Nitti and other top Outfit leaders were seized by police in a 1940 gambling investigation and subpoenaed to appear before a federal grand jury. Nitti was also indicted for violations of the U.S. Radio Communications Act for operating a racing wire service. All these official charges were made without any practical effect on Outfit gambling operations.[84] Another grand jury investigating Nitti's slot-machine operations into 1942 was unable to come to any conclusive results or press charges, although Nitti, Guzik, Vogel, and others were subpoenaed, and allegations of police corruption were made.[85]

Undoubtedly, the profitable use by the Outfit of relatively expensive gambling devices such as slot machines required the active connivance of police forces. During high-profile periods of investigations that were hyped by the media, such devices were often just temporarily removed and then brought back into full operation when things had cooled down. The Outfit under Nitti directly controlled major manufacturers of coin-operated machines.[86]

Labor Racketeering

At the end of Prohibition, the Outfit made labor racketeering a major priority. The FBI defines labor racketeering as the domination, manipulation, and control of a labor movement that affects related businesses and industries, with this domination possibly resulting in the denial of workers' rights and sometimes inflicting economic losses on workers, business, industry, insurers, or consumers.[87] The mob prefers to call it "labor-management relations" in which they often take control of health, welfare, and pension plans by offering sweetheart contracts, peaceful labor relations, and relaxed work rules to companies and by rigging union elections. Labor funds are an enormous opportunity for organized crime. New York, Chicago, Buffalo, Cleveland, Detroit, and Philadelphia are traditional centers for such scams. Decades later, the Teamsters' Central States Pension Fund would be used by the Outfit to finance the construction of its Las Vegas casinos and related amenities such as golf courses.[88]

The 1935 National Labor Relations Act (Wagner Act) provided a vehicle for organized labor to make a significant impact upon America, a development that had not gone unnoticed by the underworld. To assist in the enforcement of union territories and agreements, organized labor often turned to organized crime. This played the direct control of many unions into mob hands. Unions and their company employers often provided organized-crime members with cushy jobs where no actual work was required, access to large funds from membership dues and benefit-fund contributions, plus the capability of manipulating collective-bargaining agreements to their own ends. This union influence was combined with political influence at all levels of government through backing the "right" candidate for office, influencing legislation across the board, and influencing the selection of members of the judiciary to form an invisible all-powerful "government within a government" for all intents and purposes.

The syndicate soon realized that direct influence peddling was not always as effective as exercising indirect control through well-paid attorneys and legal business representatives. The Outfit rarely supported the placement of known public enemies into important union positions, instead employing frontmen with little or no criminal record.[89] By 1930, in one of its earliest labor-control efforts, the Outfit under Capone was making a major effort to control the California grape-juice industry and related unions, which were essential elements for the desired vertical integration of wine and spirits production.[90]

The "steamroller pressure" tactics of murders, kidnappings, acid throwing (usually against inanimate products, but sometimes against wayward people), and bombings were used by Frank Nitti to take control of Chicago's unions and their treasuries.[91] Frank F. Loesch, a president of the Chicago Crime Commission, estimated that two out of every three unions in Chicago were controlled by the Outfit, which usually terrorized its way into positions of authority. The American Federation of Labor during the same period conceded that twenty-eight of its Chicago locals were dominated by the Outfit.[92] During Nitti's term of office, there were more than one hundred greater-Chicago region business associations and trade unions under the control of racketeers.[93]

Many union leaders fled to the Chicago suburbs of Des Plaines and northern Cook County seeking the alternative protection of mob leader Roger Touhy and his brothers, Tommy and Eddie.[94] With Capone in prison, the Outfit continued the struggle under Nitti, who had Touhy business associate, political fixer, and financial backer Matt Kolb killed at his Club Morton. The Touhy brothers by the early 1930s were challenging other Chicago organized-crime factions for complete control of the lucrative Chicago teamster's union, but were really little more than a gang of mail robbers and bootleggers. Patty Burrell, vice president of the Chicago teamster's union, was in favor of the membership seeking Touhy protection as an alternative to the Capone-Nitti led Outfit. It appears that this schism was mainly drawn upon Italian versus Irish ethnic lines with the new mayor of Chicago, Anton Cermak, favoring the Touhy family and their post-Saint Valentine's Day Massacre suburban remnants of the North Side Gang.

The Outfit took extreme measures to win this struggle. Murray Humphreys had a lead role in the terror tactics used to gain control of the targeted unions such as the Chicago milk drivers' and dry-cleaners' unions during the early 1930s, being himself an expert kidnapper and strong-arm man.[95] William "Three Fingers Jack" White and James "Fur" Sammons were recruited by Frank Nitti to fight a series of labor wars against the North Side Gang under Roger Tuohy in 1933. Sammons was an unprincipled labor goon, psychotic murderer, "crazed machine-gun executioner," convicted child molester, and rapist. He had been sentenced to death for murder, but released under controversial circumstances. Years later, he died in prison, sent there as a habitual criminal.[96]

The fact that the historical Frank Nitti would actually hire such people (but undoubtedly would not have let them near his own family) was sufficient for one leftist reviewer of the 2002 Hollywood movie, *Road to Perdition*, to comment on the prominent role of the Nitti character: "The portrayal of mob czar Nitti as a respectable and fair-minded businessman is equally ridiculous and reprehensible. Nitti, known as The Enforcer, ran the crime syndicate while Capone was in prison in late 1920s and early 1930s (he eventually committed suicide in 1943). This [Sammons] is the sort of company Nitti kept."[97]

Of course, Nitti was not the only Outfit boss who employed such men. Decades later under Sam Giancana, Mad Sam DeStefano would gain the admittedly arguable reputation as the worse torturer-murderer in history.[98] As a debt collector "juice man" for the Outlet who began his mob career near the end of Nitti's tenure, DeStefano had a soundproof torture chamber built in the basement of the suburban home he shared with his wife and children. Generally, such sociopaths were found useful for the syndicate up to a certain point. When they became an embarrassing liability, they were usually disposed of in the manner of a master putting down a rabid dog. An example of such a policy was the horrible dispatch of William "Action Jackson" Kelly, also under Giancana's term.

The resulting brutal gangland conflict over the control of Chicago unions resulted in numerous deaths for the Touhy and Outfit factions (perhaps as many as one hundred during 1932 alone). By the early 1930s, the Irish labor-union leaders had pretty much turned to Roger Touhy for protection. However, this soon backfired on Touhy. On one occasion, Murray Humphreys directly informed him that he was in "hot water" with Nitti, who wanted to see him in Cicero, the equivalent of a death warrant. Touhy refused to visit Nitti, and following this threat, he employed guards to protect his children, which given the threat posed by someone like Sammons was probably wise.[99]

The 42 Gang was affiliated with the Outfit, with young future syndicate star Sam Giancana in its ranks, and did most of the street fighting against the Touhy faction. Roger Touhy was liquidated in 1959 by the Outfit following his lengthy prison sentence for what today is believed by many to have been a trumped-up kidnapping charge. As we shall see, by 1933, Roger Touhy and Ted Newberry had been removed from power in one way or another by Nitti, thus finishing the North Side Gang as a viable opposition force to the Outfit once and for all.

Some the activities undertaken during the labor-union wars were quite bizarre. In 1931, Murray Humphreys had the president of the Milk Drivers' Union, Robert G. Fitchie, kidnapped for a $50,000-ransom demand. Francis Maritote (a.k.a. Frankie Diamond and Al Capone's brother-in-law), who was part of the kidnapping scheme, made a secret offer to union officials to kill Humphreys and his men, George "Red" Barker and William "Three Fingers Jack" White, for $10,000, and to bring White's gouged right eye and Barker's severed ear as proof (Humphrey's body-part trophy was not specified). The union saw through this attempt to obtain additional money and declined the offer, but was still forced to pay the $50,000 for Fitchie's release.[100] The elderly Fitchie soon died as a result of the kidnapping ordeal. However, in the final analysis, it was Frank Nitti's leadership and perseverance that won the bloody labor union intergang wars of 1931 to 1933 for the Outfit.

In 1932, the Outfit formed the Trucking and Transport Exchange (soon christened with the dynamic label T-N-T), which levied tribute from various transportation-related unions and labor and trade associations under mob control. The scheme, apparently thought up by Murray Humphreys and supported by Nitti, was to control the overall transportation infrastructure of Chicago through seizing every related union of teamsters and chauffeurs, and forcing such union members, as well as every independent truck owner, to belong to T-N-T.

The control of the Coal Teamsters' Union and the distribution and pricing of the then-critical supply of coal-heating fuel was apparently a major underlying objective. At first, forty thousand trucks were drawn into the scheme, and initial fees and fines for infractions of "real or imaginary rules" provided at least $400,000 in profits, but the plan soon faltered after government officials got wind of it.[101] One of those involved in the scheme, Joseph Glimco, was a union trustee of Chicago Taxicab Local 777 and a close associate of Nitti. Glimco was twice indicted for murder and convicted of larceny and was a future associate of Jimmy Hoffa.[102]

Other targeted Chicago unions were the Cleaners' and Dyers' Union, the Teamsters' Union, and the Electrical Workers' Union. Chicago's cleaning, dyeing, linen, and laundry industry was for all intents and purposes taken over by the Outfit by 1931 through the use of violence and threats of violence.[103] Efforts led by Murray Humphreys to control the laundry, cleaning, and dyeing industry sectors in Chicago were quite sophisticated even by today's standards. A Cleaners and Dyers Institute, with a Dr. Benjamin M. Squires from the University of Chicago as titular director, was supported by the Outfit and used to set and stabilize the sector's prices, labor-union practices, and wages, and also as a front for inciting strikes and sabotage directed at recalcitrant cleaners and dyers business owners who refused to sign an "institute agreement."[104] Likewise, a group of lawyers connected to the syndicate formed a Chicago Laundry Owners' Association for similar purposes, and both sectors had related unions directly under Outfit control. Wiretap evidence indicated that Frank Nitti often controlled operations such as strikes from his hotel-suite headquarters.

By the late 1930s, labor-union plundering had grown into a major source of the Outfit's income, and much of it was organized by Nitti's key lieutenant Murray Humphreys. For example, in 1939, Chicago's Scrap Iron and Junk Handlers' Union, Local 20467 was renamed the Waste Handlers' Material Union, Local 20467 of the American Federation of Labor, and Outfit labor racketeer Paul Dorfman moved in to manage the union as a shakedown operation.

George Scalise, a former pimp, was elevated by Frank Nitti in 1937 to the position of president of the AFL International Building Service Employees' Union. This union had been infiltrated by Nitti during the early 1930s. Scalise was later prosecuted by New York District Attorney Thomas E. Dewey and convicted in Chicago and New York for pocketing hundreds of thousands of dollars in union funds and extorting large sums from hotel owners and building contractors. Nitti was directly linked to these activities, but escaped any prosecution.[105] At one point, two unions under Nitti's control, the International Building Service Employees' Union and the International Alliance of Theatrical Stage Employees (IATSE), were disputing which would have jurisdiction over the theatrical janitors' unions.[106]

The Outfit under Nitti gained similar control of Chicago's International Union of Operating Engineers during the early 1930s and profited more than $1 million per year through skimming union funds and wage-reduction agreements with employers.[107] By 1937, the International Union of Pavers and Road Builders and the International Hod Carriers, Building and Common Laborers' district council were led by Outfit frontman Mike Carrozzo and were under Nitti's sway with threats of strikes levied upon contractors unless regular tribute was paid. Nitti had Carrozzo corner aspects of the hod carriers, teamsters, and other unions, such as the looting of labor funds and contract rigging.[108]

Likely due to his close relationship with their family, Nitti handpicked the Esposito brothers, Frank "Frankie X" and Anthony "Tony X," to head street workers' unions and district councils, positions that they maintained for four decades. (During the 1960s, Frankie X was the target of an unsuccessful contract by Sam Giancana that used David Yaras as one of the hit men.) Louis Alterie, the corrupt (a criminal himself, involved in shootings, extortion, and kidnapping schemes) president of the Theater and Building Janitors' Union in Chicago, was shot to death by a sniper while leaving his home with his wife on July 9, 1935, possibly for somehow offending Frank Nitti. In 1933, Art Wallace of the Painters' Council Union paid Nitti $40,000 to stay out of his union, but the ultimate success of this action is unclear.[109] In 1939, Steve Sumner, the head of the Chicago Teamsters' Local Number 753, testified in a U.S. courthouse before Bollon B. Turner, member of the U.S. Tax Board of Appeals, that when Frank Nitti and his associates wanted to seize control of a Chicago union, they simply had the head of the union step aside, or if he refused, would have him killed.

Another union frontman for the Outfit was Max Caldwell (a.k.a. Max Pollack), head of the Chicago Retail Clerks' Union. Over the years, Caldwell expropriated more than $900,000 in union funds and was on close terms with Frank Nitti, having once introduced Nitti to a VIP restaurant party in Miami as a "prominent Chicagoan" and later purchasing a Miami home from Nitti.[110]

George B. McLane, former head of the Chicago Bartenders' Union, Local 278 and with a background as a criminal racketeer, testified to a Cook County circuit court, that for a period of twenty-eight years ending in 1940, he was the head of this union and was manipulated by Frank Nitti and associates from 1935 to 1940 for its takeover by the syndicate.[111] McLane was also a former bartender and professional union thug.[112] At stake were thirty thousand union members (from the local and fifteen other affiliated unions), $20,000 per month in union dues, and a $135,000 treasury.[113]

Between October 18, 1940, and November 29, 1940, Frank Nitti, Paul Ricca, Murray Humphreys, Thomas Panton, Frederick Evans, Louis Campagna, and Louis Romano (Outfit frontman and president of the Chicago Bartenders' Union) were formally indicted by a Cook County grand jury on a conspiracy charge related to their alleged control of the Chicago Bartenders' and Beverage Dispensers' Union of the

AFL (Local 278). Nitti had been arrested by prearrangement and questioned briefly in the state's attorney's office. He provided some noncommittal answers, was fingerprinted, and soon released on a $3,500 bond for which he paid in cash.

The Chicago Bartenders' Union case had its genesis in 1935 at an Outfit meeting at the Capri Restaurant on North Clark Street when Nitti, Campagna, Ricca, Joseph Fusco, Jake Guzik, and Fred Evans first threatened then-union president George B. McLane. Nitti reportedly made a direct death threat to McLane if he didn't cooperate in the takeover of his union.[114]

At the 1940 trial, Nitti and his associates were also accused of installing Outfit members in union-management positions and forcing the sale of alcoholic beverages from mob-controlled breweries.[115] It was claimed that in total, the Outfit had looted more than $1 million in union funds.[116] To undertake these racketeering activities, Nitti had gained control of all Chicago's bartenders, waiters and waitresses, cooks, and checkroom attendants through a joint council of related unions Romano had established and had planned to further his influence in the Chicago Federation of Labor and the American Federation of Labor, as well as through a Chicago Tavern and Café Owners' Association. Nitti personally masterminded and managed this overall plan, approving all letters and literature used to elect his union candidates although his control was ultimately limited to the greater Chicago region.[117]

This case well illustrated Nitti's underlying violent nature. When at a subsequent La Salle Hotel meeting where McLane had refused an earlier offer by Nitti to name a mob-union officer, Nitti made a direct threat. "We've taken over other unions. You'll put our man in, or you will get shot in the head."[118]

And in a follow-up 1935 meeting in the private third-floor dining room of the Capri Restaurant, Nitti had again intimidated McLane. "Give me the names of any [union] board members who oppose [an Outfit member on the board]. We'll take care of them. We want no more playing around. If you don't do like I say, you'll get shot in the head. How would your old lady look in black?"[119]

Thus, in July 1935, an Outfit man was put on the bartenders' union board, Louis Romano, who was a former bodyguard of Al Capone and now Nitti's stooge.

It was very likely that as a key prosecution witness, George McLane had been thoroughly intimidated and thus refused to testify and identify Nitti and the others on the convenient grounds that it might incriminate him.[120] McLane supposedly had been "promised that if he went through with his testimony, his wife would be mailed to him in small pieces, bit by bit."[121] Furthermore, double jeopardy prevented Nitti and the other defendants from being prosecuted again for the same crime, and they all walked from the case as free men.[122] It is also likely that the assistant state's attorney and the jury had been somehow "got to" by the syndicate.[123] Prosecuting attorney A. C. Lewis, who had prepared a thirty-two-page brief outlining the history of the union and the Outfit's influence on it, had this to say in the *Chicago Tribune* on November 30, 1940, concerning McLane's change of heart:

> McLane's action, at the opening of the trial, brought a smile of understanding from Murray Humphreys, one of the seven defendants, who, like Nitti, was one of the chiefs of the old Capone gang. He beamed upon the man the State had expected to crush the gangsters, put on his coat, and departed from the courtroom before most of the crowd comprehended the significance of McLane's move...I am sure the hand of Nitti reached into the courtroom and palsied McLane with terror. There is no other explanation for his action...I believed Nitti had burned his fingers in grabbing the Bartenders'

Union and had let go and would never again molest
the union members... Now I am not so sure about
it.... I believe we were making headway. If McLane
had gone through with the prosecution of Nitti his
action would have had a great influence in cleaning
up rotten union affairs in this city.[124]

THE OUTFIT'S LINK with the bartenders' union certainly did
not disappear following this trial. Claude Maddox (a.k.a. John
"Screwy" Moore), a close Nitti associate, became the unofficial
head of the Chicago Bartenders, Waiters and Waitresses' Union,
Local 450, headquartered in Cicero and is believed to have been
connected to the May 1943 shooting death of labor racketeer
Danny Stanton in a dispute over syndicate union activities that
also involved Murray Humphreys, Louis Campagna, and Paul
Ricca, shortly following Nitti's death in March 1943. Nitti and
Humphreys are believed to have supported Stanton, while the
others backed Maddox. It is possible that Nitti and Stanton had
been double-crossing Ricca and Campagna and not sharing
fully with their union-racketeering proceeds. Stanton had been
positioning himself to control all Chicago hotel employees,
bartenders, waiters, and waitresses, and was the unofficial head
of a trades and crafts council formed by George McLane to
facilitate the organization of hotel-employee union locals. The
council was taken over by Nitti to be used for related union-racketeering activities that included groups representing carpenters,
painters, laundry workers, cleaners, and others.[125]

By 1941, the Outfit leadership under Nitti had net profits
of millions of dollars per month with vice and unions rackets
providing a major part of this take.[126] This activity expanded
to the nationwide extortion of the Hollywood entertainment
industry and related unions such as the Moving Picture
Operators Union, as will be detailed in a following dedicated
chapter. While organized crime certainly did not hesitate to

pilfer union funds, their involvement provided the labor union with a clout that was particularly threatening to big business and old-money interests. Some independent businesses also appreciated the protection the mob provided them for a fee. The Outfit's links to Chicago unions apparently continues to the present with the Cicero local chapter of the Hotel Employees and Restaurant Employees International Union having been reportedly chartered by Joey Aiuppa, as well as the Teamsters, the Laborer's International, and the Longshoreman's Association having possible corrupt mob ties with Chicago and Atlantic City, according to a recent Chicago Crime Commission report.[127]

Vice and Other Rackets

Besides gambling and labor racketeering, the Outfit had other means of making money, a few of which were apparently even quasi-legitimate, such as a restaurant in Indianapolis and similar establishments in various other locations. In Chicago, Nitti had business interests in the Dante Theatre and the Naples Restaurant at 901 South Halsted Street. Nitti also had offices in the building on West Kinzie Street that now houses Harry Caray's restaurant. At the Kinzie address, Nitti had a fourth-floor apartment (living room, bathroom, kitchen, bedroom, and cedar closet) while his future in-laws, the Caravetta family, owned the building and had a main-floor cheese-packaging and distribution business called the Ehrat Cheese Company that moved there in 1939.

Nitti supposedly used this apartment, which had thick masonry walls and a heavy steel door, as a secret headquarters and vantage point to keep tabs on the nearby criminal courthouse building. As well, the building may have been connected to others throughout the city by a secret maze of tunnels constructed by Nitti and Capone. (Similar extensive tunnel systems have recently been rediscovered in Moose Jaw, Saskatchewan, Canada, where the Outfit maintained a bootlegging-production operation during Prohibition and at some point, may have been frequented by Capone and Nitti). In 1998 during renovations, a false wall was discovered in the basement with a hidden one-thousand-square-foot vaulted chamber. Behind Nitti's bedroom in the apartment is a thick masonry wall with a steel door that, perhaps, at one time connected to another secret chamber. The apartment and tunnels are still maintained as a Chicago tourist site and are decorated with photos of Nitti, Capone, and other era mobsters.[128]

Another operation used by Capone and Nitti as a front organization was a cab garage in Oak Park, Illinois.[129] Nitti owned the Paddock Lounge located in the Towne Hotel (the renamed old Capone headquarters, the Hawthorne Hotel) at 4833 Cermak Road near the Hawthorne and Arlington racetracks in Cicero during the early 1930s. Alex Louis Greenberg managed this bar for Nitti, but after a series of murders gave the Paddock a bad name, it was rechristened the Turf Lounge and was a favorite Outfit watering hole and hangout for decades to come.[130] At one point, Claude Maddox was also an owner of the lounge.[131] Other Outfit-controlled nightclubs in Chicago included Cicero's Cotton Club at 5342 Twenty-Second Street, the Yacht Club at 100 East Superior Street, the Owl Club casino in Calumet City, and Ralph's Place and the Fort casinos near Glenview.

In February 1936, Frank Nitti met with Jake Guzik, Ralph Capone, Charles Luciano from New York, and other important organized-crime figures concerning the formation of a large-scale vigorish loansharking operation in Chicago modeled after a successful operation in New York. Nitti had a related background in controlling protection money under Capone.[132] Vice operations had been expanded during the 1933-1934

Century of Progress Chicago World's Fair, often through the establishment of massage parlors.[133] Nitti continued to increase the emphasis on prostitution and vice as key profit centers and moved toward ending the wide-open bordellos of the Capone era and instead emphasizing more low-key striptease clubs and massage parlors, which were locations where sex, particularly oral sex, could still be purchased.[134]

Author Max Allan Collins developed a new theory in his recent novel, *Road to Purgatory* (the sequel to the highly successful *Road to Perdition*), that explains Frank Nitti backing off on prostitution during the early years of the Second World War at the very time Eliot Ness was in charge of the Social Protection Agency and was fighting prostitution around military bases/training centers and war industries. However, Nitti can be considered the father of modern prostitution as it is still to a large extent controlled by organized crime in North America and around the world in the manner he first introduced in a big way for the Chicago World's Fair: city-licensed massage parlor fronts, striptease clubs, and pornography shops, with a decreased emphasis on traditional prostitution (i.e. brothels) at the low end and an increased emphasis on expensive call girls (i.e. escort services) at the high end.

The Outfit diversified some of its operations into other major American cities. Frank Nitti sent Charles "Cherry Nose" Gioe to Des Moines, Iowa, in 1936 to establish a branch of the syndicate's rackets in that city, but he was replaced by Louis "Cockeyed" Fratto in 1939. Later Nitti assigned Gioe a role in the high-profile Hollywood extortion case for which he received a prison sentence. Also involved with managing Chicago gambling operations before being sent to prison in 1943, Gioe even had the audacity to found a commercial amusement enterprise called Crusaders Against Crime, Inc., during the 1939-1940 New York World's Fair. Gioe was liquidated in 1954 possibly on the orders of Tony Accardo because he had provided too much detail during testimony to the Kefauver Committee hearings on organized crime during the early 1950s.[135]

Narcotics

While there is no specific hard evidence that Frank Nitti was personally involved with illegal-drugs ventures except those concerning alcohol, the Outfit he led was certainly deeply into smuggling, processing, and trafficking narcotics of all kinds including heroin, cocaine, and marijuana. A popular belief continues that Nitti had any of his subordinates who were undertaking such activities summarily executed or that the pushing of drugs was restricted to nonwhite populations, but the accuracy of such views is questionable. A seedy Machine Gun Jack McGurn reportedly made an offer to Nitti in Florida in 1936 to run a heroin and cocaine operation from the Caribbean to Chicago, which supposedly was firmly refused by Nitti and likely contributed toward McGurn's subsequent mob execution.[136]

However, the financial incentives for the many Outfit narcotics operations during Nitti's reign were simply too significant to be easily ignored. For example, in 1923, one kilo (2.2 pounds) of heroin could be purchased for $2,000 and then cut and resold on the street for $300,000. The Mafia has also traditionally had interests in import-export businesses of bulk produce items such as cheese and olive oil delivered in large containers, where relatively small valuable packages can be hidden and smuggled, and the mundane garment industry, which perhaps coincidentally uses the chemical acetic anhydride for the production of the fabric rayon; it is also used in the conversion of raw opium into the morphine base from which heroin is further refined.[137]

In fact, it is possible that Nitti may have directly ordered the Outfit's entry into the lucrative Los Angeles narcotics market in competition with Charles Luciano, something Capone had supposedly refused to condone.[138] However, there is contradictory evidence on the Outfit's narcotics ventures. Some also believe that Paul Ricca, Nitti's successor as boss, had a son who became a drug addict, which led Ricca to decree during his term as boss that no Outfit member could have anything to do with narcotics trafficking.[139] There are additional reports that other bosses such as Tony Accardo reserved the death sentence for drug-pushers within the Outfit.[140]

It is doubtful that Nitti would have allowed any of his men to become drug addicts when he even frowned upon their excessive alcohol consumption. A similar antijunkie code is found in today's Hell's Angels Motorcycle Club, where a "no needles" policy is strictly enforced through the permanent banishment of offending members.[141] At times, exceptions were made to this Outfit rule: Al Capone himself was believed to have a perforated septum due to chronic cocaine abuse.[142] Nitti's prison records indicated that he had no personal history of drug abuse (morphine, heroin, opium, and cocaine). The Outfit has managed throughout its history to the present day to largely enforce the avoidance of directly pushing drugs at the street level through strict internal discipline.[143] Such activities are often left to urban African-American and Hispanic-American street gangs, Chinese and other Asian triads, the Russian *mafiya*, outlaw motorcycle gangs, and various South and Central American immigrant-based organized-crime groups.

Cronies

Frank Nitti had many good friends and associates, some of whom were very atypical associates of organized crime, being far removed from the run-of-the-mill made men and gunsels who usually filled the entourage requirement for the crime lords of the time. One lifelong pal and legal character reference was a mortuary owner, who might have proved useful in Nitti's line of work.[144] Of course, Nitti was close friends with various Outfit colleagues such as Al Capone and his relatively unknown brother, John; bent Chicago politician Harry Hochstein, who became Nitti's personal assistant of sorts; and his longtime sidekick and bodyguard, Lefty Louie Campagna.[145] However, in almost every instance, Nitti's friendships with Outfit colleagues were finite in nature and easily superseded by important business-interest conflicts.

One of Nitti's more unusual associates was Saul Alinsky, a young graduate student in criminology when Nitti first met him in 1930, but who eventually became a famous sociologist and social activist. Alinsky was educated by two very different institutes of higher learning. One was the University of Chicago, while the other was the Outfit under Frank Nitti. He met Nitti by hanging around the Lexington Hotel headquarters and announcing to anyone who would listen that he wanted to study gangsters as part of his research in criminology.[146] Alinsky described his initial contact with the underworld:

> My reception was pretty chilly at first. I went over to the old Lexington Hotel, which was the gang's headquarters, and I hung around the lobby and the restaurant. I'd spot one of the mobsters whose picture I'd seen in the papers and go up to him and say, "I'm Saul Alinsky, I'm studying criminology, do you mind if I hang around with you?" And he'd look me over and say, "Get lost, punk." This happened again and again, and I began to feel I'd never get anywhere. Then one night I was sitting in the restaurant and at the next table was Big Ed Stash, a professional assassin who was the Capone mob's top executioner. He was drinking with a bunch of his pals and he was saying, "Hey, you guys, did I ever

tell you about the time I picked up that redhead in
Detroit?" and he was cut off by a chorus of moans.
"My God," one guy said, "do we have to hear that
one again?" I saw Big Ed's face fall...And I reached
over and plucked his sleeve. "Mr. Stash," I said, "I'd
love to hear that story." His face lit up. "You would,
kid?" He slapped me on the shoulder. "Here, pull
up a chair."...And that's how it started.[147]

ALINSKY'S INTRODUCTION TO Stash in turn led to his meeting
Frank Nitti, who then took the university student under his
wing. Alinsky called Nitti "the Professor," and Nitti treated
him as his student. Alinsky soon became a de-facto insider
member of the Outfit for some two years. This is how Alinsky
described their relationship:

> Once, when I was looking over their records, I noticed
> an item listing a $7,500 payment for an out-of-town
> killer. I called Nitti over and I said, "Look, Mr. Nitti,
> I don't understand this. You've got at least twenty
> killers on your payroll. Why waste that much money
> to bring somebody in from St. Louis?" Frank was
> really shocked by my ignorance. "Look, kid," he said
> patiently, "sometimes our guys might know the guy
> they're hitting, they may have been to his house for
> dinner, taken his kids to the ball game, been the best
> man at his wedding, gotten drunk together. But you
> call in a guy from out of town, all you've got to do
> is tell him, 'Look, there's this guy in a dark coat on
> State and Randolph; our boy in the car will point
> him out; just go up and give him three in the belly
> and fade into the crowd.' So that's a job and he's a
> professional, he does it. But one of our boys goes
> up, the guy turns to face him and it's a friend, right

away he knows that when he pulls the trigger there's
gonna be a widow, kids without a father, funerals,
weeping—Christ, it'd be murder."... That was the
reason they used out-of-town killers. This is what
sociologists call a "primary relationship." They spend
lecture after lecture and all kinds of assigned reading
explaining it. Professor Nitti taught me the whole
thing in five minutes.[148]

ALINSKY THOUGHT NITTI was a little disappointed by his even
questioning this supposedly humane practice, which made
him seem a bit callous by the mob's way of thinking. Nitti
made Alinsky, now a type of adopted mascot, familiar with
the Outfit's entire operation, including gin mills, whorehouses,
bookie joints, and various new legitimate businesses. According to Alinsky, having a dedicated university student studying
them appealed to their egos, and they told him everything
because they felt he was harmless.

Under Alinsky, Chicago later became the birthplace of a
powerful grass-roots social movement that changed political
activism across America. Alinsky's training ground for this
was the rough-and-tumble environment of Chicago during the
1930s Great Depression when the city was under the control of
the Kelly-Nash political machine and Frank Nitti. Alinsky also
worked for sociologist Clifford Shaw at the Institute for Juvenile Research and undertook studies on the causes of juvenile
delinquency in Chicago. Through his research and workplace
experience with the Outfit, Alinsky came to realize that criminal behavior was often symptomatic of poverty and powerless-
ness.[149] Alinsky also became a labor-union activist and founded
Chicago's Industrial Areas Foundation in 1940 with the mission
of organizing strong citizens' groups across America.[150]

Alinsky was on the Outfit's payroll for years and was later,
according to some unconfirmed sources, an FBI informant for

J. Edgar Hoover. (Some have even speculated that Alinsky and Hoover had a personal relationship.) There have been other largely unfounded claims that during the 1930s, Alinsky became the Outfit's chief accountant and worked closely with Nitti in such areas as narcotics and the development of criminal youth gangs.[151]

Another unusual associate of Nitti's was the Croatian-born Josip Marusic (a.k.a. Tiger Joe Marsh), who would become the character model of the bald strongman used on the label of Mr. Clean cleaning products.[152] In addition to portraying Mr. Clean for many commercials, he wrestled in more than three thousand matches and acted in more than one hundred films, among them *On the Waterfront* (1954) and *The Joe Louis Story* (1953), and many television shows and plays. He even played the role of Nikita Khrushchev. The exact nature of his relationship with Nitti is unclear, but as a young man Marusic lived in Chicago, and it is possible that he was employed by the Outfit in some capacity that made use of his strength.

Frank Nitti was a regular at Dave Miller's Gym in Chicago and was a fan of lightweight world champion boxer Barney Ross.[153] Barney Ross also reportedly worked for the Outfit under Capone and Nitti as a runner and was implicated in meeting Jack Ruby prior to the JFK assassination in 1963.[154] After serving with distinction in the U.S. Marine Corps during World War II and suffering serious wounds, he became a narcotics addict, but recovered and had a successful business career.

Nitti made prison pals with one Othello Arturo "Arthur" Zamberletti, "the King of the Indiana Bootleggers," during his imprisonment at Leavenworth prison in 1930. Another longtime friend from Chicago, mortician James P. Marzano, testified in writing to Nitti's parole board: "During the past ten years or so that I have been acquainted with Frank, I have learned to know him as honest [sic] trustworthy citizen, a man of his word at all times. He has always been one of the first and largest givers to all deserving charity campaigns."

In further testimonial hyperbole to the board, Joseph Dire, of Chicago's railroad contractor Colianni & Dire Company, claimed, "In all my dealings with the public, both in commercial and social way, I have never met a man, whom I consider more trustworthy and honorable than Mr. Frank Nitto. He has been, at all times a liberal giver to all deserving charities. In other ways he has at all times been a good neighbor and a credit to the community in which he lived."[155]

ANOTHER NITTI CRONY was J. Livert "St. Louis" Kelly, an African-American labor leader, gambler, and political force in Chicago's South Side. An underworld boss himself, Kelly became rich from a combination of labor rackets, slot machines, and politics, and as president of Local 444 of the Chicago Bartenders' Union, he dominated five hundred black bartenders and waiters. He was shot and killed at a Democratic political brawl in 1944.[156]

Frank Nitti always valued sound financial and legal advice. One of Nitti's accountants was Izzy Zevin, who handled the books for Nitti's and Alex Louis Greenberg's Manhattan Brewing Company and other ventures.[157] Sidney R. Korshak was an important Outfit attorney. He provided mob representation since Nitti's era and provided West Coast services such as "labor relations" for racetracks and the Teamsters' Union.[158] Korshak was present at the Bismarck Hotel in 1940 in meetings concerning the Hollywood extortion case with Frank Nitti, Willie Bioff, and other top Outfit men, to whom he provided expert advice and was considered to be a syndicate associate.[159] Alex Louis Greenberg himself was an important friend, investment partner, and financial adviser to Nitti, but as we shall see, likely came to an untimely end due to business dealings with Nitti and his family.

Another Nitti associate was Morris Barney "Moe" Dalitz, a Detroit Purple Gang member, Cleveland mobster, gambling kingpin, and the so-called "godfather of Las Vegas."[160] Dalitz was present at the May 1929, pre-Mafia Commission confer-

ence at the President Hotel in Atlantic City which Capone
and Nitti had attended along with a Chicago delegation that
included Frankie Rio, Jake Guzik, special guest Moses Annenberg, and a tough young bodyguard named Tony Accardo.
Throughout his career, Dalitz was investigated by the FBI for
racketeering, bank fraud, and other criminal activities. During
Prohibition, he was active in Detroit, Akron, and Cleveland
where he became the boss of the heavyweight Mayfield Road
Gang. During the 1940s, he expanded gambling operations in
Ohio, Kentucky, and Florida, but moved to Las Vegas where he
made major investments in casinos and hotels. Although Dalitz
was indicted on federal tax-evasion charges in 1968, all charges
against him were dismissed. A generous philanthropist and
organizer of many major charities, he also heavily invested in
legitimate businesses, and when he died in 1989, was mourned
by the city of Las Vegas as a true community builder.

Such personal associations with Frank Nitti were apparently
viewed as permanent in the eyes of the law. The Hilton Hotel
chain was supposedly refused a license to operate a casino in
New Jersey during the early 1980s simply because decades earlier
one of their attorneys had been on the payroll of Frank Nitti.

"Jake the Barber"

By 1933, John Factor (a.k.a. Jake the Barber), the brother
of Max Factor, the famous cosmetics tycoon, had swindled
thousands of British and American investors out of millions of
pounds and dollars.[161] Jake was the black sheep of the Factor family. On the other hand, Jake's brother was beyond reproach:

Max Factor emigrated [sic] to the United States
in 1902 from Russia and settled in Los Angeles
with his family in 1909 where he began selling hair

goods and imported stage greasepaints to local stage actors—actors from the fledgling movie industry also came to Max for make-up advice . . . Max Factor is known as "the make-up of make-up artists" . . . the brand has a long established link with the film and entertainment world and it all started with legendary make-up artist Max Factor himself (1872-1938).[162]

MAX FACTOR'S HARD-EARNED and honest "real success came during the Second World War, when the United States Marine Corps ordered massive quantities of Factor makeup in several shades to use as camouflage."[163] John Factor's own considerable fortune would be acquired by much different means.

By all accounts, Jake the Barber was one of the most successful swindlers in history with activities over a forty-year period that spanned the 1920s to 1960s in Europe, Africa, the United States, and Canada. He was a con artist's con artist who specialized in phony stocks and bonds, shady real-estate deals, mail fraud, and larceny scams. Born Lakow Factrowitz, a rabbi's son in a large immigrant family, Jake was a confidant of master criminal Arnold "the Brain" Rothstein who is believed to have fixed the 1919 World Series. Rothstein was also a well-known New York narcotics smuggler with his psychotic partner, Jack "Legs" Diamond, who likely murdered Rothstein in 1928. Rothstein supported Jake in the largest stock swindle in European history. It involved selling worthless penny stocks to thousands of greedy, gullible British investors who were promised up to a 12-percent return on their investments when the going bank savings interest rate of the time was only 1 or 2 percent. Handsome and urbane, but with almost no formal education, Jake formed his own publishing firm in England, Broad Street Press, to advertise his phony stocks.

Jake soon accumulated millions of dollars in illegal profits from his Ponzi schemes in England. The Ponzi scheme was named after con man Charles Ponzi who defrauded people during the 1920s using a devilishly clever method that simply involves getting people to invest in some venture, usually nonexistent, for a guaranteed rate of return and then using the money of late investors to pay off the earlier ones. Hence, the only people who actually make money from such a scheme are those who buy in early, particularly the instigators. It was rumored that members of the British royal family had been taken in by John Factor's Tyler Wilson & Company front operation.

Jake fled England with more than $8 million in an era when most ordinary people earned only several thousand dollars a year if they were lucky. He landed in the U.S. in December 1930 as a phony visiting immigrant and soon faced deportation to Britain for criminal prosecution. To further complicate matters, the crazed Jack Diamond wanted to use Factor's fraudulent windfall to finance an expansion of the deceased Rothstein's lucrative European-American narcotics-smuggling operation.[164]

Luckily for him, Jake the Barber was old friends with Frank Nitti and Murray Humphreys. Some believe that Factor may have given Nitti his entry into serious organized crime through fencing hot jewelry at his barbershop. Factor continued to visit regularly with Al Capone and Nitti at the Lexington Hotel headquarters. On December 17, 1931, a drunken Diamond was executed gangland style with multiple point-blank revolver shots to the head in his New York accommodations, possibly by two Outfit hit men. By 1933, the increasingly desperate Factor fled to Chicago with the hope of avoiding extradition to Great Britain. He paid the Outfit to stage a fake kidnapping and in the process, accuse six innocent men from the North Side Gang of the crime.[165] The bogus kidnapping was arranged with the personal approval of Nitti, with Factor being "abducted" at Dell's Roadhouse in the Chicago suburb of Morton Grove on July 1, 1933.[166]

In a somewhat confusing turn of events, Jake's son, Jerome, had supposedly been kidnapped previously in April 1933 (which

conveniently had been at the same time that Jake's extradition
hearing had been scheduled to take place) and released after eight
days in captivity. It is unclear who the son's kidnappers, if any,
were and if the specified $50,000 ransom was ever paid. One hint
was that a ransom note was, in fact, written by John Factor.[167]

The incident may have provided the inspiration for the father
to stage his own kidnapping as a means of further delaying
deportation proceedings against him and to allow his statute
of limitations to expire while being held by the government as
a material witness to the "kidnapping." Under a writ of habeas
corpus, a person who is not extradited within sixty days must
be released. The framing of North Side Gangster Roger Touhy
for the unpleasant crime of kidnapping simultaneously removed
an important enemy of the Outfit.[168] However, Touhy was far
from being an innocent character and was a known kidnapper;
this, plus the very confusing nature of the case itself, always
seems to cast doubts on Touhy's complete innocence.[169]

A who's who of the Outfit was involved in the pseudo-kid-
napping operation, which seemed more like a comedy of errors
than a true underworld caper. It centered around the Congress
Hotel, one of Frank Nitti's known regular haunts, where the
Outfit had set up shop for the operation that involved Nitti,
Murray Humphreys, Paul Ricca, Tony Accardo, Frankie Rio,
Phil D'Andrea, Rocco DeGrazie, and others acting as "private
detectives." Factor was probably taken to a safe house until
the "ransom" was paid to secure his staged release. His ploy
against extradition worked, and he fled to Los Angeles to
invest his swindled fortune in real-estate ventures.

After Roger Touhy was arrested by FBI agent Melvin
Purvis on a kidnapping charge, Nitti and the Outfit waltzed
into his territory in Des Plaines. The hapless Touhy and his
five associates served a collective total of 130 years in prison, 25
of them by Touhy, for the bogus abduction, despite numerous
legal appeals, as well as escape attempts over the years.[170]

Touhy was released from prison in 1959 only to be liquidated by the Outfit after just twenty-five days of freedom,
the fourth of the Touhy brothers to be shot to death either
by fellow gangsters or the police.[171] Sam Giancana has been
identified as a possible assassin, and Murray Humphreys as
its architect. The likely instigator was probably John Factor
himself, who needed Touhy out of the way if he was ever to
present a lasting respectable public image.[172]

In 1942, the "wealthy speculator" John Factor was convicted
on new federal charges related to another confidence scam that
went awry. This one involved the mail fraud of $10 million cash.
Jake was sentenced to serve ten years at hard prison labor.[173]
Released early by 1949, the supposedly destitute Jake went on
to make further shady real-estate deals, and seven years later,
became the Outfit's frontman owner of the Stardust Casino
in Las Vegas, skimming tens of millions of dollars from the
casino's gross gambling revenues.[174] The poorly educated, but
street-smart Jake the Barber continued to undertake business
activities with such Outfit luminaries as Tony Accardo, Paul
Ricca, and Murray Humphreys.

In December 1962, the U.S. Internal Naturalization Service decided again to deport the seventy-year-old Factor to
England based upon his past fraud convictions. However, he
was pardoned by executive clemency supposedly arranged by
Attorney General Robert Kennedy. The deal may have been
struck to keep the scandalous lifestyles of the Kennedy brothers
during Camelot's heyday out of the public's eye. Factor had
provided a considerable Democratic Party cash donation to
John F. Kennedy a few years earlier, which was undoubtedly
another deciding factor for his clemency decision.

After his pardon, Jake continued to be involved in numerous
underworld scams such as trying to help Teamsters' Union
boss Jimmy Hoffa solve his Florida real-estate problems and
more shady stock transactions with Murray Humphreys. In

his old age, Jake became a benefactor to the California poor and supplied millions of dollars in funding for constructing facilities and housing for the destitute.[175] A friend to political luminaries Hubert Humphrey and Richard M. Nixon, as well as Hollywood celebrities Frank Sinatra and his Rat Pack, John Factor died in 1984 and was buried in Tinseltown.[176]

In an interesting recent development, it appears that the Factor dynasty still has the crime touch that was earlier associated with Jake the Barber. In January 2003, investigators launched a worldwide search for the thirty-nine-year-old heir to the Max Factor cosmetics fortune after he disappeared in the middle of his trial on date-rape charges. The great-grandson of Max Factor and great-grandnephew of Jake was charged with rape, sodomy, and poisoning. His legal counsels argued that he was a fugitive and suggested he could have been abducted or involved in an accident. In June 2003, he was apprehended by bounty hunter Duane "Dog" Chapman in Mexico.[177]

Modus Operandi

Unlike the gregarious Al Capone who often traveled with an entourage and much fanfare, it was often difficult to pin down the exact whereabouts of stealthy Frank Nitti. For example, a letter of April 12, 1935, from Melvin H. Purvis, FBI special agent in charge of Chicago, to J. Edgar Hoover indicated that the bureau was attempting to determine if Nitti was in Pittsburgh, Pennsylvania, but that they were unsure of his exact location.[178] Even so, Nitti had to cope with legal problems that restricted his ability to travel freely. Unlike Capone, Nitti took pains to assure that the operation of the Outfit was kept very low key and out of the public eye with its members often told to "keep your head down."[179] His typical business style could be summed up simply as "Do business with us, and you won't get hurt."

Nitti made every effort to control local political elections, as well as corrupting officials, police, and judges. He extended his reach to the state government in Springfield. However, like Capone, Nitti always had an alibi waiting to get him off the hook every time there was a murder or other serious crime that he was involved with in some way that could have sent him to prison or seen his execution. Simply put, Nitti was a slippery and shady character.

Frank Nitti may have had a little known, even darker, more direct side to his criminality that continued even after he became boss. A February 1939 anonymous letter to the FBI incriminated Frank Nitti and associates Murray Humphreys and Charlie Fischetti as being responsible and the perpetrators of a major hotel robbery in Miami that netted a large sum of cash and jewelry worth some $175,000. Nitti, his family, and associates often spent the cold Chicago winters at their Miami homes and frequented places like the Hialeah Racetrack. It is difficult to understand why Nitti would have wanted to undertake such a dangerous caper at this late stage of his career, and during a family holiday, unless it was done as a lark by some old pros simply seeking a thrill and some quick and easy money. The informant claimed that they even used Anna Nitti's car as the heist's getaway vehicle.[180]

Leadership Status?

The question of the exact nature of Frank Nitti's leadership status in the Outfit has been raised on occasion with the claim by some that he was merely a figurehead or frontman, and the syndicate was actually managed by others. The wealth of evidence points against this belief and indicates that Nitti was the boss until his death. Following Al Capone's imprisonment and the end of Prohibition, Nitti held a conference in 1933 to hand out new assignments to the top echelon of the Outfit and to solidify his leadership hold.[181]

As previously related, Capone delayed serving his prison sentence until Nitti had been released from prison just so Nitti could take control of the helm. From 1936 to 1937, Nitti undertook a purge of the Outfit of the more troublesome elements left over from the Capone era. They included Jack McGurn, Louis Cowen, George "Red" Barker, Fred Goetz, Gus Winkler, William "Three Fingers Jack" White, and others who seemed incapable of adapting to the relatively peacetime conditions Nitti favored. There is some evidence Nitti was directly involved in Barker's murder, and he had ordered the liquidation of the rest.[182]

The dapper Machine Gun Jack McGurn had been one of Al Capone's favorites, but McGurn had fallen into obscurity and became a potentially dangerous loose end linking Nitti to the Saint Valentine's Day Massacre. Following a final meeting between McGurn and Nitti in Miami, Machine Gun was executed on February 15, 1936, by three gunmen at a bowling alley. McGurn is said to have become too flashy and drank and talked too much about his work for the Outfit. Nitti and McGurn were bitter enemies, McGurn ran narcotics operations behind Nitti's back, and it is very probable that Nitti ordered his death.[183]

Nitti had also been closely linked to the unsolved December 29, 1935, slaying of Illinois State Representative Albert J. Prignano who had been friendly with McGurn. Prignano was shot to death on his doorstep during a fake holdup by three men. Nitti was never charged with the McGurn or Prignano murders, but a likely key murder suspect was Nitti's chief bodyguard, Louis Campagna. Prignano may have signed his death certificate when he defied Frank Nitti and ran again for a politically important Chicago West Side ward committeeman office.[184] This purge was undertaken to solidify Frank Nitti's leadership hold on the Outfit.

One of the myths surrounding Frank Nitti's leadership of the Chicago syndicate was that he had inherited the position due to attrition within senior gangster ranks rather than any inherent leadership qualities. One claim even went as far as stating that Nitti may have suffered lasting neurological damage after being shot by Chicago police detectives in 1932, and this handicap prevented him from "taking charge of the Outfit." (He had to use a walking cane for some time.)[185] However, others have concluded that Nitti was firmly in charge once Capone was imprisoned, and nothing important was ever allowed to happen until it was cleared through Nitti. He presided over the Outfit's frequent executive meetings and could not have chaired these unless he was seen as an authority figure by all the participants.[186]

The view that Nitti was not an actual boss is also somewhat unfair to Nitti's proven abilities as a gangland leader and strategist. Nitti was too intelligent to be used as a dupe even for a short time and certainly not for more than a decade as some have claimed. However, there is no doubt that the businesslike Nitti presented a much better and less-visible public-relations image to the authorities than did Capone.

Others claim that Paul Ricca secretly had a seat without Nitti's knowledge on the New York-based Mafia Commission where gang leaders had formed a national consortium to secretly meet to discuss joint actions and develop unified policies on their various rackets.[187] Examples are also cited where Ricca or even Murray Humphreys or Jake Guzik questioned or apparently countermanded Nitti's judgment as evidence that Nitti was not the real boss, and on occasion even John Roselli claimed Ricca had been ahead of Nitti in the Outfit's hierarchy.[188]

The most frequently cited example of this contradicting of Nitti's orders was during a 1939 meeting in Chicago between the principals of the Hollywood extortion operation when Ricca supposedly said, "From now on, Charlie Gioe will run this actors' union. Now let's hear no more about it."[189] However, it appears that this comment was aimed at Willy "the Squealer" Bioff, not Nitti, as Bioff was trying to take control of this union himself. It is, however, also likely true that by this time Ricca's strong character marked him as a potential future boss.

What most of these theories concerning the strength of Frank Nitti's leadership status ignore was the sheer length of his term of office: from 1929 to 1930 during Capone's first imprisonment and from 1932 to 1943, a total of some twelve years, one of the longest terms of a boss in the Outfit's history. Most brief written accounts of Nitti's career strangely jump from events in the early to mid-1930s to his death in 1943, almost ignoring an entire decade during which he was firmly in control of many operations and new projects. This would be an inordinate length of time to maintain the illusion of a figurehead leadership and would have been a major accomplishment for Nitti in and of itself. Moreover, Mayor Anton Cermak's unsuccessful 1932 assassination attempt on Nitti was an effort to decapitate the leadership head of the Outfit in one fell swoop—hardly the risky type of operation that would have been wasted on a facade that surely would have been known by this time to the police and competing criminal gangs. An FBI memorandum to file dated July 28, 1936, clearly identifies Nitti as the leader of the Chicago Outfit.

The real figurehead leader of the Outfit during Nitti's term in office was Al Capone. Federal officials and police were inordinately concerned over his prison activities and firmly believed that Capone was somehow continuing to run operations from prison with assistance from his brother, Ralph, and that he would assume control again upon his release.[190] However, at the time of Nitti's death, police were certain that "he (had) never lost his position as the head man of the old Capone gang, and he was much feared by all the gang's lesser lights."[191] In fact, Nitti had directly told the Chicago police in 1933 that he had, indeed, succeeded Capone.[192] This is not to say that Nitti didn't use a perceived direct personal connection to Al Capone to boost his leadership status within the Outfit although there is no documented evidence of such communications.

In regard to Nitti's participation or lack of participation on the underworld's national Mafia Commission, another view on it must take into consideration its origins and overall background. Prior to 1931, American Mafia families depended upon the most powerful boss, the *capo di capi re*, to arbitrate disputes between families, who at this time was Salvatore Maranzano. The Castellammarese War (so named because Maranzano was born in Castellammarese de Golfo in Sicily) that raged from 1928 to 1931 resulted in the death of New York boss Joseph Masseria and the rise of Maranzano. It was felt by the young up-and-coming factions within the Mafia that the first-generation immigrant American leadership was adhering too strictly to Old World customs such as familial traditions of honor, respect, and oaths of loyalty that were perceived as being outmoded and irrelevant for the place and times.[193]

In mid-May 1929, Capone and Nitti went to a conference at the President Hotel in Atlantic City where mob leaders from across America gathered to talk about possible areas of cooperation, peace, and disarmament, a nonviolent alliance against police, government agents, and informers, and amalgamation on a national scale. This meeting was a prelude of sorts to the commission because it demonstrated that the bosses could possibly cooperate and peacefully divide the nation into "spheres of influence"[194] and is considered by some to be responsible for the birth of modern American organized crime as we know it today.

Maranzano developed the lines of authority and organizational structure that are still used by the American Mafia and is believed to have coined the phrase "la Cosa Nostra" to describe the Mafia. He was liquidated in September 1931 mostly because he was not well liked by the other younger bosses and in particular because he stood in the way of Charles "Lucky" Luciano. Maranzano was murdered by four hit men dressed as uniformed police officers.[195] The progressive-minded Luciano was very keen on reforming the Mafia along modern American business lines and proposed having a new group of the top national bosses form an arbitration committee of sorts that became the commission.

The purpose of the commission and its board of directors was to avoid, through discussion and mutual agreement, the bloodshed that had characterized the underworld during the 1920s, particularly under Al Capone. It was to cover all underworld activities—alcohol, narcotics, vice, extortion, gambling, labor racketeering, etc.—and would define family territories, delineate spheres of influence, heal and broker old feuds, and in general, establish a national crime cartel. "Patterned after the hierarchical structure of modern corporations, the Commission was a tightly controlled bureaucracy of crime based on patriarchy, and empowered to settle jurisdictional disputes as they arose, particularly in cities like Las Vegas, which has always been considered 'open territory' for organized crime penetration."[196] A major function of the commission was to act as an intervener in "family disputes," approve the initiation of new Mafia members, coordinate joint ventures between families, and act as an international liaison body between the American and Sicilian branches of the Mafia. It also established various subcommittees that were tasked on specific matters such as localized disputes.

The initial charter members of this Mafia Commission that were mutually agreed upon by 1931 consisted of the bosses of the five New York City families, who were Charles Luciano, Joe Bonanno, Joe Profaci, Tom Gagliano, and Vince Mangano; the boss of Buffalo, Stefano Magaddino; and the boss of

Chicago, Frank Nitti (who was just ending a prison sentence). FBI and other sources confirm Nitti was, indeed, a founding member of this body while Paul Ricca was still his underboss.[197] Following Meyer Lansky's death in 1983, the once-considerable Jewish representation on the commission would almost disappear.[198] The same is true of the once multiethnic Outfit, which appears to have reverted back to an Italian-only Mafia syndicate. The members of the commission were to serve a five-year term with their membership up for renewal every five years beginning with 1936.[199]

By 1935, Luciano was considered to be the "boss of bosses" (sometimes also referred to as "the Man," but also, somewhat ironically, an Americanized version of the old *capo di capi re* system that Luciano had supposedly opposed; the position is believed by some to be largely honorary and a symbol of respect rather than wielding any actual national power), the number one man in command of a national syndicate that was often termed la Cosa Nostra. Luciano, in effect, chaired the Mafia Commission, but was in fact absent for many years because of lengthy prison terms. Luciano enforced his leadership with Murder Inc. Nitti and Luciano had always disliked each other to the extreme and later became direct enemies over disputes in Los Angeles during the Hollywood extortion case, and it is very possible that underboss Ricca was Nitti's designated representative at some of these commission meetings with Luciano or Luciano's subordinates after he was imprisoned for pandering in 1936.

On April 19, 1932, Luciano and Lansky supposedly made a decision and agreement not to deal directly with Nitti, but through Ricca. Despite that, they had no power in the internal affairs of the Outfit and certainly could not appoint its boss. Ricca was at this time still a relative neophyte within the Chicago syndicate and was Nitti's pupil. Luciano and Lansky perceived Nitti as a problem because of his legitimate claim to

Capone's vacant throne and because after his prison term for
income-tax evasion, Nitti felt that the commission owed him
due respect and was belligerent toward its members. Lansky
and Luciano went as far as to threaten Nitti with a gang war
in Chicago, but nothing came of this, and they were unable
to depose him.[200]

It is very likely that some of the other American underworld
bosses were intimidated by Nitti's intelligence and daring and
felt he could very well usurp Luciano's national boss-of-bosses
position. Toward this end, Nitti had organized and held a 1933
meeting in Miami with bosses from across America to coordinate a national post-Prohibition strategy, a meeting that was
not seemingly part of the Mafia Commission structure. This
national meeting, as well as others like it Nitti successfully
organized, must have increased tensions and rivalries with
Luciano. Well after Nitti's term as boss, Sam Giancana also
sensed a biased East Coast orientation to the commission, and
he also kept his involvement very much at arm's length.

The leadership hierarchy of the Outfit was relatively fluid
and constantly changing, positions being awarded due to
attrition or as rewards for distinguished performance.[201] It
is possible that as in almost any term of office, the strength
of Nitti's leadership hold waned significantly during its last
several years, and this is precisely when Paul Ricca, eventually
the next boss but previously a nobody before Nitti took him
under wing, made his play to succeed Nitti, perhaps using the
ploy that he had been "the real boss" all along.

Nitti had discovered Ricca working for his friend Giuseppi
"Diamond Joe" Esposito's Near West Side café, the Bella
Napoli, as a busboy and eventually sponsored him as a made
man into the Outfit. Ricca remained Nitti's protégé throughout
Prohibition where he learned the business aspects of organized crime because Nitti thought he had an aptitude in this
area and kept him away from most violent activities. In fact,

Ricca, often considered to have a background as a professional gambler, was described by some professional horsemen who knew him as knowing virtually nothing about the sport, his only concern being that "each syndicate book should produce a certain amount of money and if it didn't, Ricca would 'give someone the hotfoot.'"[202]

By 1941, there was also some speculation that Jake Guzik was the Outfit's boss because of Nitti's ill health, but there was never any real foundation to this theory popularized by some press accounts of the time.[203] Jake Guzik and Murray Humphreys may have been Nitti's most serious opponents for the leadership of the Outfit after Capone was imprisoned for the final time, but this opposition was brief in nature. Guzik was not Italian and could not be the boss, but was Nitti's top financial wizard. Humphreys could not be the boss for the same reason and was always subordinate to Nitti who used him as a hit man and frontman.[204] The Chicago Crime Commission also reported that Tony Accardo, a future boss, was used by Nitti and Ricca as a frontman, so the position held a certain amount of importance.[205] However, well into the Hollywood extortion scandal "while Nitti solicited counsel from all and listened patiently as each expressed his viewpoint, Nitti's was the final word."[206] It is also well documented that it was Nitti who continued to chair the regular Outfit board of directors meetings, a duty he always took very seriously.

Frank Nitti apparently became emotionally weak and depressed after his first wife died in 1940, and this may have affected his leadership hold, but he was still directly in charge of operations until his death in 1943. Nitti made most of the Outfit's profits and was ultimately responsible for the organization's crimes. In May 1942, the Chicago Crime Commission concluded that the control of labor unions, vice, and gambling in Chicago was "in the hands" of Frank Nitti and associates, and the Outfit influenced all organized crime in that city.[207]

Nitti is not the only Mafia boss who has had the reality of his leadership questioned—the Giancana and Genovese Mafia families also often sparked speculation on whether their "true" leadership was kept hidden. At his prime, Nitti was simply too powerful and with the ability to decide the life or death of too many people and involved in too many key decision-making processes to have been just a figurehead leader.

Achievements

Frank Nitti's criminal aspirations became more grandiose as his career progressed until these at last became national in scope and eventually out of his effective control with the blackmail of the Hollywood entertainment industry. Perhaps Nitti's greatest legacy to the Outfit was to have taken it from the public eye after the boisterous and bloody Capone era and closely drawn it together as a much more cohesive organization following the federal government's successful attacks upon it under Capone. Nitti was always low key compared to Capone, and he wanted the entire organization to adopt the same careful approach. The Outfit became more cost effective and profitable overall, and while smaller in personnel, it would expand on a national scale somewhat along the lines of a legitimate corporation. It was largely left alone by the law during Nitti's term, and many local law-enforcement officials were safely on the take.

While Capone was a Prohibition-made opportunist, Nitti had the intelligence and flexibility to adapt to changing circumstances. Faced by attacks from both vengeful rival gangs and a hostile police force under the control of a corrupt political establishment during the early 1930s, the Outfit could very well have been annihilated but for the steady leadership Nitti provided during a time of crisis. "Aided by the expertise of [Jake] Guzik, Nitti rebuilt organized crime in Chicago to the point where, although obviously not producing the income available during the Capone era, it remained a viable, tightly structured organization able to support its members."[208] A key Nitti lieutenant had this to say of him:

> When Capone got sent up, Frank took over the outfit and really consolidated all the rival gangs, stopped all the wars, and made room in the outfit for guys of all nationalities, but we Italians, you know, the made guys, called the shots. When Prohibition went out, we branched into other rackets. We not only got into unions, but we ran the politics in that city, and we had plenty of juice in Springfield. Frank deserves much of the credit for moving the outfit into these areas.[209]

HE WAS THE creator of the modern Outfit as it is known to this day, by 1934 having consolidated the personnel and activities of various organized-crime factions in the greater Chicago and northern Indiana area into a single syndicate.[210] The Outfit established outposts and strategic alliances across America from Detroit to Miami to Los Angeles. Operations were to be found in far-flung locations including Havana in Cuba and Moose Jaw, Saskatchewan in Canada. Nitti's criminal activities emphasized manipulating individuals, human frailties, and organizations. Outfit vice and gambling activities were packaged into forms that were essentially acceptable to the authorities and society in general while during the same period, Nitti's New York rival, Charles Luciano, was imprisoned for pandering. In many respects, Frank Nitti was a founding father of modern white-collar organized crime.

5

Lost Assassins

*1933 to 1963. Thirty years and parallel situations....
"Giuseppe was a fucking nut. Some Chicago boys
paid him to pop Cermak and take the bounce. He
had a fucking death wish, and he got his fucking
wish fulfilled. Frank Nitti took care of his family
after he got executed."*
—James Ellroy, *American Tabloid*

...you'd think people would catch on.
—Sam Giancana

Vendetta

Vendettas and feuds inherently result in tragedy. One of
the most intriguing episodes of Frank Nitti's life occurred
shortly after he succeeded Al Capone to become the boss of the
Outfit when the mayor of Chicago unsuccessfully attempted
to have Nitti murdered and was himself soon after gunned
down in Miami while standing next to the president-elect of
the United States.

Many of the official police and federal government records
of this case have now simply disappeared as far as the general

public is concerned. For decades after the event, informants were still considered vulnerable by the Chicago Police Department. Crime researcher John Tuohy believes he has proven that "Using previously overlooked Secret Service reports, for the first time, that the mob stalked Cermak and used a hardened felon to kill him."¹ Tuohy's evidence is derived from the U.S. Secret Service "The Field Agents Daily Reports" from the National Archives, Washington, D.C., that documents the daily routine of agents assigned to guard the president and other duties.

These conclusions are in many aspects confirmed by references from the online FBI public archives library through a surprising correlation of data when sifted from the large volume of bureaucratic paperwork. A strange Italian immigrant bricklayer named Giuseppe Zangara gained a moment of fame and a place in history through his commonly believed failed assassination attempt on Democratic President-elect Franklin D. Roosevelt that fatally wounded the mayor of Chicago, Anton Cermak, supposedly by mistake. Many questions concerning this case still remain unanswered, but it now appears likely that Cermak was the assassin's actual target and that the assassination had been masterminded by Frank Nitti.

Mayor Cermak

Anton J. Cermak was an antagonistic, not very well-liked Democratic city politician who had served in the Illinois State House as Cook County representative and then was elected mayor of Chicago for an abruptly short term. Cermak certainly was not the civic reformer and anticrime politician of high morals and virtue that has been portrayed in some fictionalized versions of events (e.g. the 1993-1994 television series of *The Untouchables*). He reportedly used dirty-trick methods such as physical intimidation and beatings, wiretaps, mail tampering, covert surveillance, and informants for intelligence gathering on his numerous opponents and enemies. He had publicly stated after his election that he was going to take matters into his own hands and use "tough coppers" (referring to his special squad of police detective thugs who were loyal to him personally) to take out organized-crime figures. While touted as a political reformer who opposed organized crime, he was, in fact, a thinly disguised greedy racketeer himself who formed a shakedown organization called the United Societies that solicited the membership of Chicago businesses catering to alcohol, vice, and gambling in return for police protection.[2]

Ironically, much of this business was concentrated along Chicago's Twenty-second Street that was renamed Cermak Road after the mayor's untimely death; it led from Capone's old headquarters at the Lexington Hotel straight to the Outfit's hangouts in Cicero (probably much to the amusement of many of the gangsters who traveled it). The Outfit initially had supported Cermak's successful election bid versus Al Capone's former dupe, the Republican incumbent William "Big Bill" Thompson, to become the thirty-fifth mayor of Chicago on April 7, 1931. This was in the expectation that Cermak would control the real civic reformers for the Outfit. However, Cermak began his term as mayor on an ostensibly strict anticrime platform that he addressed in his inaugural speech:

> The next matter to which I wish to direct your attention, and the importance of which is recognized by you and every good citizen of Chicago, is the so-called crime situation. I stated in my pre-election campaign that the minimizing of crime and the apprehension of criminals was a police problem. Punishment of criminals is, of course, a matter for the prosecuting agencies and the courts. I wish to

repeat that statement now, and to declare that the
administration, through its Police Department, must
accept full responsibility for the prevention of crime
so far as humanly possible, and for the prompt appre-
hension of offenders against the criminal laws.[3]

IN FACT, WHILE Cermak on the one hand had promised his
voters that he would clean up Chicago organized crime in
time for the opening of the 1933 Century of Progress Chicago
World's Fair, on the other hand he schemed to personally
profit from lucrative gambling rackets by controlling them
with elements of the Chicago police force loyal to him and
through supporting his own favorite mobsters such as George
"Bugs" Moran crony and career gangster, Teddy Newberry,
who was treated as a sort of consultant on vice and rackets.
Newberry had at one time been a member of the Outfit, but
had become an independent gangster whose services were
essentially available to the highest bidder. He led the North
Side Gang since Moran had quickly vacated the position following the Saint Valentine's Day Massacre. Newberry advised
Cermak to support Irish hood Roger Touhy rather than the
Outfit in Touhy's struggle to supplant the Chicago syndicate
and in particular to target Frank Nitti.

The murder of Nitti was reckoned to be a means of bringing all the underlings of the Outfit under Touhy's direct and
Cermak's indirect control in a partnership of convenience.[4]
Virgil W. Peterson, a head of the Chicago Crime Commission, also believed that Cermak was trying to corner Chicago's
gambling rackets, particularly those of the city's North Side.
Nitti and the Outfit stood in Cermak's way, just as they had
during Touhy's attempted control of Chicago labor unions.[5]

According to Frank Nitti's graduate student friend, Saul
Alinsky, Cermak and Newberry had approach Roger Touhy
in early 1932 to discuss the murder of Nitti and to ask Touhy to

provide the muscle, in combination with the Chicago police force, to take on and eradicate the Outfit.[6] After Cermak's election, the Outfit's overall casualties quickly soared to about one hundred members dead resulting from its irregular gangland war tactics of street fighting and ambushing Touhy and company. Chicago's Teamsters' Union and its lucrative pension fund fell under Touhy's sway at one point while key Outfit frontman Murray Humphreys was imprisoned. For a while, it looked as if Cermak and his cronies were on the road to success, and they prepared a final blow to decisively settle the matter. At this time, Nitti had been full-time Outfit boss for not even a full year.

Failed Hit

Shortly before 1:00 P.M. on December 19, 1932, two Chicago police detectives named Harry Lang and Harry Miller, part of a Chicago police detective special squad, went to Frank Nitti's downtown office with orders stemming from Chicago Mayor Anton Cermak to kill Nitti.[7] Cermak and Newberry had jointly agreed to pay the detectives $15,000 for Nitti's death, although one source indicates that Alvin Karpis claimed that Nitti had told him that Lang took the job because of a longtime grudge.[8] Both these officers were by many accounts little more than criminals themselves. Miller had a record of narcotics trafficking and had been one of the notorious Miller brothers who led the Valley Gang, while Lang had been a bagman for former Mayor Thompson and had been assigned to the police department by "special political appointment" in 1927.[9] The detectives brought a uniformed cop with them to Nitti's office, police officer Chris Callahan (and perhaps one more by some accounts), who was probably not in on the murder contract because he later was to provide incriminating evidence against Lang and Miller at the subsequent trial.[10]

Lang and Miller found Frank Nitti with several of his underlings at the Room 554 office suite of the large commercial La Salle-Wacker Building, just two blocks north of City Hall. Nitti's office was at this time being used as a gambling handbook and race-wire room.[11] Nitti associates present in the office included Louis Campagna, Tommy Hurt, Louis Massessa, Congressman Joseph "Hinky Dink" Parrillo (an Outfit-supported politician who was a U.S. congressman for two terms and specialized in fixing bribes on the Hill), Martin Sanders, and John Yarlo (a.k.a. "Johnny the Pope"). Some sources also stated that Louis Campagna, Louis Schiavone, John Yario (a.k.a. Yarlo), Charles McGee (who later claimed to be Nitti's wife's chauffeur), Martin Sanders, and Joseph Parrillo were taken in for questioning by the police, but discrepancies may be a case of aliases and misspelled names.[12] This particular Outfit headquarters had been rented by Nitti associate and bodyguard Louis Campagna under the alias "Fred Smith" for use by a legitimate front company Nitti called the Quality Flour Company. At a later trial, Nitti admitted it was actually a gambling shop, but was owned by a Joe Palumbo.[13]

Nitti had recently altered his appearance by shaving off a mustache he had grown as a disguise, wearing colored contact lenses, and changing his hair style from slicked straight back to combed to one side. The disguise must have been effective because the policemen apparently didn't recognize him at first when he was found yelling orders into a phone. Nitti became irritated at being interrupted from his work by the raid. Nitti and his men were faced against the wall with their hands over their heads, all in the same room, and were frisked. The scene was similar to the scenario of the Saint Valentine's Day Massacre except these were real cops. Nitti was searched twice and supposedly had some paper in his mouth that he attempted to swallow. The paper later turned out not to have any incriminating evidence or underworld secrets. (It was sent to the Northwestern University School of Crime Detection for analysis with inconclusive results.) Nitti was punched in the gut to make him spit out the note and frisked again by Lang and uniformed officer Callahan.

Later, the police detectives alleged that Nitti drew a gun on them first, resisted arrest, and lunged for Lang's service revolver (all of which seems improbable given the multiple friskings of Nitti), and they were forced to open fire in self-defense. Some have characterized the following events as a "fierce gun fight," but this appears unlikely.[14] One police report claimed that there were six guns found among those arrested and that Campagna had attempted to shoot Lang, but was forcibly prevented from doing so.[15] Nitti was likely unarmed when Lang coldly and deliberately shot him three to five times at point-blank range from behind, wounding him in the abdomen, leg, groin, right side of the chest, back near the spinal cord, and right side of the neck. Some sources indicate that Nitti was wounded only three times—in the back near the spinal cord, after he spun around in the right side of the neck and the right chest —but a total of five shots were fired, and others said that up to six shots were fired, but five shots and five wounds seems to be a likely maximum figure.[16] The wounded Nitti asked Lang, "What's this for?"[17] After shooting Nitti, Lang then shot himself once in the left hand in an anteroom causing a minor flesh wound to a finger.[18]

Frank Nitti lay on the floor bleeding to death as a police physician tended Lang's self-inflicted wound.[19] Nitti was taken to Chicago's Bridewell Hospital where at his request, he was operated on by his father-in-law, Dr. Gaetano Ronga. Nitti supposedly pleaded to God for his life before the operation. He recovered consciousness long enough to state, "I didn't shoot Lang. I didn't have a gun."[20] A Roman Catholic priest, Father John Peterson of St. Casimir's parish, administered Nitti the last rites.[21]

The next day, although still in critical condition, Nitti was transferred to Jefferson Park Hospital where his father-in-law practiced. The initial prognosis was that he would soon die, but he somehow managed to pull through and then slowly almost completely recovered from his serious injuries over the following months. Nitti's astonishing physical constitution plus his father-in-law's careful treatment were the key factors in his near-miraculous recovery. This incident greatly increased the public visibility of Nitti and reinforced his growing legend as a tough guy and leader of the Outfit and in fact, produced exactly the opposite results that Cermak and his gangster friends had intended.

Retribution

All those involved with Nitti's attempted assassination made a major mistake in not finishing the job and making sure he was dead. The lasting effects of Nitti's wounds, however, would be a burden for the rest of his life and were the likely cause of debilitating side effects such as stomach ulcers that may have contributed to his early death. Far from spooking the Outfit into submission, Cermak and Newberry's botched plan ensured direct retaliation. While some claim Paul Ricca took complete charge of this retaliation while Nitti was recuperating, at this point, Ricca had only studied under the master for several years, and it is almost certain given Nitti's trademark penchant for planning complicated hits that he had in some capacity devised and supervised this entire revenge operation first upon Newberry and then Cermak. Nitti masterfully planned a devious hit against Cermak, with the instrument of this vengeance being just what was required to make it appear that Cermak's death was entirely unrelated to the Outfit.

At some point, likely within two weeks following his shooting, Nitti made the decision that the mayor of one of America's most important cities was to die, and the time and place of the death were to coincide with Cermak being in the presence of a Democratic president-elect who could quite possibly also die.[22] Nitti also correctly believed that Cermak's death would bring an end to Chicago's so-called crime crusade and the de-facto police alliance with the North Side Gang. Tough-guy Ricca likely had the senior role for implementing the plan while Nitti was recuperating, but Louis Campagna was probably also closely involved because he was Nitti's most trusted enforcer.

It should be noted that Nitti was not afraid of having bent politicians whacked as necessary. Nitti would also be linked to the December 29, 1935, slaying of Illinois State Representative Albert J. Prignano and the July 9, 1936, murder of State Representative John M. Bolton, both likely killed by Campagna. Bolton had been deep into the Chicago West Side race-handbooks and slot-machine gambling rackets and had attempted to have handbooks legalized and licensed in Illinois, while Prignano had defied Nitti when ordered not to run for office. Bolton was suspected of complicity in the Saint Valentine's Day Massacre. His brother, Joseph "Red" Bolton, leader of the Red Bolton Gang, was also the victim of an unsolved gangland-style execution in 1938.[23] Like Cermak, all these politicians were considered to be the underworld's own and therefore fair game. Nitti may have decided not to use Campagna to hit Cermak because of his star hit man's role as a witness in the Nitti-Lang trial.[24]

Teddy Newberry was found dead on January 7, 1933, dumped in a Porter County, Indiana, ditch near Bailey Town.[25] Newberry was reportedly wearing a diamond-studded belt buckle that had been given to him by Al Capone years before.[26] Newberry's body was near the same location that Tony "the Ant" Spilotro's tortured body would be found more than five decades later.[27] Tony Accardo probably murdered Newberry on the Near North Side of Chicago, and dumped his body out in the country. In reward, Nitti promoted Accardo to capo with about a dozen soldiers running a gambling racket, putting Accardo in the top echelon of the Outfit.[28] Some sources indicate that Nitti also soon placed Accardo in command of all the Outfit's Chicago gambling operations.

As Nitti recovered, Lang and Miller soon wanted to leave town while the mayor became too edgy to do any work.[29] Lang had a temporary hero status in the Chicago Police Department for shooting Frank Nitti and had even received a cash reward of $300 for this "meritorious service." At Nitti's trial during April 1933, in which he was initially charged with assault with intent to kill for supposedly wounding Lang, it would quickly be revealed that Nitti had, indeed, been set up, and he was found not guilty of any wrongdoings. The other Outfit members present at the shooting had been charged with vagrancy and disorderly conduct, and after posting bonds of $1,100, each was called to testify in court. These witnesses denied that any of them had been armed in the office. They claimed that Nitti had been shot in cold blood and that they had just been present in Nitti's office to place gambling bets and collect winnings.

Louis Campagna refused to sign an official statement that claimed to detail the shooting.[30] Miller testified that Lang had been paid the then-tidy sum of $15,000 to kill the unarmed Nitti after the uniformed police officer, Chris Callahan, had testified against Lang, claiming that Lang had shot himself and that Nitti had been twice searched with no weapon found. Lang would not testify while Nitti was in court, claiming his answers would incriminate himself. The trial ended in a hung jury, and Nitti was completely exonerated.

Following Nitti's trial, Lang was indicted on a charge of assault with a deadly weapon, attempted murder, and perjury. His case was dismissed on May 31, 1934, "for want of prosecution" because Nitti would not press charges. True to the Mafia code of conduct, he merely considered Lang a soldier following his boss's orders. Lang was dismissed from the police force, as was Miller who testified against his partner, Lang. Not surprisingly, their meritorious service awards were revoked.[31]

Even before these trials, Mayor Cermak had understandably become increasingly nervous concerning his long-term life expectancy, but apparently thought the method of revenge in Chicago would be in the form of Nitti's longtime bodyguard and hit man, Louis Campagna, who had lost some face because he had been unable to protect his boss during the attempted murder. There may have been a failed attempt to blow up Cermak in his car, leading the mayor to increase his personal security arrangements, as well as his family's. He began wearing a bulletproof vest and moved into a penthouse apartment with a private guarded elevator. He increased his bodyguard from two men to five and had guards placed at the homes of his two daughters.[32]

As Nitti recovered, Cermak decided to temporarily move from Chicago to a home he owned in Miami and to wait until things cooled down somewhat. Cermak also planned to conduct political work in Miami for Franklin Delano Roosevelt. By some accounts, detectives Lang and Miller accompanied Cermak, but their performance as bodyguards was as much a failure as their efforts at assassination.[33] However, Cermak's efforts at self-preservation were ultimately in vain as the Outfit under Nitti devised an innovative solution for his demise and the means of implementing this solution: an Italian immigrant and sociopath with serious gambling debts to the mob, Giuseppe Zangara.[34]

Giuseppe Zangara

Giuseppe Zangara was a thirty-three-year-old immigrant from Calabria, Italy, who had been sponsored to America by Giuseppe "Diamond Joe" Esposito, the same gang leader Nitti worked for during the early 1920s.[35] Hence, his connections to the Mafia were evident at an early stage of his new life in America. Zangara was an uneducated, unhappy laborer with serious physical and mental health problems. His photos show the mere shell of a man by the time he was imprisoned for murder in Miami. He was only about five feet tall, weighed about one hundred pounds, and had bushy hair that gave him a "shocked" appearance.[36] He was thought to be poor and openly bitter at the world for his fate in life, an assumption that would later become very apparent at his trial for murder. A major incident in his life occurred at age seventeen when he was conscripted into the Italian army as an infantryman. He became proficient with firearms, according to some reports becoming a marksman and pistol expert, having won prizes for his pistol shooting.[37] He remained in the Italian military for five years during which time he was arrested for carrying a knife as a concealed weapon. In 1923, he immigrated to the United States where he first stayed with relatives in New Jersey and obtained employment as a construction worker. In 1929, he became an American citizen and was earning quite a decent living with his unionized construction job.

However, all during his landed immigrant period, Zangara was cementing his underworld ties, and while it's unlikely he was a made man, he was well connected. By this time, his criminal inclinations included the use of a number of false identities. He began consorting with known organized-crime racketeers, and in 1929, Zangara was arrested and convicted for bootlegging. He served seven months of a one-year prison sentence at the Atlanta Federal Prison after which he did not resume his construction job. Instead, he moved to Florida to become a full-time gambler losing considerable sums of money at pony and dog races, and in the process becoming heavily in debt to the mob.

FBI records indicate that Zangara was a member of the Federation of Italian World War Veterans in the United States, or *Associazone Nazionale Combattenti Italiani Federazione Degli*

Stati Uniti D'America.[38] Zangara was a perfect mob assassin. He was described by Sam and Chuck Giancana as "a patsy, set up to appear to be a political fanatic, but…in reality nothing more than a rumrunner who'd owed the Mob too much money to refuse a job."[39] To disobey would mean a slow and terrible death under torture and possible similar retaliation against family members.

Fate and the hand of the Outfit would bring Giuseppe Zangara together with Mayor Anton Cermak on February 15, 1933, as the mayor's executioner with Paul Ricca soliciting Zangara's services through Outfit representatives in Florida.[40] A Democrat, Cermak was planning to attend a political convention in Miami to greet President-elect Franklin D. Roosevelt in front of a crowd of thousands of people. The Outfit's point man in Miami, a young pugilist by the name of David Yaras, was on top of the situation and, according to Sam Giancana years later, identified Zangara as a useful patsy for just such an assassination attempt.[41] The twenty-one-year-old Yaras ran a heroin smuggling-and-processing operation in south Florida for the Outfit and was linked to Frank Nitti through Paul Ricca. In Chicago he was involved with Outfit vigorish loans, sports betting, and coin-operated machine rackets. Decades later, he was linked to Mafia operations in Cuba.[42]

Zangara also worked for this heroin-processing operation.[43] Yaras had hired Zangara in 1932 as a mule to transport smack to New York City where he would collect money from mobsters such as Bugsy Siegel before returning to Florida. Zangara also went by the name of Luigi DiBernardo during this period in Florida.[44] Clearly, at this point, Zangara was a low-level associate of the Outfit, but soon acquired a reputation as an unreliable worker. In addition, Zangara still owed large organized-crime gambling debts.[45]

No mob wise guy, Zangara was soon labeled as expendable. He was given the choice of being tortured and whacked by the mob or assassinating Cermak, taking his chances escaping, and in the process, gaining some wealth and respect. He was also known to be concerned about the welfare of his mother in the event of his death.[46] His erratic background made an insanity plea a viable option if he was caught, and for the time, Florida had some very lenient laws for the criminally insane, which meant Zangara thought he could conceivably avoid a death sentence if captured. Zangara may have naively believed that he could come out of this charged situation a winner.

Successful Hit

The basic idea behind the use of Zangara for assassinating Cermak was to make it appear as a politically motivated action conducted by a lone crackpot with no apparent link to the underworld. John William Tuohy's extensive research through U.S. Secret Service records of the case indicates that following the hit, only a few personal items were found in Zangara's room in his travel bag, mostly some clothes, English-Italian-Spanish language books, newspaper clippings about FDR's Florida visit, and material about the Lincoln assassination conspiracy. However, the Outfit actually intended to use a second and possibly a third gunman to kill Zangara after he killed Cermak, as well as using these reserve gunmen (possibly Frankie Rio and William "Three Fingers Jack" White) to back up Zangara's attack on the mayor. The local police or U.S. Secret Service would get credit for killing Zangara, and the general ploy was to make it seem like a psychotic killer's attempted murder of FDR had gone bad with the accidental resulting death of Anton Cermak. A few days before the Cermak hit, Rio, White, and Outfit-linked Chicago politician Harry Hochstein had been searched and released by police prior to taking a "short vacation" in Miami.

In fact, the subsequent investigation revealed that on the day of the shooting, eighteen individuals from Chicago were in Miami, twelve of whom were known underworld associates. After questioning, they were all released.

The potential participation of Harry Hochstein in this assassination conspiracy is interesting because of his close personal relationship with Frank Nitti. Hochstein strangely began his career as a public morals inspector in Chicago, but soon became a bent city politician and de-facto member of the Outfit, Frank Nitti's close friend and neighbor, chauffeur and personal masseur until Nitti's death. In 1931, Hochstein was charged with conspiracy to embezzle City Hall funds intended for Christmas distribution to the poor at the end of Big Bill Thompson's term as mayor.[47] He was indicted in 1943 by the federal government with Nitti and other top Outfit associates over their big Hollywood shakedown racket and perjured himself after being threatened by labor racketeer Willie Bioff.[48] He gained some brief fame during the course of an infamous political murder-mystery of his brother-in-law, Clem Graver, an Illinois State representative and Twenty-first Ward Republican committeeman. Graver was dragged from his garage at 976 West Eighteenth Street in Chicago and kidnapped on June 11, 1953, by unknown assailants driving a black 1950 Ford sedan that had been stolen in the South Side. His wife, Amelia, watched helplessly from inside their house. Strangely, no ransom demand was ever made, and his body was never recovered despite an intensive search of local rail yards, coal piles, and dead-end streets. Graver was said to have had dealings with organized-crime figures and was likely whacked despite Harry's appeals to Outfit boss Tony Accardo.[49] Hence, given his colorful history, it is not unlikely that Hochstein was closely involved with Nitti's plot against Cermak.

On the day prior to the Cermak assassination, Zangara purchased a cheap .32-caliber revolver and ten bullets at a

Miami pawnshop where he was known and then began to stalk the mayor.[50] It is a modern Hollywood myth that hit men always prefer expensive sophisticated weapons, particularly customized handguns. True long-distance handgun marksmen are somewhat rare, and the tried-and-true method is to use a discreetly purchased Saturday-night special that can be emptied into the victim at extremely close range if possible and later safely discarded or even left at the scene of the hit if no prints are on the weapon. A revolver is also often a preferred weapon over a semiautomatic pistol because the former is less likely to jam. Zangara then rented a room at the Bostick Hotel at 217 South Miami Avenue the day of the shooting because it is believed that he was informed that the owners of this hotel were friends of Cermak, giving him a good opportunity to kill Cermak at this location. The Bostick Hotel was also near Bayfront Park, edging Biscayne Bay, where the Democratic Party rally was to be held.

Zangara had no luck at the hotel. He next focused his activities on the political rally that night. During the day, he had also supposedly met with a number of local Sicilian immigrants, all of whom were later cleared of any connection to the murder although they may have been with Zangara at the rally. The Bayfront Park political rally provided a perfect venue for an assassination, with an amphitheater with eight thousand seats, a flat bandstand, and a stage area where Cermak and other dignitaries would be situated. Cermak had a stomach ailment and refused the police offer of a bulletproof vest. Roosevelt was to make a speech from his touring car to avoid difficulties in accessing the stage area with his wheelchair.

The evening was warm and humid. At 9:25 P.M., FDR arrived wearing a conspicuous white suit in his open-topped touring car. It was parked adjacent to Cermak and the other V.I.P.s in the bandstand area, which was bathed in bright lights. A crowd of more than ten thousand was present. Zangara approached quite close to FDR's car, from which the politician made a speech for about eight minutes, and could have been easily killed at this point if the president-elect had been the assassin's actual target. Zangara worked his way even closer to the area where Cermak subsequently joined Roosevelt at his car without his bodyguards at about 9:35 P.M.[51]

Some accounts indicate that Cermak may have at some point spotted Harry Hochstein or other members of the Outfit in the crowd, which startled him and caused him to move away from the stage and even closer to Zangara's position among the crowded spectators. Zangara pushed his way to the front of the crowd and rapidly fired three to five rounds from his revolver at Cermak to his left, rather than Roosevelt toward his right. He had also waited until Roosevelt sat down before firing. None of the six people wounded by the hail of bullets was nearer to FDR than thirty feet, but were all within several feet of Cermak. Eyewitnesses, including FDR himself and other high-ranking politicians, subsequently agreed that Cermak, not Roosevelt, was the assassin's obvious target. Zangara's initial shot hit Cermak in the right armpit, while other people were hit by the ensuing volleys. A nearby reporter was supposed to have said to the severely wounded Cermak, "Just like Chicago, eh mayor?" Cermak whispered to Roosevelt, "I'm glad it was me instead of you."[52] This phrase appears on Cermak's gravestone.

The subsequent official investigation claimed that Zangara never fired more than three rounds, but seven spent bullets were recovered from the scene. Zangara was a practiced marksman, and there was no evidence that his aim had been deflected by the crowd as claimed by some.[53] There is also a report that the bullet that struck Cermak was a .45-caliber round possibly from another Outfit assassin in the crowd who had taken advantage of the confusion, not from Zangara's .32 caliber revolver.[54] Some believe that other Outfit assassins may have been dispersed in the crowd wearing police uniforms.

Initial media reports indicated that the Chicago underworld had, indeed, targeted Cermak. Subsequent reports omitted all such references, perhaps indicating an official cover-up although President Roosevelt openly maintained till his death that Chicago gangsters had deliberately killed Cermak. The Chicago Police Department was obviously also convinced that Cermak had been killed by the Outfit. Gangster Roger Touhy told the Illinois Parole Board in the 1950s that the mass confusion caused by Zangara's fire allowed Jack White and Frankie Rio, posing as uniformed police officers, to unsuccessfully attempt to kill Zangara with .45-caliber revolvers, wounding some innocent bystanders and police, and allowing the gunsels to slip away.[55]

The stunned Zangara was beaten by the crowd, which had turned very ugly, and arrested by the police. Safely in jail, Zangara supposedly made statements to the effect that the attempted murder was arranged and that he had to undertake it and not rat out his confederates, or he would be killed also. Despite very erratic behavior that included delusions and blaming his stomach pains on capitalists (an autopsy would later reveal that his stomach was normal), prison doctors declared him sane enough to face trial.

The U.S. Secret Service and FBI espoused a somewhat far-fetched theory that the uneducated Zangara was a communist activist or an anarchist bomber and that he was even a member of a large international group promoting ideologies it is doubtful he even comprehended let alone followed as a revolutionary. The final official conclusion was that Zangara had been politically motivated when he attempted to assassinate FDR, but had fatally wounded Anton Cermak instead. Decades later, the Warren Commission investigation of the assassination of President John F. Kennedy would conclude that Zangara was a model lone assassin and natural prototype for its characterization of Lee Harvey Oswald.[56]

Cermak lingered in a Miami hospital for several weeks until he died on March 6, 1933, as a result of complications brought on by his wound. Shortly after his death, Prohibition was repealed. Zangara was to have two very short trials, and before Cermak died, was sentenced to an eighty-year sentence of four twenty-year counts of attempted murder. Zangara was retried for Cermak's murder two weeks after the mayor died. He was defended by inexperienced lawyers, pleaded guilty to first-degree murder, and sentenced to death by the electric chair. Zangara never confessed that Cermak was his target for three important reasons: the Mafia code of silence, *omerta*, which is a real and terrible thing to those sworn to it; his family members were to be well provided for by the underworld, which would be forfeited if he talked; and ratting out would surely result in a terrible death for all his immediate family members. Relatively few questions were asked during and after the proceedings that could have led to the real conspiracy against Cermak.[57] Zangara was executed on March 20, 1933, and reportedly provided a small hint when he shouted "*Viva Italia!*" and "*Viva Camorra* [Mafia]!" just before he died (although other versions had him saying, "Pusha da button").

The prison's warden, Leo Chapman, had talked with Zangara during his brief incarceration and had become convinced that the strange little man was, indeed, a member of an underworld organization. The president of the Chicago Crime Commission during the 1930s, Frank F. Loesch, believed that Cermak was the victim of an organized-crime plot, as did Judge John H. Lyle, a political figure and friend of Cermak.[58] On his deathbed, Cermak had supposedly said that he had been targeted by the Outfit before he left Chicago and that his shooting was an underworld hit.[59]

Nitti's friend Saul Alinsky in 1959 corroborated the widely held view that the bullet that entered Cermak was from a .45-caliber pistol from another Outfit assassin in the crowd who took advantage of the confusion caused by Zangara. Alinsky maintained that a Cermak-Newberry-Touhy alliance was causing the Outfit hundreds of men lost due to gang warfare, sometimes at the rate of one per day, and threatened its very existence. After Cermak and Newberry were murdered and Touhy began serving a lengthy prison sentence on the phony kidnapping charge of John "Jake the Barber" Factor framed by Nitti, these losses stopped.[60] In addition, famous syndicated columnist Walter Winchell is said to have discovered that Zangara was a hit man for the Outfit.[61]

Paul Robsky, of Eliot Ness's Untouchables, was also convinced that Cermak was the victim of an Outfit assassination plot. Robsky confirmed the Cermak-Newberry connection and that $15,000 had been paid Lang and Miller to kill Nitti. Lang had stopped at Cermak's office for instructions just prior to the raid on Nitti's office. Robsky also confirmed that Zangara had been a marksman in the Italian army and that there was no doubt that Zangara "was a mafia killer... sent to Miami for the express purpose of eradicating Cermak."[62] *Omerta* had forced Zangara to remain silent until his execution.

Mayor Ed Kelly followed Cermak, after an interim one-year term in 1933 for Frank Corr, and Kelly had little to say about crime during Nitti's remaining term of leadership, nor did Pat Nash, who was the chairman of the Democratic Party of Cook County. The Outfit put its considerable influence behind the Kelly-Nash machine. Nitti also supported Mayor Kelly in the 1935 election because Kelly came out for the legalization of gambling in Chicago.[63]

Local government was once again safely in the pocket of the Outfit where many in Chicago thought it belonged. In any case, Frank Nitti was fully avenged and at this stage, had gained a legendary status to a growing number of people. Teddy Newberry was dead just nineteen days after the attempt on Nitti's life, and Cermak had followed after a little more than two months. Ironically, after Cermak was murdered and the various trials were over, Nitti went to Miami to continue his recovery in the Florida sun.[64]

Or Coincidence?

Some historians maintain that it is revisionist thinking to claim that the madman Zangara's target was actually Cermak rather than Roosevelt and that the shooting of Cermak a few months after the unsuccessful attempt on Nitti's life was merely a fortunate happenstance for the Outfit, and "there is almost no evidence to support that Capone's men [sic] would undertake a mob hit in this manner," John A. Lupton has written.[65] The common explanation is that Zangara's arm was deflected by a woman in the crowd and that he had carefully prepositioned himself to have a clear shot at Roosevelt at a range of less than thirty feet. Cermak just happened to be in the way of the cone of widely stray shots.[66]

It is also proposed that the cautious Nitti would never have used such a strange and possibly unreliable individual as Zangara to do a hit of this importance, but as we shall see, he was an almost-ideal component for such an assassination conspiracy. Moreover, official federal records offer significant support for the view that Cermak was, indeed, Zangara's intended target all along. No competent investigation of Cermak's assassination has ever been undertaken, particularly from the perspective of the motivations of those who benefited from his death. How did the uneducated and apparently destitute Zangara undertake the preplanning for this hit?

The official FBI archives on the "Franklin D. Roosevelt Assassination Attempt" provide a number of pieces of key information in connection with this case that include apparent direct links to the Outfit. The paper flow of evidence starts out prior to Zangara's execution with a March 1, 1933, memo to the FBI agent in charge for Jacksonville, Florida, by none other than the FBI Special Agent in Charge for Chicago Melvin H. Purvis, who states: "Mr. Green, the United States Attorney at Chicago, informs me that he has received information to the effect that a check signed by an alleged hoodlum or gangster of Chicago, the name of which is unknown, was found on the person of GIUSEPPE ZANGARA, who attempted to assassinate President elect Roosevelt.

"Mr. Green requested that I determine if you had any information in this regard, and as a matter of cooperation with him, it will be appreciated if you will advise me about this matter."[67]

An FBI follow-on to this memo dated March 28, 1933, (after Zangara's execution) indicated that the check could not be found, but still provided previously undisclosed information that this unknown check "was drawn on a closed Chicago bank" and that some incriminating mail to Zangara may also have been intercepted, but with these specifics somehow unavailable. A careful reading of this correspondence indicates some investigative tensions between the U.S. Secret Service, FBI, Dade County Florida Sheriff's Office, Miami Police Department, and most interestingly, the Chicago Police Department that also had an active hand in the investigations in Florida in the form of several investigating *detectives*. It is not inconceivable that among these agencies, incriminating evidence could have been either deliberately or accidentally misplaced, particularly remembering that the Chicago and probably also the Miami police forces were at the time thoroughly corrupted by organized-crime factions and that Chicago detectives were precisely the group of people who had sparked the Cermak hit through their attempted murder of Frank Nitti. The same memo of March 28 almost casually states "that Secret Service operatives indicated that their investigation disclosed that Zangara also had in mind the assassination of Mayor Anton Cermak at the time of his attempted assassination of President Roosevelt," but doesn't follow up this incredible admission.[68]

A February 18, 1933, anonymous letter had been mailed to the U.S. Secret Service stating that a "Louis Gleckman, St. Paul Minn underworld character, racketeer, licker [sic] runner, etc. was in Florida at the time of the attack on President elect Roosevelt. If it was intended to kill Cermak for activities against Chicago underworld why not find out what he was doing in Florida."[69]

A March 18, 1933, memo from FBI Director J. Edgar Hoover states, "I called [deleted] this morning regarding the Guiseppe Zangara investigation, and advised him substantially as follows: That [deleted] had informed me that he had saw former Vice President [Charles] Curtis at the funeral of former Senator [Thomas J.] Walsh, and at that time Curtis had told him that in the event we conducted investigation of Zangara, he had in his possession some information which may be of value; that today the Attorney General had informed me that former Vice President Curtis had in his possession some information regarding Zangara, that Zangara had a postal savings account somewhere in New Jersey, and that it is claimed that Zangara is a member of some gang and has a considerable amount of money in back of him…"[70]

It is not clear whether the "gang" that Hoover referred to was an organized-crime or a radical political group. FBI files indicate that in the roughly year and a half prior to Cermak's assassination, Zangara had been able to accumulate and send to someone in Italy some $3,000—a considerable sum for the time. A letter of June 16, 1933, from Hoover to W. H. Moran, chief of the Secret Service Division of the U.S. Treasury Department, indicates a possible connection between Zangara and the "Italian Black Hand Society," which was the New York City faction of the Mafia where Frank Nitti and Al Capone started their careers. Another memo dated June 11, 1933, had alerted Hoover to possible criminal irregularities concerning the more than $300,000 estate of the late Anton Cermak. However, the file's possible *pièce de le résistance* is a copy of a January 19, 1940, letter from an Ernest Hix of Hollywood, California, to Walter Winchell, who was then a syndicated gossip columnist, that had been forwarded to Hoover:

> Cermak was muscling in on the beer racket in Chicago. The various mobs knew they had to do something to stop him as their beer was being thrown out and Tony's beer put in. Zangara was living on borrowed time. He had an incurable disease. The mob told him that if he would get Cermak, they would take care of his family; otherwise, on his death the family would be penniless. The opportunity came at Miami. Zangara got his man as he was not after Roosevelt.

It would be interesting to know just where the Zangara family is now and how they are faring.

I have been shown a lot of reports on this case by a former G-man. You might ask J. Edgar about it the next time you see him.[71]

J. EDGAR HOOVER, apparently, had scribbled in the margin of the copy of the letter to Winchell what looks like "That this is really not true"!

A February 13, 1950, memo from Hoover to the U.S. attorney general summarized all the loose links the FBI and Secret Service had found between Zangara and organized crime, but indicated that its investigation had concentrated on Philadelphia and Chicago, and did not appear to be aware of his mob activities between New York and Miami. Hoover also recounts that the New York-based *America Weekly* had killed a story in September 1947 linking Zangara to an Outfit contract on Cermak, likely on Hoover's recommendation. An FBI memo of November 2, 1950, to Hoover indicates that "Further allegations that Secret Service operatives investigation [of the] attempted assassination of President Roosevelt had allegedly revealed to former local officials that Secret Service investigation had disclosed information indicating Zangara intended assassinating Cermak..."[72] A final August 3, 1951, memo indicated that the official lid on the case was so tight that the actual gun or even a picture of the weapon used by Zangara was unavailable from the Secret Service or the FBI to be used in an assassins' display at the Lincoln Museum.

The 1950 request for information on the case from the attorney general's office and the resulting paper flow appears to have been brought on by some unknown party attempting to reopen the case, perhaps merely for a news story. Hoover, an expert at this type of thing, appears to have been successful keeping the lid shut to avoid, as stated in yet another 1950 interdepartmental memo, "a revival of the whole story in a sensational and undesirable manner."[73] One must wonder in an undesirable and sensational manner for whom, and why was the FBI so concerned with eliminating an organized-crime angle to Cermak's death? There was that longstanding rumor concerning Hoover's private life and organized-crime elements having incriminating pictures of him and Clyde Tolson. One can only speculate that such a hidden loaded gun was why Hoover was reluctant to come out and attempt an open-minded investigation.

Parallels with JFK Assassination

Now, flash forward to November 22, 1963. A president of the United States has been assassinated in Dallas while riding exposed to a crowd in a motorcade. Witnesses will later swear that unidentified men dressed as policemen and tramps were positioned all around Dealey Plaza at the grassy knoll and other locations such as buildings and sewer manholes. Many believe that the president was killed by a withering cross fire from several well-positioned gunmen.

The official investigation by the Warren Commission went to great lengths to develop complicated explanations of how a lone gunman accomplished difficult shots in a seemingly impossible short period of time, as well as denying the possibility of any involvement by the American underworld, although the syndicate had some of the most likely motivations and best capabilities—in terms of professional killers, organization, and weapons—to commit the crime. For example, "lend-lease assignments" of expert hit men are often provided between Mafia factions, reminiscent of Murder Inc.[74]

Theories that vary from official explanations concerning both the Anton Cermak and John F. Kennedy assassinations often belong to an area popularly known as "conspiracy theory." Conspiracy theory commonly proposes that one or more elite groups are secretly manipulating important events as part of a grand design to rule society. The important elements of this perspective are: members of a powerful, secret cabal shape history for their own agenda; the media often doesn't report on these elite cabals because they control the media by having their own people in places of influence or through buying off others; the government cannot effectively stop them because they control the government in the same manner that they control the media; the *agents provocateurs* of these elite cabals are ubiquitous, but are largely unrecognized because they appear to be part of conventional society; these *agents provocateurs* are themselves unaware of the overall details of the master plan that their own activities are part of because they act in blind obedience to their superiors while only an inner elite circle of cabal leaders know these full details. In addition, the activities of the conspirators are frequently made to seem so outlandish and ridiculous by conventional standards so as to discredit those attempting to "reveal" these activities to society in general. In Umberto Eco's 1988 esoteric novel *Foucault's Pendulum*, the author paints a scenario in which all of human history is one vast manipulated conspiracy between shadowy secret organizations of which the majority of the general population, or to use Eco's terminology the *lumpen proletariat*, are almost totally oblivious.[75]

Obviously, the activities of organized-crime syndicates such as the Outfit and government-intelligence agencies such as the CIA often fit quite nicely into conspiracy-theory frameworks, and unlike some secret societies that conspiracy theorists allege exert a great hidden influence upon society, it is known that these covert organizations are, indeed, very real and exert many tangible influences.

By definition, the Mafia is a type of conspiracy and in many ways resembles a "shadow government." For example, as one theorist proposes: "In the Cold War years, the Mafia conspiracy theory gave an ethnic identification to the newly reconceptualized problem at a time when fear of 'un-American' thinking and behavior was at its peak and new limits were added to the range of permissible discussion."[76] However, as with the Cermak murder, there are many detractors who seemingly attempt to debunk the idea of any JFK assassination conspiracy that involves the Mafia and shadowy government agencies.[77]

As mentioned, assassinations are commonly known in intelligence terminology as "wet work." A Central Intelligence Agency study of assassination methods was prepared as part of the CIA's training for "Operation PB Success," a covert operation that overthrew the democratically elected government of Jacobo Arbenz in Guatemala in June 1954, and was released under the Freedom of Information Act in May 1997.[78] This report provides a conceptual framework that classifies an assassin who is to die with the subject of the assassination plot as a "lost assassin" and an assassin who is to escape as a "safe assassin." No compromise is allowed between these two categories because the actual assassin must never fall alive into enemy hands under any circumstances.

An assassination that requires publicity to be effective is termed "terroristic" and where the subject is unaware of its imminent possibility as "simple." The CIA study specifies that a lost assassin "must be a fanatic of some sort" and unstable psychologically, with politics, religion, and revenge being his major motives. The lost assassin must be handled with extreme care and not know the identities of most other members of the assassination organization "for although it is intended that he die in the act, something may go wrong." Instructions are provided to the assassin orally by one handler only, and this handler should also be used to cover any unforeseen complications arising from the assassination. Transience in the assassination area is also a desirable characteristic for an assassin. Patriotism, bribes, blackmail, and operant conditioning (i.e. brainwashing) are all used to secure the loyalties of suitable assassins by organized crime and intelligence agencies—failing this, a prospective assassin must often be killed to maintain security.

Following these definitions, Nitti's would-be assassins were safe and the failed action simple in intent, although its aftermath was intended to be terroristic. Giuseppe Zangara was a lost assassin, and Cermak's assassination was also terroristic in intent, but not simple because Cermak clearly feared for his life at the time and took some precautions. Zangara's handler remains unknown, but could have been one of a number of Outfit associates, most likely David Yaras, who became during the following decades a well-known professional hit man, go-between, and associate of Sam Giancana, Carlos Marcello, Santo Trafficante, Johnny Roselli, and Jack Ruby.[79] Yaras's longtime crime partner, Lenny Patrick, likely was not involved with the Cermak assassination because he was incarcerated from 1933 to 1940 on a bank-robbery conviction.[80] Yaras was a cold-blooded professional killer, the suspect for many officially unsolved murders. In a February 1962 wiretap, FBI agents listened in on a conversation between Yaras and fellow hit man Jackie "the Lackey" Cerone during which they discussed murder and corpse-disposal methods, with Yaras commenting about an intended victim, "Leave it to us. As soon as he walks in the fucking door, boom! We'll hit him with a fucking ax or something. He won't get away from us."[81]

Yaras was possibly not a made man per se because he was Jewish, but was still highly connected with the multiethnic Outfit and was eventually a capo in rank.[82]

Another possible category for Zangara's assassin type is the so-called "zombie assassin" who has a mental state with significant memory gaps concerning his actions and which is often the product of reinforcing secret belief structures.[83] In modern psychology, this reinforcement process is known as operant or Pavlovian conditioning where a positive or negative stimulus is used by a controller (or handler) to modify a subject's behavior in a desired direction. In practice, this is often accomplished by reinforcing a suitably pliable assassin candidate with money, narcotics, and alcohol, having the candidate repeatedly perform seemingly important (but often nonsensical) "jobs" for which they are rewarded with more money, narcotics, and alcohol, reinforcing the candidate's distorted sense of reality that often includes feelings of paranoia particularly against authority figures, and in the process have the candidate develop a dependency on his handler (whose true identity is often unknown to the candidate so that in the event of capture, the dupe's story appears incoherent and irrational) so that the candidate's sense of paranoia can be directed against an assassination target.

A mentally weak or simple individual, as well as a socially ostracized and habitual loser such as a Giuseppe Zangara or a

Lee Harvey Oswald, would be particularly vulnerable to such operant conditioning, particularly if he was also a member of a cultlike organization, which in many ways the Mafia resembles.[84] The effects of alcohol and narcotics would further distort such a candidate's already confused sense of reality. The zombie assassin was popularized in John Frankenheimer's controversial 1962 movie, *The Manchurian Candidate*, which was based on the 1959 novel by Richard Condon of the same name. ("Raymond, why don't you pass the time by playing a little solitaire?")[85] The Mafia could easily have available the medical and scientific capability to condition such an assassin because, as we have seen in the case of Dr. Saul Alinsky, Dr. Benjamin M. Squires, and Dr. Gaetano Ronga during Nitti's term in office, and even Dr. Reinhardt Schwimmer who was murdered as part of George Moran's gang in the Saint Valentine's Day Massacre, they have historically had ready access to highly educated associates holding doctorates in medicine and other fields.

The assassination of President John F. Kennedy thirty years later can be described as lost, simple, and terroristic. The full scope of Kennedy assassination conspiracy theories and related circumstantial evidence presents an investigative quagmire that is certainly beyond the scope and objective of this study—the intent here is just to reveal commonalities between the two assassinations and the possible role of key Outfit members who had served under Frank Nitti at the time of the Cermak assassination and who could also have been involved in the JFK murder decades later. Indeed, the parallels between the Cermak and JFK assassinations are amazing and could conceivably indicate that both followed a similar set formula. Others have commented on the similarity and apparent methodological relationship between the two murders, as well as how dumbfounded many Outfit insiders felt that the authorities had so easily fallen for such an obvious and proven scheme twice.[86]

Several key underworld characters actually have important connections with each of these assassinations even though these were undertaken three decades apart. A plausible methodology of the Kennedy assassination in some respects also resembles the 1926 Hymie Weiss hit with its use of overlapping zones of fire by multiple shooters; the Cermak hit may have also employed multiple shooters. While the names of Jack Ruby and Lee Harvey Oswald, unlike David Yaras and John Roselli, are familiar to almost everyone in connection to the JFK assassination, their links to the Outfit still remain little known.

Nitti's Errand Boy: Jack Ruby

Jack "Sparky" Ruby (Rubenstein) was born in Chicago in 1911 in a house near Newberry and Fourteenth streets, and in his youth, had run numbers and delivered payoff parcels to crooked public prosecutors and policemen. As a young man, Ruby was employed by Frank Nitti to run such errands and later qualified as a hit man.[87] While these mob connections were later glossed over by the Warren Commission and follow-on Congressional investigations, there is now little doubt that Ruby was at least a low-level Outfit associate.[88] Ruby, originally an uneducated street thug, later became involved with the lucrative mob marijuana-smuggling operation out of Mexico into Los Angeles, but by 1937 had become a "union organizer" (that is, a strong-arm goon and enforcer) for Chicago's Scrap Iron and Junk Handlers Union, Local 20467, and the city's Waste Handlers' Material Union.[89] He was soon made the Outfit's bagman within the union likely under the command of close Nitti associate Murray Humphreys who was at the time the syndicate's "master fixer" and frontman.

Ruby was a prime suspect in the murder of senior Scrap Iron union official Leon Cooke, a murder that was reinvestigated years later by Attorney General Robert Kennedy. In the 1930s, Ruby may also at some point have been involved with the Trans-American Publishing and News Service, Inc., and later in related gambling activities in California with John Roselli for a few years.

In the 1940s, Ruby was recruited to represent Outfit interests in Dallas and make payoffs to the local police department. Ruby opened various nightclubs in Dallas, first the Singapore Club and later the Carousel striptease club, which were often used as local headquarters by the Outfit. Two small-time fixers from the Outfit, Paul Roland Jones and Romeo Jack Nitti, were sent to Dallas to help Ruby organize syndicate operations likely related to gambling (e.g. dice, roulette, handbooks, policy games, bingo, and slots), vice, and narcotics. This was probably done under the direction of Murray Humphreys and Jake Guzik. Romeo Jack Nitti is thought to have been related to Frank Nitti, possibly a nephew, and in some sources is named as Jack Knappi, Jack Knapp, or Jack Nappi. As a result of illegal activities and attempted police bribes, Jones was sentenceed to three to five years in prison. While Romeo Jack Nitti was indicted by a grand jury, Dallas authorities were never able to take him into custody.[90]

Jack Ruby apparently became a member in some capacity of U.S. overseas military counterintelligence operations after he joined the U.S. Army Air Corps in May 1943 and served until February 1946. He may also have been involved with Cuban smuggling activities involving narcotics and weapons after he left the service. Ruby was known to have serious psychiatric problems. It was rumored he had a sexual fetish for dogs, as well as possible homosexual tendencies.[91] Of course, Ruby eventually made history as the assassin of President John F. Kennedy's assassin Lee Harvey Oswald.

Throughout his life, Ruby had numerous Chicago underworld links, but it is not generally known that Oswald, a supposed leftist like Zangara, also was connected through very close family and personal ties to New Orleans Mafia boss Carlos Marcello and possibly, like Zangara, was all the time just an unrecognized low-level Mafia associate.[92] Marcello, a contemporary of Nitti's and also a boyfriend of Nitti's ex-girlfriend, Virginia Hill, has been named by many sources as a key organizer of the JFK assassination. Longtime Chicago mobster Sam "Teets" Battaglia's business partner, Irwin Weiner, a bail bondsman and friend of Jack Ruby's, was one of those who assured the Warren Commission that Ruby had no possible link to the Outfit.[93] The Warren Commission itself strangely concluded:

> Based on its evaluation of the record, however, the Commission believes that the evidence does not establish a significant link between Ruby and organized crime. Both State and Federal officials have indicated that Ruby was not affiliated with organized criminal activity. And numerous persons have reported that Ruby was not connected with such activity.[94]

IN FACT, THERE can be very little doubt that Ruby was a member of the Outfit in long standing and possibly a Mafia "sleeper agent" who had purposefully kept on good terms with the law for a long time. Sam Giancana had praised Ruby "for a job well done" in arranging the release of Santo Trafficante from Cuban custody after the communist takeover and was going to reward him with a small piece of a Havana casino if their Cuban holdings had been recovered from the communists.[95] Ruby was very possibly a made man within the Outfit under Sam Giancana at the time of the JFK assassination, and if not so because he wasn't Italian, he was still exceptionally well connected.[96]

In ways, Jack Ruby was a similar sort of man to Dave Yaras, while Lee Harvey Oswald was a confused patsy just like Giuseppe Zangara. In fact, Ruby and Yaras were Outfit colleagues and may have worked on the JFK assassination together. Johnny Roselli was a member of the Outfit during both assassinations and while linked to the JFK murder, had no known role with the Cermak hit. Roselli did have a close link to Jack Ruby and admitted to Senate investigators and news columnists shortly before his murder in 1976 that Ruby had been ordered to liquidate Oswald to prevent him from testifying. Ruby and Roselli may have first met in 1933 when both were involved with the newly opened Santa Anita Racetrack in Los Angeles and decades later are believed to have met twice in Miami during the fall of 1963 before the JFK assassination.[97]

Jack Ruby had no prior record of doing wet work for free or for ideological reasons. Sources indicate that a month prior to murdering Oswald, Ruby had met or talked with old Nitti associate John Roselli in Miami, Frank Caracci, a member of Carlos Marcello's New Orleans mob family, and Irwin Weiner, a senior frontman for the Outfit who had lost major gambling holdings in Havana, among many other organized-crime personalities who may have had a grudge against the Kennedy administration. In the weeks prior to the JFK assassination, it is documented that Ruby made a large number of telephone calls to syndicate leaders across the United States.[98] Many believed that after he participated in President Kennedy's assassination, the naive Lee Harvey Oswald was supposed to have faded away into the confused Dallas crowd in Dealey Plaza and then made his way to Jack Ruby's apartment or some other rendezvous location where Ruby would provide him with a passport, cash, and transportation to Mexico.

However, Oswald was actually a lost assassin like Zangara before him. In this scenario, after the police had caught Oswald—before he was quietly whacked as had likely been planned—it was Ruby's responsibility as Oswald's handler to eliminate him. Wearing a dark suit and the customary pearl-gray hat with black hatband, Ruby gunned down Oswald at point-blank range in true Outfit hitman style. The weapon Ruby used for the hit was the .38 Colt Cobra, a specialized assassination piece designed to be fired from inside a coat pocket with its hammer covered by a shroud to prevent it from catching on a coat pocket's lining and misfiring. The use of this weapon requires specialized training because when the pistol is fired from within a pocket, the assassin has no way of aiming his shots and must place the index finger of his gun hand flush with the cylinder and his middle finger on the trigger, allowing the weapon to fire where the index finger is pointed. The photographic evidence of Ruby shooting Oswald indicates that this is exactly the technique he used in Dallas.

All this occurred in the basement of the Dallas Court House and Police Station for the entire world to see on live television. It has never been determined exactly how Ruby gained entrance to this secure facility and what others thought he was supposed to be doing there, but he was likely assisted in this by his longstanding favorable relationship with the Dallas Police Department. Before being murdered by Ruby, Oswald had shouted to the press corps "I'm just a patsy." At the same crime scene, Ruby had yelled just before being led away, "I've been used for a purpose."

Ruby was likely a dead man in any case because he had just fouled up the largest mob contract in history by allowing Oswald to be captured.[99] Ruby was found guilty of murder on March 14, 1964, and sentenced to death, but this sentence was never carried out. He was reportedly paranoid and delusional before his death on January 3, 1967, as a result of a blood clot. However, Oswald's murder at Ruby's hands (apparently just one "lone nut" killing another) had essentially ended the JFK assassination case without a public trial. Today, on the outside front wall of the Texas School Book Depository building, from where Oswald supposedly shot Kennedy from a sixth-floor windowsill, there is a small plaque that states the date of the assassination as "when Lee Harvey Oswald allegedly shot and killed President John F. Kennedy."

Outfit Conspiracy?

Much has been written about alleged underworld involvement with the JFK assassination, as well as its purported Byzantine interactions with government intelligence agencies such as the CIA and FBI that are also accused by some as having been party to the plot. Certainly the liquidation of President Kennedy, and later his brother, Attorney General Robert Kennedy, had virtually ended the massive federal government war on organized crime.[100] However, some very knowledgeable people are adamant that the underworld had nothing to do with the president's death, and that just as in the Cermak murder, the official "lone nut" explanation is correct.[101] There is much evidence that the Outfit regarded John and Robert Kennedy, because of the syndicate's long business association with father Joe Kennedy, as "one of their own" and answerable to the underworld's code of justice.[102]

It is also interesting to observe the lengths that some syndicate members themselves went to to deny any involvement with the JFK assassination. One Outfit member who had possibly been connected to the murder as a member of an assassin team, Lenny Patrick, stated to the House Select Committee on Assassinations in 1978 when questioned whether the Mafia was behind President Kennedy's or Lee Harvey Oswald's murders:

> In my opinion, I don't think they are crazy. I know I wouldn't. I wouldn't have nothing to do with nothing like that or any public official or anybody.

It is silly. They know that. They wouldn't do that.
They would have no reason to do that there, as far
as I know. You know, you never know anything. If
they were, they weren't going to tell me nothing.
I would say definitely not...I don't know. They
wouldn't stick their nose out like that. What are
they going to get?[103]

PATRICK'S TESTIMONY TO this committee seemed to consist of
little more than denials and avoidance tactics in true omerta
fashion, but unlike John Roselli who provided more detailed
answers and was soon found dead, and his partner David Yaras
and his boss, Sam Giancana, who also might have provided
highly interesting testimony, but were murdered before they
could testify, Patrick was to live on for many years.

The Outfit has historically been very capable of maintaining
secrets from police forces and federal agents and has often used
its intelligence network of paid informers and plants within
government bureaucracies to manipulate information on
their activities that is deliberately leaked to law-enforcement
officials. Various Outfit members such as Johnny Roselli were
extremely knowledgeable on modern wiretapping and surveillance methods, and it is possible that some FBI surveillance
operations directed against high-level syndicate leaders such as
Sam Giancana were fed selective and false information—*disinformation* in intelligence operations terms.

Outfit members were often quite aware of being wiretapped
by the authorities. Murray Humphreys, for example, was
in the habit of picking up his telephone receiver and saying
good morning to the FBI agents on surveillance duty. There
is enough uncertainty on the whole subject that a post-War-
ren Commission congressional select committee that investigated the JFK assassination felt it prudent to conclude that
elements of the American Mafia had the motive, means, and

opportunity to conduct the hit, even if they had not, in fact, formed a conspiracy.[104] Elements of the American Mafia, including Santo Trafficante, Carlos Marcello, Johnny Roselli, Sam Giancana, and Jimmy Hoffa, all had the motivation and means to kill President Kennedy.[105]

The gist of this lore is that the Outfit's boss at the time, Sam "Momo" Giancana, worked with Tampa boss Santo Trafficante, New Orleans boss Carlos Marcello, and the local Dallas boss, Joe Civello, on the assassination plot, which had been sanctioned by the national Mafia Commission. These were the individuals identified in a 1978 report by the House Committee on Assassinations as being most likely to have been involved in a JFK assassination conspiracy. Civello ultimately controlled the nightclubs that Ruby ran, and Ruby reported to him on a regular basis on loansharking and racketeering activities. Jack Ruby had been a close friend in Chicago with David Yaras since the 1930s. Yaras was also a founder of the Miami Teamsters' Local and a key go-between for Trafficante and Marcello.[106] This, of course, was the same David Yaras who had been the Outfit's representative in Miami and Cuba for decades, performed various undercover operations, was reputed to be a professional killer and mob-union liaison man, and ran a heroin-smuggling operation for the Outfit under Frank Nitti when he had helped put together the Anton Cermak assassination using Zangara as a patsy three decades earlier.[107]

Giancana had also studied under the old master, Nitti, and while Giancana may have given the orders, it was almost as if the spirit of Nitti had reached out of his grave and across time, so similar was the method used to murder both Cermak and JFK. Johnny Roselli, a veteran of the Outfit's Hollywood extortion case under Nitti, is also believed by many to have been deeply involved in the JFK assassination. Roselli, Ruby, Yaras, and Giancana have all been linked to the Combination Network, a reincarnation of Murder Inc. Giancana had been friends from the old days with Joe Kennedy, and Giancana had been disappointed when President Kennedy and his brother, Attorney General Robert Kennedy, began an antimob war. The Kennedy family's Achilles heel was its history of being associated with American organized crime. Old man Joe Kennedy had supposedly bargained for the Outfit's support in having his son elected president in return for the mob having "a guy on the inside."

Frank Costello also reportedly had a contract on Joe Kennedy's life that Sam Giancana lifted in exchange for future political favors.[108] This political support did not proceed as hoped, and organized crime had a related grudge against President Kennedy for letting its important assets in Cuba fall into the hands of the communist regime of Fidel Castro and for mishandling the botched Bay of Pigs invasion by refusing to provide the all-important air cover for the operation.[109] There have been longstanding suspicions by many segments of the public that at some point the CIA-Outfit-Cuban exiles joint preparations for toppling the Castro regime in Cuba—the so-called "ZR Rifle" group—became focused instead on President Kennedy, the resulting government investigations of the assassination were improper, and the complete truth has never been revealed.[110]

Far from being the ally the syndicate had hoped for, the Kennedy administration's war against organized crime resulted in related convictions rising from 35 in 1960 to 288 in 1963. During this period, the IRS also netted a quarter of a billion dollars from top racketeers; and just a month before his brother's assassination, Attorney General Robert Kennedy requested Congress to pass an electronic-surveillance law to be used against the Mafia. Sam Giancana was constantly being tailed and wiretapped by FBI agents requested to do so by Robert Kennedy. In addition, John Kennedy and Giancana supposedly had mutual girlfriends such as Marilyn Monroe and Judith Campbell, which may have further aggravated bitter rivalries and testosterone-fueled personal jealousies at some stage.[111] The Mafia's justification and rationale for the assassination has been made with the analogy of killing a mad dog—cutting off the tail (Robert Kennedy) would not kill it, but chopping off its head (JFK) would.

Furthermore, if Robert Kennedy had been killed first, President Kennedy could have exercised an option to use military force in a state of national emergency to destroy the Mafia once and for all. On the other hand, they had confidence that once President Kennedy was killed, his brother would soon be replaced by a new administration. According to his longtime attorney, Santo Trafficante swore on his deathbed more than two decades later that he had, indeed, been behind the president's death.[112] Another intriguing piece of the puzzle—if there is a puzzle—was the fact that J. Edgar Hoover was the director of the FBI during both the Cermak and JFK assassinations and was responsible for aspects of both follow-up investigations.

In 1975, Giancana was killed in the basement of his home with a silenced .22-caliber pistol, possibly a High-Standard Duromatic, by shots to the back of the head and throat.[113] The .22 rimfire cartridge family of weapons with silencer is one of the weapons of choice for clandestine wet work when it can be done up close because of their low signature and accuracy, plus small size and lack of recoil. One of Giancana's daughters claimed he was murdered by the same people responsible for assassinating John and Robert Kennedy.[114] Some propose that it was John Roselli who had coordinated Giancana's murder to clean up the loose ends shortly before his own liquidation.[115] The underlying fear was that Giancana might have been planning to tell all to the authorities, with the same rationale also being used to justify Roselli's subsequent murder.

Dave Yaras was possibly the most important direct link between the Cermak and Kennedy assassinations, and some reports indicate that Yaras was one of the gunmen used in Dallas. If so, he may have contributed an historical legacy of methods used for the JFK assassination. Yaras had only been twenty-one years old in 1933 and was fifty-one in 1963. President Kennedy visited Florida, Yaras's old outpost for the Outfit, just prior to arriving in Dallas where he was assassinated. Yaras has been described as one of "more than a score of top-rated exterminators who work strictly on contracts for the board of directors," with "board of directors" likely referring to the national Mafia Commission.[116] Yaras and his partner, Lenny Patrick, were well-known Mafia hit men and Teamsters' enforcers. Patrick and Jack Ruby had a prior mob relationship acknowledged by the FBI, while information on Ruby's ties to Yaras was provided to the Warren Commission by Jack Ruby's sister, but was ignored because of a typographical error that spelled Yaras's name as "Yeres."[117] Yaras's name has also been misidentified by federal authorities as "Yarras" and as "Yaris" during the 1978 House Select Committee on Assassinations hearings.[118]

The specific connection of David Yaras to the Cermak and Kennedy assassinations some three decades apart has apparently been previously overlooked along with the implications of this for the similar methodologies used for both killings. Crime writer John W. Tuohy has similarly observed, "The fascinating thing about this killing [Cermak's] is its eerie similarity to the Kennedy assassination in Dallas thirty years later, made even more macabre by the fact that several of the names associated with the Cermak killing were later aligned with the Kennedy killing."[119]

Yaras was a close Outfit associate of Giancana and Roselli, a narcotics kingpin and a cold-blooded professional murderer who basically would do anything for money. If the Kennedy assassination was a mob hit, it would have required the coordination of a special team formed from the Mafia's national network of professional killers, tied together by someone who could also coordinate communications among the various elements of the conspiracy without leaving an incriminating trail. This coordinator was possibly Jack Ruby.[120] Roselli was used as a liaison between different bosses and Ruby to coordinate the assassination itself. Ruby's relationship with the Dallas police force was "unusually good" and would have assisted these efforts.[121]

David Yaras and Lenny Patrick had very colorful, but extremely brutal criminal careers. It is quite possible that David Yaras was the greatest mob hit man of all times. Yaras was thirty-five in 1947 when he was linked to the murder of James A. Ragen Sr. He was also tied to the murder of Ted Roe, a black policy-lottery kingpin, on August 4, 1952, and was suspected of others killings, as well as the planned, but ultimately unsuccessful 1962 Miami hit on Laborers' International Union official and former Nitti crony Frank "Frankie X" Esposito ordered by Sam Giancana.[122] David Yaras and a brother were active in Dallas racketeering operations for the Outfit during the 1940s, and he had involvement with Jack Ruby during and after this period into the early 1960s. Lenny Patrick, according to federal and state law-enforcement files, was responsible for the murders of more than a dozen mob victims, was in later years to become a lieutenant under Sam Giancana, and was on personal terms with Jack Ruby.

In 1946, the Chicago FBI office indicated that Yaras and Patrick might have had a part in the killing of Willie Tarsh and "Zukie the Bookie" Zuckerman, West Roosevelt Road gamblers who were murdered in gangland style several years earlier, along with other Chicago underworld slayings. In 1957, the FBI was aware that Yaras and Patrick were operating a gambling establishment on Chicago's North Avenue and having diversified responsibilities for gambling activities in the Summerdale and Rogers Park districts among many other mutual gambling, "juice loan" shylocking, and narcotics interests that continued well into the 1960s, by which time both were considered senior members of the Outfit.

The Chicago Crime Commission reported in February 1953 that Yaras and Patrick operated the Sans Souci Casino in Havana, Cuba, the same establishment that Johnny Roselli had been linked with years earlier. By the late 1950s, Yaras was again residing in his old stomping grounds of Miami, but kept in close business association with Patrick in Chicago. On February 18, 1963, Chicago Alderman Benjamin F. Lewis was found shot to death in a ward that Patrick and Yaras controlled, reportedly because he was not cooperating with the syndicate.[123] Other members of the Yaras crime family have also been closely linked to the Outfit by federal and police authorities, in some cases as recently as the mid-1990s.[124]

Another source from the intelligence world concurs with the Jack Ruby hit-team theory with David Yaras a key player. A 1993 Brazilian-directed TV documentary called *ZR-Rifle: The Plot to Kill Kennedy and Castro* that was aired in Cuba and subsequently published in book form outlined CIA attempts to assassinate Cuban President Fidel Castro and a purported related conspiracy that undertook the assassination of President Kennedy. The film's director, Claudia Furiati, is a Brazilian journalist and filmmaker with government connections in Cuba. After seeing Oliver Stone's movie, *JFK*, she made inquiries with Cuban intelligence about their views on Kennedy's assassination. She then worked with Gen. Fabian Escalante Font of Cuba's Interior Ministry and head of Cuban counterintelligence from 1976 to 1982, who provided her research access to classified Cuban intelligence archives. General Font reported that investigations by Cuban intelligence agencies had concluded that four to five gunshots from various positions were fired at Kennedy in Dallas. General Font gave the names of the shooters as David Yaras, Leonard Patrick, and

Richard Gaines—whom Font identified as members of the Chicago organized-crime syndicate—and Cuban exiles Eladio del Valle Gutierruz and Herminio Diaz Garcia.

In this version of events, there were two teams in Dealey Plaza that day: one under Jack Ruby's direction for sniper operations with Yaras and the others; and a second headed by anti-Castro agent Frank Sturgis in control of communications. Sturgis later became chief of the so-called "plumbers" in the Watergate scandal that led to the impeachment of President Richard M. Nixon.[125]

ZR Rifle itself was a special clandestine operations group the CIA had established to eliminate enemy foreign leaders. At the time of the JFK assassination, this unit enjoyed very close relations with the Outfit. Richard Cain, a.k.a. Ricardo Scalzitti or Richard Gaines, was, in fact, one bright Outfit man who Sam Giancana temporarily "transferred" to the CIA during preparations for the Bay of Pigs invasion operation and who may also have participated in the JFK assassination team as a sniper. Cain, reportedly a mathematical genius, was murdered under unusual circumstances on December 20, 1973.[126] While certainly not conclusive, and from an unexpected and possibly suspect source, this information joins a growing library discrediting the Warren Commission's final report and also agrees with other sources such as statements by family members of Sam Giancana.[127] The link to David Yaras does lend credibility to the Cuban report when correlated with other sources as to the possible members, source, and motives of the conspiracy.

In a 1964 FBI interview, David Yaras stated that he had last seen Jack Ruby more than ten years prior to the assassination, but apparently evidence of more recent telephone conversations between the two refuted this claim. The U.S. House Select Committee on Assassinations determined that Leonard Patrick and Ruby had a telephone conversation during the summer of 1963. What seems to be missing from the investigation by the

Warren Commission and subsequent congressional inquiries was a clear understanding of the importance of the record and capabilities of Yaras as a professional hit man *extraordinaire* throughout the United States and how this impacted on his relationship with Ruby at the time of the assassination. By the mid-1950s, Yaras was basing his operations out of Miami and Havana, and a link to anti-Castro operations was possible.[128] Chicago Police Department records indicate that Yaras had been arrested twenty-eight times from 1933 to 1947 mostly for general principles, disorderly conduct, and other related investigations. Still, the FBI considered Yaras and his partner Patrick as the primary "torpedoes" or hit men for the Outfit.[129]

The full extent of Yaras's activities between the Cermak and Kennedy assassinations will probably never be known, but the open police records are likely only the tip of the proverbial iceberg. In 1972, Yaras was still identified as a member of the Outfit under Sam Giancana, as was Leonard Patrick.[130] Yaras apparently died of a heart attack in 1974 when he was sixty-two years of age, while a year later, both Giancana and Roselli were murdered.[131] Unlike most of those closely involved with the Kennedy assassination, Leonard Patrick lived on and eventually became an informant to the FBI in 1992 at the age of eighty.[132] Yaras may well have been a crucial figure in the Cermak and Kennedy assassinations (conceivably the gunman who actually shot the president), a master craftsman in wet work dating from Nitti's era. However, relatively little is still publicly known about this enigmatic Outfit man, a true stone-cold killer.

Master of Assassination

Being used and being a patsy remain part and parcel of the standard mob modus operandi for high-level hits, and this tried-and-true formula likely owes much of its success to Frank Nitti's planned revenge against Anton Cermak. Yet another even-earlier possible example of the Outfit's use of a patsy for an assassination was the conviction of Leo Brothers for the high-profile murder of *Chicago Tribune* reporter Alfred "Jake" Lingle, a murder that Nitti was directly associated with according to some sources.[133] Robert Kennedy's assassin, Sirhan Sirhan, also seemingly fits the patsy and supposed lone-nut mold, as does Martin Luther King Jr.'s murderer, James Earl Ray.[134] Yet another political assassination that fits the conspiracy mold was that of Louisiana wildcat politician Huey Pierce Long in 1935.

TODAY IT IS easy to forget that in the early twentieth century, the techniques of clandestine operations for the most part remained close to the crude images of lunging, crazed assassins or anarchists throwing a lit short-fused bomb. However, powerful nations such as Great Britain had been engaging in intelligence operations abroad for centuries. Joseph Conrad's 1907 novel, *The Secret Agent*, was perhaps the first work to seriously examine the area of espionage, the psychological makeup of agents provocateur, and conspiracy theory.[135] The Mafia is believed to have supported the wartime U.S. Office of Strategic Services (OSS), the precursor of the modern CIA, by providing burglars and assassins, experimentation with drugs, the security of American ports from German and Japanese agents, and intelligence for the invasion of Sicily. Overall, Frank Nitti likely contributed considerable operational knowledge to the tactics of wet work employed by modern intelligence organizations.

The detailed operational planning that Nitti, as Al Capone's security expert and chief enforcer, used to execute the Saint Valentine's Day Massacre that included gunmen dressed as policemen and the Hymie Weiss hit with gunmen at rooftop level covering the target with interlocking fields of fire, as well as the use of conditioned patsy assassins, all became part and parcel of the operational techniques used by the newborn OSS and similar British, Russian, German, and Japanese intelligence services during and after World War II. The Cermak hit set the standards for covert, clandestine operations that had become doctrine by the time of the JFK assassination: invisibility, plausible deniability, and compartmentalization. Activities that are common to both organized crime and intelligence agencies include wiretaps, bribes, bag jobs (covert entries into offices and residences to obtain information through lock-picking, safe cracking, photography, electronic surveillance bugging, fingerprinting etc., and so named because tool bags were used to carry the necessary equipment), smears, deception operations, currency scams, tax fraud, industrial espionage, torture, and assassinations. The interrelationship and extent of the ongoing Mafia and CIA partnership has been often so close that at the time of the JFK assassination, Sam Giancana claimed it "had become—for all practical purposes—one."[136]

Frank "The Enforcer" Nitti in 1930 at the time of his arrest for income tax evasion. He is wearing his short-lived mustache and displaying "the look." His relatively small stature is quite evident. *Chicago History Museum DN-0093637 / Chicago Daily News*

Frank Nitti in 1941 during a court appearance. Unlike Al Capone, Nitti tried to avoid the public eye as much as possible. *Bettmann / Corbis*

Frank Nitti in 1943 just before his death. Note that he has aged noticeably since the 1941 photo, lending some credence to the theory that he was suffering from a serious illness. *Bettmann / Corbis*

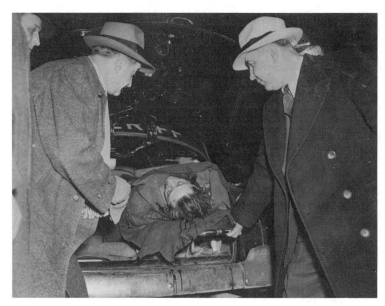

Frank Nitti's body being removed from a police squad car. Suicide or assassination? The hurried autopsy provided no definitive information to resolve this question. *Bettmann / Corbis*

Louis "Little New York" Campagna (right) and Paul "The Waiter" Ricca. Campagna was Nitti's main henchman and Ricca his underboss and successor. *Bettmann / Corbis*

Frankie Rio. Rio (right) was loyal but unimaginative, and, as this photo with his attorney illustrates, like Nitti, he did not seem to appreciate having his picture taken. *Troy Taylor Collection*

John Roselli. Roselli (right) was Capone and Nitti's point man in Hollywood, and later Sam Giancana's officer with the CIA, among other duties. *Library of Congress / NYWTS*

Phil D'Andrea. D'Andrea was actually the one who had carried a concealed firearm into the courtroom during Capone's trial, not Nitti, who at the time was imprisoned at Leavenworth. *Tom Hunt Collection / Chicago Police Dept.*

Mayor Anton Cermak. He tried to have Nitti clipped, but was dead himself some two months later. *Library of Congress / Underwood & Underwood*

David Yaras as a nineteen-year-old boxer in 1931. Yaras was Giuseppe Zangara's handler for the 1933 assassination of Mayor Anton Cermak. This photo is extremely rare and reproduced here for the first time. *Liz Latrobe Collection*

Giuseppe Zangara—lone nut? It is believed by some that he was recruited by David Yaras to kill Anton Cermak and take the rap as revenge for Cermak's assassination attempt on Nitti. The same technique may have been repeated three decades later with Lee Harvey Oswald. *Florida State Archives*

Virginia Hill. Recruited by Nitti to be an exotic dancer at the 1933 Chicago World's Fair, she was possibly his short-time girlfriend as she was with almost every other key mobster from New York to Los Angeles, at one time or another. *Library of Congress / NY-WTS*

David Yaras (right) seated with Santo Trafficante Jr., likely in the early 1960s. Trafficante is believed by some to have been, along with Sam Giancana and Carlos Marcello, a key conspirator in the John F. Kennedy assassination, while Yaras may have been one of the actual gunmen at Dealey Plaza. *Liz Latrobe Collection*

Harry Caray's Restaurant today. This building is the former location of Nitti's secret headquarters that then overlooked the nearby criminal courthouse building. *Harry Caray's Restaurant Group*

Sam "Momo" Giancana. A gunman under Nitti, Giancana rose to become an infamous boss of the Chicago Outfit in the 1960s. *Library of Congress / NYWTS*

Jack "Sparky" Ruby. An errand boy for Nitti, he was a long-time associate of the Chicago Outfit and likely communicated with David Yaras, John Roselli, and other underworld figures shortly before the JFK assassination. *Library of Congress / NYWTS*

Billy Drago as Frank Nitti in Hollywood's big-screen version of *The Untouchables*. While the story script he worked with had little to do with historical reality, Drago's stellar performance firmly entrenched Nitti in the public mind as a type of super-villain. *Silvio Gallardo and Billy Drago*

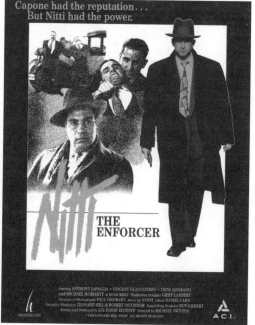

Nitti: The Enforcer — "Loving husband, good father, successful business man, ruthless killer. The true story of the rise and fall of the mob's most notorious enforcer." *Leonard Hill Films*

Anthony LaPaglia as Frank Nitti in the movie *Nitti: The Enforcer*. This film is overall the most historically accurate and complete account of Frank Nitti's life on film, placing his life and times in a realistic social and political context. *Leonard Hill Films*

6

Hollywood Shakedown

*This is the way they pay me back; after all I've done
for them.*
—Bruce Gordon as Frank Nitti at the
conclusion of the Hollywood extortion
case in "The Frank Nitti Story,"
The Untouchables (April 28, 1960)

The Mob Enters Show Biz

Frank Nitti's career was destined to supernova in a truly
grandiose scheme to corner the entire American entertainment
industry through the control of its unions and the extortion
of top industry executives. The relationship between the
underworld and the entertainment industry has often been a
close arrangement of convenience. According to the Web site
ipsn.com, "Historically the wise guys have always found the
movie industry ripe for an extorted buck or two—especially
by the Chicago mob."[1] The syndicate supplied the booze for
the clubs where live entertainers worked and eventually came
to own a good portion of this segment of the industry. Frank
Nitti had direct involvement in this area from an early stage.
One Irish-American musician of the era reminisced that after
refusing to be bullied by the mob-controlled musician's union,
Nitti ordered, "Leave the Micks alone; they got guts."[2]

Naturally, as the end of Prohibition squeezed the profit margin of illegal alcohol dry, the Outfit searched for new areas to replace lost revenues. As related, a whole series of unions had been targeted in Chicago, including those in food and beverages, transportation, construction, and services such as cleaning and laundry.[3] The dynamic opportunities of the entertainment industry plus organized labor with its ripe coffers of union funds fit the new bill of activities exactly. However, it was Nitti who first decided to undertake the actual exploitation of this prize on a truly national scale, directly combining union and entertainment racketeering, and contributing further to his legendary stature. Nitti was an avid moviegoer, enjoying gangster films such as *Little Caesar*, *Scarface* (1932), *Public Enemy*, and many others. His love of movies may have been a personal motivation to become closely involved with the parent industry.[4]

The origins of the underworld struggle to control Hollywood by criminals in Chicago and New York began as early as 1920 when union racketeer Tommy Maloy took control of Local 110 of the Motion Picture Machine Operators' Union in Chicago, shortly followed by the sector's electricians' union.[5] A tough, roly-poly Irishman, Maloy used intimidation, assault, arson, and even murder to ensure that his people were hired to operate motion-picture theaters. Pragmatic by nature, he formed alliances with Al Capone and George "Bugs" Moran. After Capone was sent to prison, Frank Nitti picked up the ball with Maloy. The Chicago Police Department suspected that Nitti's close associate Murray Humphreys was responsible for the 1931 gangland-style, six-bullets-to-the-head execution of Jacob Kaufman, a dedicated union organizer who persistently attempted to have Tommy Maloy and his thugs removed from the unions.

However, the Outfit wasn't really seriously interested in the potential of the motion-picture industry until the advent of soundtracks greatly increased its commercial potential, and then Nitti began to give it his close personal attention.

Eventually in his quest to control the American entertainment industry, Frank Nitti moved on to undertake what arguably remains the largest extortion case in the history of American criminal justice, an operation that set the pattern for modern organized crime, but led ultimately to Nitti's downfall while boosting his status as a true criminal legend.

Maloy was important to Nitti because he controlled the movie projectionists, without whom no motion-picture theater could operate. The entire industry at this time was deeply in debt, and even a short strike by the projectionists had the potential to financially ruin it. Maloy soon had another labor dissident, Fred F. Oser, beaten and finally executed after Oser attended a meeting in New York where he complained to the national union president, Fred Green, about Maloy's improprieties. After this murder, which occurred during a meeting in Maloy's office, Maloy went into hiding in a union-paid suite at the Congress Hotel in Chicago. Tubbo Gilbert, the Illinois State's Attorney chief investigator, soon seized all the union's records. However, those records quickly ended up in Frank Nitti's possession. He then used this information to begin taking direct control of the union in March 1933.

Nitti had known Maloy for many years, and in 1934, Maloy requested favors from Nitti in helping to put off a U.S. Treasury Department tax-evasion case for $81,000 in back taxes by having the case thrown off the books through political influence, and to provide the Outfit's backing for his run at the presidency of the International Alliance of Theatrical Stage Employees (IATSE). As Nitti was already backing George E. Browne, the business agent of IATSE Local 2, for the IATSE presidential position, he at first somewhat tentatively offered Maloy the vice presidency.[6]

Frank Nitti soon double-crossed Maloy, stalling on his assistance so Maloy would get convicted on tax-evasion charges, and the Outfit could then simply take over the projectionists' union. However, in November 1934, it appeared that Maloy would walk away from his tax case and stronger solutions were sought. On Christmas Eve 1934, Nitti held a party for the Outfit's top management, as well as his entertainment-union extortion men, George Browne and Willie Bioff, that had the problem of Tommy Maloy as a major discussion topic. Browne and Bioff were at this point being groomed by Nitti to become key players in the Outfit's major move on Hollywood, which required total control of Maloy's union to consolidate the syndicate's domination of various unions related to the entertainment business. It soon became apparent to the Outfit that Maloy was expendable, and he became as good as dead.[7]

Frank Nitti and some of his top boys, Charlie Fischetti, Frankie Rio, and Paul Ricca, soon met again at one of their regular executive sit downs during an extravagant dinner party at Harry Hochstein's house in Riverside. One can almost picture them following a fine meal when they were all puffing on Cuban cigars, drinking brandy, and generally feeling satisfied with life when Nitti again broached the subject of the takeover of Maloy's racket and the need to move on this quickly. Rio is thought to have promised to take care of Maloy at the beginning of the new year and is supposed to have hired two hit men from New York for the job.[8]

Nitti had earlier made a series of escalating demands that kept Maloy busy dipping into his union treasury.[9] First, Nitti's men kidnapped somebody outside Maloy's home that they thought was Maloy, but turned out to be one of his bodyguards. After calling Maloy and asking if his man's life was worth $10,000, Maloy said he wasn't worth anything to him and hung up. Nitti's men soon released the bodyguard anyway. A maid was also kidnapped in an unsuccessful attempt to gain entry into Maloy's home, although a subsequent robbery of Mrs. Maloy at their summer home may have resulted in the theft of $65,000 in cash and a large amount of jewelry.[10]

By January 1935, Maloy was under indictment for the extortion of movie theater owners and failure to pay income tax for the years 1929 to 1932.[11] On February 4, 1935, as the forty-two-year-old Maloy was on his way to visit his chorus-girl mistress, driving his Cadillac near the new Century of Progress Chicago World's Fair building on Lake Shore Drive, a car pulled alongside and in classic underworld hit fashion, riddled Maloy with shotgun and submachine gun fire, removing the entire left-hand side of his face and causing his car to crash into a fire hydrant. George Browne was one of the funeral pallbearers at Maloy's funeral, which was attended by two thousand curious people.[12] Maloy's murder also provided a clear signal to other union leaders of what to expect if they resisted the Outfit.[13] George Browne soon officially appointed Nitti's man Nick Circella (a.k.a. Nicky Dean) to take over Maloy's labor-union functions for the Outfit, which now had complete control of the strategically important movie projectionists' union.[14]

Bioff and Browne

Nitti's main operatives for his big move into Hollywood were the aforementioned Willie "the Squealer" Bioff and George Browne, Chicago pimps, minor labor racketeers, and union goons who specialized in shakedown rackets and who had formed a partnership they unofficially called "B&B Inc."[15] Willie Bioff had a criminal history that included stints with gangs such as those of the notorious Genna brothers and the brutal Battaglia brothers.[16] Bioff had at one time also made a valiant, but ultimately doomed attempt at unionizing Chicago's kosher butchers in a price-fixing scheme.[17] However, Bioff was a brutal pimp at heart, a disciple of fellow panderers Mike de Pike Heitler and Jack Zuta. Bioff reportedly used torture with pliers and acid to control his girls and once claimed that he had discovered a new surefire method for controlling recalcitrant whores:

> If you slug a girl half silly and then tie her down, you can stuff her cunt with powdered ice. They tell me it's so cold in there it feels like fire. You got to gag the girl, she screams so loud, but you don't really hurt her permanent. But after ten minutes of that, she will get down on her knees to you any time you say the word "ice."[18]

BIOFF BEGAN WORKING with George Browne around 1933 when Browne, a big, boozing slob and former stagehand, was a business agent for Chicago's Local 2, Stagehands' Union.[19] Browne was an alcoholic who claimed to be able to drink one hundred bottles of beer a day, each and every day, and had many escapades of drunken rowdiness. At times, he would place $1,000 in $100 bills on a bar and start ordering drinks for all his cronies.[20]

Browne did not share the Outfit's work ethic for senior members that often called for twelve or more hours of work every day with few real holidays. Once in a 1935 meeting at Miami, Browne had pleaded with Nitti for some time off so he could take in the sun and do serious beer drinking. Nitti was baffled that someone important like Browne would not be eager to return to work as quickly as possible, but offered a small and what he probably felt was a generous reward: "OK. Go ahead. Have a night on the town."[21] However, George Browne was an outwardly personable character, described by a *New York Times* correspondent in 1940 when he was still IATSE president as follows:

> Mr. Browne can charm you off your feet if he so chooses, and is as alert as they come. Among labor union officials he is unique, scorning all the oratory...which in public is the stock-in-trade of some

of them. He boasts a rare sense of humor, even if it works to his personal disadvantage, and [he] is not being fooled very often. With newspaper reporters he is a square-shooter, and when he gives them his word he stands by it. At the moment, he is not a well man, and living for the most part on a diet of milk. At one time he could drink with the best of them, but he is devoted now to an imported beer. Much of the year he passes in the loneliness of a hotel room.[22]

ORIGINALLY BIOFF AND Browne had operated separately from the Outfit with scams such as a soup kitchen for unemployed union members that was used to launder their graft-derived incomes, but this soon changed.[23] The local theater stagehands' union was one in which Bioff and Browne had arbitrarily increased dues in a profitable shakedown operation, and they soon planned other like schemes such as strike threats requiring monthly payments from theater owners for "no strikes guarantees." By the mid-1930s, Barney Balaban, along with his partner Sam Katz, was the owner of Chicago's largest and most successful movie theater chain, known as Balaban and Katz Theaters. Self-reliant entrepreneurs, Balaban would one day own Paramount Studios while Sam Katz would head MGM Studios, and they had been pioneers in the production of silent films and the operation of nickelodeons.

Balaban was targeted by Bioff and Browne, but initially directly rebuffed their pay-or-strike extortion threats. They continued threatening to orchestrate a union strike unless $20,000 was paid (originally $50,000 was requested, but Balaban bargained down the payoff price).[24] Bioff lied to Balaban that the payoff would go toward a fund for helping unemployed union members and the hoaxy soup kitchens that were supposed to help feed the unemployed, but in actuality, were cash cows for Bioff and Browne. (Browne had at one point solemnly donated

$5 worth of canned soup for the needy.) However, all parties soon came to the mutually satisfactory realization that money donated toward such an ostensibly charitable cause could be used as a corporate-tax write-off and public-relations ploy. It was hoped that records of such donations did not need to be kept meticulously so that Balaban and Katz could claim a much lower amount donated and pocket the balance for themselves. Balaban's lawyer handled the $20,000 payment to Bioff and Browne, but retained several thousand dollars for so-called "carrying costs." Balaban's payment to organized crime set a precedent with much wider implications for the industry.[25]

Bioff and Browne soon squandered much of this cash windfall on expensive clothing and foreign cars, as well as gambling away thousands of dollars in an Outfit-run casino inside the Loop district of Chicago called the Club 100 that was managed by Nick Circella, a wise guy who worked for Nitti through Frankie Rio.[26] Rio and Circella had known Bioff for years and soon noticed him and Browne in the club losing large amounts of cash. Curious where such small-time hoods had acquired so much money, Rio closely questioned them and shortly after, scheduled a meeting for Bioff and Browne with Frank Nitti.[27] Browne had casually met Nitti previously in the office of Tommy Maloy.[28]

There is some confusion in the various accounts of meetings that took place between Nitti and Bioff and Browne, and some record that the initial meeting took place in Harry Hochstein's house with Louis "Lepke" Buchalter from New York representing Charles Luciano's interests among the guests. FBI files also confirm that Nitti frequently used his own home or Hochstein's for such important meetings. However, the Outfit's board of directors met on a very frequent basis, and Bioff and Browne likely had attended a whole series of meetings during 1933-1934 with Nitti and his senior management, including one at Guey Sam's Chinese restaurant. Nitti may have also met with Browne at his office.[29] At his trial in 1943, Bioff testified that there were, indeed, a number of such planning meetings where the conspiracy was plotted out during 1934, 1935, and 1936, usually at Nitti's or Hochstein's homes. They were mostly attended by Nitti, Louis Campagna, Nick Circella, Paul Ricca, Frank Fischetti, as well as various others (with Hochstein providing bar services).

However, one can easily visualize Bioff and Browne arriving early for this initial meeting, perhaps fearing for their lives as the result of some unknown slight against Nitti (although it was very unlikely that Nitti would ever order a hit done in his own or a close friend's residence), but also hopeful that it presented a business opportunity with the shrewd Outfit boss. Small-time hoods, they were perhaps awed during the meeting with immaculately attired senior underworld characters including Nitti, his lieutenant Paul Ricca, Phil D'Andrea, Charles "Cherry Nose" Gioe, and Nitti's top enforcer, Louis "Little New York" Campagna.[30]

After Bioff and Browne had explained their local shakedown scam, Nitti immediately translated this information to the strategic "big picture" potential of similar larger-scale operations that could include scores of movie theaters in the Chicago area alone, thousands throughout Illinois, and tens of thousands across the nation, as well as the Hollywood studios themselves that produced the movies for distribution. The first step toward this would be the Outfit's control of the relevant entertainment unions, such as the recently acquired and key movie projectionists' union.[31]

Nitti ordered that the Outfit would totally absorb Bioff and Browne's operations, taking an initial 50 percent of profits, but eventually increasing the syndicate's share to 75 percent and then 90 percent as the scale of operations increased, with 10 percent of these excised gross profits going into the Outfit's general treasury and the balance being divided up with the scheme's mob investors. Browne had asked Nitti if he and Bioff could talk this "offer" over, and Nitti had replied, "Sure. But we're gonna cut in for half anyway..."[32]

This partnership arrangement with Nitti was to include George Browne's quick rise in the IATSE hierarchy; he had run for senior office once before and failed. Browne was at one point quizzed by Nitti on his willingness to cooperate with the Outfit if he became IATSE president:

> Suppose this time we saw to it that you had enough votes to win. Hands down. No contest. Would you like that?...In this world if I scratch your back, I expect you to scratch mine. If you can win by yourself, you don't need us. But if you want our help, we'll expect you to cooperate. Is that fair enough?[33]

BROWNE DID NOT hesitate to accept this offer. While Browne would become president, Bioff would play an even more important role as Browne's lieutenant and a union enforcer in Hollywood. Nitti, henceforth, expropriated effective control of the relevant entertainment unions and reduced Bioff and Browne to the position of his union bagmen and day-to-day union problem solvers with standing orders to report any really serious problems to Outfit members Nick Circella and John Roselli.[34] There is a possibility that Nitti eventually promoted Browne and Bioff to non-Italian made-men status in the Outfit as a reward for their services.[35]

Given the unfortunate turn of events that would follow, one must question the usually clear-thinking Nitti's decision to use the somewhat erratic Bioff and Browne team to so closely implement and manage a major Hollywood operation and to specifically use Bioff who had a known criminal record that included a Chicago jail sentence for pandering, which he had never served.

The Outfit Moves West

The Outfit already had its hand directly in Chicago's entertainment sector through the direct ownership of companies such as the World Amusement Corporation (chartered in 1933) and its World Play House club, as well as the Dante Theatre in Little Italy that Nitti himself had managed from 1926 to 1927 in partnership with a J. Vicedomini.[36] The Outfit was now after much larger prey. By early 1935, Bioff and Browne's shakedown operations for the Outfit had grossed more than $332,000 from the Chicago area alone.[37]

However, its Midwest operations were not enough. The Outfit had, in fact, long targeted Hollywood as an area for new operations. Al Capone had prioritized this expansion in 1929 before he went to prison, but Frank Nitti had undertaken the actual planning for the move. Some claim that as early as 1928, Nitti had joined forces with New York mobster Frank Costello and Prohibition tycoon Joe Kennedy to pool speakeasy profits and covertly purchase movie studios.[38]

Bioff and Browne's Chicago activities had provided the Outfit a convenient opening for much larger national operations. Nitti developed a subtle strategy for infiltrating all entertainment-related unions.[39] He conducted research on the potential of the entertainment racket and concluded that despite the negative effects of the Depression, the movie industry was still a major sector in America and that many of the major production studios were divisions of theater chains over which the Outfit was now gaining control through related labor unions. Nitti also realized that many key players in Hollywood were vulnerable to blackmail and extortion and that L.A. was a hotbed of organized-crime activities that included election tampering, bent politicians, and violent union disputes.

The L.A. district attorney, Baron Fritts, was reportedly corrupt as was the city's chief of police, Jim Davis, and its mayor,

Frank Shaw. From his ongoing research, Nitti had concluded that the movie business, only about fifteen years old at this point, was open to extortion and union-wage shakedowns because of profit downturns resulting from the Depression and the lack of stability and cash reserves to weather bad times that other more established industries enjoyed. However, even with these structural weaknesses, the motion-picture industry was growing and had a large daily cash flow across the United States that amounted to tens of millions of dollars. Nitti and the Outfit were determined to have a long-term piece of this action through the intimidation and control of national entertainment unions. The tactic would simply be that once the unions were under their control, the Outfit would threaten strike actions across the entire movie industry unless a regular tribute was paid. Nitti had high hopes for the success of this operation and had concluded a 1934 strategy meeting in Miami stating: "They are just waiting for us to walk in the door and ask for money...I think we can expect a permanent yield of a million dollars a year."[40]

Shortly after the Bioff and Browne takeover meeting, Nitti again met with some of his key associates including Ricca, Campagna, Circella, and Rio, to discuss the takeover of entertainment unions at the national level. Over a luncheon meeting at the Capri Restaurant, Nitti discussed his research on Barney Balaban's national movie business and a recent discussion he had with Charles Luciano on how the Chicago and New York underworlds could cooperate on the Hollywood project. Even though Nitti disliked Luciano (and the feeling was mutual), he knew that because the East Coast mob already controlled the key eastern stage workers' and projectionists' local unions, as well as the vast scale of the U.S. movie industry itself, it would be better to cooperate with Lucky rather than attempt direct competition. Balaban's operations would be the initial Bioff and Browne target for a 20-percent wage increase for movie

projectionists with the threat of a general strike and movie-
theater shutdown across the Midwest and East Coast.

Officially, Bioff would be the key Hollywood representative
for the IATSE and the Motion Picture Machine Operators'
Union. The studios would pay protection money because otherwise the Bioff-and-Browne-controlled unions would simply
go on strike and close down theater operations. In a game of
"good crook" "bad crook," Bioff would threaten a strike action
while Browne would be a conciliatory peacemaker suggesting
as an alternative a relatively small wage increase. In addition,
the studio heads were known to be physically intimidated by
Bioff because of his underworld status.[41]

George Browne had been successfully propped up as the
IATSE president in the key 1934 union election.[42] The IATSE
was formed in 1893 to provide organized-labor benefits for
stage and vaudeville workers, but it was immediately eager to
spread its membership to the relatively new medium of film.
During the mid-1930s, the union arranged a Hollywood-wide
strike to organize film workers and sound engineers, as the era
of silent film was now finished.[43] Organized-crime intimidation helped end this strike, and Browne was portrayed as a
peacemaker by both sides and in the bargain, got the union
membership a not too unsatisfactory 10-percent raise. The
strike had seen the IATSE's active membership plummet.
Once Bioff and Browne were in power, they quickly saw to it
that twelve thousand studio workers from twenty-seven studio
unions quickly affiliated with it once more.[44]

Browne's election at the June 1934 IATSE meeting in Lou-
isville, Kentucky, was basically accomplished through a feat of
arms. Present were all the top leaders of the Outfit, headed by
Nitti and accompanied by large numbers of gunsels, as well as
important gangsters from New York, including Charles Luciano,
Meyer Lansky, Ben Siegel, Lepke Buchalter, and others.[45] Some
accounts claim that mob gunmen actually wandered about the

convention with Tommy guns propped on their hips to suitably intimidate any possible opposition. Bioff was given the position of "special representative" for Browne, but what he did, in effect, was strong-arm Browne's edicts for Nitti. "Bioff muscled his way into Hollywood where he extorted millions for the Chicago Syndicate after threatening the movie moguls that he would close down every theater from New York to California through assorted acts of violence and intimidation."[46] To further increase his control of the union, Nitti had also appointed his accountant, Isidor Zevin, as the IATSE bookkeeper.[47]

Frank Nitti ordered Willie Bioff to move operations to L.A. where the nation's most important movie-production studios were located in Hollywood. The initial official excuse by the union for this transfer was to rectify past management's across-the-board salary reductions for IATSE members and the threat of a retaliatory general strike that Bioff and Browne had finessed into George Browne's election as president.[48] In return for payoffs from the Hollywood studio heads, Bioff and Browne would control the threat of future strikes. Within three months, some $250,000 in cash had been extorted from major firms such as Twentieth Century Fox, Warner Brothers, RKO Studios, and Paramount Studios without any major difficulties, which Nitti found to be almost too easy.

In 1936, a 2-percent "tax" for a union defense fund was also levied against the wages of employees of the IATSE, the Motion Picture Machine Operators' Union, and other entertainment unions under syndicate control. This special tax collected $2 million or more over two years before it was reversed, most of which likely went directly to Bioff and Browne's and the Outfit's coffers. The federal government never attempted to trace its ultimate dispensation although it was initially included in the indictments against Nitti and his team.[49]

Eventually, well more than $2.5 million was exhorted from various activities (in addition to the special tax), and according to some sources, the actual total amounts ran from six million to tens of millions of dollars that were never recovered and on which no income tax was ever paid.[50] The major sources of these extorted funds were: collections from theater companies in the Chicago, New York, Newark, and California areas; collections through commissions on raw-film purchase contracts; and direct collections from movie-production companies.[51] Bioff claimed that by the time he was arrested, some 20 percent of the industry was paying extortion money, and this would have soon risen to 50 percent. He glibly claimed, "I had Hollywood dancin' to my tune."[52] All this money was divided among the top Outfit men involved with the scam, as well as a smaller portion that went into the Outfit's general treasury as a mutual fund, as had been planned by Nitti.[53]

Fred Evans is thought to have been the expert behind the laundering of the Hollywood extortion money for the Outfit.[54] Evans, who was murdered in 1959 after providing information on the mob to the FBI, had also been the "mystery man" financial genius of the Outfit who had taken control of Chicago's laundry and cleaning businesses.[55]

A recently released secret history of the top cases of the U.S. Internal Revenue Service from 1919 to 1994 revealed that Frank Nitti's shakedown of the motion-picture industry actually "demanded two thirds of [their] profits" and that such criminals were usually difficult to convict "because they often bribed and used corrupt political influence to escape charges, as well as intimidated prosecution witnesses."[56] Bioff and his team often left their "calling card" on the front door of those who offered opposition in the form of a stick of dynamite, and soon they were accepting bribes from the studios for keeping union demands in line.[57]

The names of Nitti, Browne, and Bioff have left a bitter taste to this very day in the mouths of many IATSE members who see the control of the union "founded in greed, and the most blatant example of that greed was the establishment—and subsequent perversion—of a two percent assessment on the earnings of all IA members to create a defense fund which was supposed to be for the purpose of fighting the unscrupulous employers."[58] Browne had an almost complete control of this fund, some $60,000 per month, and an accurate accounting of it was never kept.

Johnny Roselli

The story of Frank Nitti in Hollywood is also the strange story of one John Roselli, an almost fantasylike series of events that covers more than four decades.[59] Johnny Roselli was a mysterious character whose life and career, like Frank Nitti's true story, was not well known to the general public. Roselli was Nitti's point man posted in L.A., Bioff's nominal superior holding the rank of capo, and he briefed the Outfit's board of directors on a regular basis concerning all the important angles in Hollywood and Beverly Hills. In fact, Roselli's job was to constantly observe Willie Bioff, who Nitti felt often talked too much, particularly when he was drunk.[60] Nick Circella played a similar supervisory role with the hard-drinking George Browne, who was based mostly in New York and Washington, D.C.[61]

The official records are somewhat hazy on his early life, but Roselli by various accounts was born either Giovanni Roselli in Chicago in 1904 or Anthony D'Acunto or Felippo Sacco in Italy at about the same time. Even the official FBI files on John Roselli indicate that authorities were uncertain of the specifics of his early background, including his real name, even after his death, because of the numerous aliases and assumed histories he adopted throughout his colorful criminal career.[62] His real name was probably Felippo Sacco, and he probably was born in Esteria, Italy.[63]

After joining Al Capone's inner circle at a young age, Roselli is believed to have been an Outfit "sleeper agent" on the West Coast since he was sent there by Capone at about 1924-1925 for the purpose of prospecting opportunities in gambling, extortion, and vice rackets. He likely had an important hand in the Outfit's ongoing shakedown of expensive Los Angeles nightclubs and restaurants that was firmly established by the mid-1930s, and helped thwart New York competition led by Charles Luciano.[64] Following Capone's imprisonment for the final time, Nitti had kept on Roselli as his *representante* on the West Coast.[65]

Roselli helped establish the Trans-American Publishing and News Service, Inc., the national wire service operated by Moses Annenberg, whose family would later go on to publish *TV Guide* magazine, and Gus Greenbaum, a Phoenix socialite and gambler.[66] In particular, Roselli headed operations at the Santa Anita Racetrack, likely at one point with a young Jack Ruby. In 1938, Roselli had a short stint as the Outfit's representative to the Sans Souci Casino in Havana, but he always returned to the West Coast to pursue his career.[67]

Roselli was superb for the Hollywood role because he was an intelligent, shrewd, aggressive hustler with very good looks and an affected style and charm, including a predilection for expensive suits and a house in an exclusive neighborhood favored by many leading stars of the era such as supposed tough guys Humphrey Bogart and Edward G. Robinson. By 1936, Roselli was thought to have taken control of most West Coast organized gambling, as well as the wire service at Santa Anita for Trans-American.[68] During the 1950 Kefauver Committee hearing on organized crime, Roselli admitted to having been a confederate of Frank Nitti and Moses Annenberg in the establishment of the Trans-American gambling wire service and other West Coast gambling activities.[69]

Roselli had been one of those who helped mastermind the nationwide Hollywood extortion scam in meetings at

Al Capone's Palm Island estate in Miami during March 1934 with Frank Nitti, Paul Ricca, Ralph Capone (who simply acted as host while his brother was in prison), George Browne, Willie Bioff, Nick Circella, Charles Gioe, Louis Campagna, Ralph Pierce, Francis Maritote, Charles Fischetti, and Phil D'Andrea.[70]

Roselli came to think of himself as a "labor conciliator" and was, in fact, an expert at influencing public officials.[71] However, Roselli was still essentially an Outfit wise guy at heart—an L.A. hit man, bootlegger, drug peddler, vigorish loan shark, and bookmaker to the Hollywood stars, as well as having been a convicted arsonist in his youth. Besides key members of the Outfit, among his Mafia connections were Frank Costello, Charles Luciano, Ben Siegel, and Meyer Lansky from New York, Sam Maceo from Texas, "Dandy" Phil Kastel from New Orleans, Tony Gizzo from Kansas City, and many others.

According to some prison medical and FBI reports, Roselli exhibited an extreme paranoid personality, sometimes very friendly, but often displaying a violent temper.[72]

Roselli was what Frank Nitti termed "an all-around hustler," a man who could figure out illicit and profitable angles on almost anything. During his long stay in L.A., he had fully bought into the elite Hollywood and Beverly Hills lifestyle and was generally accepted within elite social circles with casual acquaintances often remarking that he looked like a "movie character." At one point, Roselli had seriously considered an acting career, became quite knowledgeable about the movie industry in general, and was involved in the production of the 1948 cult classic film, *He Walked by Night*, and such noir-gangster classics as *T-Men* and *Canon City*, working with legendary Warner B-grade movie producer Bryan Foy.[73] However, Roselli's staple organized-crime activities in L.A. over the decades continued to be gambling, prostitution, drugs, loansharking, enforcement, and union racketeering.[74]

Roselli successfully avoided arrest in California (except for one charge of carrying a concealed weapon) and acted as a tour guide providing introductions to movie stars for Al Capone during Capone's 1930 trip to Hollywood, so he was very well placed for his job.[75] The provision of illegal narcotics (usually opium, heroin, cocaine, and marijuana) and vigorish loans (perhaps totaling as much as $5 million) to those in high Hollywood positions was a primary means by which the Outfit cemented its deep influence over the entertainment industry.[76]

Included in the stories that Roselli had supposedly briefed Bioff on during his personal introduction to Hollywood was the allegation that the young rising MGM Studios star, Joan Crawford, had previously appeared in pornographic films, and in 1935, she had been blackmailed through MGM for some $100,000 by freelance extortionists who claimed to have prints of her adult films. MGM decided to offer $25,000 to protect their star's reputation and put Roselli in charge of the transaction. Roselli simply threatened to murder the small-time hoods if they ever contacted Crawford or MGM again (they never did) and kept the ransom money for himself.[77] Roselli had also been a key player in the 1932 war between brothers Jack and Harry Cohn over control of Paramount Studios.[78]

Roselli's loansharking operations involving millions of dollars may have included loans to stars Ronald Reagan and Ed Sullivan.[79] Roselli's entertainment friends and gambling acquaintances over the years are said to have included Clark Gable, Gary Cooper, Frank Sinatra, Charlie Chaplin, George Raft, Jean Harlow, Phil Silvers, Zeppo Marx, Georgie Jessel, Dean Martin, Peter Lawford, and Marilyn Monroe.[80] He was on a first-name basis with Jack Warner, Harry Cohn, Sam Goldwyn, and Joe Schenck. He would later work with the infamous Hollywood private detective, Fred Otash, who was the private investigator for the notorious 1950s gossip rag, *Confidential*. For a period of time, he was married to actress June Lang. Roselli dated Hollywood actresses such as Betty Hutton, Lana Turner, and Donna Reed, and reportedly had an affair with Nitti's ex-girlfriend and Bugsy Siegel's paramour, Virginia Hill (who didn't?).[81]

Roselli was the Outfit's West Coast hit man of choice for many years, perhaps into the early 1970s.[82] According to some legendary accounts, Roselli helped murder Marilyn Monroe as part of a warped mob plot that involved John and Robert Kennedy, who allegedly both had affairs with Monroe that had soured. Monroe also had a long and stormy relationship with Sam Giancana and the Outfit. She began drinking heavily and taking pills when her career and love life took a dive and increasingly became a liability. Named "Number One Sex Star of the 20th Century" in 1999 by *Playboy* magazine, her alleged suicide or possible murder merely added to her mystique and legend.[83]

Roselli became known as "John Rawlston" when he took part in Outfit-CIA plots to overthrow Castro and as we have already seen, may even have been directly involved in a JFK assassination plot. Shortly before his violent death, he had provided testimony to government inquiries into at least some of these matters.[84]

As the decades passed, Roselli just would not give up on his criminal career and was constantly on the make till the end of his life. It is highly interesting that in 1975, Roselli tried to promote a script for a motion picture about "a patriotic mobster who becomes entangled in a White House-CIA plot to assassinate Fidel Castro … [but] the scheme backfired when Castro hires his own mobsters to kill the American President."[85] The idea was rejected as being "too implausible"! In government testimony during the early 1970s, Roselli had, in fact, claimed that he acted from patriotism when participating in clandestine United States intelligence operations aimed at assassinating Castro.[86] Roselli and Murray Humphreys had also become quite adept at electronic eavesdropping and wiretapping techniques, and later did such work for mob boss Sam Giancana using FBI and CIA standard equipment. Roselli remained a top representative of the Outfit on the West Coast well into the 1960s.[87]

While most American cities are specifically designated as being under the sovereignty of a Mafia family, Las Vegas is considered an "open city" theoretically open to participation by all, but in practice dominated by New York and Chicago. The Outfit's first Las Vegas casino was the Stardust and was built under the direction of Murray Humphreys. The Fremont, Desert Inn, and Riviera casinos were for a time directly controlled by the Outfit.[88] Starting in the late 1940s after having served prison time for his part in Nitti's failed Hollywood extortion scam and then working for local mob boss Jack Dragna in L.A., Roselli was an ambassador of sorts to Las Vegas for the Outfit under Ricca and Accardo to collect their portion of the "skim" (skim is money taken off the top of the gross revenues from casino gambling before it was legally accounted for) and to enforce the mob edicts along the Strip and downtown's Glitter Gulch on Fremont Street.

The Outfit expected Roselli to be its version of Bugsy Siegel in Las Vegas, but he never quite seemed to meet their expectations in this role, likely because he was always too involved with his own sideline activities that interfered with his Outfit work.[89] For example, Roselli had opened a talent-booking agency from the Desert Inn called Monte Prosser Productions that had a virtual monopoly with all Las Vegas casinos, and he even arranged a contract to represent a venture that would supply all the ice machines for every hotel in town.[90] Roselli, along with Teamsters' Union President Jimmy Hoffa, tried to assist billionaire Howard Hughes's move into the ownership of Las Vegas casinos.[91]

The legacy that the Outfit established in Las Vegas was one that lasted well into the 1980s. By the late 1950s, Roselli began falling into the Outfit's disfavor and when he became too greedy for his own good was succeeded in Las Vegas by the sinister Anthony "the Ant" Spilotro, Marshall Caifano (used as a hit man by Nitti), and the bright Donald "Wizard of Odds" Angelini by order of Sam Giancana and successive bosses.[92] Roselli's attempt to squeeze increasing finder's fees in Las Vegas may have helped lead to his replacement by these others. Spilotro was notably believed to have been in on the infamous liquidation of William "Action Jackson" Kelly, a 340-pound juice man (and a sexual degenerate, rapist, thief of the Outfit's coffers, and as Sam Giancana believed, a traitor providing information to the FBI) who was impaled on a meat hook in his rectum and suspended from a chain while being slowly tortured to death –literally flayed alive—over a two-day period, reportedly the most cruel Outfit execution ever committed. The horrifying result was photographed and widely distributed as a warning to others in the underworld.[93] Spilotro was also the role model for Joe Pesci's character in the motion picture, *Casino*. Spilotro and his brother, Michael, were murdered together in 1986 by being tortured and then buried alive in an Indiana cornfield (in the same area where Ted Newberry's body had been found decades earlier after he had been ordered murdered by Nitti).[94]

Roselli would spend time in prison during the late 1960s for a 1963 high-stakes gambling scam at the Beverly Hills Friars Club where he used peepholes and electronic devices to cheat the club's many rich and famous patrons, such as Phil Silvers and Zeppo Marx, of approximately $400,000 during the course of less than a year.[95] A system similar to that employed by Roselli was portrayed at the beginning of the 1964 James Bond movie, *Goldfinger*. Roselli's membership in the exclusive Friars Club had been sponsored by Frank Sinatra and Dean Martin.[96] Coming out of prison a supposed broken man and facing deportation, he ratted to the feds in 1970 about the Outfit in return for leniency and lived in obscurity with his sister in Florida until he was liquidated onboard a yacht in 1976. Miami boss Santo

Trafficante was linked by the FBI to Roselli's homicide, which may well have been a result of Roselli's testimony in 1975 and 1976 to a Senate Select Committee on Intelligence investigating assassination plots against Fidel Castro and John F. Kennedy where he insinuated that he knew the people who were behind the JFK assassination conspiracy.[97] Roselli's strangled, shot, mutilated, and butchered body was stuffed in an oil drum, dropped into Miami's Biscayne Bay, and later contemptuously referred to by Outfit leaders as "Johnny in a drum."[98] Roselli was last seen on a boat owned by a Trafficante associate.[99]

While some of these allegations concerning John Roselli's criminal career and covert activities may verge on the fantastic, if one carefully examines the declassified FBI files on Roselli and plays fill-in-the-blanks with the censored areas using related information from other sources, it soon becomes much more believable. Roselli has one of the largest FBI files, 10,969 pages, but of these, only 1,228 have been made accessible to the public because of sensitivity concerns. Roselli's FBI criminal case number was 333986.[100]

An Incestuous Union

While Bioff and Browne operated the Hollywood extortion racket, many studio executives soon appreciated this under-world interference because they quickly came to realize that they were saving money by not providing legitimate union-wage hikes. Frank Nitti was known to always keep his word when he promised not to raise labor costs or order any work stoppages by IATSE members (in all Bioff and Browne came to control up to 46,000 unionized workers).[101] This situation resulted in an often very weak union and a strong studio man-agement that was able to fire and hire workers at will, produce lower-cost films, pay low wages, and not provide overtime and other fringe benefits—something that the IATSE remains bitter about to this day.

One estimate is that the studios saved $15 million in potential wage increases. In the process, both communist agitators and two-bit hoods had been eliminated as Hollywood labor problems by the intervention of the Outfit. Movies were produced within schedule and at lower budgets without the fear of wildcat strikes. Bioff and Browne also took action to raise the admission costs of motion-picture competitors such as live theater, operas, and other concerts. At the time, no federal, state, or local laws regulated union funds and their activities.[102]

Joseph Schenck, one of the so-called "Founding Fathers of Hollywood," furthered this underworld shakedown by representing the studios and developing a plan to satisfy Bioff and Browne's increasing extortion demands within the context of rigid studio production and budget schedules. The Schenck brothers, Joe and Nick, were the most powerful men in Hollywood because between them they controlled MGM and Twentieth Century Fox. In April 1936, Joe Schenck was reportedly prepared to pay Bioff up to $1 million, but he then, for some reason, came to believe that Bioff and Browne could be bribed for considerably less. Schenck offered Willie Bioff a 7-percent commission on the increasing raw-film business between Hollywood studios and DuPont Chemicals for acting as a designated sales agent (a position Johnny Roselli also occupied for DuPont), although any actual work would be undertaken by legitimate DuPont representatives.[103] This offer also required considerable business being switched from Eastman Kodak to DuPont. Bioff agreed to this offer on the stipulations that Frank Nitti would not be informed, the annual commission income would not be less than $50,000, and he would retain it in its entirety (also excluding George Browne).

However, once the Schencks were drawn into the overall extortion scheme, Nitti knew Hollywood was wide open for

his grand takeover plan. By the mid-1930s, Nitti had pioneered the union tactic of using a "wave of disruption" rather
than a general strike by all members of the union.[104] He also
employed scare tactics such as having his thugs throw harmless, but very annoying stink bombs into crowded theaters.
The movie moguls from MGM, Paramount, Warner Brothers,
RKO Studios, Columbia Pictures, Universal Pictures, and
Twentieth Century Fox, plus various smaller studios such as
Loew's, Inc., soon gave in to Bioff and Browne's demands at
the union's negotiating table. Such early a capitulation was
perhaps prudent. A high-explosives bomb was found in a
Loew's theater at one point during negotiations with Bioff and
Browne.[105] At this point, Nitti, for all intents and purposes,
was well on the way toward owning Hollywood.[106]

The growing relationship between the Outfit and Hollywood film moguls was quite incestuous and worked both ways.
Another perspective on what really occurred at the time was
that Bioff and Browne had engaged in actual extortion at first,
but this practice evolved into little more than accepting bribes
from the studio heads in exchange for keeping union demands
low.[107] By 1936, $2.5 million in extortion fees had been paid to
the Outfit, but shortly thereafter, the studio heads reasoned
that such extortion fees could simply be considered another
business-expense write-off, and they could even increase such
payments if a percentage of the cash payment was secretly
returned as a kickback.[108]

On April 30, 1937, Hollywood faced an entertainment-union
strike over new federal wage laws and a related 20-percent
wage increase demand that could have halted all movie productions. As it was, six thousand studio painters, plasterers,
plumbers, cooks, hairstylists, and set designers went on strike
for the recognition of their union representation, which was
not yet directly controlled by the IATSE.[109] Nitti was at first
hesitant to become directly involved using mob muscle, but

the studio heads through Bioff and Browne requested the Outfit to break the strike. East Coast mob bosses Charles Luciano and Abner "Longie" Zwillman also pressured Nitti to intervene. Nitti tasked this assignment to Johnny Roselli who sent twenty professional thugs from Chicago and San Francisco to Hollywood where they were armed with guns, baseball bats, and chains with the connivance of the local police department and then directly confronted the striking union membership at studio entrances, particularly Twentieth Century Fox's at Pico Boulevard.

Roselli's goons undertook various intimidations and beatings of the strikers over the next several weeks, but the unions countered by hiring their own team of thugs in the form of some sympathetic longshoremen. Pitched battles resulting in several deaths and numerous injuries continued over a six-week period with Roselli's men eventually prevailing.[110] As a psychological warfare-type alternative to brute force, Roselli had Bioff and Browne hold a press conference with the studio bosses during which they jointly declared the striking union's rogue leadership as being infiltrated by communists. This ploy resulted in the key Screen Actors Guild ignoring union picket lines, smaller unions being either disbanded or absorbed into the mob-controlled IATSE, and the dissident Federation of Motion Picture Crafts being completely eliminated.[111]

At this time, working conditions in Hollywood often left much to be desired for organized labor. As Tom Sito wrote on the Los Angeles Grim Society Web site, such conditions included: "Strict personal contracts, stuntmen firing live ammunition at your face for gangster pictures, studios that lay you off before Christmas and re-hire you after New Years to save themselves paying out a bonus, [and] screen credits non-existent or padded with the boss's relatives or his latest tootsie."[112] The Motion Picture Academy of Arts and Sciences established by Louis B. Mayer and Irving Thalberg in 1927 was one attempt at developing a system for the arbitration of employee-employer complaints, but was largely ineffective, particularly for union-ized labor or those aspiring to become unionized. Unions were more often than not simply considered by many of the studio heads as fronts for communist agitators.[113]

When it wasn't directly exploiting unions, the mob certainly could provide the working stiff a lot of muscle on his or her side, and there were some intelligent and not altogether unsym-pathetic men like Frank Nitti and Meyer Lansky behind the scenes. Organized labor did sometimes receive more money because of the Outfit's not-altruistic efforts.[114] Ironically, both Bioff and Browne were apparently quite conscientious in many of their regular day-to-day union duties and personally sympathetic to the plight of the individual working person while they simultaneously worked toward pilfering the coffers of the IATSE.[115]

Remarkably, Willie Bioff, the outwardly gruff Chicago gang-ster and former pimp, proved to be a gifted union organizer and negotiator and a forceful orator. He had no difficulty represent-ing men and women in trades he was totally inexperienced in and quickly adapted to the ins and outs of the clannish Hol-lywood movie industry. Even after Bioff was imprisoned, the IATSE members still hoped for his early release so that they could use him again for their next round of labor negotiations.[116] The IATSE is also said to have later unsuccessfully attempted to recruit Bugsy Siegel to replace Bioff.[117]

Under Bioff and Browne, the IATSE defeated rival unions such as the FMPC in 1937, as well as fending off various incursions onto their turf by the Teamsters' Union, the Con-ference of Studio Unions, and the International Brotherhood of Electricians who had tried to recruit sound engineers to their organization.[118] (The CSU, according to some, actually had direct links to communist organizations, while others considered it as the only truly democratic union in Hollywood history. By the late 1940s, it would become a victim of redbaiting in Hollywood.) In 1937, Bioff and Browne actually negotiated an across-the-board 10-percent raise for the IATSE membership, a feat they repeated in 1939, although working conditions generally did not improve.[119]

Consequently, the IATSE indirectly admits in its current literature that not all things undertaken by Bioff and Browne under the auspices of Frank Nitti were always detrimental to the well-being of union members:

> From the labor point of view the IATSE had created an enviable labor record in the past 25 years with regard to hours, wages and working conditions ... it was maintained and even improved during Browne's reign ... Factually, the record shows that repeatedly these confederates did things to further the legitimate aims of their union in a manner utterly inconsistent with any theory that they were acting to the detriment of union member ... Raises and union recognition were even obtained by Bioff for unions not a part of IATSE ... even a defense witness called to contradict portions of Bioff's testimony had to observe that Bioff did a good job for the IATSE.[120]

Furthermore, Nitti's influence in Chicago and Hollywood's organized-labor unions was apparently long term in effect. One 1996 view of the union practices of the modern IATSE revealed the opinion that its "constitution is largely unchanged from when it was written by the Frank Nitti crime family of Chicago in the 1940's" and that its "members are not permitted to vote for their leaders ... international officers are elected by a convention of delegates every three years (in) a rubber stamp process ... incumbents always win and the President stays until he dies or retires in mid-term ... a successor is then named by our unelected leaders and this person runs as an incumbent for a life-time term at subsequent conventions...our President has dictatorial powers, is the ultimate interpreter of our constitution, and can change or take over locals at will."[121]

However, it must be emphasized that today's IATSE is by no way affiliated with or infiltrated by organized crime as it was during Frank Nitti's era.

One union legend concerns Frank Nitti and leftist painter's union leader Herb Sorrell.[122] Sorrell was a colorful union activist with a past history as an amateur boxer who would not hesitate to fight management goons. One perhaps overly enthusiastic lady newspaper reporter had described him as "a big man from Indiana with flaming hair, intense blue eyes, and the muscles of his former profession, prize fighting."[123] In 1939, Sorrell and Willie Bioff clashed because Bioff had one of Sorrell's close friends almost beaten to death, and Sorrell reported this to the press. Bioff supposedly requested permission from John Roselli to have Sorrell killed, but Roselli kicked the request up the chain of command to Nitti. Nitti is then said to have decided to handle Sorrell personally as an example and supervised Sorrell's planned hit. This was to happen at the Taft Hotel at the corner of Hollywood and Vine where Sorrell was lured to a meeting.

Sorrell was waiting at the hotel as requested by an acquaintance and after having Nitti pointed out to him, supposedly gave the flyweight, likely physically maimed, and late middle-aged Chicago boss a severe beating in the hotel lobby. In other accounts of this or a similar incident, Sorrell beat off several goons sent by Bioff and declined to press charges with the comment, "Oh, no, I won the fight."[124] These encounters apparently resulted in Sorrell becoming a full-fledged union hero, as well as for some reason being branded a communist by FBI director J. Edgar Hoover. However, it seems doubtful that Nitti would have actually endured this thrashing, because

Sorrell surely would have been thwarted or even killed on the spot by Nitti's ever-present bodyguards, and such a slight to the Enforcer's image would surely have required the union-leader activist to be whacked sooner or later. Louis "Little New York" Campagna, Nitti's close associate, bodyguard, and a deadly hit man, was known to have been active in and about Hollywood at this time and surely would have paid Sorrell a personal call. This episode may simply be another case of an anecdote with some truthful basis of a personal confrontation that has been exaggerated over the years.

Hollywood Confidential

A remarkable collection of Hollywood celebrities is thought to have had some link to the varied activities and personalities connected to Nitti's Hollywood shakedown project. Johnny Roselli acted as the Outfit's official "talent scout" and sponsor for promising actresses and actors, and he claimed to have sponsored the early studio careers of eventual stars such as Wendy Barrie, Gary Cooper, Jimmy Durante, Clark Gable, Gary Grant, Jean Harlow, the Marx Brothers, Marie McDonald, and screen gangster George Raft. Raft had reportedly been a beer runner before he entered acting. In addition to being acquainted with Roselli, Raft was a personal friend of Ben Siegel and is supposed to have modeled his screen gangster mannerisms on Bugsy's. After his acting career faded, Raft worked in mob casinos in Havana and London.[125]

Murray Humphreys claimed that it was the Outfit's profits from Prohibition and its control of several major entertainment unions that had supported much of Joe Kennedy's investment successes in Hollywood. Kennedy's initial move into Holly-wood was to purchase a failing British film studio called Cole Studios that he reorganized into the Film Booking Offices of

America, or FBO Pictures, which manufactured a steady stream of low-cost, but profitable pictures. Kennedy then moved on toward vertical integration by purchasing the movie theaters where his films were shown to increase runs and profits.

Kennedy's motion-picture theaters were first established by obtaining a chain of old vaudeville houses owned by E. F. Albee and merging these with his own company to form the studio company RKO Studios. He also made a reputed failed attempt to obtain control of other movie theater chains, such as the small West Coast Pantages Theatre chain owned by Alex Pantages, through a trumped-up rape charge against Pantages. An innovative thinker well ahead of his time, Joe Kennedy used his mob-related profits to indulge in Wall Street insider trading to vastly inflate the value of his stock holdings, which he then dumped to recoup enormous profits.

Famed singer and actor Bing Crosby was said to have paid $10,000 to an unknown extortionist in Hollywood during the 1930s with Frank Nitti's team being a possible culprit according to FBI files.[126] Other suspects were Bugsy Siegel and small-time independent extortionists. In all, $50,000 was extorted from various stars by this particular scam including $1,600 from the mother of Ginger Rogers. Crosby was known to socialize with organized-crime figures, indulge in golfing with the Outfit's Machine Gun Jack McGurn (who packed a gun in his golf bag before Nitti had him whacked), had a penchant for women and booze, and was also an avid gambler as was his acting partner, Bob Hope.

Another respectable citizen linked to Nitti's Hollywood was the creator of the beloved children's cartoon characters Mickey Mouse and Donald Duck—Walt Disney. Little known to the general public, Disney was a "rabid Red-baiter and union-hater."[127] The right-wing, anticommunist Disney was also a secret informer for the Los Angeles office of the FBI, as well as a personal confidant of FBI director J. Edgar Hoover beginning in 1936.[128] During the great Walt Disney Strike of 1941, Bioff and Browne were major players in Disney's attempt to thwart union activities.[129] In June 1941, Disney requested Willie Bioff to call a meeting with leftist labor leader Herb Sorrell and other union strike leaders at Bioff's ranch just before Bioff was indicted by a federal grand jury on extortion charges. It was likely that Bioff and Browne were attempting to intimidate the union leaders on Disney's behalf, but the meeting never took place. Disney eventually negotiated and settled the strike to avoid a potentially disastrous public connection to Frank Nitti and the Outfit.[130]

Luciano Lucks Out

Factions of New York organized crime were also involved in the Hollywood shakedown operation, most notably Charles Luciano, Meyer Lansky, Louis Buchalter, and Benjamin Siegel. Siegel was based in Hollywood for many years.[131] Newark IATSE business agent Louis Kaufman was a direct link between Nitti and the New York Mafia families concerning the Hollywood rackets.[132] In addition to Chicago and New York, Miami and West Coast syndicates had a piece of the action because each controlled an element of the relevant entertainment labor unions.[133] While this relationship was originally intended to be cooperative, it eventually broke into outright warfare between the New York and Chicago gangs. Siegel began related operations at about the same time as Bioff and Browne and Roselli, specifically to control the movie extras' union.[134]

Charlie Luciano was nicknamed "Lucky" after surviving a gangland execution "one-way ride" in 1929. Luciano's early career centered around vice and white slavery and resulted in an extensive arrest record and prison terms. His longtime business associate and friend was Meyer Lansky. In 1936,

Luciano was convicted on sixty-two of ninety counts of compulsory prostitution and was sentenced to thirty to fifty years imprisonment. Paroled in 1946 on the condition that he be deported to his native Italy, he spent the remainder of his life there in exile, but still reportedly directed major criminal activities in the United States. He maintained that he assisted the Allied invasion of Sicily in World War II by providing key intelligence on his native turf. The FBI believed that he was involved with narcotics-smuggling operations until his death. He suffered a fatal heart attack in Italy in 1962.[135]

Luciano was at first not keen on joining Nitti, his sworn enemy, in the Hollywood racket. Initially Bioff and Browne cooperated with Luciano and Lansky so that they could be provided with access to New York-based entertainment moguls. Luciano may have attended a Miami meeting that Nitti called in March 1934 for the bosses from across America to be briefed by Johnny Roselli on the Hollywood entertainment shakedown project. Nitti may have also called a second follow-up national conference during the summer of 1934 that Luciano did not attend, having sent Louis "Lepke" Buchalter instead for East Coast representation.[136] By the mid-1930s, Luciano made a straightforward attempt to forcefully guarantee his perceived fair share of the Hollywood shakedown project and also to directly force Nitti and the Outfit out of Los Angeles. Luciano and Nitti were also supposedly competing for control of the lucrative Hollywood drug, vice, extortion, and gambling rackets. However, Nitti, with his heavyweights Roselli, Bioff, and Browne, had a clear advantage over Luciano in all organized-crime activities on the entire West Coast.[137]

At one point in September 1935, Luciano may have decided to use Buchalter and Siegel in their Murder Inc. capacity to liquidate Browne and Bioff, and perhaps even Nitti himself. Luciano probably desired Nitti's murder on a personal level, the enmity between the two bosses was so great. Specifically,

Luciano wanted his syndicate represented on the IATSE executive along with Bioff and Browne. There is a somewhat controversial claim that at a Chicago luncheon between the two bosses, Luciano had set up Nitti for a drive-by shooting. After Nitti barely escaped with his life, Luciano had to satisfy himself with placing his foot in a victory pose over the prone, but unharmed, Nitti. If true, Luciano and his men likely had a very difficult time in subsequently extricating themselves from Outfit territory. Like the claim of union leader Herb Sorrell, this story has the ring of a tall tale. However, regardless of the exact nature of the combat between the two Mafia bosses, the West Coast Outfit team under the wily Roselli proved just too much for Luciano to match, and his Los Angeles takeover efforts against Nitti ultimately failed.[138]

The name of mysteriously murdered movie actress Thelma Todd shall be forever linked with those of Luciano and Nitti during their struggle over Hollywood. A former Miss Massachusetts, Thelma Todd was found in a friend's garage slumped over the steering wheel of her Packard convertible by a hysterical maid on the morning of December 16, 1935. Known variously as "Hot Toddy" and "the Ice-cream Blonde," she was arguably the biggest sexpot of her day when she died at age twenty-nine.[139] While a grand jury handed up a verdict of death due to carbon-monoxide poisoning that had occurred in her closed garage with the car engine running, likely while she had passed out from being drunk, others thought her association with organized-crime figures had somehow led to her murder. There is no evidence that Nitti had ever had a personal relationship with her or a reason to have her eliminated, but his name kept coming up because of his ongoing feud with Luciano who was connected with Todd. The likely murder culprit was Luciano, with whom Todd had a widely known personal relationship. They supposedly once had the following revealing argument:

Todd: You'll open a gambling casino in my restaurant over my dead body!

Luciano: That can be arranged.[140]

The Beginning of the End

By the end of 1937, Joseph Schenck's commission deal with Willie Bioff had provided Bioff with large amounts of tax-free cash that he supplemented by other union-shakedown rackets and used to purchase an expensive ranch mansion that he called "Rancho Laurie" in the swank neighborhood of Westwood, a rare oriental art collection, and extravagant clothing and jewelry, all part of a deliberate effort to buy into the glamorous Hollywood lifestyle, much as Johnny Roselli had earlier become part and parcel of the film capital's scene.[141] Once when Bioff was providing a visiting Louis Campagna a tour of his estate, Lefty Louie became fascinated by its California-style water-sprinkler system, and he had a flustered Bioff buy him six hundred sprinklers, paid for by the IATSE, which were installed at his luxurious home in Chicago. Paul Ricca later ordered three hundred more through the IATSE after he saw Campagna's impressive system.[142]

There were other Hollywood perks for the Outfit. Bioff put Nick Circella on the official IATSE payroll, as was John Roselli, in 1936, both at the personal command of Nitti.[143] Former Chicago municipal judge, John H. Lyle, was to claim that relatives of Nitti and Tony Accardo were also on the film operators' union payroll drawing from $200 to $800 a week for no actual work. These nepotistic appointments included Joe Coscione, a Nitti chauffeur, and Frank Dolendi, a Nitti nephew, who were provided positions in the Chicago Local 110 of the IATSE. Nitti also placed Frank Maritote, Al Capone's brother-in-law, on the payroll of Chicago's Rialto burlesque theater for $200 a week for a nonexistent position.[144] In addition, Nitti had initially demanded half of George Browne's salary as president of IATSE because "he had a large family and heavy expenses," but this demand was rescinded much to the relief of the hard-drinking Browne.[145]

Bioff and Browne cash payments were usually made to Nitti through Circella or Campagna.[146] However, in one somewhat amusing incident related at the 1943 federal court trial of the Hollywood extortion case, a motion-picture projectionist working for New York IATSE business agent Louis Kaufman told how he was tasked in 1939 to deliver a "mystery package" to Nitti after being taken to a Chicago nightclub by an unknown blonde women and identifying himself to Nitti using the password "Number Ten."[147] However, the FBI maintained that at the time of this supposed rendezvous, Nitti was at Hot Springs, Arkansas, and the witness was subsequently charged with perjury and arrested on the witness stand.[148]

The newly formed Screen Actors Guild had faced down Louis B. Mayer in May 1937 and received official recognition as a result of a strike by most Hollywood actors, as well as by assistance from Bioff and Browne and the IATSE.[149] A year earlier, the Directors Guild of America had been formed and by 1940, had also seen official recognition. These new professional guilds did not take the Outfit's involvement with Hollywood as a given and resisted mob coercion.

In 1938, Nitti felt Bioff was becoming vulnerable and asked that he officially step down from his IATSE position although he continued to work with Browne behind the scenes with a salary.[150] Nick Circella was also required to resign as an official union representative and distance himself from operations in 1939.[151] The extortion-payment demands, or bribes depending upon how you looked at it, from the studios were also put on temporary hold, but resumed in 1941.[152]

The Outfit had planned to take over the Screen Actors Guild, Actors' Equity, and the so-called "4 A's" (Associated Actors and Artists of America) and put these under Charles "Cherry Nose" Gioe, who had become fascinated by the idea of mingling with movie stars and adopting the Hollywood lifestyle.[153] In this case, Nitti acted too late to consolidate previous gains, and actors simply did not want mob interference with their guilds even though Bioff and Browne had supported their formation. There was also some disagreement within the Outfit's high command on this plan as early as 1939 with Nitti in favor of absorbing Actors' Equity and Ricca opposed.[154] A president of the Screen Actors Guild (1935-1938 and 1946-1947), actor Robert Montgomery, was alerted to Bioff's extravagant lifestyle by his own network of studio informants and concluded that Bioff had been bribed by Joe Schenck.[155]

The Screen Actors Guild also had fears that Bioff, who was generally well known and liked by Hollywood stars impressed with the wage increases he had obtained for the unionized rank and file, could also organize its membership, possibly in affiliation with the IATSE. In 1938, Montgomery hired an ex-FBI agent to conduct a private investigation. He discovered Bioff's past as a Chicago pimp and perhaps more pertinent evidence of wrongdoings in the form of a copy of a check made from Joe Schenck to Bioff for $100,000, which Montgomery reported to the Internal Revenue Service. The IRS secretly indicted Schenck for tax evasion. Schenck claimed that he had just loaned the money to Bioff, but the IRS had sufficient evidence that the payoff was also a means of avoiding taxes, resulting in several counts of tax evasion for Schenck. He then agreed to cooperate with the government in return for lenient sentencing. Schenck outlined much of the basis of Frank Nitti's Hollywood shakedown scam before a federal grand jury and as a result, only served about a one-year jail sentence before returning to his Hollywood executive position. It was at this point that Nitti told Bioff to publicly resign as Browne's assistant for one full year, but to maintain his role behind the scenes. Things were now rapidly spinning out of control for Nitti.

By November 1939, a Chicago nationally syndicated news reporter, Westbrook Pegler, who was by some accounts a blatant anti-Semite, began investigating the rumored Hollywood-mob connections after he saw Bioff, who was Jewish, at a big Hollywood party. Pegler discovered Bioff's record of his vice-trade days in Chicago, in particular an unserved jail sentence for pandering, and questioned why he was now socializing in movie-star circles.[156] Pegler, who worked for the *New York World-Telegram*, would be awarded a 1941 Pulitzer Prize for his series of investigative reports on scandals within the ranks of organized labor.[157] Robert Montgomery passed on the results of his investigation to Pegler, who turned it into a journalistic crusade against Bioff and associates that spread to other important publications such as *Daily Variety*.[158] Pegler perhaps came very close to being hit by the Outfit, one member of which is said to have commented on the situation: "We've been Peglerized."[159]

Willie Bioff, George Browne, and Nick Circella were indicted by a federal grand jury in New York on September 9, 1941, although Circella had attempted to avoid capture.[160] Official investigations had revealed much of Bioff's role in Hollywood, and because he still had a 1922 Illinois state conviction for pandering, he was arrested and jailed for six months in early 1940. Following Bioff's completion of his sentence on this charge, he was indicted along with Browne for extortion. The discovery that Bioff owed $80,000 in back taxes was used by the authorities to further pressure him toward full cooperation. At the federal jury in New York, Bioff and Browne were both found guilty, but eventually ratted on the Outfit in an attempt at avoiding further hard time.[161]

Nick Circella's girlfriend, Estelle Carey, was found brutally tortured and torch-murdered in her burning apartment on February 2, 1943, and this may have been intended as a clear warning to Circella, Bioff, and Browne to not turn further state's evidence against Nitti and his senior associates. Carey may also have been the keeper of extorted funds that Nick Circella, who was by then in jail, had not shared with the rest of his Outfit partners.[162]

Circella promptly pleaded guilty rather than testifying any further, reportedly stoically stating, "I don't know nothing about nothing," and was sentenced to eight years in prison. The main suspect linked to Carey's highly publicized unsolved murder was Outfit hit man Marshall Caifano, possibly under Nitti's or Ricca's direct orders.[163] It was reported that Browne's wife and children were also threatened, but this and the Carey murder seemed to have had the opposite effect on Browne and Bioff, and they provided key evidence for the conviction of Nitti and the others.[164]

Browne and Bioff were each sentenced to an eight-year federal prison term for their crimes, but ended up only serving about three years at a federal prison farm in Arizona (rather than the more ball-and-chain-oriented Leavenworth) because of sentence reductions for turning state's evidence against Nitti and the other key Outfit members involved with the racket.[165] Bioff apparently enjoyed serving his sentence in Arizona so much he eventually settled down in this state.

The IATSE today makes the claim that its membership somehow rose up en masse against Bioff and Browne because of the 1936 illegal 2-percent tax paid on union dues, but there seems to be little to substantiate this claim, and a related legal suit filed by militant elements within the union membership on this issue had failed, although the 2-percent assessment was lifted in December 1937.[166] Union rank-and-file opposition to the perceived heavy-handedness of Bioff and Browne also led to the creation of a militant group of activist studio workers known as the "White Rats." The White Rats pressured for increased local autonomy and reform, but their militancy made them appear to some union members as undesirable as Bioff and Browne. In 1938, Browne had threatened a return to open-shop studio practices, and the militant movement soon lost momentum.[167]

Joe Schenck's and Bioff and Browne's testimonies resulted in a federal grand jury issuing subpoenas to all the major studio heads and eventually revealing the full extent of the involvement by organized-crime elements. In 1941, further testimony by Harry Warner provided the basis for federal indictments of Nitti, Browne, Bioff, Ricca, Circella, Gioe, Roselli, D'Andrea, and others for extortion and tax evasion issued by the U.S. District Court for the Southern District of New York. Willie Bioff soon became a full-fledged cooperating witness for the feds. It was now apparent that Nitti's decision to use Bioff and Browne for this major operation had been a key error in judgment for which he was to pay a very high price. The IATSE claims that:

> Browne himself testified briefly at the trial of these men, collapsing at the end due to a stomach ulcer. Bioff testified for nine days, and enjoyed every minute of it according to contemporary accounts of the trial.
>
> His testimony resulted in the conviction of the eight defendants. Despite the severity of their crimes, most of the men managed to negotiate their tax liabilities and win early parole. They all returned to their old profession of racketeering.[168]

ALL THE BIG studio heads were required to testify by 1941: Harry Warner, Albert Warner, Louis B. Mayer, Joseph Schenck, as well as their business representative in Hollywood, Pat Casey. These studio heads alone had likely funneled more than $1 million to Bioff, Browne, and Nitti over the previous six years. Testimonies were made of how they were all regularly required to provide wrapped bundles of tens of thousands of dollars in $100 bills as shakedown tribute at hotel meetings. Harry Warner testified that in addition to threatened strikes, he feared for his "bodily harm" and had retained armed guards for his personal protection. In addition, federal government wiretaps and eavesdropping under New York state law provided key evidence for the successful prosecution of this case.[169] Interestingly, at one point in 1941, "Major" Albert Warner revealed in court that he had retained Col. William J. ("Wild Bill") Donovan, father of the Office of Strategic Services (OSS), the predecessor of the modern CIA, for unknown duties related to the extortion case.[170]

Once Bioff turned stoolie from behind bars, he laid out the entire racket including dates, times, places, names of people, and specific dollar amounts, to U.S. Assistant Attorney Boris Kostelanetz in 1941 to avoid further prison time. A confessed perjurer, Bioff later claimed under oath that he had turned state witness and didn't want to be further imprisoned so he could help the war effort against the Axis powers following Pearl Harbor. The cold-blooded killer, Louis Buchalter, had been assigned to murder Bioff and managed to have himself arrested and placed in the same jail-cell tier as his target. Bioff got wind of the plot and had Kostelanetz move him to a secret location.[171]

Under pressure from his tax-violation charges in New York, Joe Schenck provided to Kostelanetz further important testimony concerning his involvement in the scheme and thereby frightened the other studio heads into doing the same.[172] In addition to Kostelanetz, the case was investigated and prosecuted by New York Assistant Attorney General Charles Carr, U.S. Assistant Attorney General Mathias F. Correa, and Elmer L. Irey from the Treasury Department, who it may be recalled had a major role in convicting Al Capone of income-tax evasion.[173]

Kostelanetz was never known for his leniency. Many years later at age eighty-seven, he still "count(ed) among his prosecutorial successes...the conviction of Capone's enforcer, Frank Nitti. And while it may be awhile ago, he can still remember how it was done when a witness's testimony could not be bought for any price—even, and especially, for a promise of leniency."[174] In actual fact, for his testimony, the federal government allowed Bioff to retain his illegal incomes from the previous decade and walk away from any further charges laid against him after serving a drastically reduced jail term.

Roselli took charge of the Outfit's Hollywood activities after Bioff's conviction, and Sam Giancana would take Roselli's place after he, in turn, was sent to prison.[175] Like Roselli and Bioff before him, Giancana would take a liking to the extravagant and high-profile Hollywood lifestyle to the distress of more traditional and secretive Mafia members.

As a result of this ongoing compilation of testimony, further indictments were made on March 18, 1943, for violations under Section 420a, 18 U.S. Code of the Anti-Racketeering Act and the Mail Fraud Statute for activities relating to the so-called union "Two Percent Assessment Fund," against Frank Nitti, Johnny Roselli, Paul Ricca, Louis Campagna, Charlie Gioe, Phil D'Andrea, Nick Circella (who had pleaded guilty before the trial), Louis Kaufman, Ralph Pierce, and Francis Maritote.[176] Roselli had joined the U.S. Army, but was discharged so he could face trial. Again, testifying witnesses would include major studio heads Louis B. Mayer, Harry and Albert Warner, Joseph Schenck, Nicholas Schenck, and others.[177] Defense lawyers and some cynics maintained that really what had occurred once the Hollywood extortion scam was underway amounted to bribes from the studio heads to Bioff and Browne to hold working conditions and related costs down for the production companies.[178] The cash amounts with which Bioff and Browne were provided often came from the padded personal expense accounts of these studio heads.[179] The Outfit had shown the studio heads how "everybody would make a lot of money" and had explained that it really wouldn't cost them anything because theaters would remain open and uninterrupted by strikes or labor disruptions.[180]

However, for their role as "labor-management consultants," Nitti and his senior associates were charged with the multimillion-dollar shakedown of four major motion-picture studios. The mail-fraud charges were later dropped, and none of the illegal tax fund was ever traced or recovered. During their trial that began October 5, 1943, the case was so overwhelming that none of the Outfit members charged took the stand in their own defense, and a December 23, 1943, verdict found them each guilty and sentenced to an average of ten years in federal prison, a $10,000 fine, and liability for back taxes owed. Ralph Pierce had his charges dropped during the trial and was acquitted due to lack of sufficient evidence. None of the extorted funds were ever recovered.[181]

This was the single worst blow to the Outfit in its history.[182] The lucrative shakedown operation had now become a total fiasco for Frank Nitti and his close associates, and the Outfit was in utter disarray with its top leadership about to be removed. However, Nitti never had to face his final indictment, stand trial in New York, or do prison time. Just after the March 1943 arraignment, Frank "the Enforcer" Nitti, according to popular wisdom, ended his own life by suicide in a Chicago train yard not too far from his home.

If Nitti did, indeed, commit suicide as a result of the failed Hollywood scam and a fear of spending the rest of his life in prison, he had, perhaps, acted in haste. By August 1947, Ricca, Gioe, Campagna, Roselli, D'Andrea, and the rest had been released on early parole following bribes totaling hundreds of thousands of dollar to parole boards, assorted officials, and politicians, as well as complicated legal maneuvers and "anonymous donations" to pay all their back taxes.

In what the Kefauver Committee later called "an awesome display of the syndicate power and ability to wield political influence," President Harry Truman's administration arranged for the early parole of the entire imprisoned Outfit leadership, also likely influenced by the fact that their attorney had been one of Truman's campaign managers.[183] Nitti's lieutenant, Murray Humphreys, is thought to have played no small role in these efforts, supposedly even visiting the prisoners at Leavenworth disguised as an associate attorney.[184] Some even claim that the attorney general of the United States, Tom C. Clark, was promised the next appointment to the Supreme Court for his cooperation on vacating charges and paroling the group.[185] It is also possible that Continental Press Service owner James A. Ragen Sr. was murdered in 1946 as part of an intimidation effort directed by Tony Accardo to secure the early release from prison of Paul Ricca and the others.[186]

After they were released, Gioe, Ricca, and Campagna were (unsuccessfully) warned by Chicago's mayor, Martin H. Kennelly, and Police Commissioner John C. Pendergast to stay out of the city, and an outraged public encouraged the formation of a congressional committee to investigate what was now considered a parole scandal, but all the men still remained free.[187] Paul Ricca had formally succeeded Nitti as the head of the Outfit for a short time before his sentencing and prison term and quietly returned to this position upon his release.[188] However, Ricca's reign was just in passing as a new breed of Outfit leaders with Sam Giancana at the fore were now coming into their own. Joe Schenck was pardoned by President Truman and later restored to his position at Twentieth Century Fox, while the IATSE's new president, Richard Walsh, was actually a holdover from the Bioff and Browne organization.[189]

A Continuing and Unique Relationship

Frank Nitti's extortion angle on the entertainment industry is even today too good an idea to completely die out. The "unholy alliance between the movies and the mob" is a volatile and violent longstanding relationship that likely still exists at various levels, employing the time-honored blend of manipulation, blackmail, staged union arbitration, and threatened or real violence.[190] This unique symbiotic relationship owes much to the personalities of key players on both sides. The "Chairman of the Board" Frank Sinatra was just one well-known star who was the cohort of various Mafia leaders including Sam Giancana and John Roselli, but Sinatra himself, although extremely well connected, was probably not a made man as some have long suspected.[191] Major entertainers are still often at the beck and call of their underworld financial backers and must perform when and where instructed. Today, the underworld is usually careful not to make one of Frank Nitti's major mistakes and takes pains to back up their actions with a careful legitimate paper trail that can be audited by the IRS. However, Nitti set the pattern more than anybody else for establishing this dysfunctional relationship.

7

Death of the Enforcer

There is no life but by death.
There is no vision but by faith.
> —inscription on Frank Nitti's
> family gravesite monument,
> attributed to Nitti himself

Nitti's Downfall

Popular wisdom has it that not wanting to take the rap and depressed over his personal life, Frank Nitti shortly after he was indicted on the Hollywood extortion case used his revolver to blow his brains out so he could avoid a long prison sentence. Some have said that he had previously threatened to take his own life if he ever had to go to prison again following his first prison stretch back in 1931-1932. It has also been proposed that Nitti was told by Paul Ricca to take the fall for the Outfit because he was the organization's major frontman and his conviction could take the heat off the other senior leadership members. The story goes that after Ricca, Louis Campagna, and other senior members of the Outfit were charged and faced jail time, they placed the blame squarely on Nitti as the originator of the failed, grandiose Hollywood scheme. This view has it that Ricca was by this time the Outfit's de-facto boss, and he had decided that it was now time for Nitti to culminate his role as a frontman by taking the heat for everybody.

In a March 18, 1943, sit-down meeting at Nitti's home with Ricca and others involved with the scheme shortly before the indictment was sent up, Ricca humiliated and demeaned Nitti, criticizing him for originating the scheme, entrusting stupid Willie Bioff with so important a responsibility, and letting the Outfit down in general. The police now had Nitti's home under constant observation and knew who attended this meeting.[1] Not unreasonably, it was argued that Nitti should never have let the Bioff and Browne team testify in court and should have had them hit as a precaution. Nitti was told that he should now be a "stand-up guy" and take the rap and do time for everyone the way Al Capone had for his income-tax evasion charge.[2] Capt. Dan Gilbert, chief investigator for the state's attorney's office, later claimed that Ricca, Campagna, and the others wanted Nitti to murder Bioff in a crowded courtroom in a kamikaze-type ploy to prevent him from testifying against them and to frighten Browne into silence.[3]

A dumbfounded Nitti tried to finesse his way out of the trap. His associates' hostile and cold reaction surprised him after all his years of loyal service to the mob. Nitti and Ricca had a serious argument in which Ricca basically threatened Nitti's life. Nitti hotly spouted legal precedents at Ricca and the others on why he could not be prosecuted alone on the indictment charges because they were all part of a conspiracy. Ricca stated, "Frank, you're asking for it." At this point, Nitti realized he was without support from the board of directors and was no longer the boss of the Outfit. He asked all those present to leave his house, held the front door open for them, and remained silent as his guests left—a serious breach of customary Sicilian hospitality between made men. He had in effect broken the Mafia code of honor that governed the Outfit.[4]

That same evening by some accounts, capo Tony Accardo phoned Frank Nitti and informed him that he was to meet Paul Ricca again the next afternoon at a restaurant in the Loop to further discuss the pending indictments. Nitti reportedly got very drunk the next day before the sit down with Ricca and Accardo, and they later claimed that he was almost incoherent during the meeting and had "the shakes." Nitti was by habit a teetotaler who rarely drank, and this behavior would certainly have been considered very unusual for him. It was also charged by Ricca that Nitti was skimming money from the top of the extorted gross takes from Hollywood before dispensing it to his other partners, a reason just by itself, if true, that would have resulted in Nitti facing death by the mob.[5] Charles Luciano had long complained that Nitti was devouring more than his fair share of the take from the Hollywood scam.[6] Ricca later claimed that Nitti's conduct during this last meeting disgusted him and that Nitti continued to drink after the others had left. Other accounts of Nitti's last day indicate that he had actually remained at home and gotten drunk there, and this seems to best match the timing of actual events.

Suicide?

On Friday, March 19, 1943, by about 2:00 P.M., an alienated and tormented Frank Nitti pondered a long stretch of prison time and unsuccessfully tried to think of ways out. A March 18 *Chicago Tribune* newspaper article had predicted his swift arrest.[7] In addition to Paul Ricca, Jake Guzik and Murray Humphreys could have pressured Nitti to take the pinch in prison, although Guzik and Humphreys never had much to do with or were charged on the Hollywood extortion case.[8] Nitti's attorney had telephoned the U.S. marshal's office and made arrangements to surrender Nitti after the indictment was made.

A month previously, Nitti had approached A. Bradley Eben, a former assistant U.S. Attorney, on the upcoming indictment and hired him as his legal representative. Nitti had several meetings with Eben and always claimed he was innocent of the charges and was just a legitimate businessman (likely referring to his ownership of coin-operated vending machines, racing facilities, and company stocks). Eben later said that they had made arrangements for Nitti to surrender after his arrest warrant was issued. On the day of the indictment, Eben called Nitti at his home before lunch, and Nitti promised to soon meet the lawyer at his office and did not appear to be distressed, but was not heard from again.[9]

Nitti had a quiet final lunch with Antoinette. At about 1:15 P.M., she left for Our Lady of Sorrows Church to a novena at his request and to do some shopping. It's likely that at this point, he began drink heavily again. When she returned at 3:30 P.M., her husband had left their home. She would never see him alive again.[10] After supposedly quickly drinking himself blind, Nitti packed his .32-caliber snub-nosed Colt revolver into his overcoat pocket and left his home for the North Riverside Illinois Central Railway Yard located about a mile from his Riverside neighborhood and across from the Municipal Tuberculosis Sanitarium.[11] Taking such an out-of-way stroll was not in itself unusual for him as his wife related that he frequently took long walks around the neighborhood. On his last day on earth, Nitti was dressed dapperly as usual, in a gray-checked three-piece suit, expensive shirt with button-down collar, flowered necktie, brown-plaid overcoat, a blue-and-maroon-plaid scarf, an expensive brown fedora, an expensive waterproof watch, black patent-leather shoes, rubbers over his shoes, and long woolen underwear because of the cold day.[12]

Railway workers William F. Seebauer, Lowell M. Barnett, and E. H. Moran reportedly saw Nitti walking drunkenly in front of an oncoming train and over to another track at around

3:00 P.M.[13] Some reports indicate that a matron from the nearby sanitarium was also a witness and others that only two railway men were witnesses. According to the railroaders, Nitti was staggering with a gun in one hand and a whiskey bottle in the other, and fell to the ground near a fence. Seebauer yelled at him, "Hi there, buddy!" quite unaware that the small drunken gentleman was Frank Nitti. Former FBI agent William F. Roemer Jr. describes the shocking events that followed:

> If there hadn't been two reputable witnesses who saw it, what happened next would be hard to believe...Frank Nitti, the proud successor to Al Capone, drew a pistol from his pocket, put the pistol to his head and shot himself...Nitti was the only major mob boss...to commit suicide. No wonder Paul Ricca had slowly, but apparently surely, assumed the top job, probably as early as fours years before, although there seemed to be no ceremony or other "official" act that made it apparent.[14]

SPECIFICALLY, SEEBAUER CLAIMED that he saw Frank Nitti pull the trigger of his weapon as he sat slumped amid winter-dry weeds against a six-foot-high chain-link fence near the railway right of way.[15] Several earlier shots had been heard that the railway men, both with families, first thought were directed at them, but then they discovered Nitti sitting on the ground by a railway fence and did not go near him because he was drunk with a firearm. In some accounts, two warning shots were fired by Nitti to attract attention from witnesses and prove that he had not been murdered, but had shot himself. Nitti then fired a third and final round into his head, the one Seebauer reported witnessing.[16]

The railway men quickly reported the fatality to the authorities, and the chief of police of North Riverside, Allen Rose, rushed to the scene where, along with a sergeant and several beat patrolmen, he found Nitti's corpse at the death site and immediately identified it as the syndicate leader. Rose removed his left glove and took the firearm from the corpse's hand. Nitti's body was then hastily loaded into the trunk of a sheriff's squad car with its back seat removed so the body's legs could squeeze in and was taken to the Cook County morgue.[17] The exact spot of Nitti's death was southeast of Twenty-second Street (Cermak Road) and Harlem Avenue. The site is located most recently between a Toys "R" Us and a Firestone store that were built during the early 1990s.[18] Today, Nitti's suicide site is part of a Chicago guided sightseeing package that includes the location of the Saint Valentine's Day Massacre and where bank robber John Dillinger died. Chicago's Twenty-second Street had been renamed Cermak Road in honor of the assassinated mayor.

The Cook County coroner's physician testified that one bullet through Frank Nitti's right temple had caused his death.[19] Other reports indicate that Nitti had died from a round that entered behind his right ear and lodged in the top of his skull and that he had pumped a total of two or even three shots *into his own head* with a nonautomatic revolver, clearly a very difficult feat even if some of the shots were near-misses, given the noise, shock, concussion, and muzzle blast effects produced by the close discharge of a firearm. A cylindered revolver requires considerable pressure by the shooter's trigger finger to fire the weapon and mechanically move the next round into position to be fired by yet more trigger-finger pressure, compared with a semiautomatic or automatic weapon that uses the expended gas-pressure recoil resulting from a fired round to do most of the work. The conventional explanation is that Nitti had fired three shots, the first two of which missed because of his drunken state and passed through his hat, making four holes, and only one bullet actually entered his skull.[20]

However, there are also persistent reports that he had been shot at least twice in the head: one shot had entered his right jaw and exited the top of his head, removing a lock of hair that protruded from a hole in the crown of his hat (as clearly shown in photos of the hat), and another round had entered behind his right ear and lodged in the top of his skull.[21] The exact nature of Nitti's fatal wounds remain unclear, but if two or three shots were, in fact, fired into his skull, this was clearly impossible in a suicide attempt using a nonautomatic weapon. The seemingly cavalier handling of his body at the death scene and subsequent sloppy autopsy and inquest raise further questions as to what had actually occurred on that cold March day.

The media had a sensation with Frank Nitti's death. Chicago newspaper headlines screamed: "Nitti Ends Life With Gun—Rail Men Witnesses—Gangster Kills Self After US Indictment" and "Gang Chief Dies By Gun After US Jury Charge—3 Trainmen Look On As Racketeer Fires 3 Shots." Morbid photos were produced of Nitti's body at the scene of his death and in the Cook County morgue. Other photos showed the revolver that was found beside Nitti, unspent shells, and one bullet slug removed from his head, as well as Nitti's brown fedora hat with a protruding portion of his scalp lodged in it by a bullet.

The IATSE, no friend of Nitti's, has recently claimed that when his body was found "The man who was supposedly a crime syndicate mastermind died with $1.14 in his pocket."[22] Other versions had it that he carried only $1.03 in change, but this actually had nothing to do with his financial situation, which apparently was quite secure.[23] Also in Nitti's pockets were his draft-registration card with the address of his Selbourne Road home in Riverside; an automobile driver's license that indicated an address at 1208 Lexington Street, which was said to be the current home of his in-laws by his first wife, the Rongas; a rosary enclosed in a small leather case in his vest pocket; a key;

a nail file and comb in a leather case; a twenty-seven-cent pack of cigarettes; and his wallet, which bore the name "Frank" in gold letters and held a gold pencil in one pocket.[24]

There has been much speculation as to the state of Frank Nitti's physical and mental health at the time of his death. Nitti may have been suffering from a severe depression caused by a lasting grief over the death of his first wife eighteen months earlier combined with the prospect of a lengthy stretch of prison time that was aggravated by his reportedly extremely claustrophobic personality. He often wore black following the death of Anna. However, any grief did not deter him from quickly remarrying a young woman.[25]

Other reports indicated that Nitti had stomach problems linked to a nervous disorder and ulcers, possibly a lasting effect of his near death at the hands of the Chicago police in 1932. Family members reported that he appeared to be nervous and ill tempered about four months prior to his death, and a brother-in-law reported that he "had been acting strangely lately, as if he did not have the full powers of his mind."[26] He may have had cancer, a lasting neurological illness caused by the 1932 shooting, or heart disease, according to varying sources.[27]

Whatever the exact nature of his mental and physical ailments, Nitti had been spending an increasing amount of time in hospitals during the last several years of his life. Existing photographs taken of Nitti between 1941 and 1943 indicate that he had significantly aged and exhibited signs of stress during the final several years of his life although he appeared far from being insane. The severity of the extortion charges also made it unlikely that he would receive any special treatment or early release from prison this time around. Nitti's despondence may have increased as a result of steadily losing influence with other organized-crime figures both within his organization such as Paul Ricca and outsiders such as Meyer Lansky and Charles Luciano.

However, there had been no official past records of Frank Nitti having suicidal tendencies or any hint of mental illness, and he had managed to endure his previous prison stretch, however unpalatable it was to him, and quickly resume his work upon release. He also seems to have been afflicted by a remarkable number of physical ailments for a man involved with so many fast-paced projects during the final years of his life. If he did commit suicide, he was the only Outfit boss known to have done so, and therefore his mental health would have been very questionable at the time. (Abner "Longie" Zwillman, an established boss of New Jersey's underworld from 1935 to 1959, and one of six bosses of Murder, Inc., is also believed to have committed suicide.)

Nitti loved his young son, Joseph, and it somehow seems inconceivable that he would have raised a gun to his head and left his boy alone under such sad circumstances. Likewise, he had just married a young wife. While Cook County officials were quick to close Nitti's case with a verdict of suicide, the FBI immediately conducted a more rigorous investigation without any apparent contradictory findings that were ever made public.[28] The official inquest into Nitti's death was held at the Cook County morgue, just the day after his death, on March 20, 1943, at 11:00 A.M. and was a perfunctory affair compared to most other investigations of major gang-related killings.[29] The coroner's toxicologist filed a report that Nitti's blood had contained .23 of 1 percent of alcohol, an amount sufficient for intoxication

The only friend and family member present at the inquest was Nitti's brother-in-law, who stated that Nitti was "retired" at the time of his death and was "temporarily insane." After brief deliberation, the official county verdict the following day was that Nitti had "committed suicide while temporarily insane and in a despondent frame of mind." However, there was perhaps a small hint of something amiss in the photos of Nitti's body in the morgue that revealed he had worn long underwear against the chill of that cold March day, an interesting choice for a man who had supposedly chosen the easy way out and was irrational and did not care about his health any longer.

The strange circumstances and aftermath of Frank Nitti's death are such that murder cannot be completely ruled out. Simple logic and motive point to the ambitious Paul Ricca as a potential perpetrator. Herb Sorrell, Nitti's erstwhile Hollywood union boxing opponent, maintained that he had known all along that Nitti was going to be eliminated because he "knew too much about the big time Hollywood producers to let him testify" in court, and he also expressed feigned amazement that Nitti had supposedly "shot himself twice in the head."[30] Some say that it has "been an open secret in mob circles for 50 years that he was taken out" and that Nitti simply would not have committed suicide because he was an "honorable man" and "worshiped his adoptive son." Others have come to the conclusion that to prevent Nitti from turning state's evidence against Ricca and the others, Nitti was the victim of a hit at close range that was conveniently classified as a suicide.[31] There are other rumors that Nitti had been murdered and his body found in a ditch.[32]

Crime-story author and historian Max Allan Collins has theorized after investigating the location of Nitti's death that the terrain, which at that time had tall grasses, scrub, and trees, would have been very suitable as an assassination site.[33] When one considers the extent of the disinformation that the Outfit orchestrated around the murder of Mayor Anton Cermak and possibly that of President John F. Kennedy, it is, indeed, possible that Nitti's suicide was an elaborate fabrication.

Financial Aftermath

The vultures were not satisfied just with Frank Nitti's death. Nitti had the same problem that has plagued so many of his senior underworld colleagues—while they were able to amass large fortunes as a result of their illegal enterprises, these monetary gains were often more ephemeral than tangible and seemingly hard to maintain over the long term even when successfully laundered. Soon following his death, an inventory filed in Chicago probate court claimed that Nitti's estate was valued at a somewhat low $74,000.[34] By 1948, a congressional committee was still attempting to determine the exact amount Nitti had profited from during the Hollywood extortion scandal and was liable to taxation plus interest and penalties, but while seeking up to $400,000 from his heirs, had at this point only found $100,000 of his fortune to levy and through the IRS placed a lien against his estate to the amount of $200,000.[35]

In 1949, a federal court further investigated Nitti's estate left to his widow and son, and while it concluded that Hollywood studio heads had willfully complied with the Outfit, the burden of guilt fell upon the underworld boss and his key associates. The extortion cash was never traced, recovered, or taxed.[36] The full extent of Nitti's fortune and its dispersal was never really determined, and the amounts pursued by the government seemed ridiculously underestimated.[37]

There are, however, some interesting clues. Frank Nitti's supposed old friend, Alex Louis Greenberg, had borrowed large sums of money from him without security, at one time totaling $110,000, of which he paid back $65,000 to Nitti. This money was assumed by Nitti to have been used for high-interest loansharking. After Nitti's death, Greenberg tried to avoid repaying the balance of this loan and interest to Nitti's widow and son. In addition, Nitti's widow claimed that her husband had been forwarding cash and securities in trust to Greenberg from 1919 to just before his death that totaled $2 million that was intended as a trust fund for Nitti's son. A year and a half after Nitti's death, Greenberg provided only a further $64,000 to the Nitti estate and $100,000 to Joseph's trust. Greenberg had supposedly talked Nitti's apparently naive widow, who was now the boy's legal guardian, into signing releases that confirmed that all legal claims for the estate and trust had been satisfied. Nitti's 1931 prison record indicated that he had not taken out life insurance for the protection of his family in the case of death, and this may also have been the case up to his death in 1943.

While now protected by the law, this did not afford Greenberg protection from the Outfit, which can often be very patient when it comes to settling such matters. On December 8, 1955, Greenberg and his wife, Pearl, after having dinner at the Crystal Dome Hickory Pit at 2724 South Union Avenue, were on their way back to their car when Lou Greenberg was calmly killed by two men with .38-caliber revolvers.[38] Supposedly only a few days earlier, Greenberg had openly disagreed with syndicate associates of Frank Nitti over the inheritance and estate shortfalls now that Nitti's son was twenty-one, and it was widely felt that Greenberg should pay up the balance owed. Greenberg had refused to pay any more money, and this likely resulted in his murder. Greenberg left an estate of more than $3.3 million, and a cousin of Frank Nitti had supposedly remarked at Greenberg's funeral "Now he's the richest son of a bitch in hell."[39] Others believe that he was liquidated as part of Sam Giancana's consolidation of power.[40] Greenberg had also been involved with Nitti's Hollywood extortion scheme and was a government witness in the resulting trial. Ralph Pierce had reportedly voiced a threat to kill Greenberg during the 1943 trial.[41]

Greenberg's wife and other family members, possibly fearing further reprisals, maintained that his death was just the result of a common holdup.[42] Nitti's widow filed a suit against Greenberg's estate for more than $2 million during the late 1950s, and some believe she was at least partially successful.[43] The Department of Justice on October 31, 1952, posthumously canceled Frank Nitti's naturalization certificate because of noncollectible Internal Revenue taxes and the belief that Nitti had held stocks under a fictitious name.

Murray Humphreys and Johnny Patton managed a syndicate family-pension fund for Nitti's widow, as well as for the widows of other deceased high-ranking Outfit members such as Al Capone and Jake Guzik, and one for the special case of Virginia Hill. Nitti's second wife received more than $30,000 per year for life.[44]

Whatever Happened To...?

Nitti's old mentor, Al Capone, although suffering for many years from a then-incurable disease, outlasted him. Capone died January 25, 1947, from complications that included a stroke and pneumonia in the relative peace of his Palm Island, Miami, home, still with his Irish-American wife, Mae, who remained faithful till the end. Capone had never publicly returned to Chicago following his release from prison, and some said that in his final years, he had the mind of a young child. Capone claimed during a 1939 interview with the FBI just prior to his release from prison that he had accompanied boxer Jack Dempsey to Randolph Hearst's Santa Monica beach residence where he "witnessed various sexual activities which disgusted him." Capone also said that his son, Sonny, was a lawyer who had graduated from Notre Dame (untrue, although Sonny had apparently attended there briefly before his father's past caught up with him) and that with his brother, Ralph, they were going to establish major legitimate businesses in Florida following his release (also untrue). It was the opinion of the FBI agent conducting this interview that Capone's mental processes were, indeed, quite impaired.[45]

When under questioning in court, Jake Guzik was asked if Al Capone was still connected to Chicago gambling activity, and Guzik seemed sincere when he replied, "I don't think Capone is connected with anything in the world. . . . I think he is crazy."[46] The life of Al's only child, Albert Francis "Sonny" Capone, appeared to steadily decline in later years as first his restaurant business and then his marriage in Miami faltered. At one point, he was arrested for shoplifting. He eventually changed his surname to Brown, lived an obscure life in Florida, and finally passed away in Florida in 2004—certainly not the glowing life his father, who by all accounts loved him greatly, had intended.

Mae continued to live a modest life in Florida into her old age, the Palm Island estate long ago sold, until she passed away in 1986. Al's brother, Ralph, had a sad remaining life with many family problems and died, virtually ignored by the Outfit, in 1974. None of the media fame that later was derived from Al Capone's exploits and infamy, and none of the vast fortune that many claimed he had accumulated during Prohibition, seemed to have provided lasting benefit to any of those most dear to him.

As recounted, Nitti's close associates in the Hollywood extortion case were all released on early parole, which had resulted in a public uproar and political scandal. Paul Ricca became the new boss of the Outfit for a short time before his prison sentence. When Ricca was released in 1947, he became boss again for a few more years and then a senior adviser to the Outfit under Tony Accardo. Ricca had several more brushes with the law for past crimes that led to his being imprisoned again for twenty-seven months and almost deported to Italy. Ricca died in 1972 in his impressive Chicago mansion from natural causes.

Louis Campagna, like Ricca, had lost much of his former zest for the more overt aspects of criminality upon his release from prison and like Ricca, had always feared that his parole would be revoked. Campagna died in 1955 from a heart attack

while fishing off the coast of Florida.[47] The loyal Frankie Rio
had passed away many years earlier of natural causes while
Johnny Roselli's cryptic career and gruesome fate has already
been described as far as the available facts will permit. Charles
Gioe was liquidated in Chicago by the Outfit in 1954, as was
Al Capone's brother-in-law, Francis Maritote, both apparently
victims of an ongoing leadership struggle. Phil D'Andrea passed
away from a heart ailment in Riverside, California, in 1952 at
age sixty-nine.[48] Accardo would be pushed onto the sidelines
by the up-and-coming Sam Giancana, although he fancied
himself as the elder statesman of the Outfit until his death in
1992, to all intents and purposes still untouched by the law.

The corpulent Jake Guzik died of a heart attack in 1956 while
dining in his favorite restaurant, the St. Hubert's Grill. Murray Humphreys, who was the majority owner of this exclusive
Chicago establishment, supposedly did not want Guzik's body
to be found there because of the resulting bad publicity, so
he had it brought to Guzik's home and dropped off in front
of his stunned wife.[49] After Nitti's death, some believed that
Guzik had become the Outfit's new de-facto boss. In fact, he
became increasingly marginalized and at one point in 1946,
was even supposedly kidnapped for up to $100,000 ransom,
but more likely had simply been humiliated to be put in place
by his own syndicate.[50]

In 1965, Murray Humphreys also died of a heart attack
shortly after being rousted during an arrest by the FBI. With
the deaths of Guzik and Humphreys, the Outfit essentially lost
a lot of the somewhat unique multiethnic, equal-opportunity
character that had obviously been a point of pride for both
Frank Nitti and Al Capone and which has never been restored
to this day. None of Nitti's successors ever really matched his
intelligence and vision, and, except for short-lived efforts by
Sam Giancana, the Outfit was not fated to take on the national
role to which he had aspired for it.

FBI records indicate that Benjamin Siegel had made a determined effort during the next few years following Nitti's death to take over significant Outfit activities, but naught came of this attempt. He then focused his considerable skills on the construction of the Flamingo Hotel and Casino and the creation of the Las Vegas gambling mecca until his own murder in 1947, which was likely ordered by his friend, Meyer Lansky.[51] Bugsy's friend, Louis Buchalter, was executed at Sing Sing State Prison in March 1944 for murder. Boss of Bosses Charles Luciano was exiled to Italy in 1946 where he died in 1962 of a heart attack, supposedly still working on big-time heroin deals. The wise Meyer Lansky died in Miami of lung cancer in 1982 with estimated financial holdings of $400 million (but some sources indicate he lived like a pauper) and having never spent time in prison. He was denied the right to live in his beloved Israel.

The fate of Bioff and Browne was fitting from the syndicate's perspective. Louis Campagna is thought to have warned Willie Bioff in jail during 1940 that he faced a death sentence if he turned stool pigeon in the Hollywood extortion case trial: "There ain't no resignations in this Outfit. Whoever quits us, he quits feet first." Campagna also said to Bioff in court after he was sentenced to prison the fateful words, "Our boys can wait a long time."[52] After they were paroled, Browne and Bioff quickly disappeared from sight. In 1948, they briefly entered the limelight again when they were called upon by federal authorities to repeat their Hollywood extortion case testimony during an inquest on taxes due from Frank Nitti's estate.

Bioff eventually settled in Phoenix as part of the federal Witness Protection Program under the assumed name of William Nelson, but on November 4, 1955, he was blown up in his home's driveway by a dynamite bomb attached to the starter of his pick-up truck in an explosion that was heard for miles and left debris scattered for blocks. The only means of his subsequent identification was a gold ring that was recovered on a detached finger. Prior to his death Bioff, who could just not resist the lure of the syndicate and mingling with the rich and famous, had become the manager of the Riviera Hotel in Las Vegas and fast friends with Senator Barry Goldwater.[53] Bioff's death was likely ordered by Sam Giancana, but was never officially solved.[54] Some believe that Bioff had amassed as much as $6.5 million from the 2-percent tax on Hollywood union dues and other extortion angles.[55]

The exact fate of George Browne is unknown as he completely faded into obscurity, possibly to a farm somewhere in Illinois or Wisconsin where some believe he quietly drank himself to a lonely death in the late 1950s.[56]

Nick Circella was deported to South America and may have gotten away with more of the extortion money that he didn't share with Nitti and the others, and for which his girlfriend, Estelle Carey, had likely been murdered. He is supposed to have lived in Argentina for a while and then in Mexico where he operated a score of shrimp-fishing boats.[57] As it turned out, many of those involved with Nitti's Hollywood extortion racket had been secretly skimming away portions of the extorted funds quietly behind each other's backs.

George Moran had fled Chicago after he had too close of a call at the Saint Valentine's Day Massacre. He turned to a life of petty crime and served a ten-year sentence in Leavenworth for a string of bank robberies. He died there of cancer in 1957. Bugs was buried in a pauper's grave.

As we have seen, Eliot Ness died essentially a failed man, but in death would later obtain the lasting heroic stature that had eluded him in life. IRS hotshot Elmer L. Irey made an enemy of President Harry S Truman when he alleged that the new president was connected to the mob. Irey was quickly put out to pasture with his well-earned federal pension and lived in obscurity for the twilight years of his life. Melvin Purvis, the famed FBI G-man, after making an enemy of his jealous, publicity-hungry boss, J. Edgar Hoover, left the FBI, but his career faltered and never really recovered. Purvis is believed to have died by his own hand in 1960, although some have labeled his death the result of a gun accident.

Hoover was director of the FBI for forty-eight years until his death in 1972 at age seventy-seven. He left virtually his entire estate to his assistant director and longtime companion, Clyde Tolson, who took control of Hoover's vast secret file system that included details on the sexual lives of many famous politicians and movie stars. Tolson died in 1975 and was buried next to Hoover at the Congressional Cemetery in Washington, the quintessential gay couple.

A Tragic End

Whether his death was by suicide or murder, Frank Nitti's demise was tragic at a personal level to his family and friends and remains a mystery to this day. He was "a thinking man's gangster whose emotional problems eventually overwhelmed him."[58] Just fifty-seven, he left behind his young grieving second wife, Antoinette, and his nine-year-old son, Joseph, whom he had adopted with his deceased first wife, Anna. The death came as a total surprise to Nitti's recent bride. They had just bought their home, and Nitti had made extensive renovations that he had personally planned. She provided a grief-filled, near-hysterical interview to the press in her housecoat shortly after Nitti's death:

> The first I knew of what had happened was when they [the police] came and told me he was dead. I knew something was wrong. There were always strange men watching the house. He knew some-

thing was up, too. Frank wasn't well—it was his stomach, nerves I think. They were always after him. They wouldn't let him alone. They made him do this. But why did he do this to me? He didn't have any time to do anything wrong. I was with him all the time. All the time. It's a dirty shame that they persecuted him. He was a good man. He was too good to live. Now leave me alone.[59]

THE NITTIS' UNLISTED home telephone constantly rang with calls from friends, as well as reporters seeking stories. His widow refused to speak of their son or Nitti's business activities. How different was the reality of Nitti's demise and its sad aftermath on his loved ones compared to Hollywood's later harsh fictitious portrayals of his dispatch by Eliot Ness.

Frank Nitti's funeral, unlike the public spectacles of many other Chicago gangsters, was a private affair. His family plot is in Chicago's Mount Carmel Cemetery at 1400 South Wolf Road, Hillside, Cook County, Illinois. Mount Carmel is known to some, perhaps unkindly, as Chicago's "Boot Hill" for gangsters. His gravesite plot can be found at Section 32 of the cemetery after entering from Roosevelt Road and taking a left turn. There he rests to this day along with some friends and many foes he helped bury over the years: Al Capone, Sam Giancana, Tony Accardo, Dion O'Banion, the Genna brothers, Hymie Weiss, Roger Touhy, Jack McGurn, to name just a few.

Frank Nitti's gravestone inscriptions read, "Father, Frank Nitto, 1886-1943, Rest in Peace" and "There is no life except by death. There is no vision but by faith." Frank Nitti's friends and foes alike perhaps thought that these epitaphs would be the last ever heard about the legendary gangster boss who had such a sad final chapter. As it turned out, they were all very wrong because the memory of Nitti within fifteen years would now progress from a legendary to a mythical status.

8

Rebirth on Film

Eliot Ness: You son of a bitch, you killed my friend.
Frank Nitti: He died like a pig.
Eliot Ness: What did you say?
Frank Nitti: I said that your friend died
*   screaming like a stuck Irish pig. Now you*
*   think about that when I beat the rap.*
        —Billy Drago as a psychopathic
        Frank Nitti in Brian De Palma's
        The Untouchables (1987)

The Most Glamorized Gangster in History?

In the years following his death, the legacy of Frank Nitti would spark a long-lasting fame and popularity that is unique for an underworld figure. The publicity-shunning Nitti himself would likely have been the most confused observer of all and could only have been puzzled and amazed at the wildly varying characterizations that would come to use his name.

It is true that many underworld gangsters and popular outlaws have had movies and television-series episodes produced that were based upon their criminal exploits, these including Al Capone, John Dillinger, Meyer Lansky, Bonnie and Clyde, and more recently John Gotti. However, Frank Nitti is arguably the most media-glamorized gangster in history with his character having appeared in more television-series episodes and motion pictures than any other specific modern gangster. While some crime historians may debate the strength of Nitti's final leadership hold on the Outfit, how many of today's moviegoers are familiar with Paul "the Waiter" Ricca?

First TV Series

This situation came about when Frank Nitti became a recurring staple character in the original 1950s-1960s television series of *The Untouchables* while Scarface Al Capone was only in the pilot episodes and the spin-off theatrical movie, *The Scarface Gang* and briefly in a few other episodes of the series. This was just as well since Neville Brand's portrayal of Al Capone was somewhat less than convincing. In the 1993-1994 remake of the series, Nitti was again a regular along with Capone. When total episodes featured in both series are combined, Nitti simply came ahead of Big Al. Other criminals featured in both series, such as George "Bugs" Moran and Charles "Lucky" Luciano, were only provided fleeting exposure compared to Nitti although Frankie Rio had excellent character development in the more recent series.

Nitti became perceived by the television-viewing public as Eliot Ness's major nemesis although, as has already been discussed, this is historically inaccurate. The two television series of *The Untouchables* were among the longest-running criminal-police action series dedicated to a specific historical era, and both developed a large viewing audience and a cult status for gangster buffs. Ness was pitted against everyone from John Dillinger to Ma Barker, criminals that he had nothing to do with in real life.[1] While dramatic fiction, the presentation of each episode of the original series was documentarylike, so much so that many viewers apparently considered it to be historical fact.

Eliot Ness first documented his adventures for the general public in 1957 when he wrote *The Untouchables* with his ghost-writer Oscar Fraley. Ness died unexpectedly in 1957 shortly before the book was released. Initial sales were disappointing, but it did catch the attention of television producer Desi Arnaz, the then-husband of Lucille Ball. Arnaz was most famous for his portrayal of bandleader Ricky Ricardo on the *I Love Lucy* show.[2]

Arnaz's production company, Desilu Productions, was affiliated with the CBS television network, and it produced a dramatic anthology series called *Desilu Playhouse* for the 1958 and 1959 seasons. The series would later run on ABC after this network won an intense bidding war. Arnaz decided to use a fictionalized two-part version of *The Untouchables* as an entrée for the anthology series. The first two episodes of *The Untouchables* aired in March and April 1959 with Robert Stack as Eliot Ness and Bruce Gordon as Frank Nitti, roles that were to continue throughout the series.

Real-life Capone- and Nitti-era newspaper gossip columnist and radio personality Walter Winchell narrated the series for a touch of quasi-documentary legitimacy, his voice in perfect counterpoint for the firing of the ubiquitous Tommy gun. At the time of the initial episodes of the series, Winchell still had a nationwide radio show and a syndicated newspaper column, and his unique style and voice had broad public recognition. Strangely, Winchell during the Senator Joe McCarthy Communist-witch hearings made political accusations against Lucille Ball.

In addition to the 1962 theatrical release of *The Scarface Mob* made from the two pilot episodes, another movie spun off from the series, *Alcatraz Express* (1962), also featuring Bruce Gordon in his role as Frank Nitti. The television series ran from October 15, 1959, to September 10, 1963, with a total of 118 episodes, in which Gordon acted in at least thirty-one starring as Nitti. Among the great guest stars were Robert Redford, Ed Asner, Peter Falk, Frank Sutton, Barbara Stanwyck, Dane Clark, Nehemiah Persoff, William Bendix, Lloyd Nolan, and Clu Gulager. The director for the entire series was Walter Grauman and the executive producers were Quinn Martin, Jerry Thorpe, and Leonard Freeman.

Frank Nitti rather than Al Capone was Eliot Ness's main adversary in the original series because of some very interesting personal history from Desi Arnaz's youth. Arnaz had attended high school in Miami and became close friends with Al Capone's son, Albert Francis Capone, known to most people as Sonny. When the new series was announced and was to be based upon his father's exploits, Sonny Capone maintained that he and his mother "have been bearing this cross all these years...[and] it's high time that we got a little peace."[3] Sonny contacted Arnaz and unsuccessfully attempted to persuade him to give up on the series.[4] Al Capone's widow, Mae, instigated the first of many lawsuits against the series, in one instance for $1 million, and Scarface's role in the series was de-emphasized as a result of this litigation. Some of Mae and Sonny Capone's outrage may have been due to the show using Al Capone's name and likeness without financial reimbursement for his heirs. Sonny Capone also unsuccessfully filed suit against Desilu Productions for defamation.[5]

Frank Nitti's character, who had been killed off rather early on in the series at the end of the "The Frank Nitti Story" episode, had to be revived for new episodes with a typical Walter Winchell staccato explanation to the effect "that while he would be killed in the future, he was now very much alive," which could be allowed in the series because its episodes were not in chronological order.

The reaction of actual Outfit veterans to *The Untouchables* is said to have ranged from rage, frustration at blatant inaccuracies, to laughing it off as their favorite "comedy series."

Arnaz did receive crank and threatening letters and calls concerning the series. In 1962, he had planned to take a crew to Chicago to film exterior shots, but this had to be canceled due to mob threats. Arnaz also claimed he was the target of mob hit men Jimmy "the Weasel" Fratianno and Frank "Bomp" Bompensiero on the order of Sam Giancana because of the "bad publicity" and disrespect the series gave to the memories of Nitti and Capone. However, the assassination effort was half-hearted, and nothing ever came of it likely because Giancana was known to have frequent mood swings. Arnaz probably did come close to being "clipped."[6]

The series was noir in atmosphere, filmed mostly inside studios in black and white, and somewhat gritty and claustrophobic in style, which was mostly a result of the stylistic influence of Quinn Martin.[7] The villains often appeared more human than the somewhat lifeless and somber Ness and his team. The series had great theme music by Walter Hatch and Nelson Riddle, which the theatrical release, *The Scarface Gang*, greatly suffered from not using. The series used a jagged, fusion-jazz theme song that became its well-recognized anthem of sort.

Some consider it to be one of the most violent television shows of all times, even by today's standards, because of the sheer number of shootings, knifings, bombings, corpses hanging in meat lockers, etc. However, most of the series' violence was presented in an effective style that still left much to the viewer's imagination. Nevertheless, it became the target of three Congressional investigations—the Senate Subcommittee on Violence on Television, the Subcommittee on Juvenile Delinquency, and the Subcommittee on Communications. It was also denounced by the Federal Communications Commission in 1961.[8]

In many respects, the series was a morality play in which the bad guys, best personified by Nitti, always lost to the good guys personified by Ness. It spawned spin-offs such as comic books, board games, and bubble-gum trading cards. Ness and Fraley's book finally took off in sales resulting in Fraley cashing in on the success by writing two more, *4 Against the Mob* (1961) and *The Last of the Untouchables* (1962).[9] While the original television series took liberties with history, it was to be outdone by a big-screen movie successor.

The series was a hit, so to speak, with the general public, but was viewed by the National Italian-American League to Combat Anti-Defamation as being anti-Italian for portraying the majority of its gangsters as Italian-accented, spaghetti-slurping "Goombah of the Week" stereotypes. The league's pressure resulted in a March 17, 1961, agreement with ABC that there would be no more semifictitious Italian-American wise guys and more emphasis was paid to positive contributions and roles for Italian-Americans. The series made little or no effort to stick to historical facts after the initial two-part pilot episodes that saw Al Capone vanquished and sent to prison. In fact, the further the series progressed, the more it varied from historical fact, pitting Ness against criminals he had nothing even remotely to do with in real life such as assorted bank robbers, counterfeiters, kidnappers, interstate truck hijackers, narcotics traffickers, postal-train robbers, white slavers, and Nazi spies.

Various FBI officials including J. Edgar Hoover complained about their real-life cases being credited to an increasingly fictionalized Ness. This all occurred in an apparently compressed and random chronology that often did not provide exact dates, but was in an atmosphere that consistently appeared to be very 1930ish. For example, in the episode "The Frank Nitti Story," the entire Hollywood extortion scam and its aftermath were portrayed in a homogenized version of history including a finale with Nitti's supposed death by being run over by a Chicago subway train while being pursued by Ness amid much gunfire, all in an unspecified timeframe that appears to be circa 1930 rather than the early 1940s when the actual, substantially different events occurred. While the real-life Ness had very little to do with the real-life Nitti (and certainly had absolutely nothing to do with his death), throughout the life of the series, they were comic book-like archenemies to the bitter end. While Ness always won, Nitti always gave him a good run for the money and never gave up.

Nitti was played by Bruce Gordon, a character actor born in Fitchburg, Massachusetts, on February 1, 1916. During the series, he looked more like Senator Joe McCarthy than the real Frank Nitti and was certainly a much larger man than the actual gangster although the two Nittis were possibly more alike in spirit than is commonly acknowledged by many contemporary Nitti revisionists. Gordon portrayed Nitti for the original pilot episodes with a somewhat hoaxy Italian accent ("Whatsa matter wid you? I paya you to sella beer, notta think!"), but thankfully substituted this for a more realistic Brooklyn one for the balance of the series.

Nitti in this series was portrayed as a bachelor living in a suite that was part of his "Club Montmartre" speakeasy (actually a Cicero café run by Ralph Capone) and whose lady friends were typical showgirl floozies. This Nitti was a rough-and-tough man who drank heavily, but like his boys, "not on the job." His wardrobe of loud pinstriped suits and an imposing homburg set a standard of sorts for Hollywood portrayals of gangsters. Gordon provided a very gutsy and inspired, if somewhat historically inaccurate, portrayal of the Enforcer and, for good or bad, has become associated by a large segment of the viewing public as its image of Nitti, just as Robert Stack (who died at age eighty-four on May 15, 2003) was the personification of Ness.

Throughout the series, Gordon portrayed his version of Frank Nitti as a blustering Damon Runyonesque character who was also, like the real-life Nitti, an astute businessman and who on rare occasions let some of the original's human sensitivities show through.[10] An example of the latter was portrayed in the episode "Snowball" when Nitti is nonplussed by an up-and-coming college-graduate criminal played by a young Robert Redford who incorrectly thinks that the uncouth Nitti does not know the meaning of the word "chameleon." Of course, the real-life Nitti preferred the conversation of intelligent and well-educated people, and would have had no qualms about simply hiring the college boy for his staff, just as he actually did with Saul Alinsky. Gordon's Nitti had occasional near-sociopathic propensities, but was also sometimes played for laughs, particularly in the final season of the show. George Eckstein, a casting director and writer for the show, said of Gordon:

> Bruce was wonderful, Bruce was great to write for, because he brought so much energy, and vitality, and excitement to the screen. He was a little "over the top" sometimes, but always entertainingly so.[11]

DOROTHY BROWN WAS the ABC "head of continuity acceptance" (i.e. censorship), and was a big supporter of Gordon's Nitti, likely because of the dark humor and high level of testosterone he brought to the series. Gordon's contract had stipulated that he would appear in at least four episodes a season, but he ended up doing many more.[12]

Gordon also carried the Frank Nitti role and character outside of *The Untouchables* television series and its spin-off movies. He starred in a period Gillette safety-razor commercial in which he is shaving, and then in his best Nitti tough-guy voice said, "I'm clean! Honest, I'm clean!" A March 14, 1966, episode of *The Lucy Show* called "Lucy, the Gun Moll" starred Lucille Ball, Bruce Gordon as a "Big Nick" version of Nitti, Robert Stack as Eliot Ness, and Walter Winchell in his usual narrating role. Gordon played the same comic-gangster role in other episodes of *Here's Lucy.*

Years later, a very similar version of this type of skit was tried on *Saturday Night Live,* but minus Gordon it just wasn't the same. In the 1966-1967 CBS sitcom *Run, Buddy, Run,* Gordon again packaged a comedy version of his Nitti character as a gangster known as Mr. Devere (a.k.a. "Mr. D."). Such comic adaptations were natural because of the evolution of Gordon's portrayal of Nitti in the final year of *The Untouchables* into the wisecracking, off-the-cuff gangster who was a major attraction of the series for many viewers. Gordon became known to many as Bruce "Frank Nitti" Gordon. He reportedly ran a restaurant in Kansas City, Missouri, known as "Frank Nitti's Place," and Robert Stack had jokingly threatened to put together a raiding team of the old Untouchables. The restaurant is supposed to have burned down some years later. Bruce Gordon retired from acting in the 1980s. By 2007, in his nineties, he was reported living in Santa Fe, New Mexico, with his wife Marla.

Some particularly outstanding episodes starring Bruce Gordon as Nitti remain television classics and are particularly memorable for story lines and for the young actors who co-starred with Gordon and would someday become Hollywood stars. "The Frank Nitti Story" aired on April 28, 1960, at the end of the series' first season and was a very loose interpretation of the Hollywood extortion case. It portrayed Nitti as a hard-nosed gangster who was not above throwing acid in the face of theater owners who were late with their extortion payments. It co-starred Sidney Rodgers as Zoran Besnovitch, a Willie Bioff-like character

"The Empty Chair" was essentially the continuation of the two-part pilot episode with Capone's conviction leaving a leadership void in the Outfit, which was challenged both by Nitti and Jake "Greasy Thumbs" Guzik, portrayed by Nehemiah Persoff. Of course, Nitti was up to the challenge and as he finally sits in Capone's old chair at the head of the boardroom table, offers this observation: "Big chair—big man. It fits all right. Anybody object?" Forever with a sharp tongue, on other memorable occasions, he belittled the "low-life Purple Gang" and "foreigners...who are taking over the place."

The two-part episode the "Unhired Assassin" (also titled "The Gun of Zangara") was, like the Hollywood extortion case episode, a reworked version of actual events, in this case the murder of Mayor Anton Cermak linked to an Outfit plot to take over the Chicago World's Fair. It has many fictional touches such as Eliot Ness being present during the police shooting of Nitti (which of course Nitti sparked by drawing a gun)!

The episode titled "The Speculator" was reminiscent of the John "Jake the Barber" Factor real-life case, except that Nitti himself was the victim of a Ponzi scheme during the collapse of Wall Street. Telly Savalas played a "Jake the Barber"-like confidence artist and Frank Sutton his hapless brother.

The series sometimes touched on the sensitive subject of the Outfit and narcotics. Once Nitti bellowed at his quivering subordinates, "The price of cocaine in this city is sky high, and you punks can't even get me a single ounce to sell!" The episode "Globe of Death" portrayed Frank Nitti smuggling heroin from Chinese triads into the United States, a theme that had previously been explored in "Death for Sale" and other episodes, and was the final episode featuring Gordon as Nitti.

Lesser Roles

The character of Frank Nitti has also had relatively minor appearances in relatively insignificant movies following the end of the first series, but these served to perpetuate the legend. Actor Harold Stone played Nitti in the ambitious 1967 film, *The Saint Valentine's Day Massacre*, directed by the cult-film director Roger Corman. Alan Rosenberg played Nitti in the historically inaccurate 1989 made-for-TV movie, *The Revenge of Al Capone* directed by Michael Pressman. A major flaw of the 1959 near-noir film *Al Capone*, starring Rod Steiger and directed by Richard Wilson, was the absence of Nitti's character. Likewise, the 1991 CBS made-for-TV movie, *The Return of Eliot Ness*, saw an older Robert Stack reprising his role as Ness, but without the old nemesis of Bruce Gordon's Nitti playing counterpoint the well-intentioned revival attempt was pretty much a flop.

The 1975 film, *Capone,* featured Ben Gazzara as Al Capone and Sylvester Stallone as Frank Nitti. Stallone's competent, if somewhat limited in scope, portrayal of Nitti (one of his first serious film roles) was both that of a cold killer and a sinister plotter. The film had little popular or critical recognition and is only loosely historically accurate, but strangely enough, it is the popular originator of the fictionalized version of Nitti betraying Capone and setting him up on income-tax evasion charges so he could take control of the Outfit. Nitti's personal character and life see almost no development in this film other than that he becomes a very businesslike boss of the Outfit at its conclusion. The film errs in having Nitti seemingly live past 1943. Stallone went on to become one of Hollywood's highest-paid actors, specializing in monosyllabic, antisociety, outcast, and underdog heroes.

A Major Motion Picture

The original television series of *The Untouchables* continued to be very popular in syndicated reruns, and by the mid-eighties, Paramount Pictures, which had absorbed Desilu in 1967, retained its copyright and thought it might be suitable as a new big-budget 115-minute feature film. Big-name director

Brian De Palma and Pulitzer Prize-winning playwright David
Mamet were put in charge of the project with Kevin Costner
playing Eliot Ness, Sean Connery as an entirely fictional
policeman character called Jim Malone (an Oscar-winning
role; in fact there was a Michael J. Malone who had briefly
infiltrated the Outfit at the Lexington Hotel, but he had
worked for IRS man Elmer Irey, not Ness), Robert De Niro
as an extremely evil Al Capone, and Billy Drago as a Frank
Nitti that had little resemblance to the historical person, but
was truly a classic screen villain.[13] De Palma had Nitti clad
in an almost solid white wardrobe to perhaps symbolize his
image as an "angel of death."

Unlike the original series, this 1987 $20-million motion pic-
ture was a livid-color, operatic epic filmed on location, often
quasi-surreal in its approach with an almost Dick Tracy-ish look
to it. The movie's story line gave the impression that De Palma
and Mamet almost went out of their way to not use the original
television series or little actual history as their reference source
material. In addition to Sean Connery's Oscar for best actor in
a supporting role, it received nominations for best art direction
and set decoration, best costume design, and best music and
original score. Sean Connery, as rogue Chicago policeman Jim
Malone, had some memorable dialogue as he taught Costner's
Ness to do things the violent "Chicago way."

Costner portrays Ness as a self-righteous Boy Scout throughout most of the film, but at its end, he loses all his scruples. In
its most severe divergence from fact, the film at its climax has
Ness murdering the villainous, but now apprehended, Nitti
by tossing him from the roof of the U.S. District Courthouse
building in 1929! For good measure, Ness apparently also kills
Frankie Rio in a gun battle at a train station (the slow-motion
baby carriage and steps sequence looked a lot like the classic
Odessa Steps scene in Sergei Eisenstein's *Battleship Potemkin*)
following a previous scene in which he had broken Rio's nose

while single-handedly confronting Capone and his bodyguards in the Lexington Hotel.

As in the original television series' "The Frank Nitti Story," Ness is again directly associated with Frank Nitti's death. Nitti's character in the film was taken by many members of the viewing public as something approaching fact, not the near-pure fantasy it portrayed. However, reality is further blurred because some touches were inaccurately borrowed from historical fact. The film near its conclusion had Nitti carrying a concealed firearm into the courtroom where Capone was being tried, but this offence was committed by Capone's bodyguard Philip D'Andrea, who was arrested and held without bail bond before being sent to a six-month Leavenworth prison term for contempt of court. During Capone's actual trial, Nitti was still in prison for income-tax evasion.

This film's Nitti, far from being Capone's businessmanlike *consigliere* and a family man who by all accounts loved children, was a stone-cold killer who would not hesitate to blow up a store that he knew a little girl had just entered. No attempt is made at developing Nitti's personal life, and most would question whether such a psychopath could have much of a life beyond his murderous profession. However, the film was a critical and commercial success, and its version of Nitti has often been cited as one of the most effective movie villains of all time, thereby unintentionally further building upon the Enforcer's legend.

Drago performed wonders with the very few lines of dialogue he was permitted and dominated the scenes in which he appeared with Costner and even Connery. Comparisons have been made between this character and other famous crime characters from such a diverse range of films as James Cagney in *White Heat*, Edgar G. Robinson in *Little Caesar*, to others in *Pulp Fiction*, *Reservoir Dogs*, *From Dusk Till Dawn*, and *The Usual Suspects*. Drago's acting within the film's overall context was superb, and he "received world wide recognition for his portrayal of Frank Nitti in The Untouchables."[14] While Drago's character did not resemble the real Nitti, it was perhaps a good synthesis of the type of men used to conduct the wet work Nitti often masterminded. Drago as Nitti firmly set the context for another stage of the Nitti myth: evil master villain and master gunman.

Historically Accurate Docudrama

The overall most historically accurate and authentic account of Frank Nitti's life on film to date was the 1988 ninety-five-minute made-for-TV movie, "Nitti: The Enforcer" starring Anthony LaPaglia, an Australian stage actor in his first major film role as the competently portrayed Nitti, produced by Leonard Hill, directed by Michael Switzer and written by Lee David Zlotoff (both creative alumni of the *Hill Street Blues* TV cop show). Zlotoff's movie script was originally titled "Nitti: The Story of Frank Nitto, 'The Enforcer': A Movie for Television" and was meticulously researched.

LaPaglia's portrayal was sympathetic to the character and an attempt was made to make Nitti appear as a victim of social circumstances that led to his rise in organized crime—although it could also be argued that Nitti was definitely not a victim and manipulated circumstances to his own ends right until the final days of his eventful life. While Nitti matures as the film progresses, he retains an Italian accent throughout his detailed life.

The story line of "Nitti: The Enforcer" had an underlying theme of portraying the human-rights violations against immigrant Italian-Americans as the cause rationale for their preeminence in organized crime for most of the twentieth century. The attempted murder of Nitti by Chicago police detectives and the reprisal assassination of Mayor Anton Cermak are very accurately depicted. The film did quite well in the television ratings when originally aired. It features actual footage of Nitti's gravesite at its sad ending and will likely remain the definitive cinematic account of Nitti's life for some time to come.

Second TV Series

A new syndicated version of *The Untouchables* made its debut in 1993 as part of a Paramount-package deal combined with the *Star Trek* spin-off series, *Deep Space Nine*.[15] This new series made a largely successful attempt at synthesizing the best elements of the original television series, the blockbuster 1987 motion picture, plus elements of actual history and fictionalized drama. All of its leading actors were very effective in their roles, and it captured a period authenticity often lacking in the original series and certainly almost completely absent in the 1987 big-screen version.

While the original series began with Capone's incarceration and Nitti as Ness's primary opponent, the new saga began with federal agent Ness (actor Tom Amandes) being assigned to get Capone, plus some early character development of Ness, Capone, and Nitti. Capone was very effectively played as an intelligent and multidimensional human being by William Forsythe with nice insightful touches such as Capone's quest for higher knowledge and self-actualization, and interest in hobbies such as aquarium keeping and poetry. Valentino Cimo's performance as the loyal Frankie Rio was particularly convincing (Cimo also had a brief supporting role as Rio in the 1987 movie *The Untouchables*). The series ended with Capone's conviction on tax evasion and Nitti assuming control of the Outfit.

It was a self-contained series that progressed logically and chronologically to its climactic conclusion, and throughout it all at Capone's side was Paul Regina's superb and arguably highly underrated character portrayal of Frank Nitti. Regina's version of Nitti was neither the blustering version of Bruce Gordon nor Billy Drago's psychopath, but rather an intelligent, hard-nosed, competent, and confident corporate business-type executive whose industry just happened to be organized crime.

In the series the Capone-Nitti relationship was essentially one of brothers who sometimes quarreled, but were always brought back together through deep underlying loyalties to each other. This reached its peak at the series' conclusion when Nitti betrayed Capone to Ness to capture the Outfit's leadership. Nitti eventually reconciled with the ailing boss, assisted through some tough love from Frankie Rio, before Capone was sent to prison (and again repeating the common error of having Nitti present during Capone's trial).

As the series progressed over its two seasons from 1993 to 1994, Nitti's role in turn matured until near the end, his importance was almost equal to that of Capone's. One could almost see the physical transformation of Regina's Nitti into a colder, darker figure leading to his final confrontation with Capone. This series also perpetuated the theory that Nitti set up Capone on income-tax evasion charges so he could become the boss of the Outfit. In this instance, Nitti was influenced by a power-hungry girlfriend who convinced him to turn against Capone. This and other features of Nitti's personal life are generally inaccurate in this series, but at least, he has a private life, and it is realistically projected by Regina. Regina's Nitti was probably much more of a wise guy than the real man ever was. He is usually a moderate smoker and drinker, prefers sleazy women and other men's wives (most of the events of the series supposedly occurred after the real Nitti was married in 1927), apparently lives in the Lexington Hotel, but knows how to cook like most Italian men, always (unlike Capone) considers work before pleasure, and has his men who deal in drugs whacked as a matter of policy. At the end of the series, Regina clearly portrayed Nitti's potential suicidal nature, and fortunately for once, Ness did not kill Nitti.

While attempts at historical accuracy were made for key events, with little effort, the series could have become an alternative-history parallel-universe from a science-fiction epic because it offered as "fact" events such as Ness and Capone facing each other in a prison boxing match, Ness and Capone in the midst of the Batista revolution in Cuba, Capone meeting with Italian Fascist dictator Benito Mussolini, martial law being declared in Chicago with U.S. Army tanks destroying mob speakeasies and the Outfit doing drive-by machine-gunnings of military headquarters, and at the end of the series, Capone preparing to run for U.S. Senate. While the assassination of Mayor Anton Cermak by Giuseppe Zangara and other elements of the Outfit are portrayed more or less accurately, the actual cause of the assassination—the attempted murder of Frank Nitti by Chicago police detectives under Cermak's personal orders—is completely ignored. The assassination is orchestrated by Capone who in reality was in prison at this time, while Cermak is portrayed as an anticrime reform mayor of almost saintlike virtue. Like the original series, this version also suffered from time compression in which a decade or more of history was made to appear to take place over only a few years, although key events were largely in correct chronological order.

Produced by Christopher Crowe, the series soon won critical acclaim and is still shown in syndicated reruns. It also had some very innovative entirely fictional episodes that were apparently takeoffs on film classics such as the German noir crime film *M* that explored the underworld's assistance in bringing a child murderer to justice; *The Manchurian Candidate* in which psychological brainwashing is used as a weapon; and *Fatal Attraction* in which a mentally disturbed women seeks vengeance on a married lover who has spurned her.

The major flaw of the series was that it perpetuated the Ness myth while basically ignoring the efforts of many other officials in the final conviction of Al Capone.

Sadly, Paul Regina died from cancer in February 2006.

Dramatic Portrayal

The 2002 noir motion picture *Road to Perdition* once again brought the character of Frank Nitti to the silver screen in a major way. Directed by Sam Mendes (of *American Beauty* fame) and with a screenplay by David Self, this somber motion picture is based upon a pulp-fiction crime comic by Max Allan Collins, who has also used the Frank Nitti character in other popular period mystery and detective novels.[16] The film won major acclaim from critics, particularly for its convincing portrayal of Nitti as a corporate CEO-style organized-crime leader by actor Stanley Tucci. Anthony LaPaglia, of *Nitti: The Enforcer* fame, was to have portrayed Al Capone in the film, but his scenes with Tucci were cut from the script.

The story is basically one of a Depression-era mob soldier out to avenge his wife and son's "fratricidal" murder resulting from a gang war, during which he has a dramatic meeting with a somewhat sympathetic Frank Nitti, who also happens to be the indirect boss of his family's murderer. Collins presents a story based on character and emotion, and challenges the audience with its moral ambiguity and complexities.

This finely crafted film has an almost surreal feel to it, but one that is at the same time more convincing than that of the 1987 *The Untouchables*. The Outfit is portrayed as a business corporation managed by a board of directors, an organization that promotes its most competent personnel, and simply makes those who are incompetent disappear. Morality is made to seem ambiguous in its studied and somber depiction of Depression-era Chicago and the Illinois region. As one review of the film put it: "Nitti is not a frothing homicidal fiend, but a creature far more dangerous: a placid businessman who silently signs legitimate contracts, deeds and bills of sale with blood enemies, and on occasion, friends."[17] However, the story is essentially one about human relationships and their consequences and as such, is very different from most earlier films concerning Nitti.

There have been some serious criticisms of the glamorization of gangsters such as Nitti in this film and Nitti's actual use of killers such as the psychotic James "Fur" Sammons. Joanne Laurier wrote:

> Whether Nitti was also a psychopath (like Capone and Sammons), or merely employed them, Mendes' characterization is a travesty. In the film's production notes, the director justifies his irresponsible glamorization: "I wanted to put a lie to some of the perceived notions about gangsters. You will see no double-breasted pinstripe suits, no spats, only one machine gun, and that has a very specific and unusual presence in the movie." One wants to ask: whence comes this desire to prettify thugs and murderers?...neither Sullivan nor Rooney nor Nitti is truly portrayed as a "bad man." On the contrary, they are quite sympathetically presented, as "men of honor."[18]

TO A LARGE extent, Tucci's cameo portrayal is the most cerebral and Machiavellian Frank Nitti ever captured on celluloid ("a whispering Borgia" in the words of one reviewer), and in this respect, he has perhaps presented the closest yet version of the real man. Nitti is shown as a human being, not a two-dimensional villain, and as one wanting to help the protagonist, but who cannot for reasons of business. Tucci was at first hesitant to take on a role that might stereotype Italian-Americans:

Once I read [the script], though, I changed my mind,
he says. Nitti is intelligent, and he's not a caricature.
You know—meaner for no apparent reason, not as
smart as the other guys.[19]

NITTI IS SHOWN to be a rational villain who is not entirely evil,
but is pressured to act in evil ways because of his position. He
is a businessman in the business of crime. Tucci invested his
small, but important role with a suave dignity that has rarely
before been provided for the character of Frank Nitti.

Which Nitti Was Best?

The character of Frank Nitti's appearance in both series of
The Untouchables plus six full-length motion pictures is equal to
more than eighty hours of combined story time—a record for any
historical underworld figure. While the quality varied between
each production, the majority of it was of a very high standard
with the Nitti character having an important story role.

It is difficult to decide which portrayal of Nitti has been the
best because each was in such a different movie or television-series
context. Bruce Gordon's, of course, provided a milestone and a
benchmark for all others. One of the best all-round fictionalized character development and entertaining portrayals goes to
Paul Regina with Stanley Tucci's brilliant cameo performance
as perhaps the single most sophisticated interpretation.

Bruce Gordon and Billy Drago's caricatures must occupy
special places in the development of Frank Nitti as a fictional
gangster icon in the public mind. Anthony LaPaglia's serious
version, perhaps, hit almost too close to the truth of Nitti's
tragic life and is as a result overly sad, but was without a doubt
the most accurate and true to life. Obviously, Nitti as a character role still holds much promise for future development.

9

Frank Nitti in Popular Culture

Being angry with Nitti was like getting pissed off with God. You could do it, but it wouldn't get you anywhere. Except hell maybe.
  —Private detective Nate Heller in
    Max Allan Collins's *True Crime*

The most famous enforcer in history never skated a shift in the NHL. Frank Nitti, known as "The Enforcer," helped Al Capone rule the street of a lawless Chicago some 70 years ago. The police might not have been able to maintain order, but Nitti, legend has it, could. Nitti and men of his stripe were necessary in that era because the police often were bought off by the mob and subsequently had no power in controlling the criminal element.
  —Bob Smizik, *Pittsburgh Post-Gazette* (2007)

Pulp Fiction, Drama, and Sci-fi

Elements of Frank Nitti's fictionalized life story were serialized in pulp-fiction magazines such as *Special Detective* (that story titled "Gangsters Grip in Chicago") during the 1940s and 1950s. Fictional publications and other promotional materials were also spun off from the original *The Untouchables* television series.

More recently, author Max Allan Collins has written numerous fictionalized detective novels with Frank Nitti as a central character. Collins's crime novels featuring fictional Chicago private eye Nate Heller are considered by many to be among the best historical mysteries available today. Most notable were "The Frank Nitti Trilogy" in *True Detective* (1983), *True Crime* (1984), and *The Million-Dollar Wound* (1986) with Nitti returning in *Stolen Away* (2001), a story of the Lindbergh baby kidnapping, as well as frequent references in a "post-Nitti" Chicago novel, *Chicago Confidential: A Nathan Heller Novel*.[1]

Nitti also has numerous mentions in Collins's Eliot Ness series and a more unusual role in a short story by Collins and Matthew V. Clemens set in the Buffy the Vampire Slayer universe called *Stakeout on Rush Street, Chicago, Illinois, 1943*. These novels present fictionalized accounts of the Nitti- Newberry-Cermak shootings for which Collins offers a convincing conspiracy theory that involves big-city politics, the Outfit, powerful Chicago business interests, the Hollywood extortion case, and Nitti's death, along with a whole cast of other period real-life characters such as Eliot Ness, Al Capone, Willie Bioff, J. Edgar Hoover, Melvin Purvis, John Dillinger, and many, many others. The core story of the trilogy is Heller's "awkward, sometimes frightening relationship with surrogate father Frank Nitti."[2] While fiction, the novels are so remarkably well researched and structured that they read almost as biographies, and each provides a detailed annotated bibliography at its end. These novels truly blur the line between Nitti's historical reality and fiction.

Today, Max Allan Collins is also a major name in novel-movie tie-ins, having written the novelizations for major theatrical releases. The 2002 hit movie, *Road to Perdition*, was based on an original 1998 short story of the same name by Collins that was illustrated by the famed artist, Richard Piers Rayner, and researched by George Hagenauer. The graphic novel was essentially a noir comic book that prominently featured Frank Nitti and soon developed a cult following. The graphics renderings of Nitti, based upon his actual appearance and rare photographs, are a joy to behold and bring the real man to life again.[3] This graphic novel is an Americanized version of the Japanese manga comic-book genre. In the case of *Road to Perdition*, Collins wrote a novel based upon the movie's screenplay.[4] As we have already seen, the motion picture provided the vehicle for one of the most stunning screen portrayals of Nitti to date.

Collins obviously considers Nitti a major legendary figure of the twentieth century and has done much to perpetuate a version of the character that is both historically accurate and entertaining. *Road to Perdition* is loosely based on the true story of Irish mobster John Looney from Rock Island, Illinois, who was associated with Frank Nitti (the Looney family is renamed Rooney in the movie version of the story). A sequel novel, *Road to Purgatory*, further builds upon the Nitti character who becomes much more central to the story, and a third novel, *Road to Paradise*, completes the trilogy. Nitti is to appear in all three new *On the Road to Perdition* graphic novellas by DC Comics. These are to be collected into a companion volume to the original graphic novel.[5]

Collins's landmark treatment of the Frank Nitti persona in a popular fiction context is far from being alone although it remains in a class by itself. Nicholas von Hoffman's 1984 novel, *Organized Crimes*, offered an often darkly amusing coming-of-age story of a young sociology student from the University of Chicago who in 1931 undertakes fieldwork on the Outfit and becomes taken up by a fascinated Frank Nitti. Clearly influenced by the true-life experiences of Saul Alinsky, it is a story of power and corruption that mixes fiction with factual episodes such as the Chicago police shooting Nitti, a Jake the Barber-like kidnapping, and the assassination of Mayor Anton Cermak.

Nitti is characterized as a cunning "Napoleon of Crime" and plays an important background role throughout the novel.[6]

A novel by Marvin Albert was based upon David Mamet's screenplay for the 1987 film *The Untouchables* and like the movie, presented fictitious characterizations of Nitti, Capone, Ness, and others from the period.[7]

In an alternative-history story of a communistic United States of America following a socialist revolution, "ideology agents" Eliot Ness and Melvin Purvis hunt for a legendary agitator and end up confronting "Chairman Capone's" enforcer Frank Nitti.[8] In another online version along this same theme, Nitti is Chicago Mayor Joseph Stalin's henchman and is tasked with murdering Stalin's rival, Anton Cermak.

Today there is a whole realm of self-published fiction on Frank Nitti on the World Wide Web. Frank Nitti is "Capone's chief stooge" in the post-World War I flying-ace story, *Aces High*.[9] In the online *Tales of the Red Skull*, Nitti is portrayed as a vicious psychopath a la Billy Drago's characterization:

> Nitti shrugged and slowly pulled a razor from his pocket. With one quick slice, I collapsed to the floor in agony. "Looks bad, boss," one of the goons stated as he backed up Nitti with his shotgun.[10]

OTHERS HAVE PLACED Nitti even more directly in a science-fiction genre. In the *Aeneas Boddy Chronicles*, the setting is October 1929 at Chicago's Metropole Hotel where the space- and time-traveling protagonist, Aeneas Romulus Boddy, encounters Nitti while attempting to recover his stolen Leonardo da Vinci painting:

> Aeneas is led to a corner booth where three men sit. The two on the ends are large and obviously armed,

while the one in the middle is thin and bookish with a weak moustache. "That's Frank Nitti?" Aeneas whispers to the waiter. "Don't underestimate 'im," the waiter warns.[11]

Rare art-collector Nitti tells Aeneas to get out of town, but the hero attempts to save both the painting and Nitti's seemingly captive girlfriend, Bonnie Venture, in a late-night raid on Nitti's penthouse with much ensuing high adventure with Nitti as the primary villain.

THE FICTIONALIZED NITTI becomes even more bizarre in other self-published stories on the Web. In yet-another epic sci-fi adventure, apparently set in the universe of the *Star Wars* series, Frank Nitti is "the right hand man of one Alphonse James Capone, and if this information was accurate, Capone was the new leader of the criminal Empire that once belonged to Jabba the Hutt!!"[12]

An entry on Frank Nitti is included in the 1996 version of *A Who's Who, Where's Where, When Was When and What's from What of the Story Books of Red Dwarf*, the popular British sci-fi novel and television series created by Grant Naylor. In the *Ironic Times*, a brief scene is visualized in one of Hell's bars in which "sitting within gunshot of each other: Frank Nitti and Bill 'Hopalong Cassidy' Boyd."[13]

Nitti is also referenced in Dennis E. Power's *Melvin and Howard: A Tale of the Riverworld*, Andrew M. Greeley's *Irish Whiskey: A Nuala Anne McGrail Novel*, Stuart M. Kaminsky's *You Bet Your Life* (where Nitti interacts with the Marx Brothers over gambling debts), and who knows how many other science-fiction works because he is a character that consistently generates interest as a villain and seems applicable to almost any type of exciting situation.[14]

Media Influences

Various film and television characters seem to have been directly influenced by media portrayals of Frank Nitti. The psychotic gangster Frank Booth played by Dennis Hopper in director David Lynch's 1986 cult movie *Blue Velvet* is often confused with the villainous Nitti character from other movies. Clint Eastwood's *The Enforcer* (1976) chapter of the Dirty Harry rogue police-detective saga also comes to mind, as does the character Bela Oxmyx portrayed by Anthony Caruso (often confused by *Star Trek* fans with Bruce Gordon) in the original *Star Trek* series 1968 episode "A Piece of the Action."

A more recent permutation was the 1995 kung-fu, nonstop action flick, *The Enforcer*, starring Jet Li as an undercover cop ordered to infiltrate a triad gang. Of course, these dramas have not used the actual or fictional Nitti persona per se, but rather the image of a tough, ruthless enforcer that he came to symbolize. The label "enforcer" now has a permanent correlation with Nitti for a large segment of the populace.

David Chase, creator of "the hit" HBO series, *The Sopranos* that chronicles the lives of a North New Jersey mob family, credits Frank Nitti as portrayed in the original series of *The Untouchables* as an early creative influence, particularly in regard to stereotyping Italian-Americans as being the major force behind organized crime.[15]

Woody Allen's 1994 film, *Bullets Over Broadway*, has more than a passing similarity to some of the real-life hijinks between Frank Nitti, Charles "Lucky" Luciano, and the movie studio heads during the Hollywood extortion case (which federal agent Elmer L. Irey once described as "a burlesque of all the Hollywood gangster movies that have been foisted on us for two decades") in that it effectively portrays the intense love-hate relationship between organized crime and the entertainment industry.[16]

In an Internet discussion on Italian-American movie character gangster stereotypes, Nitti's real impact on Hollywood was
remembered: "'Naaaa, your wife shes-a safe with Tonnetti—he
prefers-a spaggetti!' All us Eye-Tie Americans laugh at that
one—and then sent Nitti over to lean on the studio head."

SOME POPULAR CULTURE film references to Frank Nitti are quite
arcane. For example in the 1983 comedy movie *Easy Money*
starring Rodney Dangerfield and Joe Pesci, a character orders
"Frank Nitti" pizza specials from an Italian pizzeria. A 1975
spoof of the original *The Untouchables* TV show on *Saturday
Night Live* hosted by special guest Desi Arnaz featured a
skit on Eliot Ness tracking down Lucille Ball who had been
kidnapped by Frank Nitti. A recent dinner theater, murder-
mystery theatrical production in Philadelphia called *Gangland '29* saw the Frank Nitti character used as an authority
figure to help elicit audience participation during the play. A
black-and-white photo of the real Frank Nitti slumped dead
against a railway fence was shown in the 1972 motion picture,
The Godfather (Part One), after the Virgil "the Turk" Sollozzo
murder as part of a montage of violently deceased mobsters.
Other movies that have referenced Nitti include *Passion and
Paradise* (1989) and *Bugsy* (1991).

Universal Nitti?

An American garment firm offers hand-dyed *#432 Frank
Nitti "The Enforcer" Blue* for men's custom suits along with an
array of other gangster-inspired fabrics.[17] The television and
movie image of Frank Nitti has been described as a fashion
statement on the Internet discussion group *alt.fashion* as being
one of the best-dressed characters on film in the context of
pinstriped double-breasted suits. In fact, like the real man,

the film images of Nitti have been extremely stylish, particularly those of Billy Drago, Paul Regina, Stanley Tucci, and Bruce Gordon. The coach for the Kentucky State football team, Winston Bennett, wore a pinstriped zoot suit for the 1996 national championship game that somehow combined Curtis Mayfield's seventies Superfly look with Frank Nitti's 1930s gangland style.

Finnish NHL Flyers goalie Antero Niittymaki is known to his teammates as "Niitty" and "Frank" and has an image of Frank Nitti painted on his face mask.

One can purchase an etched "Frank Nitti—The Enforcer" bowie knife, with either gray, black-and-white, black-and-purple, or green-striped celluloid handles.[18] Another site offers custom T-shirts with the actual image of Frank Nitti, and still another, Frank Nitti "the Enforcer" brand cigars.

Some modern social contexts for Nitti are totally unexpected. A number of hip-hop and gangsta' rap singers have adopted the pseudonym of "Frank Nitti" or used him for imagery in lyrics.

Referenced on *Amazon.com*'s Web shopping site, an artist named Frank Nitti has formed a rap group with Lil' Kee and produced an album called *Dem Thugs* with explicit lyrics. In a related vein, the motion picture, *Scarface* (1983), is today largely credited with the rise of such violence-crazed gangsta' rap movements.

In Internet discussion group topics as diverse as the U.S. Internal Revenue Service, mandatory sentencing, legal licensing enforcement, gun control, radical-left politics, anti-Semitism, revisionist history, religion and philosophy (in the context of "enforcing internal discipline"), professional gambling, child adoptions, episodes of the various *Star Trek* series, politics in the Philippines, and professional hockey ("Frank Nitti is a name that's hard to forget..."), the image of Frank Nitti is evoked in comparisons with contemporary figures.

A management expert discussing online the role of "the enforcer" type in modern organizational-team role analysis states that this type of person "would relate well to the old mobster, Frank Nitti, of *The Untouchables* fame. It was Frank who took care of Al Capone's collection problems. He was aggressive, unsympathetic, and very direct. He also kept close tabs on Al's accounts to make sure they were collected on time."

In an online debate on the ethics of libertarianism as an ideology, it is remarked that "if the stockholders of a murderous corporation choose to elect directors who don't publicly report their actions, then the stockholders are in the same moral position as Al Capone choosing Frank Nitti to be his agent, with the instructions, 'See to it that this person is no longer a problem to us—how you do it is up to you,' resulting in a murder."

Nitti is the subject of online urban legends, one of the most interesting being that "Prohibition-era gangster Frank Nitti, the one Kevin Costner threw off a roof in the movie, moved to Galveston in real life and became a respected bootlegger." This reference may well be somehow related to Frank Nitti's erstwhile nephew, the elusive Romeo Jack Nitti, who was known to be actively promoting Outfit interests in Texas during the 1940s.

In Web newsgroup on relationships between the sexes, a war rages between an online participant who goes by the name "Frank Nitti" until another participant remarks: "I kinda doubt whether the real Frank Nitti hid behind a forged address."

In a competitive role-playing game featuring famous gangsters and their associates, the identity of Frank Nitti is found along with Charles "Lucky" Luciano, Thelma Todd, Joe Valachi, Bonnie and Clyde, and Abe "Kid Twist" Reles from Murder Inc. A German computer game simply named "Al Capone" features a "player play[ing] the role of Frank 'The Enforcer'

Nitti, the right-hand man of Al Capone...Frank Nitti and his men conquer the city of Chicago quarter by quarter..."

During the 2000 American presidential debate, a question was posed for Democratic candidate Al Gore. "If you haven't been corrupted after working eight years for Bill Clinton, isn't this like Frank Nitti claiming not to have picked up any bad habits working for Al Capone?" Or: "Your government extorts far more wealth by force than the Mafia ever did, although I can hardly envision Frank Nitti threatening to knee-cap General Motors for manufacturing a pickup truck with exploding gas tanks." When a state government had funding cut by the U.S. Congress because the voters "elected the wrong candidate," they are told they should "Do business with us and you won't get hurt; it's the Frank Nitti style of government.'"[19]

"Frank Nitti" is also a moniker that has been adopted by macho American athletes and sports broadcasters, although this is a family name for a surprisingly large number of individuals today. In pro wrestling, a character named Frank Nitti is matched against one called Super Nova. Another professional wrestler touts himself as "the 'enforcer' of the Men of Respect...in fact, you can call me the Frank Nitti of the Men of Respect." One wag compared not voting for somebody with a nickname like Jesse "the Body" Ventura for governor of Minnesota in 1998 as being "like voting against Frank 'The Enforcer' Nitti." African-American basketball star Frank Williams was nicknamed "Frank Nitti" because he's as deadly on the basketball court as the "white-suited assassin" of the same name in the 1987 film, *The Untouchables*.[20]

When commenting on a racketeering lawsuit against him that had been thrown out by a lower court, professional boxing promoter Don King observed, "They made this law for Gotti and Gambino, for Frank Nitti and Al Capone. It's for organized crime, a law against criminal conspiracies."[21]

Social Influence

Various Web discussions often reference the fictional film images of Frank Nitti as a great villain, which reflects a growing blurring between his real and fictional personae. Nitti is compared with such great film bad guys as Darth Vader from the *Star Wars* trilogy, Mr. Blonde from *Reservoir Dogs*, Angel Eyes from *The Good, the Bad, and the Ugly*, and Tony Montana from *Scarface* (1983).

In a Web discussion on the morality of killing in the line of duty, the imagery of Eliot Ness murdering Frank Nitti in Brian De Palma's *The Untouchables* is evoked "as a degradation of a heroic character, with set beliefs, who gives them up just for the visceral response of the audience."

In an editorial written by Bob Greene decrying the current moral state of the city of Chicago where even innocent young children are at risk playing in their own neighborhoods, he is motivated to comment that "Frank Nitti would be ashamed of us—unable to understand how a city could sink to this level," as if Nitti is somehow a benchmark of urban morality. The same writer further remarks that "Capone and Nitti and their gangs may have been completely without redeeming qualities—but they didn't go out onto the streets of Chicago to shoot children.... Capone, Nitti and their men relied on paying people off, setting up intricate organizations, arranging to be protected."[22]

In a full circle back to Frank Nitti's original criminal roots, an FBI task force on today's inner-city violent street gangs reported that a narcotics-distribution-financed African-American street gang known as the New Breed that began within the Illinois prison system prefers famous criminal nicknames for its members. These include Frank Nitti, John Gotti, and Al Capone. In a recent ominous urban gang-related development, a fourteen-year-old girl in Northwest Washington,

D.C., who was a murder witness was brutally shot and killed by a 22-year-old member of a drug trafficking gang who called himself "'Frank Nitti' after a notorious enforcer for Al Capone." An editorial on the case laments: "There should be no leniency for the Frank Nittis of the world...they will be prosecuted under the full letter of D.C. law. The feds never got that opportunity with the real-life Frank Nitti."[23]

Furthermore, the Hollywood and literary glamorization of underworld characters such as Frank Nitti has influenced whole new generations of Mafia members, providing them role models on how to look, act, and talk.[24] Comparisons extend beyond North America: a Tokyo yakuza member dressed from head to toe in white is described as a "Japanese Frank Nitti," a character out of the big screen *The Untouchables*.[25] The memory of Frank "the Enforcer" Nitti has now progressed beyond legendary and mythical to become iconic in scope in Western society.

10

Legend, Myth, and Underworld Icon

I know it is the fashion to say that most of recorded history is lies anyway, but what is peculiar to our own age is the abandonment of the idea that history could be truthfully written.

—George Orwell

WHILE A LEGEND is a widely accepted, but unverifiable story, a myth is a legendary story verging on fiction that is embellished over time. An icon in this context becomes a larger than life, almost sacred personage, if this interpretation can be forgiven as being somewhat contradictory when applied to a criminal character. However, the real and fictional Frank "the Enforcer" Nitti was and is a composite of many contradictory images, and this may be one of the attractions that has sustained his enduring public fame and long media popularity. Few today really know where the historical truth ends and the legend and fiction begin, as reality and fantasy become increasingly difficult to separate. After all, while he may be the most glamorized gangster in history, most people today do not even know that his original surname was Nitto rather than Nitti and that he possibly ended his own life in a fit of insanity rather than being murdered by Eliot Ness as portrayed by Hollywood.

Beyond movies and television series, some of the more fantastic interpretations and fictional spin-offs from Frank Nitti's underworld career are today found on the World Wide Web. As we have seen, Frank Nitti's legend had steadily morphed into something much wider culturally. Like many legendary characters, Nitti died, but was reborn, in this case into the dimension of fictionalized television series and motion pictures. Like a reversal of art imitating life, the Nitti character has been manipulated by the same Hollywood entertainment industry that the real man did so much to twist to his own ends.

There are many myths concerning Frank Nitti, a product of elements of his real life, gangland oral histories and rumors, fictionalized television and motion-picture portrayals, novelizations, and many fantastic interpretations of these elements circulated mostly on the Internet telecommunications and multimedia network. The life of the historical Frank Nitti was certainly worthy of the rare stuff legends are made from, even if these legendary figures are antiheroes such as Hermes, the classical Greek patron god of thieves.

While Nitti may have shown disdain for many of his underworld colleagues, this was because he was truly an intellectual criminal. Nitti's life was the portrait of a man of many contradictions. He was a person who could be warm and loving with his family, making his adopted son the heir to his life savings; and heartless and cruel with his enemies to the extent that he married a woman who was the fiancée of a man he had murdered; or in the case of his first wife, marrying her just two days after orchestrating the bloody Saint Valentine's Day Massacre; or pulling a jewelry heist apparently for sport during a family vacation.

Frank Nitti is truly a father of modern corporate-style white-collar crime and made significant contributions to modern intelligence and organized-crime covert operations methods—the art of wet work. As a process leading to mythical and iconic stature, these elements are gradually becoming merged to a point where reality and fiction are both blurred and unimportant in the context of a widely perceived image.

The Enforcer's permanent place in history as a criminal icon, a dark paladin, is now undoubtedly assured, in the same league as the purely fictional characters Lex Luthor, Goldfinger, Dr. No, and Ernst Stavro Blofeld.

While Frank Nitti may not really have been the greatest gunman of all time, many people continue to believe he was, and when enough people believe something for a long enough time, it becomes a truth of sorts, particularly in today's environment of instantaneous and integrated communications and entertainment media where historical records are becoming to a large extent digital electronic in form and potentially easily subject to revision (a modern touch on Nazi propaganda minister Dr. Joseph Goebbels's "big lie" method).

Furthermore, advanced virtual-reality and digital-filmmaking systems will accelerate this trend by being able to re-create on-screen cybernetic "actors" based upon databases of historical figures who will be capable of performing with live or re-created deceased actors in totally seamless performances. For an example of this future, see William Gibson's now classic *Idoru*, which explored what has quickly become the actual Japanese trend of computer-generated pop music and film stars that are so realistic that many assume they are real people.[1]

There can be little doubt when all the historical evidence is objectively weighed that Frank Nitti truly was a rarity, an actual criminal mastermind, a genius of sorts, but perhaps not a totally evil genius. Nitti's crimes were not the cruel crimes against humanity of a modern dictator or terrorist, but were focused crimes of a fundamentally American freewheeling nature that preyed upon the many human desires and vices. In some ways, the real Nitti for all his refinement could be more sinister than any of his screen counterparts. He did not hesitate to use brutal psychopaths such as James "Fur" Sammons or David Yaras when the need arose.

However, while many career criminals are forced to lead such a life, Nitti was self-educated and intelligent and could have succeeded on any path of his choosing. At some point in his early life, he made a conscious decision to be an underworld figure. One can only imagine what Nitti could have achieved if he had selected the right opportunity to focus his innovative talents in more socially productive avenues, perhaps in sectors such as the legitimate Hollywood entertainment industry or global corporate finance and management.

Nitti's life was a network of interrelated conspiracies: a Chicago mayor and a rival gangster made a failed attempt on his life; these enemies, in turn, were quickly dispatched; Nitti eventually died under rather mysterious circumstances that could very well have been a successful assassination rather than a suicide; and two decades after his death, some of the criminal human residue from his era might have participated in the murder of an American president using assassination methods Nitti pioneered.

While Nitti may or may not have been a member of a ruling national Mafia Commission, Murder Inc., or the mysterious Combination Network, he had the power to establish and chair national meetings at the time and place of his choosing just on the basis of his charisma and accomplishments. Nitti was part of a subculture where the ultimate solution to every problem was to kill somebody. If crime was just a business for Nitti, it was also a high-stakes game. He had worked his way up until he had the "world by the tail with a downhill start," but in the end, his luck somehow ran out.

Frank Nitti's greatest crimes were of such a scale and within the context of such unusual circumstances to be almost beyond the bounds of conventional morality. Nitti undoubtedly felt his actions were justified because they were part of an ongoing struggle akin to warfare between nations or hostile business takeovers. Yet compared to the "legitimate" financial excesses of modern corporate robber barons, Nitti's white-collar crimes today pale in comparison.

As a folklore outlaw, Frank Nitti's popular American image is now more akin to that of Old West outlaw Jesse James or Hell's Angels Motorcycle Club founder Ralph "Sonny" Barger. Barger has achieved an iconic rebel-hero status of his own through a widespread dissemination of his personal history and philosophy of life in printed book form and on dedicated Web sites.[2] These are the antihero types beloved by much of the American public, but vilified by the nation's forces of law and order during any given period in history.

Frank Nitti's amazing actual life and controversial fictional portrayals have now together spanned more than 110 years within three centuries, and his memory is quite unlikely to end at any time soon. Frank "the Enforcer" Nitti was born in the nineteenth century, gained notoriety and fame during a dark period of the twentieth, and will undoubtedly continue in legend and myth in the twenty-first and beyond.

APPENDIX A

Frank Nitti Chronology

January 27, 1886—Francesco Raffaele Nitto born in Angori, Sicily, Italy, to Rose and Luigi Nitto.

July 1, 1891—The young Nitti immigrates to the United States onboard the steamship *Guerra*, with his family.

Circa 1907—In Brooklyn, Nitti leads the Navy Street Boys teenage gang where he meets Al Capone. Later he joins New York's infamous Five Points Gang.

Circa 1911—After helping to support his mother and sister for many years by working menial jobs, he leaves home in Brooklyn because he cannot get along with his stepfather. Likely continues gang-related activities and is introduced to the Mafia underworld.

1919 to the early 1920s—Nitti moves to Chicago with Capone, works as a jewelry fence with John "Jake the Barber" Factor and then for Johnny Torrio and Giuseppi "Diamond Joe" Esposito, becoming an expert gunman, enforcer, and bootlegger. Nominally is employed as a barber for $40 to $42 per week.

March 9, 1921—Nitti declares his intention for U.S. naturalization.

1923 to 1924—Nitti works with Al Capone and Johnny Torrio in the takeover of the Chicago suburb of Cicero and is now a full member of the Outfit.

Circa 1924 to 1926—Nitti is Al Capone's bodyguard and is soon promoted to enforcer. He successfully protects Capone against at least four major attempts on his life from 1925 to 1929.

February 25, 1925—Nitti is naturalized as an American citizen.

October 11, 1926—The Hymie Weiss hit planned by Frank Nitti for Al Capone takes place.

July 1, 1928—Nitti takes part in the Frankie Yale hit.

February 14, 1929—The infamous Saint Valentine's Day Massacre planned by Nitti for Capone takes place.

February 16, 1929—Frank Nitti is married to his first wife, Anna Ronga, in St. Louis, Missouri.

Circa 1929 to 1930—Nitti becomes Capone's *consigliere* and underboss.

May 1929 to March 1930—Frank Nitti takes command of the Outfit when Al Capone and Frankie Rio are charged in Philadelphia on a concealed-weapons charge and sentenced to twelve months in prison. Nitti is now well established as Capone's underboss.

Circa 1930—Frank Nitti hires graduate sociology student Saul Alinsky to his personal staff.

1930 to 1937—Frank Nitti becomes president of the *Unione Siciliano*, a key position in the national Mafia hierarchy.

March 1930 to March 1932—Nitti is indicted in the U.S. district court on charges of income-tax evasion for the years 1925 to 1927, is arrested on October 31, 1930, and on December 20, 1930, is sentenced to eighteen months in Leavenworth prison in Kansas, but ultimately receives several months off for good behavior. He enters on January 11, 1931, and is discharged on March 24, 1932.

October 25, 1931—Al Capone is convicted of income-tax evasion and sentenced to ten years in prison. Frank Nitti takes effective control of the Outfit during early 1932 after his release from prison, although Capone for a short time still maintains some control from prison.

Circa 1932—Nitti's Trucking and Transport Exchange (T-N-T) initiative to control the overall transportation and coal-fuel infrastructure of Chicago meets some initial success, but eventually falters.

Circa 1932-1933—Frank Nitti leads the Outfit to victory in the bloody intergang wars over the control of organized labor unions in Chicago.

December 19, 1932—Chicago police detectives Harry Lang and Harry Miller unsuccessfully attempt to murder Frank Nitti under orders from Chicago Mayor Anton Cermak and rival gangster Teddy Newberry.

January 7, 1933—Teddy Newberry is found dead, crippling the senior leadership structure of the Outfit's major rival, the North Side Gang.

February 1, 1933—Nitti begins a seventy-five-day bombing campaign to reassert his authority throughout Chicago.

February 15, 1933—Giuseppe Zangara mortally wounds Mayor Anton Cermak in Miami, Florida, likely on Frank Nitti's order. Cermak dies on February 27.

Circa 1933—Prohibition is repealed on March 15, 1933, and Frank Nitti solidifies his mantle of command and cuts the imprisoned Al Capone from the chain of command.

April 1933—Nitti is charged with assault with intent to kill for supposedly wounding Detective Harry Lang, is found innocent, and the tables are turned on Detectives Lang and Miller at a subsequent trial.

July 1933—Frank Nitti arranges for the fake kidnapping of John "Jake the Barber" Factor, con-artist brother of cosmetics tycoon Max Factor. This leads to the lifelong imprisonment of Roger Touhy, thus once and for all eliminating the North Side Gang as a viable opposition force to the Outfit.

Circa 1933-1934—Nitti leads a successful effort by the Outfit to maximize profits from the Chicago "Century of Progress" World's Fair and is hailed by Mafia leaders at a Miami meeting where a national strategy is formed. Syndicate leaders from across America meet with Nitti there and pay homage to him for his actions against Mayor Cermak and Nitti's lead role in coordinating the lucrative Chicago World's Fair operations.

Circa 1934—Frank Nitti and wife Anna adopt a son, Joseph.

February 4, 1935—Nitti has Chicago union leader Tommy Maloy whacked and takes effective control over the Chicago motion-picture projectionist's union.

December 29, 1935—Nitti is believed linked to the murder of Illinois State Representative A. J. Prignano, but is never charged.

Circa 1935—Nitti successfully avoids a second income-tax evasion charge.

Circa 1935-1936—Nitti associates begin the Hollywood shakedown racket in earnest.

July 9, 1936—Nitti is believed linked to the murder of State Representative John M. Bolton, but is never charged.

Circa 1937—Nitti purges the Outfit of troublesome leftover elements from the Capone era to solidify his leadership hold and expands operations into new post-Prohibition fields.

April 30, 1937—Nitti associates begin a successful crackdown on a Hollywood union general strike.

December 1937—Robert Montgomery's investigation of Willie Bioff's extravagant lifestyle eventually leads to the collapse of Nitti's entertainment-extortion racket.

February 1939—Nitti possibly participates with his men in a Miami hotel robbery that nets $175,000.

Circa 1940—Nitti and other top Outfit leaders are seized by police during a gambling investigation and subpoenaed to appear before a federal grand jury. Nitti is also indicted for violations of the U.S. Radio Communications Act in the operation of a racing-wire service, but all official charges are made without any practical effect.

October 18, 1940—Frank Nitti and senior associates are indicted by a Cook County, Illinois, grand jury on a conspiracy charge related to controlling the Chicago Bartender's Union, but are found not guilty.

November 19, 1940—Frank Nitti's wife, Anna, dies at age thirty-eight from an internal ailment.

Circa 1941—A federal grand jury lays the groundwork for the prosecution of Nitti and key associates in the Hollywood extortion case.

Circa 1942—A federal grand jury investigating Nitti's slot-machine operations is unable to come to any conclusive results.

July 1942—Frank Nitti marries his second wife, Antoinette M. Caravetta, the former fiancée of associate Edward J. O'Hare who was murdered by the Outfit, likely on Nitti's orders.

March 18, 1943—Frank Nitti and senior associates are indicted by a federal grand jury for violations under the Anti-Racketeering Act and the Mail Fraud Statute related to the Hollywood extortion case. Nitti has a falling out with Paul Ricca and other top members of the Outfit.

March 19, 1943—Frank Nitti dies at age fifty-seven, supposedly by his own hand, but possibly as the result of foul play.

December 23, 1943—Paul Ricca and other key Nitti associates are found guilty on federal indictment charges.

June 24, 1946—Race-wire-service entrepreneur James A. Ragen Sr. is shot in his car by unknown persons in a moving truck, likely stemming from actions undertaken by Frank Nitti years earlier during the establishment of the Trans-American Publishing and News Service, Inc., national race-wire service.

October 31, 1952—The Department of Justice posthumously cancels Frank Nitti's naturalization certificate because of noncollectible Internal Revenue taxes and the belief that he held stocks under a fictitious name.

October 15, 1959 to September 10, 1963—Actor Bruce Gordon portrays Frank Nitti in the television series, *The Untouchables*, as well as related spin-off movies.

November 22, 1963—President John F. Kennedy is assassinated in Dallas, Texas, and Nitti alumni including Jack Ruby, Outfit boss

Sam Giancana, and hit man David Yaras are implicated in the murder, but never charged. Three decades earlier, Yaras had been a key player in the Cermak assassination under Nitti.

Circa 1967—Actor Harold Stone portrays Frank Nitti in the movie, *The Saint Valentine's Day Massacre.*

Circa 1975—Actor Sylvester Stallone portrays Frank Nitti in the movie, *Capone.*

Circa 1983-1986—Author Max Allan Collins writes the landmark "Frank Nitti Trilogy": *True Detective* (1983), *True Crime* (1984), and *The Million-Dollar Wound* (1986), beginning a long and continuing literary fascination with the character.

Circa 1987—Actor Billy Drago portrays Frank Nitti in the movie, *The Untouchables.*

Circa 1988—Actor Anthony LaPaglia portrays Frank Nitti in the 1988 made-for-television movie, *Nitti: The Enforcer.*

Circa 1989—Actor Alan Rosenberg portrays Frank Nitti in the made-for-television movie, *The Revenge of Al Capone.*

Circa 1993-1994—Actor Paul Regina portrays Frank Nitti in the television series, *The Untouchables.*

Circa 1998—Author Max Allan Collins writes the illustrated novel, *Road to Perdition*, which uses Frank Nitti as a central character.

Circa 2002—Actor Stanley Tucci portrays Frank Nitti in the movie version of *Road to Perdition.*

Circa 2004—Author Max Allan Collins writes and publishes *Road to Purgatory*, the definitive story of Frank Nitti's downfall and death.

Circa 2008—Frank Nitti's biography is published six decades after his death.

APPENDIX B

Organizational Structure of the Outfit under Frank Nitti

Note: Names followed by (D) were deceased by 1936-1937.

BOARD OF DIRECTORS
- Frank "the Enforcer" Nitti (boss)
- Paul "the Waiter" Ricca (a.k.a. Paul DeLucia) (underboss and Nitti's successor)
- Jake "Greasy Thumb" Guzik (finance, accounting and personnel, senior bagman)
- Louis "Little New York" Campagna (security—longtime Nitti bodyguard, dispatcher, and traffic manager)
- Murray "the Camel" Humphreys (consigliere, chief strategist, milk-drivers' union racketeer, bagman, master fixer, and political corrupter)
- Philip "Dandy Phil" D'Andrea (bodyguard, sniper, kidnapper, train and bank robber, promotion, and sales)
- Frankie "Slippery" Rio (security and street gang liaison) (D)

CAPOS, KEY INSIDERS, AND SPECIALISTS
- Tony "Big Tuna" or "Joe Batters" Accardo (future boss)
- James Aducci (a.k.a. William Pion) (member of the state legislature)
- Dr. Saul Alinsky (criminologist and Outfit courier)
- George "Red" Barker (D)

- James "Bomber" Belcastro (explosives expert)
- Willie "the Squealer" Bioff (a.k.a. William Berg; Henry Martin) (union frontman)
- George E. Browne (union frontman)
- Max Caldwell (a.k.a. Max Pollack) (Chicago Retail Clerks Union)
- Anthony "Tough Tony" Capezio (Frank Nitti's brother-in-law)
- Ralph "Bottles" Capone (general assistant in liquor, vice, and gambling rackets)
- Nick Circella (a.k.a. Nicky Dean)
- Dennis "Duke" Cooney (café and brothel chain owner)
- Mike Carrozzo (street sweeper's, International Union of Pavers and Road Builders and the International Hod Carriers, Building and Common Laborers' District Council union racketeer)
- Louis Cowen (propagandist and owner of the *Cicero Tribune* newspaper) (D)
- Jack Dragna (Mafia boss in Los Angeles, sometimes allied with the Outfit and other times with Bugsy Siegel and the New York families, and manager of the Trans-American gambling wire service)
- Jimmy Emory (relative of Al Capone, racetrack owner, boss of Chicago Heights)
- Giuseppi "Diamond Joe" Esposito (senior adviser)
- Frederick Evans (fiscal and money laundering expert)
- John "Jake the Barber" Factor (confidence artist and stock swindler)
- Charles Fischetti, Frank Fischetti, and Rocco Fischetti (Al Capone's cousins) (bodyguards, assassins, beer distribution)
- Louis "Cockeyed" Fratto (*representante* for Des Moines)
- Joseph Fusco (bodyguard, police official payoffs, liquor and beer)
- Joseph Genaro (explosives expert)
- Charles "Cherry Nose" Gioe

- Joseph Glimco ("Little Tim Murphy") (Chicago Taxicab Local 777)
- Fred Goetz (D)
- Alex Louis Greenberg (financial advice, real estate, and breweries)
- Harry Hochstein (city politician, Nitti's aide-de-camp and confidant)
- "Golf Bag" Sam Hunt (enforcer)
- Alex Korecek (arms merchant)
- Sidney R. Korshak (legal)
- Hymie "Loud Mouth" Levine (race-wire collections)
- Tony Lombardo (president of the Unione Siciliano guild in Chicago)
- Claude Maddox (a.k.a. John "Screwy" Moore) (one of the owners of the infamous Paddock Lounge in Cicero)
- Francis Maritote (a.k.a. Frankie Diamond; Al Capone's brother-in-law)
- "Machine Gun" Jack McGurn (enforcer/gunman) (D)
- Frank Milano (enforcer/gunman)
- Ralph O'Hara (unions and Trans-American Publishing and News Service, Inc.)
- Edward "Fast Eddie" O'Hare (gambler, lawyer and business adviser)
- U.S. Congressman Joe "Hinky Dink" Parrillo
- Johnny Patton (political ally, mayor of Burnham, big brewery owner, political fixes)
- Pete Penovich, Jr. (floating casinos)
- Ralph Pierce (owner of the Carlton Hotel gambling club)
- Frank Pope (gambling)
- Dr. Gaetano Ronga (Frank Nitti's father-in-law and mob physician)
- Johnny Roselli (*representante* in Havana, Los Angeles, Las Vegas)

- William R. Skidmore (corruptor and political fixer)
- Dr. Benjamin M. Squires (Cleaners and Dyers Institute)
- John Torrio (ex-boss, took early retirement in 1925, but continued to provide advice)
- Eddie Vogel (coin-operated machines)
- Anthony "Mops" Volpe (gambling, originally a trusted bodyguard and chauffeur)
- Peter von Frantzius (arms merchant)
- David Yaras (*representante*, hit man, labor relations, narcotics and rackets man in Miami and Cuba)
- Isidor Zevin (Nitti's accountant)

NOTABLE OTHER RANKS

- Jake Adler
- Sylvester Agolia
- Joey "the Doves" Aiuppa (future boss)
- Felix "Milwaukee Phil" Alderisio (future boss)
- Gus Alex
- Samuel Alex
- Mike Allegretto
- August "Genero" Annereno
- Joe "Pappi Genero" Annereno
- Johnny "Genero" Annereno
- Theodore "the Greek" Anton
- Tony Arasso
- John Armondo
- Tony Balcastro (D)
- Dominick Ballo
- Louis Barko (a.k.a. Louis Valeria)
- Bobby Barton (Jake Guzik's chauffeur)
- Sam "Teets" Battaglia (future boss)
- Johnny Begen
- Rocco Belcastro
- Frank Biege (a.k.a. Frank Perry) (bodyguard)

- Charles Blakely
- William Block
- Dominick Brancato
- Ralph Buglio
- P.C. "Denver Blackie" Burchan
- Fred Burke (St. Louis hit man)
- Mike Butero
- Marshall Caifano (hit man)
- Mathew Cappalario
- Charlie Carr
- Jackie "the Lackey" Cerone (future boss)
- Louis Clemente
- William Clifford
- Santo Collebron
- Charlie Costello
- Michael Costello
- Samuel Costello
- Louis Cowan (D)
- Tony Curingione
- Rocco DeGrazie (driver and alcohol)
- Nick DeGrazio
- Robert DeGrazio
- Tony DeGrazio
- Bert Delaney (breweries and warehousing facilities)
- Frank Derrico
- "Mad Sam" DeStefano
- "Big Dave" Earsman (teamster-union racketeer)
- Rocco Fanelli (procurer)
- Fred Farley
- Carlos Fontana
- Ernest Fontana
- James Forsyth (a.k.a. James Fawcett)
- "Big Earl" Fraher
- John Genaro (D)

- Sam (Salvatore) "Momo" Giancana (future boss)
- Ralph Gillette
- Marty Guilfoyle
- Joseph Guinta (D)
- Harry Guzik (white slaver and procurer for vice rackets)
- Sam Guzik
- Willy Heeney (bodyguard)
- Jack Heinan (owner of Paddock Inn)
- "Mike de Pike" Heitler (D)
- Tommy Hurt
- Lawrence Imburgio (gambling operator)
- Nick Juffra
- Marty Kane
- Julian "Potatoes" Kaufman
- Louis Kaufman (New York labor rackets)
- Frankie Kelly
- Mike Kelly
- Tom Kerwin
- Henry Kimmel
- Philip Kimmel
- Al Lambert
- Joe Lolordo
- Pasqualino Lolordo (D)
- Tony Lombardo (D)
- Marcus "Stuffy" Looney (vice monger)
- Frank Mangano
- Lawrence "Dago" Mangano (West Side leader and kidnapping expert)
- Sam Marcus (bodyguard)
- Bill Marshall
- Josip Marusic (a.k.a. Joe Marsh)
- Louis Massesso
- Robert Larry McCullough
- Charles McGee (chauffeur)

- Jimmy Mondi (Cicero dive keeper)
- Joe Morici (a.k.a. Joe Moreli; Joe Ferraro) (bodyguard)
- Martin O'Leary
- Thomas Panton
- Leonard Patrick
- Nick Perry
- Frank "West Side Frankie" Pope (brothel and gambling-house owner)
- Fred Ries
- Louis Romano (frontman and head of the Chicago Bartender's Union)
- Jack "Sparky" Ruby (Rubenstein) (Chicago, Dallas)
- David William Russell (gambler and racketeer)
- James "Fur" Sammons (former member of the West Side O'Donnell gang and psychopathic union thug)
- Martin Sanders
- George Scalise (pimp and later president of the AFL International Building Service Employees union)
- Louis Schiavone
- Nick Sorella (bodyguard)
- Tony "the Chevalier" Spano (a.k.a. Joseph Nerone) (bodyguard, assassin)
- Charles Albert Spizzeri
- Mike Spranza (Kelly)
- Danny Stanton (labor racketeering)
- "Big Ed" Stash (assassin)
- Frank Sullivan
- Thomas Sullivan (a.k.a. Tom Cullen)
- "Billygoat" Taglio (plumber's-union racketeer)
- Clement Tatton
- Danny Vallo (D)
- William "Three Fingers Jack" White (D)
- Maxie Williams
- Gus Winkler

- John "Johnny the Pope" Yarlo (a.k.a. John Yario)
- Giuseppe Zangara (D)

(References: U.S. Federal Bureau of Investigation, *Alphonse Capone*, *(http://foia.fbi.gov/capone/capone.htm)*; Anon., "Start 'Vag' Law Roundup of 59 More Hoodlums; 'Spike' O'Donnell Is First Arrested—Killers Guilty," *Chicago Tribune*, (September 1, 1933); Guy Murchie Jr., "Prohibition to Blame for Al's Rise; How Chicago Was Ruled By Guns," *Chicago Sunday Tribune*, (February 9, 1936); William F. Roemer, Jr., *Accardo: the Genuine Godfather*, (New York, Ivy Books, 1995), pp. 55-56 and p. 66; Gus Russo, *The Outfit: The Role of Chicago's Underworld in the Shaping of Modern America*, (New York: Bloomsbury, 2001), pp. 67-68; and others.)

NOTES

CHAPTER ONE

1. Some sources also cite Nitti's first name as Franco, his second name as Raffele or Ralph, and his date of birth variously as either 1883, 1888, or 1889. However, his prison-record reference for the date January 27, 1886, appears to be the most accurate as it is written in Nitti's own handwriting. The town of Nitti's birth has also been cited as Augori and Angri. See National Archives and Records Administration, *Frank R. Nitto, 38021-L: "Failing to file Income Tax return"*; US Federal Bureau of Investigation, *Subject: Frank Nitti*; US Federal Bureau of Investigation, *St. Valentine's Day Massacre*, (foia.fbi.gov/ stvalen/); Robert J. Schoenberg, *Mr. Capone*, (New York: William Morrow, 1992), p. 245; and Anon., (*www.alcaponemuseum.com*).

2. National Archives and Records Administration, *Frank R. Nitto, 38021-L: "Failing to file Income Tax return"*; and John William Tuohy, "The Enforcer: Frank Nitti & The Chicago Mob," (*www.gamblingmagazine.com*). Tuohy makes the claims of Nitti having an education in "advanced chemistry" and watchmaking while Nitti's prison record indicates only a grade-seven education and no other special education or training. Nitti stated in these records he left school at age fourteen because he "had to work."

3. William F. Roemer, Jr., *Accardo: the Genuine Godfather*, (New York: Ivy Books), 1995, p. 42.

4. National Archives and Records Administration, *Frank R. Nitto, 38021-L: "Failing to file Income Tax return"*; Elmer L. Irey and William J. Slocum, *The Tax Dodgers: The Inside Story of the T-Men's War with America's Political and Underworld Hoodlums*, (New York: Greenberg, 1948), p. 45; and Lee David Zlotoff, *Nitti: The Story of Frank Nitto, "The Enforcer": A Movie for Television*, (Second Draft, September 18, 1987), p. 6. Giuseppi "Diamond Joe" Esposito was a political powerhouse in Chicago's Little Italy for decades and likely sponsored Al Capone's and Frank Nitti's initial move to Chicago.

5. Anon., (*www.gambino.com*).

6. US Federal Bureau of Investigation, *Subject: Frank Nitti*; Orville Dwyer and George Hartmann, "List Gangsters Who Prey on Chicago Unions: Three Capone Mobster Boss Extortionists Nitti, Ricca, and Campagna Rule," *Chicago Tribune*, (March 18, 1943); and Anon., "Nitti Long Held Business Chief of Underworld: Showed Cunning in All Racketeering Fields," *Chicago Tribune*, (March 20, 1943).

7. Kenneth Allsop, *The Bootleggers: The Story of Chicago's Prohibition Era*, (London: Arrow Books Ltd., 1970), p. 392.

8. US Federal Bureau of Investigation, *FBI Homepage*, (www.fbi.gov/homepage.html, September 2002).

9.   Hank Messick, *Lansky*, (New York: Berkley Medallion Books, 1971), p. 58. See Burton B. Turkus and Sid Feder, *Murder, Inc.: The Story of the Syndicate*, (Cambridge: Da Capo Press, 1951), for a complete account of the rise and fall of this syndicate contract-killer organization.

10. George Murray, *The Legacy of Al Capone*, (New York: G.P. Putnam's Sons, 1975), p. 28; Tuohy, "The Enforcer: Frank Nitti & The Chicago Mob"; and Zlotoff, *Nitti: The Story of Frank Nitto, "The Enforcer": A Movie for Television*, p. 8.

11. Schoenberg, *Mr. Capone*, p. 245.

12. US Federal Bureau of Investigation, *Subject: Frank Nitti*; US Federal Bureau of Investigation, *St. Valentine's Day Massacre*, (foia.fbi.gov/stvalen/); and Jim Dent, *Monster of the Midway: Bronko Nagurski, the 1943 Chicago Bears, and the Greatest Comeback Ever*, (New York: Thomas Dunne Books, 2003), p. 106. Dent makes the claim for the nicknames "Screwy" and "Chi-chi," but these have not been confirmed by other sources. If accurate, they may be an indication of the more violent aspect of Nitti's nature.

13. National Archives and Records Administration, *Frank R. Nitto, 38021-L: "Failing to file Income Tax return"*; US Federal Bureau of Investigation, *Subject: Frank Nitti*; Ronald Koziol and Edward Baumann, "How Frank Nitti Met His Fate: Return With Us Now to the Scene of the Mobster's Suicide," *Chicago Tribune*, (June 29, 1987); Carl Wiegman, "Nitti Kills Himself! Gang Chief Dies By Gun After US Jury Charges 3: Trainmen Look On as Racketeer Fires 3 Shots," *Chicago Tribune*, (March 20, 1943); Murray, *The Legacy of Al Capone*, p. 289; and John William Tuohy, *When Capone's Mob Murdered Roger Touhy: The Strange Case of Touhy, Jake the Barber and the Kidnapping That Never Happened*, (Fort Lee, NJ: Barricade Books Inc., 2001), p. 86. Nitti's official FBI description was cited as reported in 1930; they considered him to be of medium build. Nitti's 1931 prison record indicated that he was five feet, five inches in height and weighed 133 pounds, had flat feet, and three dental crowns.

14. US Federal Bureau of Investigation, *Subject: Frank Nitti*; and Max Allan Collins, *True Detective*, (New York: St. Martin's Press, 1983), p. 119.

15. National Archives and Records Administration, *Frank R. Nitto, 38021-L: "Failing to file Income Tax return"*; US Federal Bureau of Investigation, *Subject: Frank Nitti*; and Schoenberg, *Mr. Capone*, p. 245.

16. Ovid Demaris, *The Last Mafioso: The Treacherous World of Jimmy Fratianno*, (New York: Times Books, 1981), p.122; and John William Tuohy, "The Guns of Zangara," (*www.gamblingmagazine.com*).

17. Wiegman, "Nitti Kills Himself! Gang Chief Dies By Gun After US Jury Charges 3: Trainmen Look On as Racketeer Fires 3 Shots."

18. US Federal Bureau of Investigation, *Subject: Frank Nitti*; Irey and Slocum, *The Tax Dodgers: The Inside Story of the T-Men's War with America's Political and Underworld Hoodlums*, p. 45; and Schoenberg, *Mr. Capone*, p. 245.

19. Andy Edmonds, *Hot Toddy: The True Story of Hollywood's Most Sensational Murder*, (New York: William Morrow and Company, Inc., 1989), p. 198.

20. Schoenberg, *Mr. Capone*, p. 245.

21. John Morgan, *Prince of Crime*, (New York: Stein and Day, 1985), p. 122.

22. Schoenberg, *Mr. Capone*, p. 246.

23. See Charles Rappleye and Ed Becker, *All American Mafioso: The Johnny Rosselli Story*, (New York: Doubleday, 1991), pp. 70-71. For an account of the archetypal Mafia made man, wise guy, or good fellow see Nicholas Pileggi, *Wise Guy: Life in a Mafia Family*, (New York: Pocket Books, 1985).

24. Quoted in Murray, *The Legacy of Al Capone*, p. 183; and quoted in Gus Russo, *The Outfit: The Role of Chicago's Underworld in the Shaping of Modern America*, (New York: Bloomsbury, 2001), p. 133. Murray is often a popular source of dialogue, usually unreferenced, for crime historians, but because Murray himself used no footnotes or reference, it is unknown if it is authentic or a journalistic fabrication on his part.

25. Murray, *The Legacy of Al Capone*, pp. 192-193.

26. National Archives and Records Administration, Frank R. Nitto, 38021-L: *"Failing to file Income Tax return"*; Schoenberg, Mr. Capone, p. 245; and Curt Johnson, R. Craig Sautter, and Roger Ebert, *The Wicked City: Chicago from Kenna to Capone*, (New York: DaCapo Press, April 1998), p. 313.

27. Anon., "Nitti Long Held Business Chief of Underworld: Showed Cunning in All Racketeering Fields"; and John William Tuohy, "Guns and Glamor," (*www.gamblingmagazine.com*).

28. Dwyer and Hartmann, "List Gangsters Who Prey on Chicago Unions: Three Capone Mobster Boss Extortionists Nitti, Ricca, and Campagna Rule."

29. Anon., "Brother of Al Is Found Guilty of Tax Fraud: Maximum Penalty Is 22 Years," *Chicago Tribune*, (April 26, 1930).

30. Richard J. Dyer, (*hymieweiss.com*).

31. Murray, *The Legacy of Al Capone*, p. 276.

32. National Archives and Records Administration, *Frank R. Nitto, 38021-L: "Failing to file Income Tax return"*; US Federal Bureau of Investigation, *Subject: Frank Nitti*; Anon., "Hunted by US: Frank Nitti," *Chicago Tribune*, (October 8, 1930); Laurence Bergreen, *Capone: The Man and the Era*, (New York: Simon and Schuster; August 1996), p. 16; and Anon., (*www.csasi.org/October2001/earl_townsend.htm*).

33. US Federal Bureau of Investigation, *Subject: Frank Nitti*; Illinois Association for Criminal Justice, *The Illinois Crime Survey*, (Montclair, NJ: Patterson Smith, 1929 and 1968), p. 1,081; and John J. Binder, *The Chicago Outfit*, (Charleston, SC: Arcadia Publishing, 2003), p. 19. The FBI files show that in 1930 even samples of Nitti's handwriting were rare.

34. National Archives and Records Administration, *Frank R. Nitto, 38021-L: "Failing to file Income Tax return"*; and Schoenberg, *Mr. Capone*, p. 274.

35. National Archives and Records Administration, *Frank R. Nitto, 38021-L: "Failing to file Income Tax return"*; US Federal Bureau of Investigation, *Subject: Frank Nitti*; and US Federal Bureau of Investigation, *Alphonse Capone*, (*foia.fbi.gov/capone/capone.htm*).

36. National Archives and Records Administration, *Frank R. Nitto, 38021-L: "Failing to file Income Tax return"*; and Murray, *The Legacy of Al Capone*, p. 178. Nitti's 1930 FBI record indicated his occupation as that of "Liquor dealer." See US Federal Bureau of Investigation, *Subject: Frank Nitti*.

37. John H. Lyle, "The Mob Recoils Before a Wave of Warrants," *Chicago Tribune*, (December 17, 1960).

38. National Archives and Records Administration, *Frank R. Nitto, 38021-L: "Failing to file Income Tax return"*; and Anon., "Nitto, Freed by US on $50,000 Bond, Is Seized as Vagrant," *Chicago Tribune*, (November 8, 1930); and Lyle, "The Mob Recoils Before a Wave of Warrants."

39. Anon., "Gangbusters Gather, Swap 'War Stories', Talk About Mob, Recall Christmas in Canarise," *Chicago Tribune*, (October 10, 1975).

40. US Federal Bureau of Investigation, *Subject: Frank Nitti*; and Russo, *The Outfit: The Role of Chicago's Underworld in the Shaping of Modern America*, p. 508. Nitti's FBI record indicates that his fingerprints were obtained in November 1927 but were destroyed by court order in January 1930. While it was felt Nitti also had a New York police record, apparently the FBI could not obtain details of it.

41. Anon., (*www.cookcountysheriff.org*).

42. James Doherty, "Three Gambling Bosses Seized; New US Probe: Summoned to Grand Jury Quiz Tomorrow," *Chicago Tribune*, (April 30, 1940).

43. James Doherty, "Extortion Cash Splitups Told in Nitti Tax Case," *Chicago Tribune*, (October 2, 1948).

44. William F. Roemer, Jr., *War of the Godfathers: the Bloody Confrontation Between the Chicago and New York Families for Control of Las Vegas*, (New York: Ivy Books, 1990), p. 25.

45. Roemer, *Accardo: the Genuine Godfather*, pp. 65-66.

46. National Archives and Records Administration, *Frank R. Nitto, 38021-L: "Failing to file Income Tax return"*; US Federal Bureau of Investigation, *Subject: Frank Nitti*; US Federal Bureau of Investigation, *Alphonse Capone*; Allsop, *The Bootleggers: The Story of Chicago's Prohibition Era*, p. 485; and William F. Roemer, Jr., *The Enforcer—Spilotro: The Chicago Mob's Man Over Las Vegas*, (New York, Ivy Books, 1994), p. 70. However, the claim that Nitti was Capone's first cousin continues to this day. For example, see Binder, *The Chicago Outfit*, p. 19.

47. US Federal Bureau of Investigation, *Subject: Frank Nitti*; Anon., "'Tough' Capezio Is Freed of Bank Robbery Charge: Cashier Not Positive in Identification," *Chicago Tribune*, (September 17, 1932; Anon., "Mrs. Marie Capezio," *Chicago Tribune*, (April 1, 1943); and Anon., "Orders Retrial of Suit Against Nitti's Sister," *Chicago Tribune*, (May 1, 1943). There is apparently no other confirmation that she was Nitti's sister.

48. National Archives and Records Administration, *Frank R. Nitto, 38021-L: "Failing to file Income Tax return"*; *Warren Report*, (September 24, 1964); *US House Select Committee on Assassinations*, (July 1978); Sam and Chuck Giancana, *Double Cross*, (New York: Warner Books, Inc., 1992), p. 194; and James K. Olmstead, "Ruby/Jones Beginnings," *alt.assassination.jfk*, (July 22, 2000).

49. Irey and Slocum, *The Tax Dodgers: The Inside Story of the T-Men's War with America's Political and Underworld Hoodlums*, pp. 48-49.

50. Allan May, "Chicago Unione Siciliana 1920: A Decade of Slaughter (Part Three)," *AmericanMafia.com*, (May 2000).

51. Allan May, "Late for the Opera—Samoots Amatuna," *AmericanMafia.com*, (May 1999).

52. James Doherty, "Bioff Bares Nitti Role in Shakedowns: Heavily Guarded with Browne," *Chicago Tribune*, (October 1, 1948); and Anon., "Bioff Reveals Power of Nitti in Shakedowns," *Chicago Tribune*, (October 2, 1948).

53. Anon., "Mrs. Anna Nitto, Frank Nitti's Wife, Dies at 38," *Chicago Tribune*, (November 20, 1940). Antonio Napoli cites access to a report by an FBI informant who claims Nitti "caught his wife cheating" in Florida and divorced her. He also mistakenly claims that Nitti had a child by her, rather than adopting, in addition to various other factual errors. See Antonio Napoli, *The Mob's Guys*, (*Virtualbookworm.com* Publishing, March 2004), p. 21

54. Murray, *The Legacy of Al Capone*, p. 35; John William Tuohy, "Artful Eddie O'Hare," (*www.alleged-mafia-site.com*); Schoenberg, *Mr. Capone*, pp. 346-347; and Napoli, *The Mob's Guys*, p. 21. She is also sometimes referred to as Sue Granata and as having had a brother who sat in the Springfield state legislature.

55. Estes Kefauver, *Crime In America*, (New York: Doubleday and Company, Inc., 1951), pp. 70-71.

56. Anon., "Deal to Send Gang Chieftain to Prison Told: Forms Motive for Revenge Killing," *Chicago Tribune*, (November 16, 1939).

57. Kevin Kobelsky, "Interesting Business History in the Context of the Enron Scandal," (*www.trinity.edu/rjensen/*).

58. National Archives and Records Administration, *Frank R. Nitto, 38021-L: "Failing to file Income Tax return"*; and June Geserick, "Nitti Sent Wife to Church at Hour of Suicide: Gangster Too Good to Live, She Sobs," *Chicago Tribune*, (March 20, 1943).

59. Anon., "Louis Caravetta," *Chicago Tribune*, (February 27, 1951); and Anon., "Mrs. Campagna Dies; Widow of Gambling Boss," *Chicago Tribune*, (August 16, 1955).

60. Anon., "Bennett Tells of Loans; Johnston Takes Stand," *Chicago Tribune*, (December 21, 1950); Anon., "Give Extension to 4 Asked to Leave Tracks," *Chicago Tribune*, (November 14, 1951); and Anon., "A Real Twist—The US Owes Accardo Cash," *Chicago Tribune*, (February 18, 1959).

61. Mark R. Leper, *Bugsy: A Film Review*, (1991); and Messick, *Lansky*, pp. 145-152. However, in Andy Edmonds's biography of Virginia Hill, she claims that Hill's assignations with Nitti were little more than party antics with other gangsters at the San Carlo Italian Village and the Plantation Club, where she supposedly was soon accepted as "one of the boys." See Andy Edmonds, *Bugsy's Baby: The Secret Life of Mob Queen Virginia Hill*, (New York: Birch Lane Press, 1993), p. 35.

62. Ed Reid and Ovid Demaris, *The Green Felt Jungle*, (New York: Pocket Books, 1962), p. 28.

63. Ben Best, "Schemers in the Web: A Covert History of the 1960's Era," *www.benbest.com/history/schemers.html*, (1990). This story may just be an urban legend or inaccurate in its detail, although it certainly conveys the actual predatory spirit of the woman. Also see, Hank Messick and Joseph L. Nellis, *The Private Lives of Public Enemies*, (New York: Dell Publishing Company, Inc., 1973), pp. 149-153. Andy Edmonds's biography lends credit to the vulger nature of Hill. For example, see Edmonds, *Bugsy's Baby: The Secret Life of Mob Queen Virginia Hill*, pp. 41-42.

64. US Federal Bureau of Investigation, *Bugsy Siegel*, (*foia.fbi.gov/siege.htm*).

65. Messick and Nellis, *The Private Lives of Public Enemies*, p. 45.

66. *US House Select Committee on Assassinations*, (July 1978); Roemer, *War of the Godfathers: the Bloody Confrontation Between the Chicago and New York Families for Control of Las Vegas*, pp. 41-42 and pp. 49-50; and Roemer, *The Enforcer—Spilotro: The Chicago Mob's Man Over Las Vegas*, p. 64.

67. US Federal Bureau of Investigation, *Bugsy Siegel*.

68. Kefauver, *Crime In America*, pp. 295-297.

69. Best, "Schemers in the Web: A Covert History of the 1960's Era"; Messick, *Lansky*, p. 152; and Russo, *The Outfit: The Role of Chicago's Underworld in the Shaping of Modern America*, p. 459.

70. US Federal Bureau of Investigation, *St. Valentine's Day Massacre*.

71. Murray, *The Legacy of Al Capone*, p. 182.

72. US Federal Bureau of Investigation, *Subject: Frank Nitti*; and Anon., "Mrs. Anna Nitto, Frank Nitti's Wife, Dies at 38."

73. Lloyd Wendt, "Capone's Cohorts Carry On," *Chicago Tribune*, (August 31, 1941); and Anon., "Nitti Long Held Business Chief of Underworld: Showed Cunning in All Racketeering Fields."

74. Murray, *The Legacy of Al Capone*, pp. 274-275; and Bergreen, *Capone: The Man and the Era*, p. 555.

75. National Archives and Records Administration, *Frank R. Nitto, 38021-L: "Failing to file Income Tax return"*; and Koziol and Baumann, "How Frank Nitti Met His Fate: Return With Us Now to the Scene of the Mobster's Suicide."

76. Anon., "Suicide Reveals Riverside to be Gangster Haven," *Chicago Tribune*, (March 20, 1943); and Napoli, *The Mob's Guys*, p. 341.

77. Wiegman, "Nitti Kills Himself! Gang Chief Dies By Gun After US Jury Charges 3: Trainmen Look On as Racketeer Fires 3 Shots."

78. National Archives and Records Administration, *Frank R. Nitto, 38021-L: "Failing to file Income Tax return"*; and Anon., "3 Barkeep Union Agents Ousted; Nitti Gives Up: Receiver Moves to Block Romano Coup," *Chicago Tribune*, (October 10, 1940).

79. Anon., "Nab John Capone in Raid on Bookie Clearing House: Police Seize Five Others at Telephones," *Chicago Tribune*, (April 4, 1941); and Jane Stern and Michael Stern, *The Harry Caray's Restaurant Cookbook: The Official Home Plate of the Chicago Cubs*, (Nashville: Rutledge Hill Press, June 14, 2003), p. 11 and p. 88.

80. Anon., "Raiders Find Police File in Gang Hangout: Secret Paper Lists 31 for Arrest," *Chicago Tribune*, (September 26, 1930); Murray, *The Legacy of Al Capone*, pp. 186-187, p. 192, p. 271; and Russo, *The Outfit: The Role of Chicago's Underworld in the Shaping of Modern America*, pp. 96-97.

81. Laurence Bergreen, *Capone: The Man and the Era*, (New York: Simon and Schuster; August 1996), pp. 392-393. Other accounts indicate that the birthday party, which had been infiltrated by a federal agent, was held at the Lexington Hotel itself. See John Kobler, *Capone*, (New York: G. P. Putnam's Sons, 1971; Da Capo Press edition, 2003), p. 280.

CHAPTER TWO

1. Michael Woodiwiss, "Organized Crime—The Dumbing of Discourse," The British Criminology Conference: Selected Proceedings. Volume 3. Papers from the British Society of Criminology Conference, (Liverpool: July 1999).

2. US Federal Bureau of Investigation, *FBI Homepage, (www.fbi.gov/homepage.html*, September 2002).

3. William F. Roemer, Jr., *Accardo: the Genuine Godfather,* (New York: Ivy Books, 1995), pp. 400-401.

4. Woodiwiss, "Organized Crime—The Dumbing of Discourse."

5. See David E. Scheim, *Contract On America*, (New York: Zebra Books, 1993), pp. 407-410.

6. US Federal Bureau of Investigation, *FBI Homepage*, (*www.fbi.gov/homepage.html*, September 2002).

7. Anon., "The Mafia Homepage," *www.geocities.com*, (2002); and Gary W. Potter, Eastern Kentucky University, "Unit # 1: Organized Crime and the Mafia—Organized Crime in Social Context," (*www.policestudies.eku.edu/POTTER/crj401_1.htm*).

8. Ed Reid, *The Grim Reapers: The Anatomy of Organized Crime in America*, (New York: Bantam, 1969), p. 5.

9. Anon., (*www.gambino.com*).

10. Ed Reid and Ovid Demaris, *The Green Felt Jungle*, (New York: Pocket Books, 1962), p. 185.

11. Reid and Demaris, *The Green Felt Jungle*, p.16.

12. Anon., (*www.gambino.com*).

13. Andy, "The Gambino Crime Family: The First Century," *(www.ganglandnews.comgambino.htm).*

14. Anon., "Inquiry Shown: Questions Parried On His Activities," *Chicago Tribune*, (September 10, 1947).

15. William F. Roemer, Jr., *Roemer: Man Against the Mob*, (New York: Ivy Books, 1989), p. 30 and p. 255; William F. Roemer, Jr., *War of the Godfathers: the Bloody Confrontation Between the Chicago and New York Families for Control of Las Vegas*, (New York: Ivy Books, 1990), p. 71; and Richard Lindberg, "Origins and History of the Mafia 'Commission'," *Search International, www.search-international.com*, (September 2002).

16. Anon., (*lacosanostra.whaticollect.com*).

17. See Roemer, *War of the Godfathers: the Bloody Confrontation Between the Chicago and New York Families for Control of Las Vegas*, p. 69; and Scheim, *Contract On America*, pp. 244-246.

18. US Federal Bureau of Investigation, *Mafia Monograph: Section II United States*, (Washington DC: July 1958).

19. See Estes Kefauver, *Crime In America*, (New York: Doubleday and Company, Inc., 1951), for a summary of the major findings and conclusions of the committee hearings.

20. Kefauver, *Crime In America*, p. 18 and rear cover page.

21. Kefauver, *Crime In America*, pp. 295-298.

22. Kefauver, *Crime In America*, p. 300.

23. Kefauver, *Crime In America*, p. 55.

24. James Doherty, "Accardo Called Capone Gang's Chicago Boss: Senators Want to Know Scope of Operations," *Chicago Tribune*, (October 1, 1950).

25. See Curt Gentry, *J. Edgar Hoover: The Man and the Secrets*, (New York: W.W. Norton & Company, 1991), and Anthony Summers, *Official and Confidential: The Secret Life of J. Edgar Hoover*, (New York: Putnam Publishing Group, 1993), for detailed accounts.

26. Potter, "Unit # 1: Organized Crime and the 'Mafia'—Organized Crime in Social Context."

27. US Federal Bureau of Investigation, *FBI Homepage*.

28. Anon., (*thesmokinggun.com*).

29. Reid, *The Grim Reapers: The Anatomy of Organized Crime in America*, pp. 6-7; and Potter, "Unit # 1: Organized Crime and the 'Mafia'—Organized Crime in Social Context."

30. Reid, *The Grim Reapers: The Anatomy of Organized Crime in America*, p. 95.

31. Reid, *The Grim Reapers: The Anatomy of Organized Crime in America*, pp. 12-14; and Ovid Demaris, *The Last Mafioso: The Treacherous World of Jimmy Fratianno*, (New York: Times Books, 1981), pp. 18-19.

32. Edmund Mahony, "Mob Initiation Tape Spellbinder in Court," *The Hartford Courant*, (July 5, 1991); and William F. Roemer, Jr., *The Enforcer—Spilotro: The Chicago Mob's Man Over Las Vegas*, (New York: Ivy Books, 1994), p. 34.

33. Roemer, *Roemer: Man Against the Mob*, p. 159.

34. Roemer, *War of the Godfathers: the Bloody Confrontation Between the Chicago and New York Families for Control of Las Vegas*, p. 25.

35. Reid and Demaris, *The Green Felt Jungle*, pp. 184-185; and Kenneth Allsop, *The Bootleggers: The Story of Chicago's Prohibition Era*, (London: Arrow Books Ltd., 1970), p. 357 and pp. 371-372.

36. Joseph K. O'Brien and Andris Kurins, *Boss of Bosses—the Fall of the Godfather: The FBI and Paul Castellano*, (New York: Island Books, 1991), p. 15.

37. Reid, *The Grim Reapers: The Anatomy of Organized Crime in America*, p.1.

38. Anon., (*lacosanostra.whaticollect.com*).

39. A similar police hostility verging on rivalry toward motorcycle clubs organized along paramilitary lines, in particular the Hell's Angels Motorcycle Club, is also very pronounced.

40. Reid and Demaris, *The Green Felt Jungle*, p. 186.

41. Scheim, *Contract On America*, pp. 96-97.

42. Scheim, *Contract On America*, pp. 448-449.

43. George Murray, *The Legacy of Al Capone*, (New York: G.P. Putnam's Sons, 1975), p. 261.

44. Anon., "The Sicilian Mafia: A State Within the State," *The Economist*, (April 24, 1993), pp. 21-24; and Anon., "US Mafiosi prefer to recruit among less chatty Sicilians," *Associated Press*, (March 14, 2004).

45. Brian Daly, "Mafia's Growing Power Evident," *Canadian Press*, (September 9, 2002).

46. Scheim, *Contract On America*, p.393.

47. Lindberg, "Origins and History of the Mafia 'Commission'."

48. Quoted in Woodiwiss, "Organized Crime—The Dumbing of Discourse."

49. US Federal Bureau of Investigation, *FBI Homepage*.

50. Sam and Chuck Giancana, *Double Cross*, (New York: Warner Books, Inc., 1992), p. 248.

51. Elmer L. Irey and William J. Slocum, *The Tax Dodgers: The Inside Story of the T-Men's War with America's Political and Underworld Hoodlums*, (New York: Greenberg, 1948), p. 271; and Murray, *The Legacy of Al Capone*, p. 190.

52. Kefauver, *Crime In America*, p. 35.

53. Anon., (*www.gambino.com/bio/alcapone.htm*).

54. US Federal Bureau of Investigation, *Alphonse Capone*, (*foia.fbi.gov/capone/capone.htm*); and Ronald Koziol and John O'Brien, "Reputed Mob Boss Accardo Dead at 86," *Chicago Tribune*, (May 28, 1992).

55. Alex Rodriguez and Andrew Zajac, "Feds Trace How Cicero Plot Began; Mayor's Late Husband Labeled Architect of Scam," *Chicago Tribune*, (June 17, 2001).

56. Illinois Association for Criminal Justice, *The Illinois Crime Survey*, (Princeton, NJ: Patterson Smith, 1929 and 1968).

57. Illinois Association for Criminal Justice, *The Illinois Crime Survey*, p. 816.

58. Reid, *The Grim Reapers: The Anatomy of Organized Crime in America*, p. 254.

59. John H. Lyle, "Al Capone," *Chicago Tribune*, (December 4, 1960).

60. Chesly Manly, "US Jury Hits $200,000,000 Beer Combine: Gang Chief Named with 68 Aids," *Chicago Tribune*, (June 13, 1931); and US Federal Bureau of Investigation, *Alphonse Capone*.

61. Roemer, *Accardo: the Genuine Godfather*, p. 38.

62. US Federal Bureau of Investigation, *Alphonse Capone*; and Anon., (*www.mapinc.org/drugnews/v01/n000/a003.html*).

63. Chesly Manly, "US Jury Hits $200,000,000 Beer Combine: Gang Chief Named with 68 Aids," *Chicago Tribune*, (June 13, 1931).

64. Anon., (*www.mapinc.org/drugnews/v01/n000/a003.html*).

65. Anon., "Tribune to Publish Ledger Sheets of the Syndicate," *Chicago Tribune*, (October 25, 1941).

66. Roemer, *Roemer: Man Against the Mob*, p. 27.

67. Anon., "Inquiry Shown: Questions Parried On His Activities."

68. Doherty, "Accardo Called Capone Gang's Chicago Boss: Senators Want to Know Scope of Operations."

69. Scheim, *Contract On America*, p. 465.

70. For example, see Douglas Bukowski, *Big Bill Thompson, Chicago, and the Politics of Image*, (Urbana: University of Illinois Press, 1998).

71. Clark R. Mollenhoff, *Strike Force: Organized Crime and the Government*, (New York: Prentice-Hall, 1972), p. 171.

72. Anon., "Courtney Urges City Hall Quiz in O'Donnell Case: Ask Why Can Victim Beat Politician," *Chicago Tribune*, (March 22, 1943).

73. Kefauver, *Crime In America*, p. 86.

74. Virgil Peterson, "Capone," *Chicago Tribune*, (October 28, 1956).

75. The term associate is used here to denote close and key members of an organized crime syndicate, but is also sometimes used as a term for non-Italian members of the mafia who are not "made men."

76. Roemer, *Roemer: Man Against the Mob*, p. 2; Roemer, *The Enforcer—Spilotro: The Chicago Mob's Man Over Las Vegas*, p. 2; and Roemer, *Accardo: the Genuine Godfather*, p. 56.

77. Koziol and O'Brien, "Reputed Mob Boss Accardo Dead at 86."

78. Koziol and O'Brien, "Reputed Mob Boss Accardo Dead at 86."

79. US Federal Bureau of Investigation, *Alphonse Capone*; and Russo, *The Outfit: The Role of Chicago's Underworld in the Shaping of Modern America*, p. 68.

80. Roemer, *Accardo: the Genuine Godfather*, pp. 314-315.

81. John Kobler, *Capone*, (New York: G. P. Putnam's Sons, 1971; Da Capo Press edition, 2003), p. 142; and Murray, *The Legacy of Al Capone*, p. 28 and pp. 144-145.

82. US Federal Bureau of Investigation, *John Roselli*, *(foia.fbi.gov/roselli.htm);* and US Federal Bureau of Investigation, *Mafia Monograph: Section II United States*.

83. Herbert Aller, *The Extortionists*, (Beverly Hills: Guild-Hartford Publishing Company, Inc., 1972), p. 80.

84. US Federal Bureau of Investigation, *Alphonse Capone*; Paul Robsky and Oscar Fraley, *The Last of the Untouchables*, (New York: Popular Library, 1962), pp. 176-177; and Allsop, *The Bootleggers: The Story of Chicago's Prohibition Era*, pp. 446-447.

85. Irey and Slocum, *The Tax Dodgers: The Inside Story of the T-Men's War with America's Political and Underworld Hoodlums*, pp. viii-ix and p. 64.

86. Peterson, "Capone."

87. US Federal Bureau of Investigation, *Mafia Monograph: Section II United States*.

88. Murray, *The Legacy of Al Capone*, p. 140.

89. Robert J. Schoenberg, *Mr. Capone*, (New York: William Morrow, 1992), p. 198.

90. Russo, *The Outfit: The Role of Chicago's Underworld in the Shaping of Modern America*, p. 68.

91. Allsop, *The Bootleggers: The Story of Chicago's Prohibition Era*, pp. 342-343.

92. Irey and Slocum, *The Tax Dodgers: The Inside Story of the T-Men's War with America's Political and Underworld Hoodlums*, p. 43.

93. Anon., "Johnson Bares Capone 'Deal' in Income Case: Defends Wilkerson at Hearing," *Chicago Tribune*, (April 3, 1932).

94. Anon., "Tribune to Publish Ledger Sheets of the Syndicate"; Anon., "Hint Pay-off Keeps Al a Friend of New Bosses: Previous Disclosures!," *Chicago Tribune*, (October 28, 1941); and Murray, *The Legacy of Al Capone*, p. 277.

95. Potter, "Unit # 1: Organized Crime and the Mafia—Organized Crime in Social Context."

96. Illinois Association for Criminal Justice, *The Illinois Crime Survey*, p. 840.

97. Herbert Asbury, *The Gangs of Chicago: An Informal History of the Chicago Underworld*, (New York: Thunder's Mouth Press, 1986) (reprint of 1940 Alfred A. Knopf, Inc. edition), pp. 357-358; and Schoenberg, *Mr. Capone*, pp. 159-160 and p. 237. Capone paid for the medical care of an innocent mother and child who were injured in this attack.

98. Kobler, *Capone*, p. 258; and Schoenberg, *Mr. Capone*, pp. 233-234.

99. For a detailed account see Schoenberg, *Mr. Capone*, pp. 234-240.

100. Allsop, *The Bootleggers: The Story of Chicago's Prohibition Era*, pp. 402-403; Hank Messick and Joseph L. Nellis, *The Private Lives of Public Enemies*, (New York: Dell Publishing Company, Inc., 1973), p. 24; and Richard J. Dyer, (*hymieweiss.com*).

101. Schoenberg, *Mr. Capone*, p. 328.

102. Murray, *The Legacy of Al Capone*, p. 141 and p. 260.

103. Irey and Slocum, *The Tax Dodgers: The Inside Story of the T-Men's War with America's Political and Underworld Hoodlums*, pp. 275-276.

104. Murray, *The Legacy of Al Capone*, p. 266.

105. Anon., "Capone Henchman Arrested in Bed: Frank Nitti, Said to Be Treasurer for Gang Leader, Faces Income Tax Indictment," *Washington Daily News*, (October 31, 1930); Anon., "Heitler 'Death Letter' Puzzle to Prosecutor: Fails as Instrument of Vengeance," *Chicago Tribune*, (September 17, 1931); Anon., "A Rusted Safe Exposes Old Mob Secrets," *Chicago Tribune*, (January 23, 1960); Schoenberg, *Mr. Capone*, p. 309; and Roemer, *Accardo: the Genuine Godfather*, p. 48.

106. Anon., (*www.crimelibrary.com*); and Antoinette Giancana and Thomas C. Renner, *Mafia Princess: Growing Up In Sam Giancana's Family*, (New York: William Morrow and Company, Inc., 1984), p. 87. According to one of Giancana's daughters, he had worked for Nitti for at least a short time, but they were not on particularly good terms.

107. Scheim, *Contract On America*, p. 404.

108. Samuel Eliot Morison, *The Oxford History of the American People*, (New York: Oxford University Press, 1965), p. 901.

109. Illinois Association for Criminal Justice, *The Illinois Crime Survey*, p. 594.

110. Illinois Association for Criminal Justice, *The Illinois Crime Survey*, p. 610.

111. Russo, *The Outfit: The Role of Chicago's Underworld in the Shaping of Modern America*, p. 477.

112. Anon., *clari.news.law.crime, clari.news.features, clari.news.gov.agency*, (June 16, 1990); and John J. Binder, *The Chicago Outfit*, (Charleston, SC: Arcadia Publishing, 2003), p. 65.

113. Russo, *The Outfit: The Role of Chicago's Underworld in the Shaping of Modern America*, pp. 474-478.

114. For example, see Anon., (*lacosanostra.whaticollect.com*).

115. Alex Rodriguez and Andrew Zajac, "Feds Trace How Cicero Plot Began; Mayor's Late Husband Labeled Architect of Scam," *Chicago Tribune*, (June 17, 2001).

116. Anon., *clari.news.law.crime, clari.news.features, clari.news.gov.agency*). In a surprise April 2005 move, fourteen reputed Chicago Outfit figures were indicted by the FBI and IRS on charges of plotting at least eighteen murders including the 1986 slaying of Tony "the Ant" Spilotro, as part of a decades-old mob conspiracy involving loansharking and bookmaking.

CHAPTER THREE

1. See, Samuel Eliot Morison, *The Oxford History of the American People*, (New York: Oxford University Press, 1965), pp. 899-904 and p. 948.

2. Elmer L. Irey and William J. Slocum, *The Tax Dodgers: The Inside Story of the T-Men's War with America's Political and Underworld Hoodlums*, (New York: Greenberg, 1948), pp. 7-8.

3. H.G. Wells, *The Outline of History, Vol. II*, (New York: Garden City Books, 1956), pp. 907-908.

4. Sam and Chuck Giancana, *Double Cross*, (New York: Warner Books, Inc., 1992), p. 101.

5. Allan May, "Chicago Unione Siciliana 1920: A Decade of Slaughter (Part Three)," *AmericanMafia.com*, (May 2000).

6. Anon., (*www.gambino.com*).

7. Orville Dwyer and George Hartmann, "List Gangsters Who Prey on Chicago Unions: Three Capone Mobster Boss Extortionists Nitti, Ricca, and Campagna Rule," *Chicago Tribune*, (March 18, 1943); and Lee David Zlotoff, *Nitti: The Story of Frank Nitto, "The Enforcer": A Movie for Television*, (Second Draft, September 18, 1987), p. 5.

8. Gus Russo, *The Outfit: The Role of Chicago's Underworld in the Shaping of Modern America*, (New York: Bloomsbury, 2001), pp. 54-55.

9. National Archives and Records Administration, *Frank R. Nitto, 38021-L: "Failing to file Income Tax return"*; Giancana, *Double Cross*, pp. 22-23; and Curt Johnson, R. Craig Sautter, and Roger Ebert, *The Wicked City: Chicago from Kenna to Capone*, (New York: DaCapo Press, April 1998), p. 240, p. 259, and p. 261.

10. Hank Messick and Joseph L. Nellis, *The Private Lives of Public Enemies*, (New York: Dell Publishing Company, Inc., 1973), p. 33; and Richard J. Dyer, (*hymieweiss.com*).

11. Laurence Bergreen, *Capone: The Man and the Era*, (New York: Simon and Schuster; 1996), p. 178, p. 180, and pp. 183-184; and Dyer, (*hymieweiss.com*). According to Ber-

green, a nervous Capone came near to shooting Nitti one late evening at the door to his Round Lake cabin, where he was cooped up with a mistress, when he was unsure of Nitti's identity after Nitti and some others were in a car accident. Nitti is supposed to have exclaimed with Capone's revolver pointed in his face, "Jesus Christ, Al, don't shoot! It's me! Jesus Christ!"

12. Anon., (*www.gambino.com*).

13. Robert J. Schoenberg, *Mr. Capone*, (New York: William Morrow, 1992), p. 198.

14. Anon., "Hunted by US: Frank Nitti," *Chicago Tribune*, (October 8, 1930); and Richard T. Enright, *Al Capone, Master Criminal*, (Lakeville, MN: Northstar Maschek Books, 1931), p. 10.

15. US Federal Bureau of Investigation, *Mafia Monograph: Section II United States*, (Washington, DC: July 1958).

16. US Federal Bureau of Investigation, *Alphonse Capone*, *(foia.fbi.gov/capone/capone.htm)*.

17. Guy Murchie, Jr., "Prohibition to Blame for Al's Rise; How Chicago Was Ruled By Guns," *Chicago Sunday Tribune*, (February 9, 1936).

18. William F. Roemer, Jr., *War of the Godfathers: the Bloody Confrontation Between the Chicago and New York Families for Control of Las Vegas*, (New York: Ivy Books, 1990), p. 32.

19. Irey and Slocum, *The Tax Dodgers: The Inside Story of the T-Men's War with America's Political and Underworld Hoodlums*, p. 40.

20. Irey and Slocum, *The Tax Dodgers: The Inside Story of the T-Men's War with America's Political and Underworld Hoodlums*, p. 59.

21. US Federal Bureau of Investigation, *Alphonse Capone*.

22. John H. Lyle, "The Mob Recoils Before a Wave of Warrants," *Chicago Tribune*, (December 17, 1960).

23. Andy Edmonds, *Hot Toddy: The True Story of Hollywood's Most Sensational Murder*, (New York: William Morrow and Company, Inc., 1989), p. 198.

24. John Kobler, *Capone*, (New York: G. P. Putnam's Sons, 1971; Da Capo Press edition, 2003), p. 127 and p. 142; John J. Binder, *The Chicago Outfit*, (Charleston, SC: Arcadia Publishing, 2003), p. 19; and Ronald Koziol and Edward Baumann, "How Frank Nitti Met His Fate: Return With Us Now to the Scene of the Mobster's Suicide," *Chicago Tribune*, (June 29, 1987).

25. Irey and Slocum, *The Tax Dodgers: The Inside Story of the T-Men's War with America's Political and Underworld Hoodlums*, p. 27, p. 37, p. 45, and p. 276.

26. Quoted in Irey and Slocum, *The Tax Dodgers: The Inside Story of the T-Men's War with America's Political and Underworld Hoodlums*, p. 38.

27. Quoted in Irey and Slocum, *The Tax Dodgers: The Inside Story of the T-Men's War with America's Political and Underworld Hoodlums*, pp. 43-44.

28. George Murray, *The Legacy of Al Capone*, (New York: G.P. Putnam's Sons, 1975), p. 277.

29. John Morgan, *Prince of Crime*, (New York: Stein and Day, 1985), p. 122.

30. Edmonds, *Hot Toddy: The True Story of Hollywood's Most Sensational Murder*, p. 109.

31. Quoted in Morgan, *Prince of Crime*, pp. 99-100.

32. US Federal Bureau of Investigation, *St. Valentine's Day Massacre, (foia.fbi.gov/stvalen/).*

33. Anon., *(www.gambino.com).*

34. Illinois Association for Criminal Justice, *The Illinois Crime Survey*, (Princeton, NJ: Patterson Smith, 1929 and 1968), p. 593.

35. Illinois Association for Criminal Justice, *The Illinois Crime Survey*, p. 594.

36. Morgan, *Prince of Crime*, p. 150.

37. Illinois Association for Criminal Justice, *The Illinois Crime Survey*, p. 834.

38. Kenneth Allsop, *The Bootleggers: The Story of Chicago's Prohibition Era*, (London: Arrow Books Ltd., 1970), p. 123; Kobler, *Capone*, p. 127; Schoenberg, *Mr. Capone*, p. 116; and Allan May, "Chicago Unione Siciliana 1920: A Decade of Slaughter (Part Three)," *AmericanMafia.com*, (May 2000). Those present at the Ship that night included Johnny Torrio, Nitti, Capone, Frankie Rio, Frank Maritote (Diamond), O'Banion, and Hymie Weiss.

39. Dyer, *(hymieweiss.com).*

40. Dyer, *(hymieweiss.com).*

41. Herbert Asbury, *The Gangs of Chicago: An Informal History of the Chicago Underworld*, (New York: Thunder's Mouth Press, 1986) (reprint of 1940 Alfred A. Knopf, Inc. edition), p. 358; Enright, *Al Capone, Master Criminal*, pp. 25-26; Allsop, *The Bootleggers: The Story of Chicago's Prohibition Era*, pp. 168-171; and Schoenberg, *Mr. Capone*, pp. 162-163.

42. Allan May, "Chicago Unione Siciliana 1920: A Decade of Slaughter (Part Seven)," *AmericanMafia.com*, (May 2000).

43. US Federal Bureau of Investigation, *Alphonse Capone*.

44. Anon., *(www.gambino.com).*

45. Enright, *Al Capone, Master Criminal*, p. 65; Allsop, *The Bootleggers: The Story of Chicago's Prohibition Era*, pp. 189-191; Morgan, *Prince of Crime*, pp. 68-69 and p. 129; and Schoenberg, *Mr. Capone*, p. 187.

46. US Federal Bureau of Investigation, *John Roselli, (foia.fbi.gov/roselli.htm).*

47. Dwyer and Hartmann, "List Gangsters Who Prey on Chicago Unions: Three Capone Mobster Boss Extortionists Nitti, Ricca, and Campagna Rule."

48. Allan May, "Louis Campagna—Done in by a Grouper," *AmericanMafia.com*, (May 1999).

49. Anon., "Keep Campagna 'Books' Closed, Cicero Orders," *Chicago Tribune*, (October 3, 1947).

50. Anon., *(garnet.acns.fsu.edu/~cmp3335/biography.htm).*

51. US Federal Bureau of Investigation, *John Roselli*; US Federal Bureau of Investigation, *Purple Gang, (foia.fbi.gov/purpgang.htm);* Allsop, *The Bootleggers: The Story of Chicago's Prohibition Era*, pp. 199-200; Bergreen, *Capone: The Man and the Era*, p. 555; and John

William Tuohy, *When Capone's Mob Murdered Roger Touhy: The Strange Case of Touhy, Jake the Barber and the Kidnapping That Never Happened*, (Fort Lee, NJ: Barricade Books Inc., 2001), p. 121.

52. Bernard Wasserstein, *Secret War in Shanghai*, (New York: Houghton Mifflin Company, 1998), p. 47. For a complete account, see Paul R. Kavieff, *The Purple Gang: Organized Crime in Detroit 1910-1945*, (Fort Lee, NJ: Barricade Books, 2005).

53. Messick and Nellis, *The Private Lives of Public Enemies*, p. 40.

54. Ronald Koziol and John O'Brien, "Reputed Mob Boss Accardo Dead at 86," *Chicago Tribune*, (May 28, 1992).

55. Anon., "Chicago Police Department Homicide Record," *www.cyberdriveillinois.com/ departments/archives/massacre.html*, (2002).

56. Allsop, *The Bootleggers: The Story of Chicago's Prohibition Era*, p. 197.

57. Anon., "Chicago Police Department Homicide Record"; and Anon., (*garnet.acns.fsu. edu/~cmp3335/biography.htm*).

58. National Archives and Records Administration, *Frank R. Nitto, 38021-L: "Failing to file Income Tax return"*; and Lyle, "The Mob Recoils Before a Wave of Warrants."

59. William F. Roemer, Jr., *Accardo: the Genuine Godfather*, (New York, Ivy Books, 1995), p. 50.

60. Schoenberg, *Mr. Capone*, p. 234; and Allan May, "Chicago Unione Siciliana 1920: A Decade of Slaughter (Part Eight—Final)," *AmericanMafia.com*, May 2000.

61. Quoted in May, "Chicago Unione Siciliana 1920: A Decade of Slaughter (Part Eight—Final)." Also see Enright, *Al Capone, Master Criminal*, p. 73; Murray, *The Legacy of Al Capone*, pp. 113-117; and Allsop, *The Bootleggers: The Story of Chicago's Prohibition Era*, pp. 206-207.

62. Irey and Slocum, *The Tax Dodgers: The Inside Story of the T-Men's War with America's Political and Underworld Hoodlums*, p. 44.

63. Roemer, *Accardo: the Genuine Godfather*, p. 41; and Anon., (*www.gambino.com*).

64. Allsop, *The Bootleggers: The Story of Chicago's Prohibition Era*, pp. 229-230; and Schoenberg, *Mr. Capone*, p. 279, p. 286, and pp. 225-226.

65. Kobler, *Capone*, p. 258; May, "Chicago Unione Siciliana 1920: A Decade of Slaughter (Part Eight—Final)"; and Johnson, Sautter, and Ebert, *The Wicked City: Chicago from Kenna to Capone*, p. 303.

66. US Federal Bureau of Investigation, *Alphonse Capone*.

67. Asbury, *The Gangs of Chicago: An Informal History of the Chicago Underworld*, p. 373; Murray, *The Legacy of Al Capone*, p. 139; Johnson, Sautter, and Ebert, *The Wicked City: Chicago from Kenna to Capone*, p. 305; and Bergreen, *Capone: The Man and the Era*, p. 340.

68. US Federal Bureau of Investigation, *St. Valentine's Day Massacre*.

69. US Federal Bureau of Investigation, *John Roselli*.

70. US Federal Bureau of Investigation, *Alphonse Capone*; US Federal Bureau of Investigation, *St. Valentine's Day Massacre*; and John William Tuohy, *The Enforcer: Frank Nitti & The Chicago Mob*, (*www.gamblingmagazine.com*).

71. Anon., "Massacred Gangsters' Ghosts Live in Some Chicago Minds," *Associated Press*, (February 14, 1989).

72. US Federal Bureau of Investigation, *Subject: Frank Nitti*; Anon., "Brother of Al Is Found Guilty of Tax Fraud: Maximum Penalty Is 22 Years," *Chicago Tribune*, (April 26, 1930); and Irey and Slocum, *The Tax Dodgers: The Inside Story of the T-Men's War with America's Political and Underworld Hoodlums*, pp. 27-35.

73. Anon., "Johnson Bares Capone 'Deal" in Income Case: Defends Wilkerson at Hearing," *Chicago Tribune*, (April 3, 1932).

74. Anon., "Jack Guzik Now Is No. 1 Man of Gang Overlords: Here Are the Records of 4 Syndicate Heads; Personalities of the Syndicate," *Chicago Tribune*, (October 25, 1941); Dwyer and Hartmann, "List Gangsters Who Prey on Chicago Unions: Three Capone Mobster Boss Extortionists Nitti, Ricca, and Campagna Rule"; and Anon., "Nitti Long Held Business Chief of Underworld: Showed Cunning in All Racketeering Fields," *Chicago Tribune*, (March 20, 1943).

75. US Federal Bureau of Investigation, *Subject: Frank Nitti*; and Roemer, *Accardo: the Genuine Godfather*, p. 52.

76. US Federal Bureau of Investigation, *Subject: Frank Nitti*; Anon., "Hunted by US: Frank Nitti," *Chicago Tribune*, (October 8, 1930); Anon., "Seize Frank Nitti, Capone Treasurer: Roche Traps Gang Leader Sought by US," *Chicago Tribune*, (October 31, 1930); Anon., "Capone Henchman Arrested in Bed: Frank Nitti, Said to Be Treasurer for Gang Leader, Faces Income Tax Indictment," *Washington Daily News*, (October 31, 1930); Anon., "Capone Aid Arrested as Federal Tax Evader," *The Washington Post*, (November 3, 1930); Anon., "Nitto, Freed by US on $50,000 Bond, Is Seized as Vagrant," *Chicago Tribune*, (November 8, 1930); Irey and Slocum, *The Tax Dodgers: The Inside Story of the T-Men's War with America's Political and Underworld Hoodlums*, pp. 48-50; and Schoenberg, *Mr. Capone*, pp. 255-256.

77. Anon., "State Prepares for Next Gang Vagrant's Trial," *Chicago Tribune*, (November 19, 1930); Irey and Slocum, *The Tax Dodgers: The Inside Story of the T-Men's War with America's Political and Underworld Hoodlums*, pp. 45-46; and Allsop, *The Bootleggers: The Story of Chicago's Prohibition Era*, p. 416.

78. US Federal Bureau of Investigation, *Subject: Frank Nitti*; National Archives and Records Administration, *Frank R. Nitto, 38021-L: "Failing to file Income Tax return"*; and Anon., "100 Witnesses Brave Death in Capone Trial: Thirty Hoodlums Called; Which Ones Talked?," *Chicago Tribune*, (August 30, 1931).

79. Irey and Slocum, *The Tax Dodgers: The Inside Story of the T-Men's War with America's Political and Underworld Hoodlums*, p. 45; and Schoenberg, *Mr. Capone*, p. 246.

80. US Federal Bureau of Investigation, *Subject: Frank Nitti*; National Archives and Records Administration, *Frank R. Nitto, 38021-L: "Failing to file Income Tax return"*; Schoenberg, *Mr. Capone*, p. 246; and Tuohy, *The Enforcer: Frank Nitti & The Chicago Mob*. The official FBI file reported that "it was pointed out that Ralph Capone, brother of Al Capone, when indicted for evading his income tax was placed under a bond of $35,000.00 and that he was considered of a more desperate type than Subject Nitti."

81. US Federal Bureau of Investigation, *Subject: Frank Nitti*; National Archives and Records Administration, *Frank R. Nitto, 38021-L: "Failing to file Income Tax return"*; Dwyer and Hartmann, "List Gangsters Who Prey on Chicago Unions: Three Capone

Mobster Boss Extortionists Nitti, Ricca, and Campagna Rule"; Anon., "Nitti Long Held Business Chief of Underworld: Showed Cunning in All Racketeering Fields"; Irey and Slocum, *The Tax Dodgers: The Inside Story of the T-Men's War with America's Political and Underworld Hoodlums*, p. 46; and Murray, *The Legacy of Al Capone*, pp. 152-154. The official FBI records give the exact amount of nonreported income as $742,887.81 with $158,823.21 due in avoided taxes, mostly occurring during 1925 when Nitti was single with no dependents. In transcripts of his parole hearings, Nitti claimed that the actual amount of income tax owing was never determined and the amounts indicated in court were just approximations. Nitti claimed that the federal-income determinations were made from gross revenues deposited in banks and did not take into consideration "losses and things like that," but he "never kept any books or anything," he was "working for another person," and only drew a salary of some $80,000 to $90,000 plus "a small interest in the profits."

82. US Federal Bureau of Investigation, *Subject: Frank Nitti*; US Federal Bureau of Investigation, *St. Valentine's Day Massacre*; and Schoenberg, *Mr. Capone*, p. 246.

83. Schoenberg, *Mr. Capone*, pp. 255-256.

84. Some sources reference his first name as Billy. Parrillo would be present at Frank Nitti's office in 1932 when Chicago police detectives under the orders of Mayor Anton Cermak attempted to murder Nitti.

85. Irey and Slocum, *The Tax Dodgers: The Inside Story of the T-Men's War with America's Political and Underworld Hoodlums*, p. 56.

86. Dwyer and Hartmann, "List Gangsters Who Prey on Chicago Unions: Three Capone Mobster Boss Extortionists Nitti, Ricca, and Campagna Rule."

87. National Archives and Records Administration, *Frank R. Nitto, 38021-L: "Failing to file Income Tax return"*; US Federal Bureau of Investigation, *Subject: Frank Nitti*; Schoenberg, *Mr. Capone*, p. 329; Bergreen, *Capone: The Man and the Era*, p. 518; and Russo, *The Outfit: The Role of Chicago's Underworld in the Shaping of Modern America*, p. 55.

88. National Archives and Records Administration, *Frank R. Nitto, 38021-L: "Failing to file Income Tax return"*; Murray, *The Legacy of Al Capone*, p. 22; and Ken Schessler, "Unusual Guide to Chicago," *members.aol.com/KSchessler/wizzn.html*, (September 2002).

89. Russo, *The Outfit: The Role of Chicago's Underworld in the Shaping of Modern America*, p. 55.

90. James Doherty, "Slot Machine 'Take' of Nitti Told Probers: Data Made Available to Sheriff Walsh," *Chicago Tribune*, (September 12, 1948).

91. Anon., "Gangsters' Tax Hearings Start Here Tomorrow," *Chicago Tribune*, (March 10, 1935); Anon., "US Cuts Income Tax Claims Against Three Ex-Gangsters," *Chicago Tribune*, (March 12, 1935); and James Doherty, "Extortion Cash Splitups Told in Nitti Tax Case," *Chicago Tribune*, (October 2, 1948).

92. James Doherty, "Bioff Bares Nitti Role in Shakedowns: Heavily Guarded with Browne," *Chicago Tribune*, (October 1, 1948).

93. US Federal Bureau of Investigation, *Subject: Frank Nitti*; Anon., "Raiders Find Police File in Gang Hangout: Secret Paper Lists 31 for Arrest," *Chicago Tribune*, (September 26, 1930); Anon., "Charge Capone Censored Cops' Gangster List: Alcock Seeks Spy in Detective Bureau," *Chicago Tribune*, (September 27, 1930); Roemer, *Accardo: the Genuine*

Godfather, p. 50; Bergreen, *Capone: The Man and the Era*, p. 398; and Russo, *The Outfit: The Role of Chicago's Underworld in the Shaping of Modern America*, p. 85. Originally, the police list had the names of forty-one gangsters from various Chicago gangs, but ten Outfit members had been edited out, presumably by Capone.

94. US Federal Bureau of Investigation, *Alphonse Capone*.

95. Russo, *The Outfit: The Role of Chicago's Underworld in the Shaping of Modern America*, p. 47.

96. Max Allan Collins, *The Million-Dollar Wound*, (New York: St. Martin's Press, 1986).

97. US Federal Bureau of Investigation, *Alphonse Capone*.

CHAPTER FOUR

1. US Federal Bureau of Investigation, *Alphonse Capone*, *(foia.fbi.gov/capone/capone.htm)*.

2. US Federal Bureau of Investigation, *Alphonse Capone*.

3. Ovid Demaris, *The Last Mafioso: The Treacherous World of Jimmy Fratianno*, (New York: Times Books, 1981), p. 122. Roselli also had this to say of the original television series of *The Untouchables*:

> Millions of people all over the world see this show every fucking week. It's even popular in Italy. And what they see is a bunch of Italian lunatics running around with machine guns, talking out of the corner of their mouths, slopping up spaghetti like a bunch of fucking pigs. They make Capone and Nitti look like bloodthirsty maniacs. The guys that write that shit don't know the first thing about the way things were in those days. Eliot Ness, my ass. The tax boys got Al, not Ness.

4. Quoted in Sanford D. Horwitt, *Let Them Call Me Rebel: Saul Alinsky—His Life and Legacy*, (New York: Alfred A. Knopf, 1989), p. 21.

5. William F. Roemer, Jr., *Accardo: the Genuine Godfather*, (New York: Ivy Books, 1995), p.50.

6. Chesly Manly, "US Jury Hits $200,000,000 Beer Combine: Gang Chief Named with 68 Aids," *Chicago Tribune*, (June 13, 1931).

7. US Federal Bureau of Investigation, *Eliot Ness*, *(foia.fbi.gov/ness.htm)*.

8. Eliot Ness and Oscar Fraley, *The Untouchables: The Real Story*, (New York: Pocket Books, 1957), pp. 93-94, pp. 162-163, p. 203, p. 238.

9. Robert J. Schoenberg, *Mr. Capone*, (New York: William Morrow, 1992), p. 297.

10. Oscar Fraley, *4 Against the Mob*, (New York: Popular Library, 1961), p. 53.

11. Paul Robsky and Oscar Fraley, *The Last of the Untouchables*, (New York: Popular Library, 1962), p. 37, pp. 179-181.

12. See Elmer L. Irey and William J. Slocum, *The Tax Dodgers: The Inside Story of the T-Men's War with America's Political and Underworld Hoodlums*, (New York: Greenberg, 1948); and Timothy W. Maier, "IRS Tax Cops," *www.insightmag.com*, (2002). Irey's book is one of the best-written, detailed, and most entertaining accounts of the struggle between federal government agents and organized crime during Nitti's era. It is unfortunate

that today Irey's memoir is so little known, although at times it clearly displays the underlying WASP prejudices that were then popular.

13. Kenneth Allsop, *The Bootleggers: The Story of Chicago's Prohibition Era*, (London: Arrow Books Ltd., 1970), p. 415.

14. Anon., "Rites Set Tuesday for Lt. Tierney," *Chicago Tribune*, (August 8, 1971).

15. William F. Roemer, Jr., *War of the Godfathers: the Bloody Confrontation Between the Chicago and New York Families for Control of Las Vegas*, (New York: Ivy Books, 1990), p. 53.

16. John H. Lyle, "Al Capone," *Chicago Tribune*, (December 4, 1960).

17. See Dennis E. Hoffman, *Scarface Al and the Crime Crusaders: Chicago's Private War Against Capone*, (Carbondale and Edwardsville: Southern Illinois University Press, 1993); and US Federal Bureau of Investigation, *Alphonse Capone*.

18. Jim Doherty, *A Tale of Three Nesses*, *(www.mysteryreaders.org)*; and Ness and Fraley, *The Untouchables: The Real Story*, p. 22.

19. Doherty, *A Tale of Three Nesses*; Paul W. Heimel, "The 'Real' Eliot Ness Emerging From Behind Hollywood Myth," *www.eliotness.com*, (2002); and US Federal Bureau of Investigation, *Eliot Ness*.

20. US Federal Bureau of Investigation, *Eliot Ness*; and Max Allan Collins, personal correspondence to author (December 4, 2003).

21. US Federal Bureau of Investigation, *Alphonse Capone*.

22. George Murray, *The Legacy of Al Capone*, (New York: G.P. Putnam's Sons, 1975), p. 97.

23. Chesly Manly, "Gangs to Fight for a Share in Beer Business," *Chicago Tribune*, (March 29, 1933).

24. Murray, *The Legacy of Al Capone*, pp. 186-187.

25. Murray, *The Legacy of Al Capone*, p. 98.

26. Richard J. La Susa, "Atlas Prager, Got It? Atlas Prager, Get It!," *Chicago Tribune*, (April 24, 1977); and Roemer, *War of the Godfathers: the Bloody Confrontation Between the Chicago and New York Families for Control of Las Vegas*, p. 23.

27. Allan May, "The Guileless Gangster," *crimemagazine.com*, (2002).

28. Virgil Peterson, "The Mob Goes Legit: Hoods Muscle Into Business and Sports, and the Profits Pour In; But the Old Bloodshed Continues," *Chicago Tribune*, (November 11, 1956); Murray, *The Legacy of Al Capone*, p. 21 and pp. 34-36; William F. Roemer, Jr., *Roemer: Man Against the Mob*, (New York: Ivy Books, 1989), p. 37; and Ken Schessler, "Unusual Guide to Chicago," *members.aol.com/KSchessler/wizzn.html*, (September 2002)

29. La Susa, "Atlas Prager, Got It? Atlas Prager, Get It!."

30. Anon., *(www.rootsweb.com/~flbaker/lore.html#agent)*.

31. Quoted in John Morgan, *Prince of Crime*, (New York: Stein and Day, 1985), p. 83.

32. Murray, *The Legacy of Al Capone*, p. 181; and Gus Russo, *The Outfit: The Role of Chicago's Underworld in the Shaping of Modern America*, (New York: Bloomsbury, 2001), p. 54.

33. Murray, *The Legacy of Al Capone*, p. 182.

34. Illinois Association for Criminal Justice, *The Illinois Crime Survey*, (Princeton, NJ: Patterson Smith, 1929 and 1968), p. 834 and p. 838.

35. Murray, *The Legacy of Al Capone*, pp. 182-183.

36. Andy Edmonds, *Hot Toddy: The True Story of Hollywood's Most Sensational Murder*, (New York: William Morrow and Company, Inc., 1989), pp. 154-155.

37. Murray, *The Legacy of Al Capone*, pp. 183-184.

38. Anon., "Rogues' Gallery as Presented by Mr. Courtney: Thumbnail Sketches of Those Named," *Chicago Tribune*, (December 2, 1937); and Anon., "Nitti Long Held Business Chief of Underworld: Showed Cunning in All Racketeering Fields," *Chicago Tribune*, (March 20, 1943).

39. Anon., "Missing Capone Tax Witness Found By US: La Cava Before Jury; Alterie Makes Bond," *Chicago Tribune*, (March 6, 1931).

40. Schoenberg, *Mr. Capone*, p. 246.

41. Frank Cipriani, "Court Hearing Puts Gambling Chief on Spot," *Chicago Tribune*, (April 14, 1944).

42. Roemer, *Accardo: the Genuine Godfather*, p. 60 and pp. 400-401.

43. Anon., "Capone's Gang Rises Again in Votes and Vice," *Chicago Tribune*, (July 11, 1936); Anon. "3 Fair Skinned Killers Sought in Bolton Death," *Chicago Tribune*, (July 13, 1936); and David E. Scheim, *Contract On America*, (New York: Zebra Books, 1993), p. 465.

44. James Doherty, "'Deal' Explained; Jack Guzik," *Chicago Tribune*, (November 2, 1946).

45. Roemer, *War of the Godfathers: the Bloody Confrontation Between the Chicago and New York Families for Control of Las Vegas*, p. 252.

46. Illinois Association for Criminal Justice, *The Illinois Crime Survey*, p. 1,012.

47. Estes Kefauver, *Crime In America*, (New York: Doubleday and Company, Inc., 1951), p. 35.

48. Roemer, *Accardo: the Genuine Godfather*, p. 64.

49. Anon., "Inquiry Shown: Questions Parried On His Activities," *Chicago Tribune*, (September 10, 1947).

50. Anon., "Order Witness to Serve Term for Balkiness: Decision Is Considered Help to Prosecutors," *Chicago Tribune*, (May 7, 1943).

51. Anon., (*www.crimelibrary.com*); and John J. Binder, *The Chicago Outfit*, (Charleston, SC: Arcadia Publishing, 2003), p. 66.

52. Howard Schwartz, "Off the Shelf: Some Answers to Questions We Often Get at Gambler's Book Shop," *CasinoGaming.com*, (June 28, 2000).

53. Quoted in Anon., "The History of Gambling in East Chicago, Indiana," *online.sfsu.edu*, (2002).

54. James Doherty, "Handbook Raids Slash Income of Nitti Gangsters: 300 Arrested in Week's Drive on Rackets," *Chicago Tribune*, (May 19, 1941); Anon., "Hint Pay-off Keeps Al A Friend of New Bosses: Previous Disclosures!," *Chicago Tribune*, (October 28, 1941);

and Anon., "Grand Jury Told How Syndicate Splits Profits: 20 Tavern Keepers Say They Get 40 Pct.," *Chicago Tribune*, (November 8, 1941).

55. Peterson, "The Mob Goes Legit: Hoods Muscle Into Business and Sports, and the Profits Pour In; But the Old Bloodshed Continues"; Laurence Bergreen, *Capone: The Man and the Era*, (New York: Simon and Schuster; August 1996), pp. 364-365; and John William Tuohy, *When Capone's Mob Murdered Roger Touhy: The Strange Case of Touhy, Jake the Barber and the Kidnapping That Never Happened*, (Fort Lee, NJ: Barricade Books Inc., 2001), p. 239.

56. Anon. "3 Fair Skinned Killers Sought in Bolton Death."

57. Anon., "Courtney Raps Police as Aids to Bookie Ring: Charges Capone Mob Rules Racket," *Chicago Tribune*, (September 2, 1938); and Anon., "Nab John Capone in Raid on Bookie Clearing House: Police Seize Five Others at Telephones," *Chicago Tribune*, (April 4, 1941).

58. Anon., "Inquiry Shown: Questions Parried On His Activities"; and Anon., "Tuohy Bares Guzik Story in Ragen Case," *Chicago Tribune*, (September 10, 1947).

59. Irey and Slocum, *The Tax Dodgers: The Inside Story of the T-Men's War with America's Political and Underworld Hoodlums*, pp. 215-224; Ed Reid and Ovid Demaris, *The Green Felt Jungle*, (New York: Pocket Books, 1962), p. 34; and Sam and Chuck Giancana, *Double Cross*, (New York: Warner Books, Inc., 1992), pp. 194-196.

60. Kefauver, *Crime In America*, pp. 35-52; and Anon., *www.dcia.com/marley.html*).

61. Allan May, "The History of the Race Wire Service—Part One: Mont Tennes and the Birth of Race Wire," *AmericanMafia.com*, (May 1999).

62. Anon., "Inquiry Shown: Questions Parried On His Activities."

63. Kefauver, *Crime In America*, p. 51.

64. Allan May, "The History of the Race Wire Service—Part Two: M. L. Annenberg and the Growth of the Race Wire," *AmericanMafia.com*, (May 1999).

65. Anon., "Heitler 'Death Letter' Puzzle to Prosecutor: Fails as Instrument of Vengeance," *Chicago Tribune*, (September 17, 1931); Roemer, *Roemer: Man Against the Mob*, p. 276; and Demaris, *The Last Mafioso: The Treacherous World of Jimmy Fratianno*, pp. 173-174.

66. Irey and Slocum, *The Tax Dodgers: The Inside Story of the T-Men's War with America's Political and Underworld Hoodlums*, pp. 223-224.

67. Allan May, "The History of the Race Wire Service—Part Three: Ragen and McBride and the End of the Race Wire," *AmericanMafia.com*, (May 1999).

68. Quoted in Christopher Ogden, *Legacy: A Biography of Moses and Walter Annenberg*, (New York: Little Brown and Company, 1999), p. 109; and quoted in Russo, *The Outfit: The Role of Chicago's Underworld in the Shaping of Modern America*, p. 206.

69. May, "The History of the Race Wire Service—Part Two: M. L. Annenberg and the Growth of the Race Wire."

70. Ogden, *Legacy: A Biography of Moses and Walter Annenberg*, p. 110; and Russo, *The Outfit: The Role of Chicago's Underworld in the Shaping of Modern America*, p. 199.

71. Anon., "Inquiry Shown: Questions Parried On His Activities"; Anon., "Tuohy Bares Guzik Story in Ragen Case"; and Anon., "Move to Link Ragen Ambush to Parole Plot: Crime Commission Data Sent Congressmen," *Chicago Tribune*, (February 25, 1948).

72. Anon., "Inquiry Shown: Questions Parried On His Activities."

73. Anon., "Move to Link Ragen Ambush to Parole Plot: Crime Commission Data Sent Congressmen."

74. James Clarkson, "Police Heroes Under Attack for Arrests," *Chicago's America*, (August 14, 1947); James Clarkson, "Tell Inside of Fight to Oust Pair," *Chicago's America*, (August 15, 1947); Carl Wiegman, "Guzik Activity in Ragen Quiz Told at Trial," *Chicago Tribune*, (August 21, 1947); Carl Wiegman, "Denies Police Charges; Vows War on Guzik: State's Attorney on Stand," *Chicago Tribune*, (September 6, 1947); and *US House Select Committee on Assassinations*, (July 1978).

75. US Federal Bureau of Investigation, *Bugsy Siegel*, *(foia.fbi.gov/siege.htm)*; US Federal Bureau of Investigation, *Mafia Monograph: Section II United States*, (Washington DC: July 1958); Scheim, *Contract On America*, pp. 136-137; and Russo, *The Outfit: The Role of Chicago's Underworld in the Shaping of Modern America*, pp. 208-209.

76. Clark R. Mollenhoff, *Strike Force: Organized Crime and the Government*, (New York: Prentice-Hall, 1972), p. 88.

77. Anon., "The History of Gambling in East Chicago, Indiana."

78. Anon., *(www.dcia.com/marley.html)*.

79. John William Tuohy, "Battaglia Brothers," *(www.alleged-mafia-site.com)*.

80. Anon., "Nitti Long Held Business Chief of Underworld: Showed Cunning in All Racketeering Fields."

81. Anon., "Tribune to Publish Ledger Sheets of the Syndicate," *Chicago Tribune*, (October 25, 1941); Anon., "Grand Jury Told How Syndicate Splits Profits: 20 Tavern Keepers Say They Get 40 Pct."; and James Doherty, "Slot Machine 'Take' of Nitti Told Probers: Data Made Available to Sheriff Walsh," *Chicago Tribune*, (September 12, 1948).

82. Doherty, "Handbook Raids Slash Income of Nitti Gangsters: 300 Arrested in Week's Drive on Rackets"; and Anon., "Inquiry Shown: Questions Parried On His Activities."

83. Anon., "Tribune to Publish Ledger Sheets of the Syndicate"; Anon., "Hint Pay-off Keeps Al A Friend of New Bosses: Previous Disclosures!"; and Anon., "Huge Gambling Graft Bared By Tribune in 1941," *Chicago Tribune*, (December 11, 1946).

84. James Doherty, "Three Gambling Bosses Seized; New US Probe: Summoned to Grand Jury Quiz Tomorrow," *Chicago Tribune*, (April 30, 1940).

85. Anon., "Slot Probe Goes On and On—So Does the Racket: All Sheriff's Men Can't Find Key Hoodlums," *Chicago Tribune*, (July 28, 1942).

86. Wayne Thomis, "Says He Fought Gang Attempts to Take Control: Background for a Murder!," *Chicago Tribune*, (January 12, 1960); and Demaris, *The Last Mafioso: The Treacherous World of Jimmy Fratianno*, p. 170.

87. US Federal Bureau of Investigation, *FBI Homepage*, *www.fbi.gov/homepage.html*, (September 2002).

88. Ben Best, "Schemers in the Web: A Covert History of the 1960's Era," *www.benbest.com/history/schemers.html*, (1990).

89. Anon., "Cites Gilbert Link to Labor Rackets," *Chicago Tribune*, (August 10, 1954).

90. US Federal Bureau of Investigation, *Alphonse Capone*.

91. Irey and Slocum, *The Tax Dodgers: The Inside Story of the T-Men's War with America's Political and Underworld Hoodlums*, p. 175.

92. Scheim, *Contract On America*, p. 435; Tuohy, *When Capone's Mob Murdered Roger Touhy: The Strange Case of Touhy, Jake the Barber and the Kidnapping That Never Happened*, pp. 73-75; and John William Tuohy, "The Guns of Zangara," *www.gamblingmagazine.com*, (April 2000).

93. James Doherty, "Accardo Called Capone Gang's Chicago Boss: Senators Want to Know Scope of Operations," *Chicago Tribune*, (October 1, 1950); and Morgan, *Prince of Crime*, pp. 79-80.

94. Thomis, "Says He Fought Gang Attempts to Take Control: Background for a Murder!"

95. Irey and Slocum, *The Tax Dodgers: The Inside Story of the T-Men's War with America's Political and Underworld Hoodlums*, pp. 174-180.

96. Anon., "Start 'Vag' Law Roundup of 59 More Hoodlums; 'Spike' O'Donnell Is First Arrested—Killers Guilty," *Chicago Tribune*, (September 1, 1933); Schoenberg, *Mr. Capone*, p.147, p. 150 and p. 170; Tuohy, *When Capone's Mob Murdered Roger Touhy: The Strange Case of Touhy, Jake the Barber and the Kidnapping That Never Happened*, p. 89; and John William Tuohy, "Just Plain Crazy," *AmericanMafia.com*, (March 2001).

97. Joanne Laurier, "Filthy Lives Have Filthy Consequences: *Road to Perdition*, Directed by Sam Mendes," *World Socialist Website*, (July 25, 2002).

98. See William F. Roemer, Jr., *The Enforcer—Spilotro: The Chicago Mob's Man Over Las Vegas*, (New York: Ivy Books, 1994), pp. 12-19.

99. Anon., "Cites Gilbert Link to Labor Rackets"; Thomis, "Says He Fought Gang Attempts to Take Control: Background for a Murder!"; and John William Tuohy, "The Last Gangster: The Life and Time of Roger Touhy, John Factor and the Mob," (*www.gamblingmagazine.com*).

100. Lyle, "Al Capone."

101. Anon., "Gang Big Shots, Heads of Truck Racket, Freed; Accused of Conspiracy: Let Out On Bail," *Chicago Tribune*, (November 5, 1932); Anon., "Federal Drive on Racketeers Nears Climax: Business Men Called as Witnesses," *Chicago Tribune*, (May 21, 1933); and Anon., "Jack Guzik Now Is No. 1 Man of Gang Overlords: Here Are the Records of 4 Syndicate Heads; Personalities of the Syndicate," *Chicago Tribune*, (October 25, 1941).

102. William Moore, "Probers Lash His Failing Memory on Rackets," *Chicago Tribune*, (August 24, 1957).

103. Lloyd Wendt, "Capone's Cohorts Carry On," *Chicago Tribune*, (August 31, 1941); Anon., "Mob Menace in Chicago: Union Rule by Terror," *Chicago Tribune*, (September 2, 1954); US Federal Bureau of Investigation, *Alphonse Capone*; and US Federal Bureau of Investigation, *Mafia Monograph: Section II United States*.

104. Joseph Ator, "Tapped Phone Talks Told in Racket Trial: Humphreys Is Connected with Trade Groups," *Chicago Tribune*, (February 14, 1934).

105. James Doherty, "Union's Board Ousts Scalise, Indicted Czar: McFetridge in Line for Presidency," *Chicago Tribune*, (April 28, 1940); Doherty, "Three Gambling Bosses Seized; New US Probe: Summoned to Grand Jury Quiz Tomorrow"; Anon., "Cites Gilbert Link to Labor Rackets"; Thomis, "Says He Fought Gang Attempts to Take Control: Background for a Murder!"; and Murray, *The Legacy of Al Capone*, p. 208.

106. Anon., "Labor Troubles in Detroit Laid to Union Raiding," *Chicago Tribune*, (January 10, 1941).

107. Orville Dwyer and George Hartmann, "Bloody Record: Gangs' Seizure of Engineers," *Chicago Tribune*, (March 26, 1943).

108. Wendt, "Capone's Cohorts Carry On"; Anon., "Courtney Urges City Hall Quiz in O'Donnell Case: Ask Why Can Victim Beat Politician," *Chicago Tribune*, (March 22, 1943); and Antonio Napoli, *The Mob's Guys*, (*Virtualbookworm.com* Publishing, March 2004), p. 8 and pp. 69-70.

109. Thomis, "Says He Fought Gang Attempts to Take Control: Background for a Murder!"; and Rose Keefe, *Guns and Roses: The Untold Story of Dean O'Banion, Chicago's Big Shot Before Al Capone*, (Nashville: Cumberland House Publishing, 2003), p. 215.

110. Wendt, "Capone's Cohorts Carry On"; Anon., "Quotes Clerk's Ex-Czar: 'Nitti a Chicago Leader'," *Chicago Tribune*, (January 17, 1942); and Anon., "Nitti Long Held Business Chief of Underworld: Showed Cunning in All Racketeering Fields."

111. Wendt, "Capone's Cohorts Carry On"; and US Federal Bureau of Investigation, *John Roselli, (foia.fbi.gov/roselli.htm)*.

112. Murray, *The Legacy of Al Capone*, p. 184.

113. Wendt, "Capone's Cohorts Carry On"; and Russo, *The Outfit: The Role of Chicago's Underworld in the Shaping of Modern America*, pp. 138-139.

114. Anon., "3 Barkeep Union Agents Ousted; Nitti Gives Up: Receiver Moves to Block Romano Coup," *Chicago Tribune*, (October 10, 1940); Murray, *The Legacy of Al Capone*, pp. 193-194; and Allan May, "Louis Campagna—Done in by a Grouper," *AmericanMafia. com*, (May 1999).

115. Morgan, *Prince of Crime*, pp. 100-101; and US Federal Bureau of Investigation, *John Roselli*.

116. Murray, *The Legacy of Al Capone*, p. 184.

117. Murray, *The Legacy of Al Capone*, pp. 190-193.

118. Quoted in Murray, *The Legacy of Al Capone*, p. 185.

119. Quoted in Murray, *The Legacy of Al Capone*, p. 185.

120. Wendt, "Capone's Cohorts Carry On."

121. Murray, *The Legacy of Al Capone*, p. 193; Anon., (*www.gambino.com*); and May, "Louis Campagna—Done in by a Grouper."

122. Roemer, *Roemer: Man Against the Mob*, p. 77; and Roemer, *Accardo: the Genuine Godfather*, p. 70.

123. Roemer, *Roemer: Man Against the Mob*, p. 87.

124. Quoted in Morgan, *Prince of Crime*, pp. 97-98 and p. 105.

125. Anon., "Charges Nitti Suicide Tagged Stanton to Die: Barnes Says Hoodlum Defied New Setup," *Chicago Tribune*, (May 7, 1943).

126. Wendt, "Capone's Cohorts Carry On."

127. Anon., "Movies. Mayhem, the Mob...and All the Players in Between," *www.ipsn.org/movies.html*, (Fall 1995).

128. National Archives and Records Administration, *Frank R. Nitto, 38021-L: "Failing to file Income Tax return"*; Jane Stern and Michael Stern, *The Harry Caray's Restaurant Cookbook: The Official Home Plate of the Chicago Cubs*, (Nashville: Rutledge Hill Press, June 14, 2003), p. 11 and p. 88; Steve Neal, "Landmark Building for a Landmark Restaurant," *Chicago Sun-Times*, (April 7, 2003); Anon., (*www.csasi.org/October2001/earl_townsend.htm*); and Clifford Kraus, "Capone May Have Slept Here, Too, Canadian Town Says," *Moose Jaw Journal*, (November 16, 2004).

129. Anon., (*www.enteract.com/~alindzy/Bellwatts.html*).

130. Murray, *The Legacy of Al Capone*, p.33.

131. Anon., "Suicide Reveals Riverside to be Gangster Haven," *Chicago Tribune*, (March 20, 1943).

132. Herbert Asbury, *The Gangs of Chicago: An Informal History of the Chicago Underworld*, (New York: Thunder's Mouth Press, 1986) (reprint of 1940 Alfred A. Knopf, Inc. edition), p. 369; and US Federal Bureau of Investigation, *Alphonse Capone*.

133. Murray, *The Legacy of Al Capone*, p. 97.

134. Roemer, *Accardo: the Genuine Godfather*, p. 58.

135. May, "The Guileless Gangster"; and Allan May, "Charles 'Cherry Nose' Gioe," *AmericanMafia.com*, (May 2000).

136. John William Tuohy, "Pal Joey," *Search International, www.search-international.com*, (2001); and Russo, *The Outfit: The Role of Chicago's Underworld in the Shaping of Modern America*, p. 68.

137. Allsop, *The Bootleggers: The Story of Chicago's Prohibition Era*, p. 373.

138. Edmonds, *Hot Toddy: The True Story of Hollywood's Most Sensational Murder*, p. 140.

139. Anon., (*www.suntimes.com/special_sections/crime/cst-nws-mobtop18r.html*).

140. Anon., (*gangstersinc.tripod.com/ChicagoHistory.html*); Binder, *The Chicago Outfit*, p. 111.

141. Ralph "Sonny" Barger, *Hell's Angel*, (New York: HarperCollins Publishers, 2000), pp. 74-75.

142. Russo, *The Outfit: The Role of Chicago's Underworld in the Shaping of Modern America*, p. 105.

143. National Archives and Records Administration, *Frank R. Nitto, 38021-L: "Failing to file Income Tax return"*; and Russo, *The Outfit: The Role of Chicago's Underworld in the Shaping of Modern America*, p. 476.

144. Russo, *The Outfit: The Role of Chicago's Underworld in the Shaping of Modern America*, p. 55.

145. Anon., "Nab John Capone in Raid on Bookie Clearing House: Police Seize Five Others at Telephones."

146. Anon., (*comm-org.utoledo.edu/papers96/horwitt.html*).

147. Quoted in Horwitt, *Let Them Call Me Rebel: Saul Alinsky—His Life and Legacy*, p. 20.

148. Quoted in Horwitt, *Let Them Call Me Rebel: Saul Alinsky—His Life and Legacy*, p. 21. Also see Alinsky's interview by *Playboy* in Anon., "Interview With Saul Alinsky, Part Four," *The Progress Report*, (www.progress.org/2003/alinsky5.htm).

149. Anon., "Life of Saul Alinsky," (www.itvs.org/democraticpromise/alinsky.html).

150. Michael Tomasky, "Saul Survivors Byline," *The Village Voice*, (April 4, 1995).

151. Executive Intelligence Review, *Dope, Inc.: The Book That Drove Henry Kissinger Crazy*, (Washington DC: Executive Intelligence Review, 1992), p. 137.

152. Vladimir Novak, "Mr. Clean (Josip Marusic a.k.a Joe Marsh) Is Croatian," *The Zajednicar*, (May 1, 1996).

153. Scheim, *Contract On America*, p. 100.

154. Scheim, *Contract On America*, pp. 262–263.

155. Mike McCormick, "King of Indiana Bootleggers Turned into Legit Family Man," *Terre Haute Tribune Star*; and National Archives and Records Administration, *Frank R. Nitto, 38021-L: "Failing to file Income Tax return."*

156. Anon., "St. Louis Kelly Slain in Brawl Over Politics," *Chicago Tribune*, (April 8, 1944).

157. Irey and Slocum, *The Tax Dodgers: The Inside Story of the T-Men's War with America's Political and Underworld Hoodlums*, p. 280; and Murray, *The Legacy of Al Capone*, p. 276.

158. Ed Reid, *The Grim Reapers: The Anatomy of Organized Crime in America*, (New York: Bantam, 1969), p. 268; Roemer, *Roemer: Man Against the Mob*, p. 33 and p. 40; and Roemer, *The Enforcer—Spilotro: The Chicago Mob's Man Over Las Vegas*, p. 144.

159. Roy Gibbons, "Bioff Reveals Death Threats By Capone Gang: Is Warned Not to Try to Quit Mob," *Chicago Tribune*, (October 9, 1943); Demaris, *The Last Mafioso: The Treacherous World of Jimmy Fratianno*, p. 203; and Roemer, *War of the Godfathers: the Bloody Confrontation Between the Chicago and New York Families for Control of Las Vegas*, p. 104.

160. Roemer, *Roemer: Man Against the Mob*, p. 121; and Roemer, *War of the Godfathers: the Bloody Confrontation Between the Chicago and New York Families for Control of Las Vegas*, p. 48.

161. Tuohy, *When Capone's Mob Murdered Roger Touhy: The Strange Case of Touhy, Jake the Barber and the Kidnapping That Never Happened*, pp. 129-135.

162. Anon., (www.maxfactor.com).

163. John William Tuohy, "Jake the Barber: The Story of a Successful Conman (Part One of a Two-Party Story)," *Search International, www.search-international.com.* (September 2002).

164. Tuohy, "Jake the Barber: The Story of a Successful Conman (Part One of a Two-Party Story)." See Donald H. Dunn, *Ponzi: The Incredible True Story of the King of Financial Cons*, (New York: Broadway Books, 1975), for the full history of Charles Ponzi and his pyramid schemes that were adopted by successors such as John Factor.

165. Thomis, "Says He Fought Gang Attempts to Take Control: Background for a Murder!"; and Demaris, *The Last Mafioso: The Treacherous World of Jimmy Fratianno*, p. 106.

166. William Edwards, "State Witness Against Touhy Gang Vanishes: Another One Shows Fear On Stand," *Chicago Tribune*, (January 30, 1934); and Tuohy, "The Last Gangster: The Life and Time of Roger Touhy, John Factor and the Mob."

167. Tuohy, *When Capone's Mob Murdered Roger Touhy: The Strange Case of Touhy, Jake the Barber and the Kidnapping That Never Happened*, pp. 139-140.

168. Thomis, "Says He Fought Gang Attempts to Take Control: Background for a Murder!"; Roemer, *Roemer: Man Against the Mob*, p. 122; and Tuohy, "Jake the Barber: The Story of a Successful Conman (Part One of a Two-Party Story)."

169. Edwards, "State Witness Against Touhy Gang Vanishes: Another One Shows Fear On Stand."

170. Allsop, *The Bootleggers: The Story of Chicago's Prohibition Era*, pp. 242-243.

171. Thomis, "Says He Fought Gang Attempts to Take Control: Background for a Murder!"; and Allsop, *The Bootleggers: The Story of Chicago's Prohibition Era*, p. 483.

172. For varying accounts see Murray, *The Legacy of Al Capone*, pp. 226-227; Morgan, *Prince of Crime*, pp. 147-151; Tuohy, "Jake the Barber: The Story of a Successful Conman (Part One of a Two-Party Story)"; and John William Tuohy, "Jake the Barber, Roger Touhy, and an Escape From the Big House: The Story of a Successful Conman (Part Two of a Two-Part Story)," *Search International, www.search-international.com*, (September 2002).

173. Tuohy, "The Last Gangster: The Life and Time of Roger Touhy, John Factor and the Mob."

174. Roemer, *War of the Godfathers: the Bloody Confrontation Between the Chicago and New York Families for Control of Las Vegas*, pp. 56-57.

175. Tuohy, "The Last Gangster: The Life and Time of Roger Touhy, John Factor and the Mob."

176. Tuohy, "Jake the Barber, Roger Touhy, and an Escape From the Big House: The Story of a Successful Conman (Part Two of a Two-Part Story)."

177. Erica Werner, "Investigators Search for Max Factor Heir," *Los Angeles Associated Press*, (January 8, 2003).

178. US Federal Bureau of Investigation, *Alphonse Capone*.

179. Roemer, *Accardo: the Genuine Godfather*, p. 58; and Doug Moe, "*Perdition* Linked to Madison," *www.madison.com*, (July 12, 2002).

180. US Federal Bureau of Investigation, *St. Valentine's Day Massacre, (foia.fbi.gov/stvalen/)*.

181. May, "The Guileless Gangster"; and May, "Charles 'Cherry Nose' Gioe."

182. Anon., "A Rusted Safe Exposes Old Mob Secrets," *Chicago Tribune*, (January 23, 1960); and Binder, *The Chicago Outfit*, pp. 55-56.

183. Tuohy, "Pal Joey"; and Roemer, *Accardo: the Genuine Godfather*, pp. 64-65.

184. Anon., "Race Handbook Clew Traced in Bolton Killing: Reveal Legislator's Gaming Interests," *Chicago Tribune*, (July 10, 1936); Anon., "Capone's Gang Rises Again in Votes and Vice"; Anon. "3 Fair Skinned Killers Sought in Bolton Death"; US Federal Bureau of Investigation, *Alphonse Capone*; and US Federal Bureau of Investigation, *John Roselli*.

185. Russo, *The Outfit: The Role of Chicago's Underworld in the Shaping of Modern America*, p. 96.

186. Schoenberg, *Mr. Capone*, p. 246.

187. See Giancana, *Double Cross*, pp. 98-99.

188. Demaris, *The Last Mafioso: The Treacherous World of Jimmy Fratianno*, p. 101; and Anon., (*www.gambino.com*).

189. Murray, *The Legacy of Al Capone*, p. 288.

190. US Federal Bureau of Investigation, *Alphonse Capone*.

191. Carl Wiegman, "Nitti Kills Himself! Gang Chief Dies By Gun After US Jury Charges 3: Trainmen Look On as Racketeer Fires 3 Shots," *Chicago Tribune*, (March 20, 1943).

192. James Doherty, "Extortion Cash Splitups Told in Nitti Tax Case," *Chicago Tribune*, (October 2, 1948).

193. Richard Lindberg, "Origins and History of the Mafia 'Commission'," *Search International, www.search-international.com*, (September 2002); and Gary W. Potter, Eastern Kentucky University, "Unit # 1: Organized Crime and the "Mafia"—Organized Crime in Social Context," (*www.policestudies.eku.edu/POTTER/crj401_1.htm*).

194. Richard T. Enright, *Al Capone, Master Criminal*, (Lakeville, MN: Northstar Maschek Books, 1931), p. 71; John Kobler, *Capone*, (New York: G. P. Putnam's Sons, 1971; Da Capo Press edition, 2003), p. 258; Allsop, *The Bootleggers: The Story of Chicago's Prohibition Era*, p. 403; Schoenberg, *Mr. Capone*, p. 234; and Scheim, *Contract On America*, p. 399.

195. Lindberg, "Origins and History of the Mafia 'Commission'."

196. Lindberg, "Origins and History of the Mafia 'Commission'."

197. Reid, *The Grim Reapers: The Anatomy of Organized Crime in America*, p. 92; and Roemer, *Accardo: the Genuine Godfather*, p. 64.

198. Lindberg, "Origins and History of the Mafia 'Commission'."

199. Anon., (*www.ganglandnews.com/column28.htm*).

200. Hank Messick, *Lansky*, (New York: Berkley Medallion Books, 1971), pp. 62-63.

201. Giancana, *Double Cross*, p. 102.

202. Doherty, "Accardo Called Capone Gang's Chicago Boss: Senators Want to Know Scope of Operations"; and Binder, *The Chicago Outfit*, p. 65 and p. 67.

203. Anon., "Jack Guzik Now Is No. 1 Man of Gang Overlords: Here Are the Records of 4 Syndicate Heads; Personalities of the Syndicate."

204. Roemer, *The Enforcer—Spilotro: The Chicago Mob's Man Over Las Vegas*, p. 38.

205. Ronald Koziol and John O'Brien, "Reputed Mob Boss Accardo Dead at 86," *Chicago Tribune*, (May 28, 1992).

206. Murray, *The Legacy of Al Capone*, p. 274.

207. US Federal Bureau of Investigation, *John Roselli*.

208. Roemer, *War of the Godfathers: the Bloody Confrontation Between the Chicago and New York Families for Control of Las Vegas*, p. 252.

209. Demaris, *The Last Mafioso: The Treacherous World of Jimmy Fratianno*, p. 122.

210. Binder, *The Chicago Outfit*, p. 56.

CHAPTER FIVE

1. John William Tuohy, "The Guns of Zangara," *www.gamblingmagazine.com*, (April 2000); and John William Tuohy, "The Last Gangster: The Life and Time of Roger Touhy, John Factor and the Mob," (*www.gamblingmagazine.com*).

2. George Murray, *The Legacy of Al Capone*, (New York: G.P. Putnam's Sons, 1975), p. 170.

3. Chicago Public Library, "Inaugural Address of Mayor Anton Cermak, April 27, 1931," *www.chipublib.org/004chicago/mayors/speeches/cermak31.html*, (September 2002).

4. See John Morgan, *Prince of Crime*, (New York: Stein and Day, 1985), pp. 149-151.

5. Allan May, "The First Shooting of Frank Nitti," *Crime Magazine: An Encyclopedia of Crime*, (February 22, 1999).

6. John William Tuohy, "Power Play: The Nitti Shooting," (*www.gamblingmagazine.com*).

7. John H. Lyle, "Was Cermak or FDR the Real Target?," *Chicago Tribune*, (December 18, 1960); and John William Tuohy, *When Capone's Mob Murdered Roger Touhy: The Strange Case of Touhy, Jake the Barber and the Kidnapping That Never Happened*, (Fort Lee, NJ: Barricade Books Inc., 2001), pp. 86-88.

8. Lyle, "Was Cermak or FDR the Real Target?"; Laurence Bergreen, *Capone: The Man and the Era*, (New York: Simon and Schuster; August 1996), p. 556; and May, "The First Shooting of Frank Nitti."

9. Murray, *The Legacy of Al Capone*, pp. 175-176; Tuohy, "The Guns of Zangara."

10. Robert J. Schoenberg, *Mr. Capone*, (New York: William Morrow, 1992), p. 358.

11. Murray, *The Legacy of Al Capone*, pp. 175-176; Schoenberg, *Mr. Capone*, pp. 358-359; and Tuohy, "Power Play: The Nitti Shooting."

12. Anon., "A Rusted Safe Exposes Old Mob Secrets," *Chicago Tribune*, (January 23, 1960); and Alan May, "The First Shooting of Frank Nitti."

13. Murray, *The Legacy of Al Capone*, p. 178.

14. Anon., (*www.gambino.com*); Kenneth Allsop, *The Bootleggers: The Story of Chicago's Prohibition Era*, (London: Arrow Books Ltd., 1970), pp. 305-306; and William F. Roemer, Jr., *Accardo: the Genuine Godfather*, (New York: Ivy Books, 1995), p. 57.

15. Anon., "A Rusted Safe Exposes Old Mob Secrets."

16. US Federal Bureau of Investigation, *St. Valentine's Day Massacre, (foia.fbi.gov/stvalen/);* Lyle, "Was Cermak or FDR the Real Target?"; Murray, *The Legacy of Al Capone*, pp. 175-177; and Schoenberg, *Mr. Capone*, p. 358.

17. Quoted in Murray, *The Legacy of Al Capone*, p. 176.

18. Lyle, "Was Cermak or FDR the Real Target?"

19. Gus Russo, *The Outfit: The Role of Chicago's Underworld in the Shaping of Modern America,* (New York: Bloomsbury, 2001), pp. 92-93.

20. Quoted in Murray, *The Legacy of Al Capone*, p. 176.

21. May, "The First Shooting of Frank Nitti."

22. Murray, *The Legacy of Al Capone*, p. 177.

23. Anon., "Race Handbook Clew Traced in Bolton Killing: Reveal Legislator's Gaming Interests," *Chicago Tribune,* (July 10, 1936); Anon., "Capone's Gang Rises Again in Votes and Vice," *Chicago Tribune,* (July 11, 1936); Anon. "3 Fair Skinned Killers Sought in Bolton Death," *Chicago Tribune,* (July 13, 1936); Frances Mundo, "Volley Kills Legislator in His Auto," *Chicago Tribune,* (July 7, 1946); Anon., "Past Killing of Politicians Are Recalled," *Chicago Tribune,* (June 6, 1959); US Federal Bureau of Investigation, *John Roselli, (foia.fbi.gov/roselli.htm);* and Roemer, *Accardo: the Genuine Godfather,* p. 63.

24. Lyle, "Was Cermak or FDR the Real Target?"

25. Lyle, "Was Cermak or FDR the Real Target?"; and May, "The First Shooting of Frank Nitti."

26. Russo, *The Outfit: The Role of Chicago's Underworld in the Shaping of Modern America,* p. 93. *Chicago Tribune* reporter Jake Lingle was also said to be wearing such a gift from Capone when he was murdered.

27. Roemer, *Accardo: the Genuine Godfather,* p. 58.

28. Anon., *(www.gambino.com).*

29. Murray, *The Legacy of Al Capone*, p. 176.

30. May, "The First Shooting of Frank Nitti."

31. Murray, *The Legacy of Al Capone*, p. 176 and pp. 178-179; and May, "The First Shooting of Frank Nitti."

32. David E. Scheim, *Contract On America,* (New York: Zebra Books, 1993), p. 24.

33. Curt Johnson, R. Craig Sautter, and Roger Ebert, *The Wicked City: Chicago from Kenna to Capone,* (New York: DaCapo Press, April 1998), p. 349; and Russo, *The Outfit: The Role of Chicago's Underworld in the Shaping of Modern America,* p. 93.

34. Murray, *The Legacy of Al Capone*, p. 176; and John William Tuohy, "The Guns of Zangara—Part II," *www.gamblingmagazine.com,* (April 2000).

35. Sam and Chuck Giancana, *Double Cross,* (New York: Warner Books, Inc., 1992), p. 89.

36. Lyle, "Was Cermak or FDR the Real Target?"

37. Lyle, "Was Cermak or FDR the Real Target?"; and Murray, *The Legacy of Al Capone*, p. 177.

38. US Federal Bureau of Investigation, *Franklin D. Roosevelt Assassination Attempt*, (*foia.fbi.gov/fdrass.htm*).

39. Giancana, *Double Cross*, pp. 450-451.

40. Giancana, *Double Cross*, p. 89.

41. Tuohy, *When Capone's Mob Murdered Roger Touhy: The Strange Case of Touhy, Jake the Barber and the Kidnapping That Never Happened*, p. 95; Tuohy, "The Guns of Zangara—Part II"; and Russo, *The Outfit: The Role of Chicago's Underworld in the Shaping of Modern America*, pp. 95-96 and p. 281.

42. Russo, *The Outfit: The Role of Chicago's Underworld in the Shaping of Modern America*, p. 284; and Antonio Napoli, *The Mob's Guys*, (*Virtualbookworm.com* Publishing, March 2004), p. 135. David Yaras was of a quite young, but not unheard of, age for such a position of responsibility. Some sources place Yaras's date of birth at November 7, 1912, others a year earlier at November 7, 1911.

43. Scheim, *Contract On America*, p. 25. Zangara's role with syndicate narcotics operations was first exposed by *Lightnin'*, a Chicago magazine that exposed various examples of Outfit-related corruption, but his mob connections have also been confirmed by other sources such as Giancana, *Double Cross*, and works by John William Tuohy.

44. Tuohy, *When Capone's Mob Murdered Roger Touhy: The Strange Case of Touhy, Jake the Barber and the Kidnapping That Never Happened*, p. 96.

45. Scheim, *Contract On America*, p. 25.

46. Lyle, "Was Cermak or FDR the Real Target?"; and Scheim, *Contract On America*, p. 25.

47. Allsop, *The Bootleggers: The Story of Chicago's Prohibition Era*, p. 302.

48. Anon., "Nitti Pal Held for Perjury in Racket Inquiry: Charges Threats by Bioff on Movie Testimony," *Chicago Tribune*, (September 25, 1943).

49. Richard C. Lindberg, "Chicago—the Way It Was: A City that Was Never Legit!," *www.ipsn.org/chiviol.html*, (1995).

50. Lyle, "Was Cermak or FDR the Real Target?"

51. Lyle, "Was Cermak or FDR the Real Target?"

52. Allsop, *The Bootleggers: The Story of Chicago's Prohibition Era*, p. 307.

53. Scheim, *Contract On America*, p. 24.

54. Scheim, *Contract On America*, pp. 25-26.

55. Tuohy, "The Guns of Zangara—Part II."

56. Scheim, *Contract On America*, p. 24.

57. Scheim, *Contract On America*, p. 24.

58. Lyle, "Was Cermak or FDR the Real Target?"

59. Murray, *The Legacy of Al Capone*, p. 177; and Scheim, *Contract On America*, p. 25.

60. Allsop, *The Bootleggers: The Story of Chicago's Prohibition Era*, pp. 243-244; Morgan, *Prince of Crime*, p. 93 and pp. 147-151; and Scheim, *Contract On America*, pp. 25-26 and pp. 329-330.

61. Russo, *The Outfit: The Role of Chicago's Underworld in the Shaping of Modern America*, p. 94.

62. Paul Robsky and Oscar Fraley, *The Last of the Untouchables*, (New York: Popular Library, 1962), pp. 179-181.

63. Roemer, *Accardo: the Genuine Godfather*, p. 60 and p. 63.

64. Murray, *The Legacy of Al Capone*, p. 178.

65. John A. Lupton, *Illinois Political Journal*, University of Illinois at Springfield, (February 11-17, 2002). For a detailed, sober and well-rounded appraisal of the Zangara case see Blaise Picchi, *The Five Weeks of Giuseppe Zangara: The Man Who Would Assassinate FDR*, (Chicago: Academy Chicago Publishers, September 1998). However, Picchi is either unaware of, or cannot sufficiently confirm, Zangara's criminal, prison, and underworld record in America.

66. Anon., (*members.tripod.com/~american_almanac/smedley.htm*).

67. US Federal Bureau of Investigation, *Franklin D. Roosevelt Assassination Attempt*.

68. US Federal Bureau of Investigation, *Franklin D. Roosevelt Assassination Attempt*.

69. US Federal Bureau of Investigation, *Franklin D. Roosevelt Assassination Attempt*.

70. US Federal Bureau of Investigation, *Franklin D. Roosevelt Assassination Attempt*.

71. US Federal Bureau of Investigation, *Franklin D. Roosevelt Assassination Attempt*. Some have hypothesized that Nitti provided for Zangara's family in Sicily, which was the native land of both men. For example, see James Ellroy, *American Tabloid*, (New York: Vintage Books, 2001), p. 533.

72. US Federal Bureau of Investigation, *Franklin D. Roosevelt Assassination Attempt*.

73. US Federal Bureau of Investigation, *Franklin D. Roosevelt Assassination Attempt*.

74. Scheim, *Contract On America*, p. 90.

75. Umberto Eco, *Foucalt's Pendulum*, (New York: Ballantine Books, 1988).

76. Michael Woodiwiss, "Organized Crime—The Dumbing of Discourse," *The British Criminology Conference: Selected Proceedings. Volume 3. Papers from the British Society of Criminology Conference*, (Liverpool: July 1999).

77. For example, see James Kirkwood, *American Grotesque*, (New York: Simon and Schuster, 1968).

78. US Central Intelligence Agency, *A Study of Assassination*, (1954).

79. Scheim, *Contract On America*, pp. 135-137.

80. *US House Select Committee on Assassinations*, (July 1978).

81. Quoted in William F. Roemer, Jr., *Roemer: Man Against the Mob*, (New York: Ivy Books, 1989), p. 266; and Russo, *The Outfit: The Role of Chicago's Underworld in the Shaping of Modern America*, p. 430.

82. Hank Messick and Joseph L. Nellis, *The Private Lives of Public Enemies*, (New York: Dell Publishing Company, Inc., 1973), pp. 39-40; Hank Messick, *Lansky*, (New York: Berkley Medallion Books, 1971), p.224.

83. Anon., (*members.tripod.com/~american_almanac/smedley.htm*).

84. See John Marks, *The Search for the Manchurian Candidate*, (New York: Time Books, 1979), for an excellent history of CIA attempts to develop such conditioned agents. Behavior-altering and cognitive-distorting drugs are today commonly used to supplement operant conditioning.

85. Richard Condon, *The Manchurian Candidate*, (New York: Dell Publishing Company, Inc., 1959), p. 291. The excellent 1974 film, *The Parallax View*, explored a similar theme, while the 1954 noir thriller, *Suddenly*, starred Frank Sinatra as the crazed leader of a trio of syndicate hit men tasked with assassinating the president of the United States. Like the motion-picture version of *The Manchurian Candidate* (1962), which also starred the in-real-life highly connected Sinatra, this film was pulled from circulation for years after the JFK assassination and according to some, had directly influenced Lee Harvey Oswald. J. X. Williams's 1965 controversial, and now-banned and out-of-circulation, docudrama *Peep Show* explored various aspects of the JFK conspiracy and is said to include actual film footage of Sam Giancana. Oliver Stone's *JFK* continued the theme.

86. See Giancana, *Double Cross*, pp. 450-451.

87. Robert J. Groden and Harrison Edward Livingstone, *High Treason: The Assassination of President John F. Kennedy—What Really Happened*, (Baltimore: The Conservatory Press, 1989), p. 357; and Ben Best, "Schemers in the Web: A Covert History of the 1960's Era," *www.benbest.com/history/schemers.html*, (1990).

88. Scheim, *Contract On America*, p. 100.

89. Scheim, *Contract On America*, pp. 101-103.

90. *Warren Report*, (September 24, 1964); *US House Select Committee on Assassinations*; James K Olmstead, "Ruby/Jones Beginnings," *alt.assassination.jfk*, (July 22, 2000); Richard C. Lindberg & John William Tuohy, "Jack Ruby, Organized Crime and the Kennedy Assassination," *Search International*, (*www.search-international.com*); and John William Tuohy, "The Lost Boy: Jack Ruby and the Murder of Lee Harvey Oswald," *AmericanMafia.com*, (April 2002). A. J. Weberman and the Kefauver Hearings are cited as references by Olmstead. A Warren Commission transcript apparently misidentified Frank Nitti as "JACK NETTI, well known Chicago hoodlum," when indicating his relationship to Romeo Jack Nitti.

91. Groden and Livingstone, *High Treason: The Assassination of President John F. Kennedy—What Really Happened*, p. 251.

92. Dan E. Moldea, *Dark Victory: Ronald Reagan, MCA, and the Mob*, (New York: Viking, 1986), p. 234; Giancana, *Double Cross*, pp. 460-461; and Scheim, *Contract On America*, pp. 64-66.

93. John William Tuohy, "Battaglia Brothers," (*www.alleged-mafia-site.com*).

94. *Warren Report*.

95. Giancana, *Double Cross*, p. 389.

96. Giancana, *Double Cross*, pp. 458-459.

97. Scheim, *Contract On America*, p. 58 and pp.133-134.

98. Moldea, *Dark Victory: Ronald Reagan, MCA, and the Mob*, p. 234.

99. Tuohy, "The Lost Boy: Jack Ruby and the Murder of Lee Harvey Oswald."

100. Ed Reid, *The Grim Reapers: The Anatomy of Organized Crime in America*, (New York: Bantam, 1969), pp. 162-163.

101. Roemer, *Roemer: Man Against the Mob*, pp. 178-180; and Russo, *The Outfit: The Role of Chicago's Underworld in the Shaping of Modern America*, pp. 451-454. It is interesting that Russo denies the JFK mob assassination conspiracy theory, but adheres to the explanation that Zangara's shooting of Cermak was part and parcel of an Outfit hit. See pp. 93-96. Also see Ovid Demaris, *The Last Mafioso: The Treacherous World of Jimmy Fratianno*, (New York: Times Books, 1981), pp. 192-193 and p. 327 where it is claimed that John Roselli denied any Mafia involvement in JFK's death.

102. Morgan, *Prince of Crime*, pp. 166-167.

103. *US House Select Committee on Assassinations*.

104. Moldea, *Dark Victory: Ronald Reagan, MCA, and the Mob*, pp. 234-235.

105. Groden and Livingstone, *High Treason: The Assassination of President John F. Kennedy— What Really Happened*, p. 357.

106. Best, "Schemers in the Web: A Covert History of the 1960's Era."

107. Claudia Furiati, *ZR Rifle: The Plot to Kill Kennedy and Castro*, (Melbourne: Ocean Press, 1994), p. 164; and Gus Russo, *The Outfit: The Role of Chicago's Underworld in the Shaping of Modern America*, (New York: Bloomsbury, 2001), pp. 95-96.

108. Giancana, *Double Cross*, pp. 318-323.

109. See Giancana, *Double Cross*, pp. 416-420 for details on CIA-Outfit cooperation in anti-Castro operations including attempts on the Cuban leader's life.

110. Anon., "JFK, King Murder Probes," *Chicago Tribune*, (September 18, 1976); and Anon., "JFK, King Probes Sift Tangled Clues; Internal Squabbles Also Hinder House Committee," *Chicago Tribune*, (June 1, 1977).

111. See Roemer, *Roemer: Man Against the Mob*, and Giancana, *Double Cross* for details of these many mutual animosities. While Giancana was at first apparently fascinated by having mutual girlfriends with JFK, this may have changed to jealousy at some point.

112. See Frank Ragano, Selwyn Raab (Contributor), and Barbara Grossman (Editor), *Mob Lawyer*, (New York: Charles Scribner's Sons, 1994), pp. 348-349; and Scheim, *Contract On America*, pp. 81-82. In addition to Trafficante and Giancana, Nitti's old crony Murray Humphreys also strongly hinted at Mafia involvement in the JFK assassination. See Morgan, *Prince of Crime*, pp. 155-167.

113. Roemer, *Roemer: Man Against the Mob*, pp. 340-341.

114. Scheim, *Contract On America*, p. 266.

115. Giancana, *Double Cross*, pp. 493-494.

116. Quoted in Scheim, *Contract On America*, pp. 135-136.

117. Roemer, *Roemer: Man Against the Mob*, p. 179; and Groden and Livingstone, *High Treason: The Assassination of President John F. Kennedy—What Really Happened*, p. 254.

118. Clark R. Mollenhoff, *Strike Force: Organized Crime and the Government*, (New York: Prentice-Hall, Inc., 1972), p. 158; and *US House Select Committee on Assassinations*.

119. Tuohy, "The Last Gangster: The Life and Time of Roger Touhy, John Factor and the Mob." However, Touhy does not specifically mention David Yaras by name. Other writers have undertaken competent analyses of the Yaras-Ruby-Kennedy links, but seem completely unaware of the Yaras-Zangara-Cermak thread. For example, see Peter Dale Scott, *Deep Politics and the Death of JFK*, (Berkeley: University of California Press, 1996).

120. Scheim, *Contract On America*, p. 258.

121. Giancana, *Double Cross*, pp. 458-459.

122. Roemer, *Roemer: Man Against the Mob*, pp. 262-269; and Roemer, *Accardo: the Genuine Godfather*, pp. 127-128 and pp. 372-373.

123. *US House Select Committee on Assassinations*.

124. Anon., "Mob-Linked Firm Bombed: Find Fuel Containers After Blaze," *Chicago Tribune*, (November 9, 1967); Mollenhoff, *Strike Force: Organized Crime and the Government*, p. 158; William F. Roemer, Jr., *War of the Godfathers: the Bloody Confrontation Between the Chicago and New York Families for Control of Las Vegas*, (New York: Ivy Books, 1990), p. 160 and pp. 261-262; and Roemer, *Accardo: the Genuine Godfather*, p. xi and pp. 104-105.

125. Furiati, *ZR Rifle: The Plot to Kill Kennedy and Castro*, pp. 162-166; and Giancana, *Double Cross*, pp. 458-468. Furiati also references Giancana, *Double Cross*, but she claims to have verified and supplemented her information through Cuban intelligence sources.

126. Giancana, *Double Cross*, pp. 486-488.

127. See Giancana, *Double Cross*, for specifics on Sam Giancana's related claims concerning a very twisted assassination plot.

128. Sandy Smith, "Prio Reputed Top Syndicate Gambling Boss; Background of Other Hoodlums Told," *Chicago Tribune*, (March 15, 1955).

129. *US House Select Committee on Assassinations*.

130. Reid, *The Grim Reapers: The Anatomy of Organized Crime in America*, p. 326; and Mollenhoff, *Strike Force: Organized Crime and the Government*, p. 253.

131. Anon., "Yaras," *Chicago Tribune*, (January 6, 1974); and Anon., "News From Cuba: Official Names Five in JFK Murder Plot," *Cuba Newsbriefs, soc.culture.latin-america*, (December 12, 1993). Other conflicting sources indicate he was murdered under mysterious circumstances, but these may have had him confused with son Ronnie who was murdered.

132. William F. Roemer, Jr., *The Enforcer—Spilotro: The Chicago Mob's Man Over Las Vegas*, (New York: Ivy Books, 1994), p. 118; and Roemer, *Accardo: the Genuine Godfather*, p. 372.

133. Anon., "Capone Henchman Arrested in Bed: Frank Nitti, Said to Be Treasurer for Gang Leader, Faces Income Tax Indictment," *Washington Daily News*, (October 31,

1930); and Anon., "Heitler 'Death Letter' Puzzle to Prosecutor: Fails as Instrument of Vengeance," *Chicago Tribune*, (September 17, 1931).

134. Scheim, *Contract On America*, p. 329. For a plausible fictional assassination-conspiracy scenario that includes both Kennedy brothers and King, see James Ellroy, *The Cold Six Thousand*, (New York: Vintage Books, 2002).

135. Joseph Conrad, *The Secret Agent*, (London: Penguin Classics, 2000). One of the major themes of Conrad's novel that remains true to this day is that many of the personalities involved with covert-intelligence activities, far from being the sophisticated James Bondian figures so popular in the public's imagination, are often borderline members of the lunatic fringe.

136. See Giancana, *Double Cross*, pp. 300-304, p. 415 and pp. 464-465; and Furiati, *ZR Rifle: The Plot to Kill Kennedy and Castro*, p. 163.

CHAPTER SIX

1. Anon., "Movies. Mayhem, the Mob...and All the Players in Between," *www.ipsn.org/movies.html*, (Fall 1995).

2. Walter M. Cummins, Jr., "Preserving Dad's Words of Wisdom," *Orlando Sentinel*, (June 17, 2001).

3. Lloyd Wendt, "Capone's Cohorts Carry On," *Chicago Tribune*, (August 31, 1941).

4. George Murray, *The Legacy of Al Capone*, (New York: G.P. Putnam's Sons, 1975), p. 229.

5. Elmer L. Irey and William J. Slocum, *The Tax Dodgers: The Inside Story of the T-Men's War with America's Political and Underworld Hoodlums*, (New York: Greenberg, 1948), pp. 180-184; Murray, *The Legacy of Al Capone*, pp. 229-242; John William Tuohy, "The Legend of Little Tommy Maloy," *www.americanmafia.com*, (February 2001); and John William Tuohy, "Tales From the City of Angels," (*www.gamblingmagazine.com*).

6. Murray, *The Legacy of Al Capone*, pp. 241-242; Anon., "The IA's Dark Era: The Browne/Bioff Years," *IATSE Home Page*, (2002); and Tuohy, "Tales From the City of Angels."

7. Tuohy, "Tales From the City of Angels."

8. Murray, *The Legacy of Al Capone*, p. 242 and pp. 265-266.

9. John H. Lyle, "Al Capone," *Chicago Tribune*, (December 4, 1960).

10. Irey and Slocum, *The Tax Dodgers: The Inside Story of the T-Men's War with America's Political and Underworld Hoodlums*, p. 183; and Lyle, "Al Capone."

11. Irey and Slocum, *The Tax Dodgers: The Inside Story of the T-Men's War with America's Political and Underworld Hoodlums*, p. 184.

12. Tuohy, "Tales From the City of Angels."

13. William F. Roemer, Jr., *Accardo: the Genuine Godfather*, (New York: Ivy Books, 1995), p. 71.

14. Irey and Slocum, *The Tax Dodgers: The Inside Story of the T-Men's War with America's Political and Underworld Hoodlums*, p. 180 and pp. 278-279.

15. Irey and Slocum, *The Tax Dodgers: The Inside Story of the T-Men's War with America's Political and Underworld Hoodlums*, pp. 271-288; Murray, *The Legacy of Al Capone*, pp. 242-257; and John William Tuohy, "Guns and Glamor," (*www.gamblingmagazine.com*). This B&B should not be confused with the law firm of Bieber & Brodkin, which was the legal mouthpiece for Chicago mobsters for many years.

16. John William Tuohy, "Battaglia Brothers," (*www.alleged-mafia-site.com*); and Allan May, "The Guileless Gangster," *crimemagazine.com*, (2002).

17. Irey and Slocum, *The Tax Dodgers: The Inside Story of the T-Men's War with America's Political and Underworld Hoodlums*, pp. 272-273; and Tom Sito, "The War of Hollywood—Part One: Hollywood Labor Unions in the 1930's," *www.grimsociety.com*, (September 2002).

18. Quoted in Murray, *The Legacy of Al Capone*, p. 251.

19. Irey and Slocum, *The Tax Dodgers: The Inside Story of the T-Men's War with America's Political and Underworld Hoodlums*, p. 272.

20. Irey and Slocum, *The Tax Dodgers: The Inside Story of the T-Men's War with America's Political and Underworld Hoodlums*, p. 272; Kenneth Allsop, *The Bootleggers: The Story of Chicago's Prohibition Era*, (London: Arrow Books Ltd., 1970), p. 109; and Tom Sito, "The War of Hollywood—Part Three: The Battle of Warner Bros.," *www.grimsociety. com*, (September 2002).

21. Quoted in Gus Russo, *The Outfit: The Role of Chicago's Underworld in the Shaping of Modern America*, (New York: Bloomsbury, 2001), p. 143.

22. Quoted in Anon., "The IA's Dark Era: The Browne/Bioff Years."

23. Herbert Aller, *The Extortionists*, (Beverly Hills: Guild-Hartford Publishing Company, Inc., 1972), pp. 35-36.

24. James Doherty, "Bioff Bares Nitti Role in Shakedowns: Heavily Guarded with Browne," *Chicago Tribune*, (October 1, 1948); and Aller, *The Extortionists*, pp. 39-41.

25. Murray, *The Legacy of Al Capone*, pp. 256-257.

26. Anon., "Gang Aid Tells How Nitti Took Union Control," *Chicago Tribune*, (October 2, 1948); Irey and Slocum, *The Tax Dodgers: The Inside Story of the T-Men's War with America's Political and Underworld Hoodlums*, pp. 274-275; Aller, *The Extortionists*, pp. 42-44; Murray, *The Legacy of Al Capone*, p. 257; Tuohy, "Guns and Glamor"; and May, "The Guileless Gangster."

27. Doherty, "Bioff Bares Nitti Role in Shakedowns: Heavily Guarded with Browne"; Irey and Slocum, *The Tax Dodgers: The Inside Story of the T-Men's War with America's Political and Underworld Hoodlums*, pp. 276-277; and Aller, *The Extortionists*, pp. 45-47.

28. Anon., "Gang Aid Tells How Nitti Took Union Control."

29. Anon., "Movie Bosses' Agony at Paying Bioff Related: Browne Tells US Jury of Riverside Meeting," *Chicago Tribune*, (October 27, 1943); Anon., "Gang Aid Tells How Nitti Took Union Control"; Murray, *The Legacy of Al Capone*, pp. 261-262; and US Federal Bureau of Investigation, *John Roselli*, (*foia.fbi.gov/roselli.htm*).

30. Irey and Slocum, *The Tax Dodgers: The Inside Story of the T-Men's War with America's Political and Underworld Hoodlums*, pp. 276-278.

31. Tuohy, "Guns and Glamor."

32. Irey and Slocum, *The Tax Dodgers: The Inside Story of the T-Men's War with America's Political and Underworld Hoodlums*, p. 276.

33. Quoted in Russo, *The Outfit: The Role of Chicago's Underworld in the Shaping of Modern America*, p. 131.

34. Dan E. Moldea, *Dark Victory: Ronald Reagan, MCA, and the Mob*, (New York: Viking, 1986), pp. 23-28.

35. Marc Eliot, *Walt Disney: Hollywood's Dark Prince*, (New York: Birch Lane Press, 1993), p. 64.

36. National Archives and Records Administration, *Frank R. Nitto, 38021-L: "Failing to file Income Tax return"*; Anon., "Tells How Gang Gunmen Milked Chicago Unions: Insider Says Theatre Men Paid Millions," *Chicago Tribune*, (March 1, 1943); Anon., "Movie Bosses' Agony at Paying Bioff Related: Browne Tells US Jury of Riverside Meeting"; and US Federal Bureau of Investigation, *John Roselli*.

37. Murray, *The Legacy of Al Capone*, p. 268.

38. Tom Dewe Matthews, "Goodfellas, Badfellas and Raging Bulls," *www.homecinemachoice.com*, (1999). This author's claims are not readily verifiable, and some are apparently inaccurate, although interesting.

39. Eliot, *Walt Disney: Hollywood's Dark Prince*, pp. 64-65.

40. Quoted in Murray, *The Legacy of Al Capone*, p. 269; and Russo, *The Outfit: The Role of Chicago's Underworld in the Shaping of Modern America*, p. 133.

41. Irey and Slocum, *The Tax Dodgers: The Inside Story of the T-Men's War with America's Political and Underworld Hoodlums*, p. 282.

42. US Federal Bureau of Investigation, *Alphonse Capone, (foia.fbi.gov/capone/capone.htm)*; and Murray, *The Legacy of Al Capone*, pp. 271-280.

43. Sito, "The War of Hollywood—Part One: Hollywood Labor Unions in the 1930's."

44. Irey and Slocum, *The Tax Dodgers: The Inside Story of the T-Men's War with America's Political and Underworld Hoodlums*, p. 281.

45. Anon., "Gang Aid Tells How Nitti Took Union Control"; Irey and Slocum, *The Tax Dodgers: The Inside Story of the T-Men's War with America's Political and Underworld Hoodlums*, pp. 277-278; Aller, *The Extortionists*, pp. 52-53; and Russo, *The Outfit: The Role of Chicago's Underworld in the Shaping of Modern America*, p. 135. Herbert Aller's insights on Bioff and Browne are particularly revealing as he was an IATSE business representative for thirty-six years and personally worked with both Bioff and Browne in an official capacity.

46. Anon., "Movies. Mayhem, the Mob ...and All the Players in Between."

47. Irey and Slocum, *The Tax Dodgers: The Inside Story of the T-Men's War with America's Political and Underworld Hoodlums*, p. 280.

48. Eliot, *Walt Disney: Hollywood's Dark Prince*, pp. 64-65.

49. Irey and Slocum, *The Tax Dodgers: The Inside Story of the T-Men's War with America's Political and Underworld Hoodlums*, p. 282; and Aller, *The Extortionists*, pp. 102-103.

50. Anon., "Tells How Gang Gunmen Milked Chicago Unions: Insider Says Theatre Men Paid Millions"; and US Federal Bureau of Investigation, *John Roselli*.

51. Aller, *The Extortionists*, pp. 154-155.

52. Irey and Slocum, *The Tax Dodgers: The Inside Story of the T-Men's War with America's Political and Underworld Hoodlums*, p. 271.

53. Murray, *The Legacy of Al Capone*, p. 277.

54. William F. Roemer, Jr., *Roemer: Man Against the Mob*, (New York: Ivy Books, 1989), pp. 77-78; and John William Tuohy, *When Capone's Mob Murdered Roger Touhy: The Strange Case of Touhy, Jake the Barber and the Kidnapping That Never Happened*, (Fort Lee, NJ: Barricade Books Inc., 2001), p. 168.

55. Allsop, *The Bootleggers: The Story of Chicago's Prohibition Era*, pp. 480-481; and Roemer, *Roemer: Man Against the Mob*, pp. 77-78.

56. Timothy W. Maier, "IRS Tax Cops," *www.insightmag.com*, (2002).

57. Anon., (*archive.salon.com/ent/movies/*).

58. Anon., "The Two Percent Assessment," *IATSE Home Page*, (2002); and Anon., "The IA's Dark Era: The Browne/Bioff Years."

59. See John William Tuohy, "Johnny Hollywood: Part One," *AmericanMafia.com*, (April 2002) for a summary and Charles Rappleye and Ed Becker, *All American Mafioso: The Johnny Rosselli Story*, (New York: Doubleday, 1991) for a full and detailed biography of this fascinating man.

60. Ovid Demaris, *The Last Mafioso: The Treacherous World of Jimmy Fratianno*, (New York: Times Books, 1981), p. 17; and Andy Edmonds, *Hot Toddy: The True Story of Hollywood's Most Sensational Murder*, (New York: William Morrow and Company, Inc., 1989), pp. 198-199.

61. Roy Gibbons, "Bioff Reveals Death Threats By Capone Gang: Is Warned Not to Try to Quit Mob," *Chicago Tribune*, (October 9, 1943).

62. US Federal Bureau of Investigation, *John Roselli*.

63. Ed Reid, *The Grim Reapers: The Anatomy of Organized Crime in America*, (New York: Bantam, 1969), p. 189; and Demaris, *The Last Mafioso: The Treacherous World of Jimmy Fratianno*, pp. 190-191.

64. Edmonds, *Hot Toddy: The True Story of Hollywood's Most Sensational Murder*, p. 155.

65. Demaris, *The Last Mafioso: The Treacherous World of Jimmy Fratianno*, p. 17, and William F. Roemer, Jr., *The Enforcer—Spilotro: The Chicago Mob's Man Over Las Vegas*, (New York: Ivy Books, 1994), p. 65.

66. Moldea, *Dark Victory: Ronald Reagan, MCA, and the Mob*, pp. 84-86.

67. Claudia Furiati, *ZR Rifle: The Plot to Kill Kennedy and Castro*, (Melbourne: Ocean Press, 1994), pp. 24-26 and p. 118.

68. James K Olmstead, "Ruby/Jones Beginnings," *alt.assassination.jfk*, (July 22, 2000).

69. Ed Reid and Ovid Demaris, *The Green Felt Jungle*, (New York: Pocket Books, 1962), pp. 188-190.

70. Anon., "Movie Bosses' Agony at Paying Bioff Related: Browne Tells US Jury of Riverside Meeting"; Murray, *The Legacy of Al Capone*, p. 273; Russo, *The Outfit: The Role of Chicago's Underworld in the Shaping of Modern America*, pp. 132-133; and Charles Rappleye and Ed Becker, *All American Mafioso: The Johnny Rosselli Story*, (New York: Doubleday, 1991), p. 68.

71. Virgil Peterson, "Capone," *Chicago Tribune*, (October 28, 1956).

72. Tuohy, "Johnny Hollywood: Part One."

73. Tuohy, "Johnny Hollywood: Part One"; and Demaris, *The Last Mafioso: The Treacherous World of Jimmy Fratianno*, pp. 109-110.

74. Murray, *The Legacy of Al Capone*, p. 274.

75. Tuohy, "Johnny Hollywood: Part One." Some sources also indicate Roselli hosted Capone in Los Angeles in 1927.

76. John William Tuohy, "Johnny Hollywood," (*www.gamblingmagazine.com*).

77. John William Tuohy, "Extortion 101," *AmericanMafia.com*, (May 2002).

78. Moldea, *Dark Victory: Ronald Reagan, MCA, and the Mob*, pp. 88-89.

79. See Sam and Chuck Giancana, *Double Cross*, (New York: Warner Books, Inc., 1992), pp. 271-273.

80. Moldea, *Dark Victory: Ronald Reagan, MCA, and the Mob*, p. 85; and Demaris, *The Last Mafioso: The Treacherous World of Jimmy Fratianno*, p. 109.

81. Tuohy, "Johnny Hollywood: Part One."

82. Tuohy, "Johnny Hollywood."

83. See Roemer, *Roemer: Man Against the Mob*, pp. 174-176; Giancana, *Double Cross*, pp. 436-441; and Russo, *The Outfit: The Role of Chicago's Underworld in the Shaping of Modern America*, pp. 432-433 for details of the Outfit's possible role and vested interest in Monroe's murder. One version of her alleged gangland murder has Roselli holding her down in bed while another assassin injected an undetectable poison enema up her rectum with a needle.

84. Roemer, *Roemer: Man Against the Mob*, pp. 149-150; Robert J. Groden and Harrison Edward Livingstone, *High Treason: The Assassination of President John F. Kennedy—What Really Happened*, (Baltimore: The Conservatory Press, 1989), pp, 121-122, p. 268 and pp. 327-328; David E. Scheim, *Contract On America*, (New York: Zebra Books, 1993), p. 58; and Moldea, *Dark Victory: Ronald Reagan, MCA, and the Mob*, pp. 231-232 and p. 246. However, it is also possible that some of Roselli's accounts of his anti-Castro activities were later exaggerated to avoid possible federal extradition charges to Italy. See Demaris, *The Last Mafioso: The Treacherous World of Jimmy Fratianno*, pp. 188-200.

85. Tuohy, "Johnny Hollywood."

86. Warren Hinckle, William W. Turner, and Bill Turner, *Deadly Secrets: The CIA-Mafia War Against Castro and the Assassination of J.F.K.*, (New York: Thunder's Mouth Press, 1993), p. 20.

87. US Federal Bureau of Investigation, *John Roselli*.

88. William F. Roemer, Jr., "Who Rules Vegas?," *IPSN, www.ipsn.org/vegas.html,* (Spring 1994).

89. Roemer, *The Enforcer—Spilotro: The Chicago Mob's Man Over Las Vegas,* pp. 64-65, pp. 68-69 and pp. 77-78.

90. Tuohy, "Johnny Hollywood."

91. Moldea, *Dark Victory: Ronald Reagan, MCA, and the Mob,* p. 246; and Demaris, *The Last Mafioso: The Treacherous World of Jimmy Fratianno,* p. 184.

92. See Roemer, *Roemer: Man Against the Mob,* p. 126; and Roemer, *The Enforcer—Spilotro: The Chicago Mob's Man Over Las Vegas,* pp. 190-191.

93. Reid, *The Grim Reapers: The Anatomy of Organized Crime in America,* p. 260; Clark R. Mollenhoff, *Strike Force: Organized Crime and the Government,* (New York: Prentice-Hall, Inc., 1972), p. 29; Roemer, *Roemer: Man Against the Mob,* pp. 269-270; Giancana, *Double Cross,* p. 413 and pp. 419-420; Roemer, *The Enforcer—Spilotro: The Chicago Mob's Man Over Las Vegas,* pp. 25-27; and Russo, *The Outfit: The Role of Chicago's Underworld in the Shaping of Modern America,* pp.429-430.

94. Roemer, "Who Rules Vegas?"

95. Reid, *The Grim Reapers: The Anatomy of Organized Crime in America,* p. 190; and Mollenhoff, *Strike Force: Organized Crime and the Government,* p. 197.

96. Reid, *The Grim Reapers: The Anatomy of Organized Crime in America,* p. 187.

97. Anon., "JFK, King Murder Probes," *Chicago Tribune,* (September 18, 1976); Anon., "JFK, King Probes Sift Tangled Clues; Internal Squabbles Also Hinder House Committee," *Chicago Tribune,* (June 1, 1977); Groden and Livingstone, *High Treason: The Assassination of President John F. Kennedy—What Really Happened,* p. 275; and Furiati, *ZR Rifle: The Plot to Kill Kennedy and Castro,* p. 121.

98. Quoted in Tuohy, "Johnny Hollywood." Also see Roemer, *Roemer: Man Against the Mob,* p. 126 and pp. 338-339; Scheim, *Contract On America,* p. 58; Demaris, *The Last Mafioso: The Treacherous World of Jimmy Fratianno,* pp. 330-331; and Russo, *The Outfit: The Role of Chicago's Underworld in the Shaping of Modern America,* pp. 484-485.

99. Scheim, *Contract On America,* p. 266.

100. US Federal Bureau of Investigation, *John Roselli;* Jack Anderson, "Castro Stalker Worked for the CIA," *The Washington Post,* (February 23, 1971); and Reid, *The Grim Reapers: The Anatomy of Organized Crime in America,* p. 299.

101. James Doherty, "Gangster Tools to Repeat Tale of Shakedown: Subpena Browne, Bioff for Atlanta Hearing," *Chicago Tribune,* (October 6, 1948); Murray, *The Legacy of Al Capone,* p. 284; and Ronald Koziol and Edward Baumann, "How Frank Nitti Met His Fate: Return With Us Now to the Scene of the Mobster's Suicide," *Chicago Tribune,* (June 29, 1987).

102. Giancana, *Double Cross,* p. 102.

103. Aller, *The Extortionists,* pp. 119-120; and Tuohy, "Johnny Hollywood: Part One."

104. Aller, *The Extortionists,* pp. 89-90.

105. Anon., "Convict Seven of Conspiracy in Film Racket: Face 10 Year Term and $10,000 Fine," *Chicago Tribune,* (December 23, 1943).

106. William Fulton, "Another Tells of Giving Movie Funds to Bioff: US Nears Close of Its Shakedown Case," *Chicago Tribune*, (October 22, 1941); and Edmonds, *Hot Toddy: The True Story of Hollywood's Most Sensational Murder*, p. 199-200.

107. For example, see William Triplett, "Busting Heads and Blaming Reds: How Movie Producers Used the Blacklist to Crack Down on Hollywood Unions," *Salon, www. buzzle.com*, (November 1, 2000).

108. Tuohy, "Guns and Glamor."

109. Sito, "The War of Hollywood—Part One: Hollywood Labor Unions in the 1930's."

110. Aller, *The Extortionists*, p. 114.

111. Tuohy, "Extortion 101."

112. Sito, "The War of Hollywood—Part One: Hollywood Labor Unions in the 1930's."

113. Anon., (*archive.salon.com/ent/movies/*).

114. Irey and Slocum, *The Tax Dodgers: The Inside Story of the T-Men's War with America's Political and Underworld Hoodlums*, p. 272.

115. Aller, *The Extortionists*, pp. 61-71.

116. Aller, *The Extortionists*, p. 144.

117. Marcia Winn, "Bioff's Shadow Is Still a Cloud on Hollywood: Painter's Star Rises as Labor Spokesman," *Chicago Tribune*, (July 27, 1943).

118. Sito, "The War of Hollywood—Part One: Hollywood Labor Unions in the 1930's"; and Anon., (*archive.salon.com/ent/movies/*).

119. Aller, *The Extortionists*, p. 110 and p. 135.

120. Quoted in Anon., "On Trial," *IATSE Home Page*, (2002).

121. Michael Everett, Jerry Ulrey, and Allen Schaaf, "Corrupt Local, Will This Work?," *alt.society.labor-unions, alt.union.iatse*, (May 28, 1996).

122. Eliot, *Walt Disney: Hollywood's Dark Prince*, pp. 122-124.

123. Winn, "Bioff's Shadow is Still a Cloud on Hollywood: Painter's Star Rises as Labor Spokesman."

124. Quoted in Winn, "Bioff's Shadow Is Still a Cloud on Hollywood: Painter's Star Rises as Labor Spokesman."

125. Giancana, *Double Cross*, p. 101; and Ben Best, "Schemers in the Web: A Covert History of the 1960's Era," *www.benbest.com/history/schemers.html*, (1990).

126. Janon Fisher, "FBI Files Show Bing Crosby Paid Extortionist $10,000; Crooner's Gambling Habit Also Got Bob Hope Into Trouble," *APBnews.com*, (December 20, 1999).

127. Triplett, "Busting Heads and Blaming Reds: How Movie Producers Used the Blacklist to Crack Down on Hollywood Unions."

128. Anon., "Disney Link to the FBI and Hoover Is Disclosed," *The New York Times*, (Thursday, May 6, 1993).

129. Sito, "The War of Hollywood—Part One: Hollywood Labor Unions in the 1930's."

130. Eliot, *Walt Disney: Hollywood's Dark Prince*, pp. 145-147.

131. Fisher, "FBI Files Show Bing Crosby Paid Extortionist $10,000; Crooner's Gambling Habit Also Got Bob Hope Into Trouble; and Anon., (*www.lvstriphistory.com/siegel.htm*).

132. Anon., "Bares Theater Union Dealings with Gang Boss: Mystery Package for Nitti Revealed," *Chicago Tribune*, (November 20, 1943).

133. Tuohy, "Guns and Glamor."

134. Sito, "The War of Hollywood—Part One: Hollywood Labor Unions in the 1930's."

135. US Federal Bureau of Investigation, *Charles "Lucky" Luciano, (foia.fbi.gov/luciano.htm)*.

136. Edmonds, *Hot Toddy: The True Story of Hollywood's Most Sensational Murder*, pp. 162-164 and p. 195. As discussed in Chapter Four, Nitti had also called a 1933 national meeting in Miami that Luciano did not attend, but was represented instead by Meyer Lansky.

137. Edmonds, *Hot Toddy: The True Story of Hollywood's Most Sensational Murder*, p. 191 and pp. 205-207.

138. Edmonds, *Hot Toddy: The True Story of Hollywood's Most Sensational Murder*, pp. 207-211 and pp. 282-283. Edmonds also provides various interesting dialog between Nitti and Luciano in support of these claims, including death threats from Luciano to Nitti, but unfortunately her sources are not referenced.

139. Bill Kelly, "A Century of Hollywood Murders," *www.cybersleuths.com*, (2002).

140. Edmonds, *Hot Toddy: The True Story of Hollywood's Most Sensational Murder*, p. 13.

141. Aller, *The Extortionists*, 105.

142. Aller, *The Extortionists*, pp. 121-122.

143. Aller, *The Extortionists*, pp. 57-60 and p. 112.

144. Gibbons, "Bioff Reveals Death Threats By Capone Gang: Is Warned Not to Try to Quit Mob"; Lyle, "Al Capone"; and Antonio Napoli, *The Mob's Guys*, (*Virtualbookworm.com* Publishing, March 2004), p. 329.

145. Anon., "Gang Aid Tells How Nitti Took Union Control."

146. James Doherty, "Extortion Cash Splitups Told in Nitti Tax Case," *Chicago Tribune*, (October 2, 1948).

147. Anon., "Bares Theater Union Dealings with Gang Boss: Mystery Package for Nitti Revealed"; and Anon., "Recall Racket Witness After Death Threat," *Chicago Tribune*, (November 23, 1943).

148. Anon., "Convict Seven of Conspiracy in Film Racket: Face 10 Year Term and $10,000 Fine."

149. Aller, *The Extortionists*, pp. 116-117.

150. Russo, *The Outfit: The Role of Chicago's Underworld in the Shaping of Modern America*, pp. 158-159.

151. Aller, *The Extortionists*, p. 131.

152. Aller, *The Extortionists*, pp. 125-126.

153. Aller, *The Extortionists*, pp. 126-128.

154. Anon., "Bioff Reveals Power of Nitti in Shakedowns," *Chicago Tribune*, (October 2, 1948).

155. Irey and Slocum, *The Tax Dodgers: The Inside Story of the T-Men's War with America's Political and Underworld Hoodlums*, pp. 283-284; Anon., "The Harder They Fall," *IATSE Home Page*, (2002); and John Morgan, *Prince of Crime*, (New York: Stein and Day, 1985), p.119.

156. Gibbons, "Bioff Reveals Death Threats By Capone Gang: Is Warned Not to Try to Quit Mob"; Irey and Slocum, *The Tax Dodgers: The Inside Story of the T-Men's War with America's Political and Underworld Hoodlums*, p. 284; Aller, *The Extortionists*, pp. 136-138; and Murray, *The Legacy of Al Capone*, pp. 283-286.

157. Anon., (*www.pulitzer.org*).

158. Anon., "The Harder They Fall."

159. Quoted in Aller, *The Extortionists*, p. 138; and Roemer, *Accardo: the Genuine Godfather*, p. 85.

160. William Fulton, "Reveal Chicago Underworld's Shakedown Cut: Witnesses Describe Bioff's Visits," *Chicago Tribune*, (October 21, 1941).

161. Anon., (*www.gambino.com*).

162. Aller, *The Extortionists*, pp. 166-167.

163. Reid, *The Grim Reapers: The Anatomy of Organized Crime in America*, p. 259.

164. Irey and Slocum, *The Tax Dodgers: The Inside Story of the T-Men's War with America's Political and Underworld Hoodlums*, pp. 286-287; Roemer, *Accardo: the Genuine Godfather*, pp. 95-96; May, "The Guileless Gangster"; and Russo, *The Outfit: The Role of Chicago's Underworld in the Shaping of Modern America*, pp. 172-173.

165. Aller, *The Extortionists*, p. 157.

166. Anon., "The Two Percent Assessment."

167. Anon., "The White Rats," *IATSE Home Page*, (2002).

168. Anon., "On Trial."

169. Fulton, "Reveal Chicago Underworld's Shakedown Cut: Witnesses Describe Bioff's Visits"; Fulton, "Another Tells of Giving Movie Funds to Bioff: US Nears Close of Its Shakedown Case"; Anon., "Movie Bosses' Agony at Paying Bioff Related: Browne Tells US Jury of Riverside Meeting"; Doherty, "Bioff Bares Nitti Role in Shakedowns: Heavily Guarded with Browne"; and Mollenhoff, *Strike Force: Organized Crime and the Government*, p. 88 and p. 171.

170. Fulton, "Reveal Chicago Underworld's Shakedown Cut: Witnesses Describe Bioff's Visits."

171. Koziol and Baumann, "How Frank Nitti Met His Fate: Return With Us Now to the Scene of the Mobster's Suicide."

172. Irey and Slocum, *The Tax Dodgers: The Inside Story of the T-Men's War with America's Political and Underworld Hoodlums*, pp. 285-288.

173. Fulton, "Another Tells of Giving Movie Funds to Bioff: US Nears Close of Its Shakedown Case"; Anon., "Tells How Gang Gunmen Milked Chicago Unions: Insider Says Theatre Men Paid Millions"; and Aller, *The Extortionists*, p. 130 and p. 140.

174. Kathryn Keneally, "White-Collar Crime," *National Association of Criminal Defense Lawyers*, *www.nacdl.org*, (April 1999).

175. Giancana, *Double Cross*, pp. 157-158 and p. 169.

176. Today they would have been charged under RICO and related legislation.

177. Allan May, "Charles 'Cherry Nose' Gioe," *AmericanMafia.com*, (May 2000).

178. Anon., "Recall Racket Witness After Death Threat"; and Aller, *The Extortionists*, p. 165.

179. Fulton, "Another Tells of Giving Movie Funds to Bioff: US Nears Close of Its Shakedown Case."

180. Anon., "Tells How Gang Gunmen Milked Chicago Unions: Insider Says Theatre Men Paid Millions."

181. Anon., "Recall Racket Witness After Death Threat"; US Federal Bureau of Investigation, *John Roselli*; Aller, *The Extortionists*, p. 166; Sito, "The War of Hollywood—Part Three: The Battle of Warner Bros."; and May, "The Guileless Gangster."

182. Morgan, *Prince of Crime*, p. 120.

183. Estes Kefauver, *Crime In America*, (New York: Doubleday and Company, Inc., 1951), pp. 61-73; Peterson, "Capone"; Giancana, *Double Cross*, pp. 198-199; and Tuohy, "Guns and Glamor."

184. For a detailed account see Morgan, *Prince of Crime*, pp. 125-133.

185. See Peterson, "Capone"; Murray, *The Legacy of Al Capone*, pp. 290-295; and Curt Gentry, *J. Edgar Hoover: The Man and the Secrets*, (New York: W.W. Norton & Company, 1991).

186. Anon., "Move to Link Ragen Ambush to Parole Plot: Crime Commission Data Sent Congressmen," *Chicago Tribune*, (February 25, 1948).

187. May, "The Guileless Gangster."

188. US Federal Bureau of Investigation, *John Roselli*.

189. Sito, "The War of Hollywood—Part Three: The Battle of Warner Bros.."

190. Matthews, "Goodfellas, Badfellas and Raging Bulls."

191. See George Jacobs and William Stadiem, Mr. S: *My Life with Frank Sinatra*, (New York: HarperCollins Publishers Inc., 2003) for details of Sinatra's involvement with Giancana, Roselli, and other mobsters, as well as the Kennedy clan and Marilyn Monroe. Sinatra's 1964 motion picture comedy, *Robin and the Seven Hoods*, was reportedly his personal tribute to the Outfit as was its signature song sung by Sinatra, "My Kind of Town" —My kind of town, Chicago is, my kind of people too . . .

CHAPTER SEVEN

1. Ronald Koziol and Edward Baumann, "How Frank Nitti Met His Fate: Return With Us Now to the Scene of the Mobster's Suicide," *Chicago Tribune*, (June 29, 1987).

2. Sam and Chuck Giancana, *Double Cross*, (New York: Warner Books, Inc., 1992), pp. 160-161.

3. James Doherty, "Gangster Tools to Repeat Tale of Shakedown: Subpena Browne, Bioff for Atlanta Hearing," *Chicago Tribune*, (October 6, 1948); and Koziol and Baumann, "How Frank Nitti Met His Fate: Return With Us Now to the Scene of the Mobster's Suicide."

4. George Murray, *The Legacy of Al Capone*, (New York: G.P. Putnam's Sons, 1975), pp. 288-289; John William Tuohy, "The Enforcer: Frank Nitti & The Chicago Mob," (*www.gamblingmagazine.com*); and Anon., (*www.gambino.com*).

5. John William Tuohy, "Guns and Glamor," (*www.gamblingmagazine.com*).

6. Andy Edmonds, *Hot Toddy: The True Story of Hollywood's Most Sensational Murder*, (New York: William Morrow and Company, Inc., 1989), p. 198.

7. Orville Dwyer and George Hartmann, "List Gangsters Who Prey on Chicago Unions: Three Capone Mobster Boss Extortionists Nitti, Ricca, and Campagna Rule," *Chicago Tribune*, (March 18, 1943).

8. Anon., (*www.crimelibrary.com*).

9. Carl Wiegman, "Nitti Kills Himself! Gang Chief Dies By Gun After US Jury Charges 3: Trainmen Look On as Racketeer Fires 3 Shots," *Chicago Tribune*, (March 20, 1943); and Koziol and Baumann, "How Frank Nitti Met His Fate: Return With Us Now to the Scene of the Mobster's Suicide."

10. June Geserick, "Nitti Sent Wife to Church at Hour of Suicide: Gangster Too Good to Live, She Sobs," *Chicago Tribune*, (March 20, 1943); and Koziol and Baumann, "How Frank Nitti Met His Fate: Return With Us Now to the Scene of the Mobster's Suicide."

11. Robert J. Schoenberg, *Mr. Capone*, (New York: William Morrow, 1992), p. 359.

12. Wiegman, "Nitti Kills Himself! Gang Chief Dies By Gun After US Jury Charges 3: Trainmen Look On as Racketeer Fires 3 Shots"; and Koziol and Baumann, "How Frank Nitti Met His Fate: Return With Us Now to the Scene of the Mobster's Suicide."

13. Wiegman, "Nitti Kills Himself! Gang Chief Dies By Gun After US Jury Charges 3: Trainmen Look On as Racketeer Fires 3 Shots."

14. William F. Roemer, Jr., *Accardo: the Genuine Godfather*, (New York: Ivy Books, 1995), p. 81.

15. Koziol and Baumann, "How Frank Nitti Met His Fate: Return With Us Now to the Scene of the Mobster's Suicide."

16. Anon., "FBI Hunts New Clews Bearing On Nitti Suicide: Inquest Witness Tells of Gangster's Ill Health," *Chicago Tribune*, (March 21, 1943); Murray, *The Legacy of Al Capone*, p. 289; Anon., (*www.alcaponemuseum.com*); and Anon., (*www.gambino.com*).

17. Wiegman, "Nitti Kills Himself! Gang Chief Dies By Gun After US Jury Charges 3: Trainmen Look On as Racketeer Fires 3 Shots"; and Koziol and Baumann, "How Frank Nitti Met His Fate: Return With Us Now to the Scene of the Mobster's Suicide."

18. Wiegman, "Nitti Kills Himself! Gang Chief Dies By Gun After US Jury Charges 3: Trainmen Look On as Racketeer Fires 3 Shots"; Koziol and Baumann, "How Frank Nitti Met His Fate: Return With Us Now to the Scene of the Mobster's Suicide"; and Ken Schessler, "Unusual Guide to Chicago," *members.aol.com/KSchessler/wizzn.html*, (September 2002).

19. Anon., "FBI Hunts New Clews Bearing On Nitti Suicide: Inquest Witness Tells of Gangster's Ill Health."

20. Anon., "Frank Nitti," *Today*, (June 28, 1972).

21. Koziol and Baumann, "How Frank Nitti Met His Fate: Return With Us Now to the Scene of the Mobster's Suicide"; and Edmonds, *Hot Toddy: The True Story of Hollywood's Most Sensational Murder*, p. 284.

22. Anon., "On Trial," *IATSE Home Page*, (2002).

23. Anon., "Frank Nitti"; and Koziol and Baumann, "How Frank Nitti Met His Fate: Return With Us Now to the Scene of the Mobster's Suicide."

24. Wiegman, "Nitti Kills Himself! Gang Chief Dies By Gun After US Jury Charges 3: Trainmen Look On as Racketeer Fires 3 Shots"; and Koziol and Baumann, "How Frank Nitti Met His Fate: Return With Us Now to the Scene of the Mobster's Suicide."

25. John Morgan, *Prince of Crime*, (New York: Stein and Day, 1985), p. 122.

26. Anon., "FBI Hunts New Clews Bearing On Nitti Suicide: Inquest Witness Tells of Gangster's Ill Health."

27. Gus Russo, *The Outfit: The Role of Chicago's Underworld in the Shaping of Modern America*, (New York: Bloomsbury, 2001), p. 96; John J. Binder, *The Chicago Outfit*, (Charleston, SC: Arcadia Publishing, 2003), p. 64; and Antonio Napoli, *The Mob's Guys*, (*Virtualbookworm.com* Publishing, March 2004), p. 12 and p. 21. It was not uncommon for cancer victims of the era to commit suicide rather than face prolonged suffering, and Nitti may have chosen this option if he had known he had cancer.

28. Anon., "FBI Hunts New Clews Bearing On Nitti Suicide: Inquest Witness Tells of Gangster's Ill Health."

29. Koziol and Baumann, "How Frank Nitti Met His Fate: Return With Us Now to the Scene of the Mobster's Suicide."

30. Anon., "Says Nitti Knew Too Much About Film Producers: Sorrell Asserts He Was Gang 'Pay-Off Man'," *Chicago Tribune*, (March 10, 1948).

31. Edmonds, *Hot Toddy: The True Story of Hollywood's Most Sensational Murder*, p. 284.

32. Kenneth Allsop, *The Bootleggers: The Story of Chicago's Prohibition Era*, (London: Arrow Books Ltd., 1970), pp. 485-486; and Morgan, *Prince of Crime*, p. 122.

33. Max Allan Collins, *The Million-Dollar Wound*, (New York: St. Martin's Press, 1986), p. 333.

34. Anon., "Court Inventory Values Nitti's Estate at $74,000," *Chicago Tribune*, (November 12, 1943).

35. James Doherty, "Slot Machine 'Take' of Nitti Told Probers: Data Made Available to Sheriff Walsh," *Chicago Tribune*, (September 12, 1948); James Doherty, "Bioff Bares Nitti Role in Shakedowns: Heavily Guarded with Browne," *Chicago Tribune*, (October 1, 1948); James Doherty, "Extortion Cash Splitups Told in Nitti Tax Case," *Chicago Tribune*, (October 2, 1948); Anon., "Bioff Reveals Power of Nitti in Shakedowns," *Chicago Tribune*, (October 2, 1948); Anon., "Gang Aid Tells How Nitti Took Union Control," *Chicago Tribune*, (October 2, 1948); and Doherty, "Gangster Tools to Repeat Tale of Shakedown: Subpena Browne, Bioff for Atlanta Hearing."

36. Russo, *The Outfit: The Role of Chicago's Underworld in the Shaping of Modern America*, pp. 176-177.

37. National Archives and Records Administration, *Frank R. Nitto, 38021-L: "Failing to file Income Tax return"*; and Anon., "Frank Nitti."

38. Virgil Peterson, "The Mob Goes Legit: Hoods Muscle Into Business and Sports, and the Profits Pour In; But the Old Bloodshed Continues," *Chicago Tribune*, (November 11, 1956).

39. Quoted in Murray, *The Legacy of Al Capone*, p. 21 and pp. 34-36; and Schessler, "Unusual Guide to Chicago."

40. Giancana, *Double Cross*, p. 315.

41. Anon., "Gang Trail Leads to Grave," *Chicago Tribune*, (December 9, 1955).

42. Richard J. La Susa, "Atlas Prager, Got It? Atlas Prager, Get It!," *Chicago Tribune*, (April 24, 1977).

43. George Tagge, "Ald. Cilella Admits Visit to Nitti Home: Says He Went as Favor to Client," *Chicago Tribune*, (May 21, 1958).

44. Ed Reid, *The Grim Reapers: The Anatomy of Organized Crime in America*, (New York: Bantam, 1969), pp. 258-259; and Russo, *The Outfit: The Role of Chicago's Underworld in the Shaping of Modern America*, p. 420.

45. US Federal Bureau of Investigation, *Alphonse Capone, (foia.fbi.gov/capone/capone.htm)*.

46. Anon., "Inquiry Shown: Questions Parried On His Activities," *Chicago Tribune*, (September 10, 1947). It is interesting that Guzik still referred to Capone in the present tense although he had at that time been deceased for a number of months.

47. Allan May, "Louis Campagna—Done in by a Grouper," *AmericanMafia.com*, (May 1999).

48. Anon., "Gang Trail Leads to Grave."

49. William F. Roemer, Jr., *Roemer: Man Against the Mob*, (New York: Ivy Books, 1989), p. 49.

50. Frank Cipriani, "Court Hearing Puts Gambling Chief on Spot," *Chicago Tribune*, (April 14, 1944); Anon., "Inquiry Shown: Questions Parried On His Activities"; and Anon., "Tuohy Bares Guzik Story in Ragen Case," *Chicago Tribune*, (September 10, 1947).

51. US Federal Bureau of Investigation, *Bugsy Siegel, (foia.fbi.gov/siege.htm)*.

52. There are various versions of exactly what Campagna had said to Bioff, but the intent was the same in each case. See: Roy Gibbons, "Bioff Reveals Death Threats By Capone

Gang: Is Warned Not to Try to Quit Mob," *Chicago Tribune*, (October 9, 1943); Elmer L. Irey and William J. Slocum, *The Tax Dodgers: The Inside Story of the T-Men's War with America's Political and Underworld Hoodlums*, (New York: Greenberg, 1948), p. 285 and p. 288; Herbert Aller, *The Extortionists*, (Beverly Hills: Guild-Hartford Publishing Company, Inc., 1972), p. 139 and pp. 148-149; and Murray, *The Legacy of Al Capone*, p. 286.

53. Ed Reid and Ovid Demaris, *The Green Felt Jungle*, (New York: Pocket Books, 1962), pp. 42-44; and Aller, *The Extortionists*, pp. 167-168 and pp. 170-174.

54. Giancana, *Double Cross*, pp. 315-316.

55. Roemer, *Accardo: the Genuine Godfather*, p. 91.

56. Aller, *The Extortionists*, pp. 167-169; Edmonds, *Hot Toddy: The True Story of Hollywood's Most Sensational Murder*, p. 284; Anon., "On Trial"; and Tom Sito, "The War of Hollywood—Part One: Hollywood Labor Unions in the 1930's," *www.grimsociety.com*, (September 2002).

57. Aller, *The Extortionists*, p. 167; and Roemer, *Roemer: Man Against the Mob*, p. 80.

58. Richard J. Dyer, (*hymieweiss.com*).

59. Geserick, "Nitti Sent Wife to Church at Hour of Suicide: Gangster Too Good to Live, She Sobs."

CHAPTER EIGHT

1. Jim Doherty, "A Tale of Three Nesses," (*www.mysteryreaders.org*).

2. Doherty, "A Tale of Three Nesses."

3. Larry Wolters, "Capone's Son Protests TV Shows On Dad," *Chicago Tribune*, (April 18, 1959).

4. See Desi Arnaz, *A Book*, (New York: Warner, 1976) for a complete account.

5. Ed Robertson, *www.edrobertson.com/the_untouchables.htm*, (1996).

6. Ovid Demaris, *The Last Mafioso: The Treacherous World of Jimmy Fratianno*, (New York: Times Books, 1981), pp. 122-125; Robertson, (*www.edrobertson.com/the_untouchables.htm*); and Russo, *The Outfit: The Role of Chicago's Underworld in the Shaping of Modern America*, pp. 353-354.

7. Robertson, (*www.edrobertson.com/the_untouchables.htm*).

8. Robertson, (*www.edrobertson.com/the_untouchables.htm*).

9. Doherty, "A Tale of Three Nesses."

10. Doherty, "A Tale of Three Nesses."

11. Robertson, (*www.edrobertson.com/the_untouchables.htm*).

12. Robertson, (*www.edrobertson.com/the_untouchables.htm*).

13. Doherty, "A Tale of Three Nesses."

14. Silvana Gallardo, "The Art of Fine Acting: Tape Overview," *www.cyberianmall.com/silvana/overview.htm*, (September 2002).

15. Doherty, "A Tale of Three Nesses."

16. Max Allan Collins, *Road to Perdition*, (New York: Pocket Books, July 2002) and (New York: ONYX, 2002).

17. Antony Teofilo "On the Road to Perdition: Human Gangsters: An Interview with Stanley Tucci," *www.moviepoopshoot.com*, (2002).

18. Joanne Laurier, "Filthy Lives Have Filthy Consequences: *Road to Perdition*, Directed by Sam Mendes," *World Socialist Website*, (July 25, 2002).

19. Celia McGee, "Stanley Tucci Is Getting Ready to Cook Again," *New York Daily News*, (September 2002).

CHAPTER NINE

1. Max Allan Collins, *True Detective*, (New York: St. Martin's Press, 1983); Max Allan Collins, *True Crime*, (New York: St. Martin's Press, 1984); Max Allan Collins, *The Million-Dollar Wound*, (New York: St. Martin's Press, 1986); Max Allan Collins, *Stolen Away*, (New York: Signet, 2001); and Max Allan Collins, *Chicago Confidential: A Nathan Heller Novel*, (New York: New American Library, 2002).

2. Max Allan Collins, *Road to Perdition*, (New York: Pocket Books, July 2002), pp. 8-9.

3. Collins, *Road to Perdition*.

4. Max Allan Collins, *Road to Perdition*, (New York: ONYX, 2002).

5. Doug Moe, "*Perdition* Linked to Madison," *www.madison.com*, (July 12, 2002); and Max Allan Collins, personal correspondence to author (2003-2004).

6. Nicholas von Hoffman, *Organized Crimes*, (New York: Harper and Row, Publishers, 1984).

7. Marvin Albert, *The Untouchables*, (New York: Ivy Books, 1987).

8. Kim Newman and Eugene Byrne, "Tom Joad," *Interzone*, #65, (November 1992). Part of the "Back in the USSA" science fiction series.

9. Mark Orr, "Aces High," *www.horrorauthors.net/gallows/cuttingedge/aces_high.htm*, (2001).

10. Anon., (*www.redskulllegion.com/Tales_of_the_Red_Skull/crimsonsky/Chapter5.htm*).

11. K.M. Wilcox, "Aeneas Boddy Chronicles: Frankie and Bonnie," *Etc. House Productions, ccwf.cc.utexas.edu*, (December 13, 1996).

12. Alan Brady Ward, "Wild Cards—Episode 4 Chapter 1," *rec.games.frp.archives*, (November 4, 1993).

13. Earl Wilson, "The Afterlife," *Ironic Times*, *www.ironictimes.com*, (November 12-18, 2001).

14. Dennis E. Power, "Melvin and Howard: A Tale of the Riverworld," (*www.pjfarmer.com/fan/melvin.htm*); Andrew M. Greeley, *Irish Whiskey: A Nuala Anne McGrail Novel*, (New York: St. Martin's Press, 1998); and Stuart M. Kaminsky, *You Bet Your Life*, (New York: Mysterious Press, July 1990).

15. Robert Lloyd, "Mob Rules: David Chase on The Sopranos, the Small Screen, and Rock and Roll," *L.A. Weekly*, (March 16-22, 2001).

16. Elmer L. Irey and William J. Slocum, *The Tax Dodgers: The Inside Story of the T-Men's War with America's Political and Underworld Hoodlums*, (New York: Greenberg, 1948), p. 271.

17. Anon., *(www.needlenecessities.com)*.

18. Anon., *(www.jbrucevoyles.com/bowieauction.htm)*.

19. Anon., "Hoodlum Politics," *www.arktimes.com/editorials/122900edit.html*, (Deccember 29, 2000).

20. Gene Wojciechowski, "Quiet Killer," *ESPN Magazine*, (2002).

21. Anon., *(www.boxinginsider.com/pressreleases/posts/1032.html)*.

22. Bob Greene, "Even Capone Would Be Disgusted," *www.jewishworldreview.com*, (September 2002).

23. David M. Alexander, "Safe Streets Task Force Cooperation Gets Results," *FBI Law Enforcement Bulletin*, (March 2001), pp. 1-2; David A. Fahrenthold, "D.C. Girl, 14, Was Killed As Witness, Police Say," *The Washington Post*, (January 25, 2004); and Deborah Simmons, "The New Nitti," *The Washington Times*, (January 30, 2004).

24. Joseph K. O'Brien and Andris Kurins, *Boss of Bosses—the Fall of the Godfather: The FBI and Paul Castellano*, (New York: Island Books, 1991), pp. 47-48.

25. Robert Whiting, *Tokyo Underworld: The Fast Times and Hard Life of an American Gangster in Japan*, (New York: Pantheon Books, 1999), p. 95.

CHAPTER TEN

1. William Gibson, *Idoru*, (New York: G.P. Putnam's Sons, 1996).

2. Ralph "Sonny" Barger, *Hell's Angel*, (New York: HarperCollins Publishers, 2000).

INDEX

Index

OTHER BOOKS IN OUR
BARRICADE CRIME SERIES

The Mafia and the Machine
Frank R. Hayde
La Cosa Nostra reaches right into the heart of America. Nowhere is that more evident than in the "City of Fountains," where the Mafia held sway over the political machine.
$22.00 • Hardcover • 1-56980-336-6

Black Gangsters of Chicago
Ron Chepesiuk
Chicago's African American gangsters were every bit as powerful and intriguing as the city's fabled white mobsters. For the first time, Ron Chepesiuk chronicles their fascinating stories.
$22.00 • Hardcover • 1-56980-331-5

The Silent Don: The Criminal Underworld of Santo Trafficante Jr.
Scott Deitche
A follow-up to Deitche's best-selling *Cigar City Mafia*, *The Silent Don* exposes the life of one of America's most powerful and feared mob bosses, Santo Trafficante Jr.
$22.00 • Hardcover • 1-56980-322-6

Blood & Volume
Dave Copeland
Ron Gonen, together with pals Johnny Attias and Ron Efraim, ran a multi-million-dollar drug distribution syndicate in 1980s New York. But when the FBI caught up, Gonen had to choose between doing the right thing and winding up dead.
$22.00 • Hardcover • 1-56980-327-7

Gangsters of Harlem
Ron Chepesiuk
Veteran journalist Ron Chepesiuk chronicles the life and crimes of Harlem's gangsters, including "Nicky" Barnes, Bumpy Johnson, and the notorious Frank Lucas.
$22.00 • Hardcover • 1-56980-318-8

Cigar City Mafia: A Complete History of the Tampa Underworld
Scott M. Deitche
Prohibition-era "Little Havana" housed Tampa's cigar industry, and with it, bootleggers, arsonists, and mobsters— and a network of corrupt police officers worse than the criminals themselves. Scott M. Deitche documents the rise of the infamous Trafficante family, ruthless competitors in a "violent, shifting place, where loyalties and power quickly changed."
$22.95 • Hardcover • 1-56980-266-1

I'll Do My Own Damn Killin'
Gary W. Sleeper
A detailed look into the life of notorious casino owner Benny Binion, which looks into his life in Dallas before his infamous Las Vegas days.
$22.00 • Hardcover • 1-56980-321-8

Thief!
William "Slick" Hanner & Cherie Rohn
The true story of "Slick" Hanner and how he gained insider access to the Mafia, starting out as a Chicago street tough and workin his way to a friendship with Tony Spilotro,

the Outfit's notorious frontman.
$22.00 • Hardcover • 1-56980-317-X

Gangster City: The History of the New York Underworld 1900–1935
Patrick Downey
From 1900 to 1935, New York City hosted more than 600 mob-land killings. No other book delivers such extensive detail on the lives, crimes, and dramatic endings of this ruthless cast of characters, including Jack "Legs" Diamond and the sadistic Dutch Schultz.
$23.95 • Hardcover • 1-56980-267-X

Il Dottore
Ron Felber
By day, he was Dr. Elliot Litner, respected surgeon at Mount Sinai Hospital; by night, Il Dottore, a sex and gambling addict with ties to New York's reigning Mafia Dons. But when Attorney General Rudolph Guiliani stepped in, Litner had to decide where his loyalties lay: with La Cosa Nostra, or the Hippocratic oath.
$24.95 • Hardcover • 1-56980-278-5

Murder of a Mafia Daughter
Cathy Scott
Not until college did Las Vegas native Susan Berman learn her father had been a notorious leader of the local Mafia. Her life took an even more bizarre turn when the wife of her college friend, real estate heir Robert Durst, disappeared, leaving Durst a murder suspect. When Berman was found dead, shot execution-style, investigators wondered if she knew more about Durst than he could afford.
$23.95 • Hardcover • 1-56980-238-6

The Life and Times of Lepke Buchalter
Paul R. Kavieff
Lepke Buchalter had a stranglehold on the New York garment industry, rising from small-scale push-cart terrorism to leadership of Murder Inc.'s staff of killers-by-assignment, until an obscure murder ended his reign as America's most ruthless labor racketeer.
$22.00 • Hardcover • 1-56980-291-2

The Purple Gang
Paul R. Kavieff
This is the hitherto untold story of the rise and fall of one of America's most notorious criminal groups. The Purple Gang was a loosely organized confederation of mobsters who dominated the Detroit underworld and whose tentacles reached across the country.
$15.95 • Paperback • 1-56980-281-5 Hardcover

The Violent Years
Paul R. Kavieff
A follow-up to Kavieff's best-selling *The Purple Gang*, this book delves deeper into the Prohibition-Era gangs of the Detroit area.
$22.00 • Hardcover • 1-56980-210-6

The Rise and Fall of the Cleveland Mafia
Rick Porrello
From obscurity, the Cleveland Mafia rose rapidly to power and position, taking its place as the third most powerful operation in the country. But the city's crime syndicates nearly decimated themselves during the Sugar War— "Big Ange" Lonardo's vendetta-driven

play to control the lucrative bootleg liquor production racket.

$15.00 • Paperback • 1-56980-277-7 Hardcover

Lucky Luciano

Hickman Powell

Written by a top investigative reporter who covered Luciano's trial from beginning to end, *Lucky Luciano* is a detailed account of Luciano's intriguing life.

$23.95 • Hardcover • 1-56980-163-0

The Animal in Hollywood

John L. Smith

The Animal in Hollywood recounts, in frank and chilling detail, Mob enforcer Anthony Fiato's explosive career in the Mafia on both coasts.

$22.00 • Hardcover • 1-56980-126-6

Mala Femina

Theresa Dalessio with Patrick W. Picciarelli

Theresa "Terri Dee" Dalessio was a Mafia daughter, pregnant teenager, barkeeper, heroin addict, murder witness, and twice-divorced mother of three. For a start.

$24.95 • Hardcover • 1-56980-244-0

COMING SOON!

The Jews of Sing-Sing

Ron Arons

Besides famous gangsters like Lepke Buchalter, thousands of Jews committed all types of crimes--from incest to arson to selling air rights over Manhattan--and found themselves doing time in Sing-Sing.

$22.95 • Hardcover • 1-56980-333-1
APRIL 2008

Human Sacrifice: A Shocking Exposé of Ritual Killings Worldwide

Jimmy Lee Shreeve

Human sacrifice still goes on today, and uncomfortably close to home. Jimmy Lee Shreeve draws on police reports and interviews with victims' families to paint a horrifying picture of ritual killing at home and abroad.

$15.95 • Paperback • 1-56980-346-3
JULY 2008